ANABAPTIST HISTORY
AND THEOLOGY:
REVISED STUDENT EDITION

ANABAPTIST HISTORY AND THEOLOGY:
REVISED STUDENT EDITION

C. Arnold Snyder

Published by Pandora Press
Kitchener, Ontario

Copublished with Herald Press
Scottdale, Pennsylvania/Waterloo, Ontario

Canadian Cataloguing in Publication Data

Snyder, C. Arnold
    Anabaptist history and theology

Rev. student ed.
Includes bibligraphical references and index.
ISBN 0-9698762-5-4

1. Anabaptists - History. 2. Anabaptists - Doctrines.
I. Title.

BX4931.2.S65 1997 284'.3 C97-931826-2

ANABAPTIST HISTORY AND THEOLOGY:
REVISED STUDENT EDITION
Copyright © 1997 by Pandora Press
     51 Pandora Avenue N.
     Kitchener, Ontario, N2H 3C1
     All rights reserved
Co-published with Herald Press,
     Scottdale, Pennsylvania/Waterloo, Ontario
International Standard Book Number: **0-9698762-5-4**
Printed in Canada on acid-free paper
Book and cover design by Clifford Snyder

This book is a second, revised edition of:
C. Arnold Snyder, *Anabaptist History and Theology:
Abridged Student Edition*
Kitchener: Pandora Press, 1995
ISBN: 0-9698762-1-1

Cover illustration:
Detail from an engraving by Jan Luiken (1649-1712) depicting the Anabaptist martyr Andries Langedul. He was arrested in Antwerp shortly following a worship service that had been held in his house. Andries was arrested while sitting on his porch, reading a Bible. He was martyred on November 9, 1559, along with two fellow Anabaptists. Used with permission of Conrad Grebel College Library and Archives, Waterloo, Ontario.

05 04 03 02 01 00 10 9 8 7 6 5 4 3 2

Contents

C. The Development of Anabaptism: 1525-ca.1600

1. Anabaptism and Political Reality

2. Anabaptism and Socio-Economic Reality

3. Anabaptism and Religious Reform

D. The Surviving Anabaptist Traditions: 1560 to the Present

Preface to the First Edition

Some books have a longer gestation periods than others. This one has been many years in the making. I was introduced to what became my perennial questions when, as an undergraduate at the University of Waterloo in the mid-1970s I enrolled in "The Radical Reformation," a course taught at Conrad Grebel College by Professor Walter Klaassen. The question was posed: How can the "Anabaptist movement" be defined and described? The question I was left with then, still preoccupies me: How best might the "Anabaptist story" be told?

I will confess, I did only moderately well in Dr. Klaassen's course. But one thing led to another, as it sometimes does: Walter Klaassen became my trusted advisor in graduate studies, and a member of my dissertation committee at McMaster University. In truth, he was my *Doktorvater*. Walter and Ruth became close friends and mentors for Linda and me during those years of study and growing families. In 1985, when I joined the faculty of Conrad Grebel College, Walter and I became colleagues. Since his retirement a few years ago, I have come full circle and found myself teaching "Walter's course," The Radical Reformation. Perhaps this book ought to be seen as my attempt to write a more credible take home exam, seventeen years later. Certainly the basic questions remain the same: How can the Anabaptist movement be described? What is the clearest and best way to tell this interesting and complex historical tale?

The text Walter had us read in 1974 was the incomparable *The Radical Reformation* by George H. Williams (Philadelphia: Westminster Press, 1962). It was an altogether impressive, encyclopedic treatment of the subject, and more than a little daunting for an undergraduate. It has since been replaced by an even more impressive third edition, of the same title, that runs to more than 1500 pages (Kirksville, Mo.: Sixteenth Century Journal Publishers, 1992). As a teacher of that subject, I quickly discovered that although there were excellent monographs on specialized aspects of the radical reformation, no comprehensive, synthetic texts, beyond the work of Williams, were available. This remained true even when the focus was narrowed to sixteenth century "Anabaptist Studies," a subset of radical reformation studies. Perhaps Williams' tour de force simply discouraged other scholars in the field from attempting synthetic overviews, even along more modest lines.

This book is the end result of the search for a text that would, first of all, provide a fairly concise narrative describing the birth and evolution of the sixteenth century Anabaptist movement. From the start I intended this book to be accessible to university students. I also hoped that this telling of the Anabaptist story would have something to say to people in the churches, and especially to those interested in the Anabaptist roots (historical and theological) of the Believers' Church tradition. All the same, the effort was made to incorporate scholarly advances in Anabaptist studies into the narrative itself, which of course complicated the narrative.

The attempt to walk this tightrope, clinging to narrative clarity on the one hand and academic respectability on the other, has not always succeeded. At times complex matters have been deceptively oversimplified in the telling; at other times, pedantic instincts have complicated unecessarily what should have been said more simply. I apologize both to those who may be confused by the intrusion of academic nit picking, and to my colleagues in the field who will find far too many nits unpicked. Nevertheless, every attempt has been made to take seriously the very rich tradition of academic research into sixteenth century Anabaptism, and to incorporate the best of that research into an accessible story.

In a further effort to make this material more accessible, two versions of the text have been prepared. This present volume is the "abridged student edition" which contains somewhat abbreviated descriptions and discussions (particularly in section C). . . . Readers interested in pursuing scholarly questions in more detail may refer to *Anabaptist History and Theology: An Introduction* (Kitchener: Pandora Press, 1995). Since both texts follow the same organization and presentation of material, cross reference should pose little problem. It is the author's hope that readers of either volume will be left with a better understanding of the complex Reformation movement we have come to call Anabaptism.

A very useful collection of Anabaptist sources in translation is Walter Klaassen's *Anabaptism in Outline* (Scottdale, Pa.: Herald Press, 1981). Cross references to this collection will be made at appropriate places in this text, in order to help readers who wish to augment the narrative with a parallel exploration of Anabaptist writings. Readers who wish to explore primary texts in more depth will want to refer to the eight volumes of the *Classics of the Radical Reformation* series (Herald Press), of which *Anabaptism in Outline* is volume three. In this series will be found the translated writings of Michael Sattler, Pilgram Marpeck, Conrad Grebel, Balthasar Hubmaier, Dirk Philips, David Joris, and most recently, Andreas Karlstadt. As always, those who read the original languages (German and Dutch) will have access to a much wider spectrum of source materials.

Various photocopied "incarnations" of this text have been used in past years in courses taught at Conrad Grebel College and other Mennonite and Baptist institutions, in locations as far afield as Ontario, Indiana, Central America (Nicaragua, Honduras, Costa Rica, Guatemala), Colombia, the Netherlands, and Switzerland. Critical feedback from those many students of history and theology has been invaluable in shaping the present book. I am indebted to them all.

I also owe a large debt of thanks to colleagues and friends who took the time to comment and correct many shortcomings at various stages in the process. Deserving of special thanks are Walter Klaassen, whose observations were invaluable as always, and my Conrad Grebel College colleague, historical researcher *par excellence*, Werner Packull, who took time away from work on his own latest monograph in order to offer help with mine. Thanks as well to C.J. Dyck, Ray Gingerich, Brad Gregory, Leonard Gross, Linda Huebert Hecht, Ted Koontz, Alan Kreider, Jerry Moon, Wayne Pipkin, John Rempel, John Roth, Shirley Showalter, James Stayer, Peter Stucky, Hildi Froese Tiessen, and Sjouke Voolstra for their invaluable encouragement to me, and their engagement with me. Also to Joe Springer, of the Mennonite Historical Library, Goshen, Indiana; to Frau Dr. B. Stadler, of the Staatsarchiv, Zürich; and to Dr. Piet Visser, Universiteitsbibliotheek, Amsterdam, for their support and assistance throughout.

Special thanks is due to the Mennonite Historical Library for graciously allowing me to reproduce illustrations from their holdings. The engravings and woodcuts in this book appear courtesy of the Mennonite Historical Library.

A sabbatical leave from Conrad Grebel College (1992/93) and a research grant from the Social Sciences and Humanities Research Council of Canada provided the necessary time and resources for the completion of this project. Gilbert Fast kindly contributed his editing skills in the final stages, and August Kroger solved a myriad of digital problems in the late going.

To my most "significant others," Linda, Carrie, Christian, Clifford, Karl, and Edna, thanks for the good-natured patience as the obsession with "the book" stretched into years. And finally, special thanks are due to my son, Clifford, who worked with me in producing this book for Pandora Press. His interest in geography and computers has taken printed form in the maps he prepared for this volume and in the general layout and production of the printed book.

C. Arnold Snyder, Conrad Grebel College, August, 1995

Preface to the Second, Revised Edition

It has been two years since this book first appeared. In that time, it has been used as a textbook by a good number of undergraduates in both Canada and the United States. I have received much valuable feedback and advice from many of these students and from some of their teachers.

The "Abridged Student Edition" of two years ago was a condensation of the larger *Anabaptist History and Theology* text. The prose in both books was essentially the same, only the Student Edition had less of it. This present version, by contrast, has been revised and re-written specifically with undergraduate readers in mind. In particular, the many "ology" words used in the first edition (which some undergraduates found confusing) have been drastically reduced in this version. Every effort has been made to render the prose accessible and clear. In addition, new narrative text (story) has been introduced wherever possible.

In the second place, some readers of the first edition found the type heavy and concentrated, and therefore difficult to read. In response, we have completely re-designed the book. It features larger and clearer type, narrower columns, and more space between lines. While the resulting book has many more pages than the previous edition, it contains only a few more words which, we hope, are more easily read.

Finally, the new edition has been enriched by the addition of number-coded sidebars. These contain sources and commentaries to supplement the text itself. It is hoped that they will add flavour, interest, and context to the book as a whole.

My thanks to all the students who contributed to this revision, and expecially to professors John Roth of Goshen College and James Juhnke of Bethel College for their helpful comments. And again, to Clifford for his help in design and production.

C. Arnold Snyder, Conrad Grebel College, August, 1997

Maps, Illustrations, Acknowledgments

Maps

Illustrations (courtesy of the Mennonite Historical Library, Goshen, Indiana, unless otherwise noted)

Acknowledgments

The extensive citations from Herald Press books, Scottdale, PA, are used with permission of the publisher. In particular, thanks is due for permission to reproduce lengthy citations from the following Herald Press books: Pipkin and Yoder, *Balthasar Hubmaier* (HP, 1989); Klaassen and Klassen, *Writings of Pilgram Marpeck* (HP, 1978); Verduin, *Complete Writings of Menno Simons* (HP, 1956); Yoder, *Legacy of Michael Sattler* (HP, 1973); Harder, *Sources of Swiss Anabaptism* (HP, 1985); Klaassen, *Anabaptism in Outline* (HP, 1982); Waite, *David Joris* (HP, 1994); Dyck, Keeney, and Beachy, *Writings of Dirk Philips* (HP, 1992).

The lengthy citations, translations, and paraphrases from C. Arnold Snyder and Linda H. Hecht, *Profiles of Anabaptist Women* (Waterloo: WLU Press, 1996) are used with permission of the publisher. Their cooperation is gratefully acknowledged.

The illustration of "The Chapel of Our Lady" on p. 32 (Copyright © The British Museum) used with permission of the Trustees of the British Museum.

Newly scanned images from the second edition of the Martyrs Mirror are used with permission of Conrad Grebel College archives. Thanks to Sam Steiner, librarian and archivist.

Thanks also to Christian Snyder for the pen and ink drawing of Dirk Philips, p. 354.

Introduction

I was born into a Mennonite home, and raised in the Mennonite church. In the church of my young adulthood it was not unusual to hear sermons that called us to remain "true to the Anabaptist vision." I heard talk of an "Anabaptist/Mennonite tradition" that challenged us to faithful living in imitation of Christ. Anabaptism, I was led to understand, was a supremely Good Thing: a badge of faithfulness, something to be imitated, preserved, and cherished.

Imagine my surprise when, some years later, I read in a contemporary church history textbook that the Anabaptists were wild-eyed fanatics, no better than weird sixteenth century cultists, satanically intent on destroying the positive gains of the Protestant reformers. Anabaptism, this text told me, was a supremely Bad Thing, a plague that was narrowly avoided in the sixteenth century to the benefit of all.

Were two different movements being described under the same name? What did nonresistant, heroic martyrs have to do with violently fanatical visionaries? How could "Anabaptism" mean such different things to different people?

"Anabaptism" in the ancient church and the sixteenth century

We can start with definitions. The word "Anabaptist" is an anglicized version of the Latin version of two Greek words that mean "rebaptizer" when they are combined. If we are being true to the definitional meaning, Anabaptism should describe a movement that emphasizes **re**-baptism. But history has overlaid several more layers of meaning on top of the dictionary definition.

In the third century AD, Christians of North Africa (followers of the bishop Donatus) rebaptized believers who had received their first baptism

Donatism

at the hands of apostate bishops. Early in the fourth century, after the Roman empire had taken an interest in church affairs, the "Donatist controversy" was heard in court and legally settled. The empire decided against the Donatists, and "rebaptism" became an ecclesiastical and criminal offense. (1) When Justinian codified ancient Roman law in the sixth century, two Christian heresies were said to be punishable by death: rebaptism and anti-Trinitarianism.

---

(1) Synodical decree from the Council of Arles, 314 AD.

"Concerning the Africans, because they make use of their own law, to the effect that they rebaptize, we have determined that if any one should come from heresy to the Church they should ask him the creed; and if they should perceive that he had been baptized in the name of the Father and of the Son and of the Holy Ghost, hands only should be laid upon him that he might receive the Holy Ghost. That if when asked he should not reply this Trinity, let him be baptized." (Petry, 1962, 59).

The sixteenth century situation was rather different. The Catholic church had lost credibility. There was a widespread suspicion that much "human invention" had crept into the church, and that it needed to be thoroughly reformed. As a result of Luther's call for biblical reform, some people became convinced that Christian baptism was one area where "human invention" had prevailed. Some became convinced that baptism was meant to be an *adult* expression of faith, and that the New Testament supported this understanding.

Adult Baptism

By the sixteenth century, virtually all European people (except for Jews and Muslims) had been routinely baptized as infants. When adults began to be deliberately baptized, by their own mature choice, some theologians and political authorities said that the practice should not be allowed: adult baptism was, they said, a "rebaptism." And of course, rebaptism already had a history as an early church heresy.

The earliest known case of adult baptism in the sixteenth century took place in January, 1525, in Zurich, Switzerland. We will describe that event in more detail in a later chapter. Written opposition to the practice of adult baptism appeared in that same year. The term used to describe someone who had been baptized as an adult was *Wiedertaufer*, a German translation of Anabaptist or re-baptizer. The term itself was both accusation and sentence, all rolled up into one. It implied that infant baptism was the true baptism, that receiving baptism as an adult was a "re-baptism," and that adult baptism was in some way connected with the Donatist heresy.

The most important decree against the practice of adult baptism was the imperial mandate published at Speyer in 1529. This decree explicitly linked the sixteenth century adult baptizers with the "old sect of Anabaptism, condemned and forbidden many centuries ago." The Speyer mandate renewed the ancient imperial law, connected adult baptism to the ancient heresy, and decreed the death penalty for the crime. (2)

By 1530 the terms *Anabaptista* or *Wiedertäufer* were interchangeable and accepted designations for the group of Christians who baptized adults on confession of faith, as reference to the Augsburg Confession of that year demonstrates. (3) In the territories of the Holy Roman Empire, the imperial law supported the death penalty. In other territories, a variety of legal arguments were used to arrive at the same conclusion.

> **(2) Imperial Mandate of April 23, 1529.**
> "We ... renew the previous imperial law ... that ... every Anabaptist and rebaptized man and woman of the age of reason shall be condemned and brought from natural life into death by fire, sword, and the like, according to the person, without proceeding by the inquisition of the spiritual judges; and let the same pseudo-preachers, instigators, vagabonds, and tumultuous inciters of the said vice of Anabaptism ... by no means be shown mercy..." *(Williams, 1992, 359-60).*

> **(3) The Augsburg Confession, 1530.**
> "They condemn the Donatists, and such like, who denied it to be lawful to use the ministry of evil men in the Church, and who thought the ministry of evil men to be unprofitable and of none effect." *(Art. VIII).*
> "They condemn the Anabaptists, who reject the baptism of children, and say that children are saved without Baptism." *(Art. IX).* *(Bente, 1921, 45-51).*

In short, in the sixteenth century the label "Anabaptist" was not simply descriptive, and in fact, as a description it missed the point of the practice of adult baptism. But the label was used as an effective theological and legal weapon. The term came to mean not only "re-baptizing heretic" but also "worthy of death." It is therefore not surprising that those who practiced adult baptism rejected the label althogether. They never called each other "Anabaptists," but rather called each other brothers and sisters, or "brethren."

Brethren

Why should modern historians continue to use the term "Anabaptism" to refer to the sixteenth century baptizing movement, given its questionable descriptive accuracy and historical misuse? In fact, the problem of terminology has been largely overcome by German scholars, and their adoption of the term *Täufer* (Baptists), and by the Dutch with their use of the term *Doopsgezinden* (Baptism-minded). In both cases the historically inaccurate prefix suggesting "re"-baptism is dropped, while the historically accurate emphasis on baptism as such is retained.

Baptizers

Unfortunately, there is no equivalently neat solution in the English language. The term "Baptist" in English suggests a direct connection with the contemporary Baptist denomination. This is not completely wrong, but what is needed is a reference to the sixteenth century movement, not the current denomination. On the other hand "Baptism-minded," which works in the Dutch language, is an awkward linguistic compound in English. Historians writing in English have continued to use the term "Anabaptism," then, because in spite of its limitations, it remains the best available word to point to the historical "baptizing" movement of the sixteenth century.

Anabaptists

Direct historical descendants of the sixteenth century Anabaptists are present day Mennonites, Hutterites, Amish, and some groups of Brethren, such as the Church of the Brethren and the Brethren in Christ; the present day Baptist denominations also can claim significant historical roots in the Anabaptist movement of the sixteenth century.

Descendants

The Historical Origins of Anabaptism

Readers wishing a more comprehensive overview of historical descriptions of Anabaptism will want to refer to the Appendix to this book. By way of introduction we must mention here at least two twentieth century developments that have coloured this present narrative.

When the Mennonite scholar and church leader Harold S. Bender published his "Anabaptist Vision" speech just over fifty years ago, he galvanized the Mennonite church with a call to emulate the "true" Anabaptists. According to Bender, genuine Anabaptism had emerged in Zurich in 1525 and, in spite of some fanatical deviants, it had survived through an unbroken line of descent in the Mennonite church. The sermons I heard in my youth were inspired by Bender's "recovery of the Anabaptist vision."

The Anabaptist Vision

More recent historical studies of Anabaptism have modified and complicated Bender's description of one true or genuine Anabaptism. Bender had emphasized one, pure, Swiss origin for all of Anabaptism. His view was challenged by historians who pointed to a diversity of historical origins, teachings, and practices among the sixteenth century Anabaptist groups. In 1975, James Stayer, Werner Packull, and Klaus Deppermann published an article that coined the word "Polygenesis." By this term they meant to indicate that the baptizing movement in Europe had several points of origin, and not just one. The polygenesis approach to Anabaptist history revolutionized the field.

Polygenesis

The beginnings of three primary Anabaptist groups have been identified and described in some detail, as follows.

Swiss Anabaptism

The earliest "baptizing" movement in the sixteenth century started in Zurich in January, 1525. Among its best-known leaders were Conrad Grebel, Felix Mantz, George Blaurock, Balthasar Hubmaier, and Michael Sattler.

By 1529 none of these leaders was still alive. Only Conrad Grebel died a natural death; Mantz, Blaurock, Hubmaier, and Sattler were martyred. The Swiss were soon noted for a sober, literal, and ethical emphasis.

Swiss Brethren

The Swiss Brethren movement continued this Anabaptist tradition. By the seventeenth century the Swiss Brethren had had many contacts with Dutch Anabaptists, and later in that century, the Swiss Brethren had come to call themselves "Mennonites." After a nasty split in 1693, the

Amish

Swiss group divided into "Mennonite" and "Amish" factions.

South German/Austrian Anabaptism.

The South German baptizing movement began early in 1526. There are no documented historical connections to the Swiss movement, but there are striking similarities in doctrine and practice. The similarities suggest the possiblity of contact between the Swiss and the South German Anabaptists. But there are also some well-marked differences between the two groups, and this suggests different sources of inspiration. The South German Anabaptist movement was more obviously "spiritualist" than "literalist,"

Apocalypticism

in its early years. It also was more apocalyptic than were the Swiss. Many of the early South German Anabaptists believed that they were living in the End Times, and that by reading the prophetic books of Scripture, they could figure out exactly when Jesus was coming back.

Three early leaders of this movement were Hans Denck, Hans Hut, and Melchior Rinck. Denck and Hut both died in 1527, Denck of the plague, and Hut through martyrdom. Rinck was arrested as a young man in Hesse. He spent most of his life in prison and died there of old age, refusing to recant, a "living martyr" to his faith.

Out of the South German Anabaptist movement came Pilgram Marpeck, several prominent spiritualist Anabaptists, and the communitarian Hutterites. Of these, only the Hutterites have survived to the present day as an identifiable group. Their distinctive teaching is a community of goods (all things owned in common).

North German/Dutch Anabaptism

This baptizing movement was begun and led by Melchior Hoffman, who became an Anabaptist in 1530, in Strasbourg. Hoffman missionized in the north, and his movement (also called Melchiorite Anabaptism) spread in North Germany and especially into the Netherlands. In its first phase, Melchiorite Anabaptism was very apocalyptic (expecting Jesus' return), but peaceful–expecting God's action to initiate the Last Days.

Strasbourg

By 1533 Melchiorite Anabaptism had entered a second phase, under the leadership of the prophetic visionary Jan Matthijs. He was a baker from Haarlem, in the Netherlands, who was convinced that he was the prophet Enoch of the Last Days. Under his direction, the Melchiorite movement became more militant. Matthijs taught that the saints of the Last Days were supposed to take the "sword of righteousness" into their own hands, to prepare the way for the return of the Lord.

Prophecy

Inspired by the prophecies of Matthijs and other visionaries, some Melchiorite Anabaptists took the city of Münster in Westphalia early in 1534, and held the city against a military siege until June, 1535. The city finally fell, and most of the inhabitants were slaughtered.

Münster

A third, more peaceful phase of Melchiorite Anabaptism began after the fall of Münster. The followers of Obbe Philips had opposed the Münsterite enthusiasm. David Joris was an important leader following Münster, but Menno Simons eventually emerged as the main leader of this movement. His followers were soon called "Mennists," and from this label we get the name "Mennonite": followers of Menno Simons.

The Stages of Anabaptist Development in the Sixteenth Century

Sorting out the question of Anabaptist origins has preoccupied historians in the past few decades. But the story of the sixteenth century baptizing movement is not exhausted by a description the historical **beginnings** of the Swiss, South German, and Dutch Anabaptist movements. There was also significant change and development in the Anabaptist groups and in the beliefs they accepted and rejected.

In order to tell not only the story of Anabaptist origins, but also of Anabaptist development, this book has been organized into four main sections, each describing a major stage in the development of the Anabaptist movement.

A. The Context: Reformation and Radical Reformation

Anabaptism emerged in the historical context of the Reformation. More particularly, the Anabaptist movement was the product of early divisions within the wider Reformation movement. There were important radical reforming leaders who provided key ideas for the baptizers. The roles of Andreas Karlstadt, Thomas Müntzer, and Caspar Schwenckfeld will be described in this section of study, as will some important issues raised by the Peasants' War of 1525.

B. The Setting of Initial Boundaries: 1525-1530.

The definition of Anabaptist core principles and practices began in 1525 and was pretty well completed by 1530. This initial phase identified a baptizing movement as distinguished from other reforming movements. It defined the Anabaptist way of being "Protestant" in the sixteenth century. It also set the stage for internal disagreements, as different and contradictory Anabaptist visions became painfully evident.

C. The Development of Anabaptism: 1525-ca. 1600.

Following the emergence of an identifiable baptizing movement there came a period of development, conversation, and disagreement among various Anabaptist groups and persons. This stage of development saw the Anabaptists trying to figure out what the proper scriptural order of reform should look like in actual practice in the world.

D. The surviving Anabaptist traditions: 1560 to the present. By around 1560, the surviving Anabaptist groups had settled the larger questions of how to interpret Scripture, and had outlined very specific "rules of discipleship" for their members. The surviving Anabaptist traditions (the Swiss Brethren, Mennonites, and Hutterites) came to agree on most crucial interpretive issues, with only minor differences. These mature Anabaptist "traditions" were then handed on to succeeding generations.

Conclusion

Who were the Anabaptists really? This book will answer that question in as simple a fashion, and in as plain a language as can be managed. But this is no easy assignment, because the reality was complex.

It now appears to me that there was some historical truth in **both** of the contrasting pictures I encountered as a young person. There were sixteenth century baptizers who were peace-loving, evangelical people who willingly submitted to torture and a martyr's death as a witness to their faith. But there were also sixteenth century baptizers who were a bit whacky, by any standard. There were Anabaptists who took two or more wives because "God told them to," as well as some who tried to establish the New Jerusalem of the End Times by force of arms.

We can sympathize with historians who have tried to simplify the Anabaptist story by choosing one kind of example, or the other, as representing the whole of "Anabaptism." What we have set out to do in this book, however, is to try to provide an overview of the entire sixteenth century baptizing movement. The principle we have followed for inclusion or exclusion in "Anabaptism" is simply whether or not the person in question believed that only *adults* (and not infants) should be baptized, following a mature confession of faith.

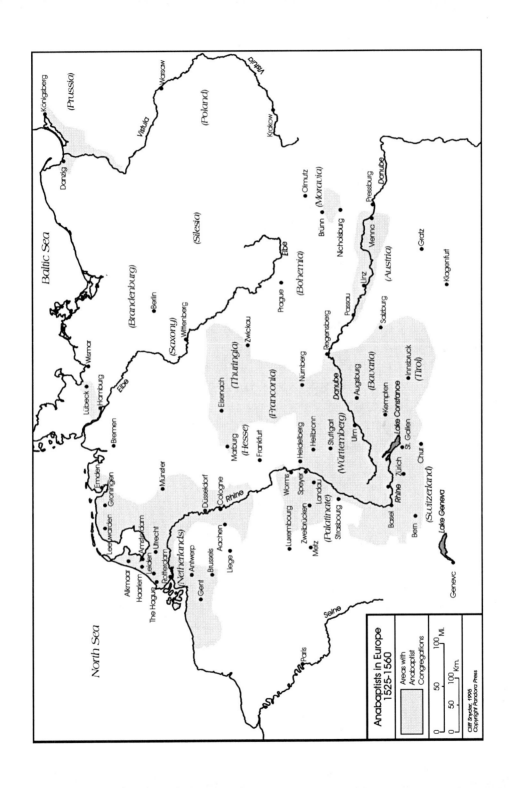

Anabaptists in Europe
1525-1560

Areas with
Anabaptist
Congregations

0   50   100 Mi.

0   50   100 Km.

Cliff Snyder, 1996
Copyright Pandora Press

A.
The Context:
Reformation
and
Radical Reformation

Chapter 1

The Late Medieval Context

In June, 1523, in the parish church of the Swiss village of Zollikon–a scant three kilometers from the cathedral in Zurich–an old bearded peasant named Jakob Hottinger listened to the learned Dr. Lorenz of Zurich preach a sermon on the passion of Christ. At the conclusion of the sermon the peasant confronted the preacher, and spoke "sharp, hard and intolerable words," demanding that the doctor stop "preaching lies about the Lord's Supper." Scripture was clear, he said: communicants were to receive both the bread and the wine when they celebrated the Lord's Supper.

When the good doctor tried to instruct Jakob on proper sacramental theology, he replied: "We don't want philosophical proofs; you should demonstrate with the Gospel; for Christ took the bread, gave it to his disciples and said: take this, this is my body; after which he took the cup and said: take this, this is my blood."

Jakob Hottinger was brought to court as a result of his outburst. The judgment handed down by the Zurich magistrates stated that Jakob must be made to admit that he had lied. He was to promise that he would desist and be quiet, and leave such lofty theological matters for the preachers to decide.

Jakob Hottinger was assessed a fine, and released. But he remained a peasant "theologian" and Bible reader to the end. Two years after this event, in 1525, he received baptism because he was convinced that this was the true biblical practice. After being arrested as an Anabaptist in 1530 outside Swiss territory, and refusing to recant, he was put to death as an unrepentant heretic.

The story of Jakob Hottinger provides a good point of departure for understanding some of the transitions that were taking place in political, social, economic, and religious life at the time of the Reformation. It was a time of fundamental readjustment, in which the old was being challenged by the new. But at the same time these challenges, for all their newness, took place in a thoroughly medieval world.

Many of us are so familiar with the Reformation story that we imagine the sixteenth century to have been a modern time. But this is misleading. The world view that dominated the sixteenth century was far more medieval than modern. The cultural air that the Anabaptists breathed was late medieval air. We need to remember this when we re-image (re-imagine) the Anabaptists. The more we know about the medieval world and medieval habits of thought, the better we we will be able to understand someone like Jakob Hottinger. He was radical, without a doubt, but he was radical in a medieval way.

The Medieval World View

(1) "The whole of the thinking and behaviour of medieval men was dominated by a fairly conscious, fairly concise Manichaeanism. As far as they were concerned, God was on one side and the devil was on the other. This great division ruled moral, social, and political life." (LeGoff, 1988, 160).

The first thing to be said about the conceptual universe occupied by Jakob Hottinger, his large extended family, and his friends, is that it was a world in which the basic **unity** of the cosmos and society was assumed. The universe in which medieval people lived was a world "under God," defined by Christian images and symbols.

At the same time, this conceptual whole was made up of two distinct parts, or worlds, that intersected and interacted in both space and time. These polar opposites represented good and evil, light and dark, heaven and hell. They did active battle on earth. (1) We can schematize this world view in the following way.

God

Heaven   **Christ**

Good   Blessed Virgin Mary

                                            Angels

Spirit   Saints

- -

Earth   [Human Beings]   Church

- -

Matter   Sorcerers
        Evil   Demons

Hell   Fallen Angels
        Satan

The unitary, and at the same time dualistic universe operated at a number of different levels, and in complex ways.

It was, on one level, a moral/religious universe in which good and evil did battle. The earthly world was a moral battleground, and human beings were lower-order participants in the cosmic struggle.

(2) "If we do not keep the obsession with salvation and the fear of hell which inspired medieval men in the forefront of our minds we shall never understand their outlook on life." (Le Goff, 1988, 187).

What was at stake was one's eternal soul, and its salvation or damnation. There was a fervent and intense concern with salvation in the medieval period which is still most evident in the sixteenth century. (2) This concern was grounded in the "two worlds" understanding of reality.

(3) Thomas Aquinas, **Summa contra Gentiles** *(ca. 1260).*

"So, therefore, in the parts of the universe also every creature exists for its own proper act and perfection, and the less noble for the nobler, as those creatures that are less noble than man exist for the sake of man, whilst each and every creature exists for the perfection of the entire universe. Furthermore, the entire universe, with all its parts, is ordained towards God as its end, inasmuch as it imitates, as it were, and shows forth the Divine goodness, to the glory of God." (In Baumer, 1970, 57).

The two-worlds universe was structural as well as moral. The heavenly and earthly worlds paralleled each other in order and form. (3) Of course, earthly society was the lesser of the two, and seen as the mirror image of heavenly society. We can depict this simply with a vertical listing.

Heaven

   God

   Christ, BVM, Apostles

   Archangels

   Angels

   Saints

Earth

[Temporal Estate]	[Spiritual Estate]
Emperor/King	Pope
[Faithful Vassals]	Cardinals
Barons	Archbishops
Knights (warriors)	Bishops
Peasants (workers)	Clergy
Craftspeople; burghers	

The medieval view of the world suggested that the feudal hierarchy (political, social, and economic) mirrored an actual heavenly hierarchy and order. (4) Consequently, any change to the human social order was a violation of the divine blueprint for society. Insofar as people and things remained in their proper "places," all was well. On the other hand, nothing but trouble resulted if proper place were ignored.

(4) "...the heavenly society of the angels was only the image of earthly society, or rather, as the men of the middle ages believed, the latter was only the image of the former..." (Le Goff, 1988, 164).

Finally, the medieval world view was overwhelmingly communal. Individuals were vulnerable, and found security in communities. People tried to ally themselves with the larger communion of saints, living and dead, with the angels, the Blessed Virgin, and Christ, against the forces of evil, who were always on the prowl, looking for the unwary. (5)

> *(5) Saint Gregory tells of a nun who ate lettuce without making the sign of the cross and swallowed a devil. When a holy man tried to exorcise him the devil said: "What fault is it of mine? I was sitting on the lettuce and she did not cross herself, and so ate me too." (In Petry, 1987, 358).*

This unified two-worlds view stood behind medieval thinking about political life, social life, economic life, and religious life. It was an understanding of the world that was in transition, but still very much dominated thinking in the sixteenth century. It was particularly influential still in the lower social orders, from which the majority of Anabaptists were drawn.

The Political Ideal: A Unified Society, under God

When historians today analyze and describe societies, it is customary to distinguish between the political, social, economic, and religious areas, each of which intersects with and affects the other areas of life to differing degrees. But these distinctions were not applied in the sixteenth century.

The medieval social ideal depicted a unified "Christian Body." (6) All of society and all of life was supposed to be under the lordship of God, with everyone and everything in that society occupying its divinely ordained place and order, in a mirror image of heavenly society.

One Christian Body

> *(6) "The reality was not that the heavenly world was as real as the earthly world, it was that they only formed one world, in an inextricable mixture which caught men in the toils of a living supernatural." (Le Goff, 1988, 165).*

Granted, by the sixteenth century this ideal picture, while still assumed, was more ideal than reality.

Jakob Hottinger's challenge to Dr. Lorenz illustrates, on the one hand, how much the "lordship of God" still functioned as a live expectation for a devout Swiss peasant, and on the other hand, how much the ideal of Christendom had disintegrated as a working option.

The Political Reality: Transition and Fragmentation

Jakob Hottinger's story, like all individual stories, needs to be put into its own political context if it is to make sense.

Zollikon

The village of Zollikon had been under the lordship of the Swiss canton of Zurich since 1357. Zurich, in turn, had become a part of the Swiss Confederacy in 1351, joining other cantons which had won, and were in the process of winning, independence from adjacent royal houses, including the Austrian house of Habsburg–the same royal line that controlled what was left of the Holy Roman Empire.

To be a peasant in Zollikon in the sixteenth century, as Jakob was, implied relatively more freedom of thought and expression than was the case in other territories. In Hapsburg lands, for example, Jakob Hottinger would have been risking life and limb if he had publicly and loudly voiced dissenting views about the Mass. The Zurich authorities, who were in the midst of plotting their own religious independence from the papacy, simply imposed a fine. Political location was everything.

Political Fragmentation

By the sixteenth century "Christendom," or a unified Christian empire and society, was nothing but a faint Carolingian memory. The political map of sixteenth century Europe was dominated by national monarchies (France, England, Spain), the Holy Roman Empire (controlled by the Austrian/Spanish house of Hapsburg), principalities of varying size and power (the Papal States, Saxony, etc.), and cities of varying size, independence, and political power. Because of this, it is impossible to generalize about political conditions "in Europe" at the time of the Reformation. Political realities varied widely, depending upon the area or territory in question.

But one thing was certain: Political fragmentation was a fact, and reforming ideas were in the process of pushing fragmentation even further.

Martin Luther's challenge was that the church should be reformed on the basis of "Scripture alone." But this raised the possibility of different political readings of what such a biblical reform might look like. In some territories, the appeal to Scripture alone encouraged peasants like Jakob Hottinger to draw their own conclusions. One of the results was the conflict historians have come to call the Peasants' War of 1525.

Martin Luther

The consequences of failing to win over any political authorities to one's reforming point of view were devastating. Without such support, a reforming movement was left in political limbo. In the end this happened to the Anabaptist movement.

Politics and Reform

Anabaptism, like all other reform visions and programmes, needed to incarnate its vision in a very real and concrete political world. But most Anabaptists still were under the older "medieval" conviction that all of life had to be brought under the lordship of God. True to the medieval spiritual ideal, social, economic, and political life needed to be brought into subjection to God's will. This is part of what church "reform" meant to most Anabaptists.

Anabaptist Political Vision

To this conviction was now added the new "evangelical" conviction, that the church needed to be reformed according to the blueprint of Scripture. Was there any state in Europe in the sixteenth century that was ready for this?

We will devote a section of our study below to "Anabaptism and Political Reality," paying particular attention to how the Anabaptist understanding of political power and participation developed over time.

Socio-economic Transition

What can we learn from Jakob Hottinger's social and economic situation, living as a peasant in Zollikon early in the sixteenth century?

Compared to situations elsewhere, conditions were quite favourable for Jakob and his extended family. In fact, Jakob Hottinger's social and economic context may help explain his apparently upstart behaviour in the parish church in 1523, when he began instructing a doctor of theology.

Tithes

By the sixteenth century and the time of the Reformation, serfdom was virtually unknown in Zollikon. Of course, all citizens were under the judicial lordship of Zurich and also owed the customary church tithes and land taxes. But except for the question of the ecclesiastical tithe and control over the appointment of the parish priest, the peasants of Zollikon were free from most of the burdens under which most peasants elsewhere still suffered. Most of the socio-economic complaints aired by the Swabian peasants in 1525 in the famous "Twelve Articles" (see below, p. 70 ff.)– with the notable exception of control over the tithe and the appointment of parish clergy–were not live issues in Zollikon.

Woods

One example of the relative freedom of the Zollikon peasants can be seen in their control over forests and wood cutting. While the Swabian peasants appealed to their lords in 1525 that ownership and control of woods "should revert to the whole community," in Zollikon the woods had been the recognized property of the village community since early in the fourteenth century, and were administered by the "Forest Corporation" (*Holzkorporation*) of the village. Jakob was a member of this corporation.

Weapons

When we add to this the fact that Jakob Hottinger, like all young men of Zollikon, owned weapons and formed part of the village militia, we see that although he worked the land and so was a "peasant," he was no browbeaten serf. The man who confronted Dr. Lorenz in the parish church was accustomed to having a say in local affairs.

Seen against the medieval ideal for the peasantry, Jakob Hottinger had long since left his proper "place" in the "divine social order." His verbal rebellion was just one more manifestation of that fact, as was his literacy and Bible reading. It was perhaps not surprising that Jakob's daughter, Margret Hottinger, also proved "rebellious," left her "proper place" of subordination, accepted baptism, and even functioned for a time as an Anabaptist prophet and leader.

Margret Hottinger

Generalizations concerning the socio-economic situation in sixteenth century Europe are subject to the same problems as generalizations concerning political reality. Local conditions were many and various. Nevertheless, some general trends can be identified.

By the sixteenth century the fundamental transition had begun from an agriculturally based feudal system (favouring the landholding aristocracy, who lived from the labour and rents of their peasants) to a capitalist system (favouring the urban bourgeoisie who controlled capital, and stimulated trade, commerce and industry).

Economic Transitions

The transitional process created social tensions. The older medieval ideal was in tune with a world run by landowning nobility and supported by a labouring peasantry. Medieval economic notions idealized agriculture, physical labour, and subsistence and at the same time denigrated the activity of traders and merchants. (7)

Merchants were often depicted as little better than thieves, consumed with avarice, charging far more than their goods were actually worth. The medieval world had not been hospitable to change, innovation, or entrepreneurial activity, but by the sixteenth century, with the increase of urban populations, this was all changing. Landowners were losing ground in the economic sphere.

(7) Thomas Aquinas, **Summa Theologica**
"[Exchange for profit] is justly deserving of blame, because, considered in itself, it satisfies the greed for gain, which knows no limit and tends to infinity. Hence trading, considered in itself, has a certain debasement attaching thereto..." (In Baumer, 1970, 90).

The great Peasants' War of 1525, which coincided with the Reformation and gained ideological legitimacy from it, can be seen as one more battle in an on-going struggle between the landowners and the peasants. Although the aristocracy won the battle decisively in 1525, ultimately they lost the war for economic supremacy to the rising bourgeosie.

Church and Economics

The church did not escape the socio-economic conflict for the simple reason that the medieval and late medieval church formed an integral part of the agrarian feudal system, as well as taking a large share of tax revenue from its parishes.

The upper clergy of the church, who were with few exceptions drawn from the nobility, were dependent, as was the aristocracy, on the revenues produced by their serfs and tenant farmers. The monasteries were particularly efficient exploiters of land and rural labour. Added to these revenues, of course, were the obligatory tithes and church taxes extracted from serfs and tenants to which the ecclesiastical lords were entitled. All of this only increased peasant resentment against the clergy.

The response of the common people to the financial exactions of the church was a strong and, at times, violent reaction against the clergy

Anticlericalism

[anticlericalism]. This manifested itself in the medieval and late-medieval heretical movements as well as in movements of lay piety and movements of outright social rebellion, often directed against ecclesiastical lords with special zeal. (8)

---

(8) A bailiff in southern France (ca. 1300) comments on the burning of a Waldensian
"Instead of this Waldensian it's the Bishop of Parmiers himself they ought to have burned. For he exacts carnelage [tithe on sheep] and makes us pay out large sums on our possessions." (Ladurie, 1979, 22).

The conservative medieval social and economic order had been put forward as the supposed expression of God's will for humankind. But it was only natural that as religious social and economic ideals (poverty, contempt for the world) came into conflict with actual church practice (efficient collection of tithes and rents), there would be a questioning of religious authority. And, in the medieval period as well as in the sixteenth century, questioning religious authority opened the door to questioning the customary social and economic order. If it could no longer be accepted that the old authorities had it right, and if Scripture was to be one's guide in all things, the question became: What does the Bible reveal about God's will for proper social and economic order?

The question may have been posed in a biblical or theological way, but very real power questions were involved.

A sixteenth century ruler could widen his economic base and strengthen his political power by "reforming" the church and appropriating church lands to himself–lands traditionally controlled by the noble families or the church itself. Likewise in the cities, the struggle between the patrician classes and the guilds (described as "the rabble" by the patrician ruling class) often centred on the question of who was to control the "reform." There was real power and real money at stake.

Church Reform and Power

Some religious ideas lent themselves more readily to the support of the elites; some lent themselves more in support of popular interests. Among the peasantry and some poorer urban classes, reform meant primarily a social change and a change in the way the church was financed and run. Very often the common people expressed a desire to control the morals of their priests and pastors by controlling appointments, and they likewise wished to use tithe revenues to help the poor in their own parishes, rather than having those tithes go to support some cathedral canon or distant scholar. And they dreamed of a more equal society where they too would have a political and religious voice.

Jakob Hottinger had learned how to read German, and he owned a New Testament. He assumed, contrary to medieval custom, that this now gave him the right, and even imposed the duty, to correct a doctor of theology on the basis of the Word of God. The Zurich magistrates, in ruling that it was not in Jakob's place to speak to theological and biblical questions, were trying to get a troublesome genie back into a medieval bottle. It didn't work in Jakob's case, nor in the case of many other dissatisfied peasants and craftspeople.

The peasants in 1525 and the Anabaptists who followed appealed to the Bible and Reformation writings. But they read the Bible in communal, levelling, and anticlerical ways that had roots (or at least precedents) in medieval communal traditions and heretical resistance movements.

Where did the Anabaptists fit in the social and economic transitions that were underway in the sixteenth century? We will devote a separate section of our study to this question, when we examine the development of Anabaptist positions on social and economic questions.

Religious Life in Medieval Context: Ideals

The framework that unified political, social, and economic life in the late middle ages was the unified, "two worlds" view outlined above. The church occupied a central role in this understanding of the cosmos. The church had defined the universal terms of reference in Christian categories, and had inculcated Christian ideals of attitude and behaviour. And the church was the one institution that claimed to have a strategy for victory.

(9) "Materially and spiritually there were no watertight barriers between the terrestrial world and that beyond." "Between heaven and earth there was an incessant coming and going. The watchful choir of angels was drawn up against the cohort of demons who swooped on men whose sins called out to them." (Le Goff, 1988, 152; 163).

For medieval people the lines between earth, heaven, and hell were not firmly drawn. Earthly life was constantly being invaded from above and below, by the divine and the demonic. (9) Or better said, daily life was populated by human beings, angels, and demons alike: no invasion was necessary. The boundary between supernatural and natural, between the spiritual and the physical, was thin, permeable, and often invisible.

The daily challenge for medieval people was to defeat the forces of evil in this life, so that they could enjoy divine protection in the here and now, and eternal bliss in heaven, in the next life. The church had succeeded in teaching medieval people the ideal ways of combatting the forces of evil, on both the personal and communal levels.

Contemptus Mundi

Nothing was clearer in the medieval scheme of things than the fact that heaven was the "higher" of the two worlds. It was the spiritual goal to be attained. Although earth was an intermediate place of pilgrimage, suspended between heaven and hell, the earthly was more of an impediment than a help. Satan used the material, the earthly, to trap and ensnare human beings. The base passions and desires all worked to the benefit of evil.

Since life on earth was conceived in this way, a primary medieval virtue, or attitude of mind, was a thorough disdain for "the things of this world." (10) Those who succeeded most thoroughly in overcoming "the world" were considered saints, living members of the community of heaven.

> *(10) "Contempt for the world,* contemptus mundi, *was one of the great themes of medieval thought. It was not a monopoly of mystics, or theologians... Contempt for the world was deeply rooted in the feelings of common people." (Le Goff, 1988, 184).*

Divine Retribution

Life on earth provided numerous opportunities for sin, and medieval people, like modern people, were only too happy to oblige. But the medieval economy of salvation decreed that sins could not go unpunished. Sin dishonoured the Lord God, and had to carry appropriate punishments.

> *Individual Salvation*

The *Ius Talionis,* or law of retribution was conceived as a divine and universal law. It decreed that one's eternal punishment would fit one's earthly sins. It was a law that was graphically depicted in countless works of art and sculpture decorating medieval buildings. Its most graphic literary description can be read in Dante's *Divine Comedy*, particularly in the depiction of the torments of hell and trials of purgatory.

Penance

According to the law of retribution, personal sins demanded appropriate repentance and atoning action, if God's honour was to be restored and the sinner returned to a state of righteousness. Acts of penance were necessary material accompaniments to one's repentant state of mind.

There were those who devoted themselves to a renunciation of the world and to acts of continual prayer and penance. They were usually, although not exclusively, the cloistered monks and nuns. Again, it was usually, although not exclusively, from among the full-time monastics that saints were acclaimed and recognized. Sainthood was theoretically open to all, but realistically, only to a few heroic individuals.

Communion of Saints

As we enter the twenty-first century, we tend to fancy ourselves independent individuals, unique, standing free before the world and before God. Nothing could have been further from the medieval mind. (11) Medieval

Communal Salvation

society was communally based, not individually based: family, kinship networks, village communities, work communities, and religious communities were all central. Membership in a concentric circle of communal

(11) *"Medieval man was not an isolated individual, facing the world on his own... It was primarily from collective beliefs and notions that he drew his convictions, including criteria for truth and falsehood. Truth was what the collective believed..." (Gurevich, 1988, 55).*

groupings was considered essential to life itself. The solitary individual was vulnerable, was bound to do wrong, and was mistrusted.

Political, social and economic ideals reinforced communal obligations. (12) So did religious teaching. Salvation was a communal venture, with each member of society having a role to play in the process. Included in the collective were the deceased, among whom Christ, the Blessed Virgin, and the saints played particularly crucial roles as advocates for the living.

(12) "The free man was the man who had a powerful protector." (Le Goff, 1988, 280).

Individualism, particularly in the matter of eternal salvation and damnation, was madness, an instance of pride, which was conceived as the progenitor of all other vices. In the cosmic battle, one needed all the forces of the community of saints on one's side.

Religious Life in Medieval Context: Realities

In fact, medieval life was far from the gloomy, austere, world-renouncing ideal sketched above. But still, it can be said that the medieval church succeeded rather well in imparting its world view to medieval people as ideals, if not always as realities. The church's success caused it no end of problems, particularly with those who took the ideals seriously.

(13) Cathar witness, ca. 1300.
"The Pope devours the blood and sweat of the poor. And the bishops and the priests, who are rich and honoured and self-indulgent, behave in the same manner . . . whereas Saint Peter abandoned his wife, his children, his fields, his vineyards and his possessions to follow Christ." (In Ladurie, 1979, 333).

Critiques of church practice and of the clergy in the medieval period were most often calls for the church to live up to the ideals it had professed and successfully taught the pagan people of Europe. (13) What conclusions were to be drawn when the church systematically fell short of living the ideals it was preaching?

(14) Cathar testimony, ca. 1300.
"It is no good confessing to the priests. They keep whores, and all they want to do is eat us up, as the wolf destroys the sheep... It is better to be received into Bélibaste's sect just before death... Then you are absolved of your sins, and in three days, after you are dead, your soul ascends to the Heavenly Father." *(In Ladurie, 1979, 298).*

The problem of the church failing to live up to its own religious, moral, and economic ideals was large enough. But the larger problem was that for many medieval people, moral failure indicated a loss of spiritual power. (14) A fallen church was a church that had lost its ability to help in the cosmic spiritual struggle against the forces of darkness and evil. (15)

We state only the obvious when we say that by the sixteenth century there was a growing and painful discrepancy between the medieval church's universal claims to religious charisma and authority and the not-so-subtle scramble for church revenue and the moral decadence of lower and higher clergy.

Any serious reform effort–and there were many in the century before the Reformation–would have to confront large practical problems, among which were:

–**Simony**: the buying and selling of church offices by higher clergy

–**Absentee clerics**: clergy receiving church income (benefices) but not providing the services paid for.

–**Poor pastoral care**: priests in smaller parishes were poorly trained and ill paid and so charged the laity extra for funerals, weddings, etc.

–**Low moral standards**: a problem top to bottom.

(15) "The less wholesome, pure and moral the country was, the more it had need of real saints. The holy lives of a few goodmen made up for the free and easy ways of the masses. They maintained contact between the small locality, with its less than fully Christian fabric, and the great God of 'real Christianity', from whom all would one day have to seek salvation." (Ladurie, 1979, 326).

From the perspective of the common people, and all larger theological issues aside, any reformation of the church would have to correct the practical failings that were witnessed daily. But at the same time, reform also would have to speak to the spiritual hunger of pious laity.

The yearning for reform arose not only from dissatisfaction with the clergy and the institutional church, but also from a substratum of fervent lay piety, spirituality, and practice. In a very real way, reform happened because the church had succeeded too well.

Conclusion

We revisit Jakob Hottinger in conclusion.

When we recreate the scene in the parish church in June of 1523, in Zollikon, Switzerland, we also need to recreate Jakob's intellectual and cultural world.

Jakob's political location allowed him to speak his mind with relative freedom, but his political ideal was more medieval than modern. Jakob was more in tune with Aquinas' theocratic views (the rule of God) than with Machiavelli's politics of princely power. Jakob's disobedience of political authorities was based on the principle that God was to be obeyed above men. God was the political Lord over all lords, political or religious. (16)

> *(16) Jakob Hottinger's testimony, March 25, 1525*
> *"He will stop baptizing— unless someone asks him [for baptism], for God's sake. Then he will do what God calls him to do. Other than that, he will be obedient to the Zurich lords."*

Jakob was freer and better off than most European peasants of the time. This fact perhaps emboldened him to speak his mind publicly. But from other evidence we know that Jakob's social and economic ideals were more medieval and feudal than modern or capitalistic. Although the incident in the Zollikon church does not demonstrate this fact, Jakob supported the medieval communal ideals of moderate equality and the economics of subsistence. Although in his person, he was a peasant emancipated from most of the bonds of serfdom, Jakob Hottinger was not poised to accumulate capital.

Finally, Jakob's mistrust of the clergy and their interpretation of Scripture placed him solidly in the Reformation period. But this mistrust had been building up for centuries. Jakob's concern with salvation, with the cosmic battle between Christ and Satan, with obedience to God's will, were long-standing concerns that were waiting for a catalyst.

Martin Luther was such a catalyst. He provided an important spark that ignited a forest fire, but the conditions had been ripe for some time.

Luther's reforming blaze swept away much of the old church, but reforms are always continuations as well as new beginnings. In many important ways, as we will see below, the Anabaptist movement retained central ideals of medieval religious piety, which Luther wished to remove. In particular we will note the importance of the following characteristics of medieval piety that continued their importance in Anabaptism:

–An ascetic understanding of salvation and the Christian life

–An idealization of the life of Christ as the model for pious Chrsitians

–A more communal understanding of life, the cosmos, and salvation

–A linking of spiritual charisma to moral purity

–A view of the world that interpreted life as a struggle between the forces of good and evil, Christ and Satan

–A spiritualized view of the world that still considered the secular realm to be a place where Satan's power held sway

The survival of these religious ideals gave a unique colour, shape, and texture to Anabaptist church reform, marking it, as Walter Klaassen said, as "neither Catholic nor Protestant." (Klaassen, 1973).

Chapter 2

Evangelical Reform

In May of 1503 a bright young man named Balthasar Hubmaier entered the University of Freiburg in Briesgau. He was from a humble family, coming to study with the famous theologian, Johannes Eck. Balthasar did very well indeed. Dr. Eck praised his brilliance, and when Eck moved to the University of Ingolstadt, Balthasar soon followed. In August of 1512, Balthasar Hubmaier received the degree of Doctor of Theology from the University of Ingolstadt. Not only had he become a theologian of note, he also was an accomplished preacher and lecturer. He was moving up.

Hubmaier appeared to have a promising university career ahead. In 1513 he was elected Prorector of the University of Ingodstadt, a post he held for three years. But in 1516 he left the university to become cathedral preacher in the city of Regensburg.

In Regensburg Hubmaier joined an anti-Jewish crusade, already underway. As cathedral preacher, his sermons contributed to the anti-Semitic fervor that led, in 1519, to the destruction of the synagogue and the expulsion of the Jewish community from the city.

As the synagogue was being torn down, a master mason suffered what appeared to be a fatal accident. By evening he had revived, and it was widely reported that the Blessed Virgin had performed a miracle. The miraculous healing was supposed to demonstrate the Blessed Virgin's pleasure at the destruction of the synagogue. A chapel was built on the spot, dedicated to the "Beautiful Mary." Hubmaier preached at its dedication, and a huge pilgrimage movement began. Many miracles were reported. In 1520 more than 100,000 pilgrims came to the chapel.

However, by January of 1521, Hubmaier was actively reading Martin Luther's writings. Luther's reform movement was broadly known as "evangelical" reform because of its appeal to the authority of Scripture and the Gospel.

By March of 1523, Hubmaier had become an evangelical reformer. By the Spring of 1525 he had become an Anabaptist.

(For the full story, see Torsten Bergsten, *Balthasar Hubmaier. Anabaptist Theologian and Martyr*, trans. by W.R. Estep, Jr. [Valley Forge: Judson Press, 1978]).

Chapel to Our Beautiful Lady, Regensburg, where Balthasar Hubmaier preached to pilgrims.

The story of Balthasar Hubmaier provides a graphic illustration of the way in which church careers underwent tumultuous changes in the early years of the evangelical reform. In the space of less than five years, Hubmaier went from being a Catholic theologian and academic, to a popular preacher and passionate devotee of the Blessed Virgin, to a possible adherent of the "pure Gospel."

In setting the medieval context, we looked through the eyes of the Swiss peasant, Jakob Hottinger. He stood outside the leadership of the institutional church, and brought some traditional grievances against it. In telling the story of the early evangelical reform we will look through Balthasar Hubmaier's eyes, from **within** the institutional church.

The Sacramental Church

It is a common refrain in the history of the church: Dissenting Christians, such as Donatists in the fourth century, or Cathars and Waldensians in the thirteenth and fourteenth, maintain that divine charisma attaches to persons. True pastors are recognized by holy lives; those who live sinful or unworthy lives are not true pastors. The institutional church from the fourth century onward maintained that charisma was attached to the pastoral **office**, not the person who occupied it. It was in this way that, in spite of moral failings of individual clerics, the medieval church could maintain that it was the exclusive means to the heavenly end.

The high claims made by the medieval church were summed up nicely at the Fourth Lateran Council (1215), were it was decreed, among other things, that outside the church and its sacraments there was no salvation. (1) This central teaching was still maintained in the late medieval church. The church, under the headship of the pope, held itself to be the sole earthly mediator of grace to a sinful humanity.

The power of the medieval church consisted in its ability to open the doors of the spiritual realm for the rest of humanity.

It was a church made up not only of the living, but also of the dead. The mystical communion of saints included those awaiting further grace in purgatory, as well as the Saviour, the Blessed Virgin, and the saints who had proceeded directly to heaven. The superfluous merits of Christ and the saints could be utilized to reduce the penalty for sin for those still living, as well as for those already dead but undergoing cleansing in purgatory.

(1) Pope Innocent III and the Fourth Lateran Council (1215)
*"There is one Universal Church of the faithful, outside of which there is absolutely no salvation. In which there is the same priest and sacrifice, Jesus Christ, whose body and blood are truly contained in the sacrament of the altar under the forms of bread and wine; the bread being changed (*transubstantiatis*) by divine power into the body, and the wine into the blood, so that to realize the mystery of unity we may receive of Him what He has received of us. And this sacrament no one can effect except the priest who has been duly ordained in accordance with the keys of the Church, which Jesus Christ Himself gave to the Apostles and their successors." (In Petry, 1987, 322-23).*

> *(2) From Bishop Lyndwood's* **Provinciale.**
> "The Mystic Treasury *is that of the merits of the whole Church, and of those made perfect in the Church, and also of Christ Himself. For this Treasure is collected from the abundance of superfluous merits which many saints have paid and weighed out . . . whereof the merit is so great as to exceed all the penalty [of sin] owed by any living man..." (In Petry, 1987, 341).*

The papacy claimed the power to draw upon the "Treasury of Merit," at its discretion. (2) The infamous indulgences that called forth Luther's 95 theses in 1517 were papal documents that were drawn on this treasury, for the remission of sin's penalty. Indulgences were only one small part of the general sacrament of penance, but as it happened, Luther's questioning of the salvific value of indulgences soon brought the entire sacramental edifice into question.

Besides claiming to be able to access the spiritual power represented by the faithful dead, the medieval church also claimed the power to convey divine grace directly, by means of the sacraments.

The medieval church finally identified seven sacraments. They were:
–Baptism
–the Eucharist
–ordination
–confirmation
–penance
–marriage
–extreme unction.

(3) Peter Lombard, Sentences, (ca. 1160) "A Sacrament is the visible form of an invisible grace." (In Petry, 1987, 321).

Sacraments brought together the visible and the invisible, the worlds of spirit and matter. (3) The waters of baptism, for example, were the visible sign that conveyed the invisible grace that removed the stain of original sin from the soul of the one baptized.

Outside of exceptional circumstances, these visible signs could only convey God's invisible grace when they were administered by someone who had been duly and properly ordained. Ordination, in turn, was only valid if administered by a properly ordained bishop standing in the line of apostolic succession headed by the pope, the bishop of Rome. So the dispensation of saving grace was entirely in the hands of the clergy of the church, under the authority of the pope. Or, said more elegantly, there was no salvation outside the church. (4)

The supernatural powers conveyed by ordination created a "clerical" class as distinct from the "laity." The spiritual powers of the clergy were displayed in the administration of all the sacraments, but they were visible particularly in the celebration of the Eucharist. At the words of institution, "This is my Body," the elements of the host (the bread) and the wine were said to be transubstantiated into the body and the blood of Christ. That is, the particular bread and wine still looked and tasted like bread and wine, but an invisible change of substance had occurred through the priestly mediation. The belief that Christ was physically (substantially) present in the consecrated host led to the common practice of adoration of the host as a form of devotion, meditation, and prayer.

---

(4) Pope Eugenius gives an account of the seven Sacraments (1438)
"...through baptism we are born again of the spirit; through confirmation we grow in grace and are strengthened in the faith; and when we have been born again and strengthened we are fed by the divine food of the mass; but if, through sin, we bring sickness upon our souls, we are made spiritually whole by penance; and by extreme unction we are healed, both spiritually and corporeally, according as our souls have need; by ordination the Church is governed and multiplied spiritually; by matrimony it is materially increased." (In Petry, 1987, 324-25).

As an ordained priest, Balthasar Hubmaier was the bearer of the church's sacramental power. But even more, as a doctor of theology he moved among the elite of the church and society. He had the philosophical and theological tools to defend the position the church had assumed in society and to explain its role in the economy of salvation. Finally, as a fiery and eloquent pilgrimage preacher, he encouraged devotion to the Blessed Virgin and fed the popular need for miraculous intervention.

Lay Piety on the Eve of the Reformation

The preceeding description of the sacramental teaching of the medieval church could lead to the mistaken impression that the spirituality of the era was dominated from above, by the clergy and the sacraments, and that the laity were just passive recipients of grace dispensed by the clergy. But the situation was much more complex than this.

Traditional Practices

Take, for example, the case of the pilgrimage church in Regensburg where Hubmaier preached to tens of thousands of excited pilgrims, three years **after** Luther posted his theses on the Wittenberg church door. Regensburg was no isolated incident. The evidence suggests that there was a marked increase in traditional religious practices, initiated and funded by the laity in the late medieval period, right up to the time of the Reformation.

The empirical evidence for an increase in traditional lay piety is a sharp upswing in the foundation of new chapels and churches, and the continuing popularity of endowed Masses for the dead, of pilgrimages and processions, and the increased commissioning of images of the saints. Added to this are the increased activities of religious confraternities who hired their own priests to celebrate Masses for the dead and occasionally endowed their own preachers. These confraternities initiated popular feasts, processsions, plays, and pageants.

The image of a silent and subservient laity dominated by an overpowering clergy does not fit the facts of lay piety in the late middle ages. Often the clergy were hired by the laity to perform sacramental functions the laity desired. Was Hubmaier leading, or following the crowds in Regensburg?

Nevertheless, the confusing fact remains that within a very few years, great numbers of these same lay people would repudiate much of what they had so recently held sacred.

Some historians suggest that the rise in traditional observances on the eve of the Reformation reflects the rising concern of the laity about salvation. Other historians have warned against extrapolating too much from Luther's personal experience of anxiety. All agree, however, that the phenomenon of increasing lay piety on the eve of the Reformation presents a complex picture.

Many practices of popular piety were based on the church's sacrament of penance. But it is important to note in addition that much of late medieval lay piety imitated monastic examples. Only ordained priests had the power to transubstantiate bread and wine, or to conduct masses for the dead, but the ascetic ideals of the monks and nuns could be duplicated by any truly zealous lay person.

Monastic models

It should not be surprising that the most religiously committed laity of the late medieval period found ways of paralleling the religiosity of the monks and nuns. The lay religious communities of Beghards and Beguines that sprang up without permission or benefit of clerical leadership are the most striking examples of lay initiative and piety in a monastic mode. The ideals they lived out were poverty, chastity, and separation from the world. The "Modern Devotion" movement also shared these same ideals.

In addition to the pervasive idealization of the renunciatory life, historians of Christian spirituality have noted a marked increase in "spiritualization" in the late medieval period and beyond. By the sixteenth century, there had been a decisive shift **inward** in Christian spirituality, away from the more "objectified" spirituality of the earlier middle ages. The shift was subtle, but significant. The emphasis began to fall on one's inner, spiritual condition, rather than on the reception of grace by means of sacramental objects and actions.

Spiritualization

Once this shift had been made, it was a short step for some to conclude that it was **only** one's inner, spiritual condition that made religious life and religious practice genuine and effective. Clerical and lay interest in mysticism and the "things of the Spirit" expressed itself sometimes in orthodox ways, but at other times and places the spiritualizing impulse directly threatened the sacramental edifice and priestly mediation.

The sacramentarian movement that began in the Netherlands was an important case of a spiritualizing tendency that opposed the church's claim to be able to sacralize material elements. The Sacramentarians openly opposed any notion of transubstantiation. In reaction against the Catholic Mass, and the claim that clergy could somehow divinize bread and wine, the Sacramentarians taught that matter could never be spiritualized at all. There was an impassable gulf between the worlds of spirit and matter.

When Anabaptism arrived in the Netherlands in 1530, it found that sacramentarian piety had prepared the way. Many Anabaptists in the Netherlands, notably Menno Simons and David Joris, had first been introduced to doubts about the efficacy of the sacraments by the Sacramentarians.

Anabaptism and Lay Piety

The Anabaptist movement must be seen against the background of the medieval institutional church, but also against the background of late medieval lay piety, from which it also emerged. Following the lead of the mainline reformers, Anabaptism did repudiate late medieval sacramental and penitential practices. But Anabaptism also continued medieval forms of piety that the mainline reformers wished to repudiate. In particular, Anabaptist piety continued to resonate to the late medieval ideals of ascetic and spiritualist piety.

There was no typical form of late medieval piety. Within the dogmatic framework of sacramental teaching and practice there flourished side by side veneration of saints, exalted mystical forms of unitive prayer, ascetic programmes of renewal, participation in bawdy street plays, pilgrimages to shrines, the purchase of indulgences as acts of penance, and spiritualistic ideas about the sacraments. Calls for reform would necessarily evoke different responses depending upon the hearer's commitments.

Nevertheless, in light of what was to come, it is fair to say that late medieval piety was shaped by fundamental presuppositions that would come under serious question with the advent of Luther's critiques. Three of these central presuppositions were:

1. The church includes the active participation of the dead as well as the living. This conviction, on which rested much of what characterized lay piety in the late middle ages, had been shared by virtually everyone in the medieval period. Salvation depended upon the penitential activity of the living, in conjunction with the benefits that could be conferred by the sainted dead. Acts of penance, deeds of virtue and self-denial, and reception of the sacramentals all played active roles in the saving process of justification before God the judge.

Presuppositions Challenged

2. Sacramental powers reside with the clergy of the church. The clergy were those duly ordained (granted spiritual power), within a hierarchy headed by the pope. Outside this sacramental structure, which existed as the only mediator of God's saving grace, there was no salvation. Furthermore, final doctrinal and interpretive authority within the church was held to reside with the papacy.

3. Truly pious laity need to live as much like clergy as possible. It was generally accepted that full time, observant clergy had an advantage in the economy of salvation, particularly in matters of penance. This conviction often led to parallel efforts among the laity.

The Challenge of Luther's Ideas

Martin Luther's 95 theses of 1517 were not calculated to overthrow the existing church. Sparked by the sale of indulgences, they were a critique of an abused practice, not of the structure that sponsored the practice. (5) But one thing led to another.

---

(5) From Luther's 95 Theses

"Thesis 27. Those who assert that a soul straightway flies out (of purgatory) as a coin tinkles in the collection-box, are preaching an invention of man.

Thesis 28. It is sure that when a coin tinkles greed and avarice are increased; but the intercession of the church is in the will of God alone.

Thesis 32. Those who think themselves sure of salvation through their letters of pardon will be damned for ever along with their teachers." (Bettenson, 1975, 187).

In his university lectures on Romans (1513-1517) Luther already had come to a radical understanding of saving faith, and it soon became evident that he was questioning the very foundations of medieval church doctrine and practice.

In 1520 Luther published a series of remarkable writings that provided many of the basic concepts and slogans for the early "evangelical" reforming movement. Luther threw down the gauntlet in public, in print, and in German, and the papacy responded with a bull entitled *Exsurge Domine*, which condemned 41 proposition extracted from Luther's publications. By January 1521 an unrepentant Luther had been excommunicated by the pope.

The revolutionary power of Luther's reforming ideas lay in its challenge to prevailing assumptions about the nature of divine authority, the church, society, and salvation. Four of these principles in particular soon were circulating as slogans at the popular level.

1. Scripture Alone. In his writings of 1520 Luther emphasized repeatedly that the authority of Scripture is above that of the papacy: it is Scripture that judges humankind, including the papacy, and not vice versa. (6) This appeal to the ultimate authority of Scripture, prepared as it had been by Wycliff, Hus, and others, challenged the interpretive powers of the church hierarchy, and appeared to place all church practices before the bar of Scripture alone.

We say "appeared to place" because Luther's appeal to Scripture failed to resolve the crucial question of who (if not the church hierarchy) was to be the authoritative **interpreter** of Scripture.

> *(6) Luther, "The Papacy in Rome," (1520)*
> *"...all that the pope decrees and does I will receive on condition that I first test it by the Holy Scriptures. He must remain under Christ and submit to being judged by the Holy Scriptures." (In Tappert, 1967, 247).*

Luther's assumption (incorrect, but shared by most evangelical reformers before 1525) was that Scripture was "clear" and would need no further interpretation.

2. Priesthood of all Believers. Luther argued that all believers are equally "priests" by virtue of baptism. Ordination, said Luther, does not mark out a special class of people. Furthermore, the authority to ordain pastors lies with the congregation. No powers were conferred through ordination, and no special spiritual estate exists. Therefore the entire papal and sacramental edifice was a house built on sand.

It appeared from this that Luther was erasing the clergy/laity distinction altogether, saying that the laity had an equal right to function as "priests" within the church, and even more, that congregations were to have authority over their pastors.

In the medieval social context (recall the parallel hierarchies of heaven and earth) Luther's teaching on the priesthood of all believers was not only theologically innovative, it had the potential for social revolution.

> *(7) Luther, "To the German Nobility" (1520)*
> *"There has been a fiction by which the Pope, bishops, priests, and monks are called the 'spiritual estate'; princes, lords, artisans, and peasants are the 'temporal estate.' This is an artful lie... [All] Christians are truly of the spiritual estate, and there is no difference among them, save of office." (In Bettenson, 1975, 193).*

3. Salvation by Grace through Faith. Whereas the medieval church held that the clergy and the sacraments were central in mediating grace, Luther argued that salvation was by "faith alone," and not by any "works." (8) This faith was a direct gift from God (grace) and could not be earned. By works Luther meant primarily the numerous works of penance as well as other good works that were supposed to confer merit and contribute to justification in the sacramental understanding. Luther's understanding of salvation emphatically removed the sacramental church from its previous mediating function, and appeared to place all individual believers directly before God.

4. At the same time Justified and yet a Sinner. Luther's understanding of salvation by faith alone challenged the ascetic rationale underlying much of medieval spirituality: it had been assumed that with proper disposition, effort, and exercise, human beings were capable of growing in virtue, and that growth in virtue would contribute to salvation. The highest exemplars of this potential growth in virtue were the saints, most of whom had devoted themselves to the religious life under a monastic rule.

(9) Luther, "Treatise on Good Works," (1520)
"But you say, how can I be absolutely sure that all my works are pleasing to God, when at times I fall, talk, eat, drink, and sleep too much...? Answer: ...[faith] blots out these everyday sins and still stands fast by never doubting that God is so favorably disposed toward you that he overlooks such everyday failures and offenses." (In Tappert, 1967, 119).

To the contrary, said Luther, human beings are justified not by any actual virtue they can attain, but only because God considers them "just" for Christ's sake. God considers sinners righteous because of their faith in Christ, period. (9) Luther's understanding of salvation "by faith alone" was a direct challenge to the ascetic rationale underlying centuries of spiritual practice.

Hubmaier Revisited

Let us revisit Baltasar Hubmaier in Regensburg, and consider what impact Luther's words might have had.

In 1520, when Luther was publishing his ideas far and wide, Hubmaier was enjoying huge success as a pilgrimage preacher. He was a priest, encouraging prayers to the Blessed Virgin, worker of miracles. He was, to all accounts, a spellbinding orator, using his talents to preach about the salvific benefits of acts of penance and pilgrimage. He regularly performed the miracle of the Mass, and provided clerical verification of the miraculous cures that had taken place at the shrine of "Our Beautiful Mary."

On becoming aware of Luther's ideas, Hubmaier experienced a painful choice, the same one faced by many other priests of his day. Either Luther was dead wrong, or he was right. If he was wrong, he was a heretic and a destroyer of the church, and needed to be opposed. That was the conclusion of Hubmaier's long-time teacher and mentor, Johannes Eck, who debated face to face with Luther in Leipzig in 1519. But if Luther was right, then Hubmaier needed to stop what he was doing, and become a different kind of pastor and preacher.

By 1523, Hubmaier had parted company with his former mentor, Johannes Eck. Witnesses claimed that on April 19, 1523 he preached a sermon in which he said that Catholic priests were "murderers of men's souls and priests of Satan who preached falsehoods, the dreams of monks and fathers of the Church, withholding the gospel from men." Of course, he did not preach this sermon in Regensburg. By 1523 he had taken up residence in Waldshut, a small city on the banks of the Rhine that was more open to evangelical reform. And he allied himself with Ulrich Zwingli, who was preaching reform in the city of Zurich. (10)

---

(10) Hubmaier speaks at the Second Zurich Disputation, January, 1523.
"In all divisive questions and controversies only Scripture ... should and must be the judge... If [images] are commanded, show us the Scripture... If they are not commanded, then they are worthless. . . . God the Son has said [Matt. 15:13]: 'Every planting that has not been planted by my Heavenly Father will be torn out.'" (Pipkin and Yoder, 1989, 23; 25).

Conclusion

Luther's reforming ideas were fruitful beyond his own expectations. But the great reform writings of 1520 were not yet a programme of reform. Luther's ideas circulated among the clergy as scholarly theses, and among the laity as popular slogans. In both cases his ideas gave rise to a variety of responses that were not always what Luther himself came to endorse.

Without a doubt the central result of Luther's critique was that the Christian church needed to be reconceived. The medieval church had been the place where the spiritual and the temporal met. It was an emphatically visible church. Luther insisted, to the contrary, that the church was essentially invisible. (11)

Following Luther's lead, the basic spiritual question appeared to be directed within, to one's personal (and invisible) faith in Christ. It was only "human invention" that had led to prayer before images of saints, the lighting of candles there, or the pilgrimages to visit holy relics.

> *(11) Luther, "The Papacy in Rome," (1520)*
>
> *"The holy church is not bound to Rome but is as wide as the world, ... a spiritual and not a bodily thing... The external Roman church we all see; therefore it cannot be the true church which is believed and which is a community or assembly of the saints in faith, for no one can see who is a saint or a believer."*
>
> *(Tappert, 1967, 221).*

All of this posed some difficult practical questions. What was to be done with holy pictures, relics, statues, and the like? Was a "biblical" church one that had been "cleansed" of these "human inventions," and should such "cleansing" proceed as soon as possible? What form of public and private piety should now take the place of those older forms?

Along with the desacralizing of holy images and objects Luther's emphasis on personal faith also appeared to desacralize the sacraments. Meditation and prayer that had focused on the "presence of Christ" in the consecrated host, and the popular celebrations and feasts associated with Corpus Christi, were now said to be much ado about nothing.

How then were sacramental practices in the church to be understood? Does baptism have any value apart from faith, given that salvation is by faith, and the water remains only water, even after a priest has blessed it? And if faith must accompany the waters of baptism, what then is the theological rationale supporting the baptism of infants, who clearly have no personal faith? How is the Supper to be understood, if Christ is not present in the elements through transubstantiation?

Luther also appeared to have removed the fundamental distinction between clergy and laity, and to have empowered the laity in spiritual matters. But Luther's understanding of salvation had at the same time removed ascetic assumptions that underlay the highest spiritual aspirations of medieval people. If human beings are saved by being considered righteous, and not by becoming righteous, how should Christian piety manifest itself? What was to become of the pursuit of virtue, of ascetic self-denial, of the avoidance of sin, of growth in humility, of a life of renunciation?

Luther's eventual answer to these practical questions gave concrete shape to the Lutheran branch of reform. Luther argued for a slow pace of reform, and that keeping many older forms was harmless. His position was "if it is not forbidden in Scripture, it is allowed in practice." In ecclesial practice the Lutheran reform looked and felt more conservative than radical.

Concerning baptism of infants, Luther said that the faith of the parents and godparents effectively substituted for the absent faith of the infant; concerning the Supper, Luther rejected transubstantiation while maintaining that Christ was physically present "with" the elements, and that the real body and blood of Christ was physically eaten with the elements, even by those who lacked faith.

These eventual Lutheran answers were not obvious in 1520, or for some years to come. In the euphoria and unclarity of those early years Luther's reforming principles and slogans were developed in a more "radical" manner by persons who also considered themselves to be part of the evangelical, or biblically-based, current of reform that Luther had championed initially. The Anabaptist movement formed part of this "Radical Reformation." We will examine the Anabaptist response to the call for church reform in various chapters and sections that follow.

Chapter 3

Radical Reform

Among the reformers who came to be labelled "radical" reformers, none was closer to Martin Luther in the early years than Andreas Karlstadt. Karlstadt had been Luther's teacher at the University of Wittenberg, and had promoted Martin Luther to the doctorate in 1512. They were then faculty colleagues until 1523. But it was Luther who took the lead in the reforming movement, and eventually the elder Karlstadt was pushed to the margins. By 1525 Martin Luther's name was identified with evangelical reform; Andreas Karlstadt, on the other hand, was regarded as a "tumultuous spirit." What happened?

There is no doubt that Martin Luther led Andreas Karlstadt to the evangelical point of view. The year 1517 was decisive: at Luther's urging, Karlstadt bought an edition of Augustine's writings. By Spring of that year, he was beginning to speak Luther's language. Karlstadt now taught that justification is a gift of God's grace, and that grace is communicated by hearing the Word.

Over the next two years, it was Luther who was the more emphatic and radical of the two. Karlstadt was cautious, and tried hard not to burn bridges. But Karlstadt accompanied Luther to the Leipzig Debate with Johannes Eck in 1519, and argued the evangelical position against Eck. This earned him a place on the papal bull of condemnation in 1520. From this point on he no longer vacillated on the question of church authority or indulgences. On the key question of authority in the church there was no looking back. He wrote in August of 1520: "Scripture judges all things, but is judged by no one."

The differences that emerged between Luther and Karlstadt were not theological differences initially, but had more to do with the pace of reform.

Immediately following Luther's dramatic confrontation with the Emperor Charles V at the Diet of Worms, when he refused to recant, Frederick of Saxony had hidden Luther away in the Wartburg castle, for his own safety. From June of 1521 until February of 1522, during Luther's Wartburg exile, Karlstadt was in charge of reform in Wittenberg.

It was a tumultuous time. There were public disputations, riots by people demanding the removal of "images" from the churches, and more. Frederick of Saxony was upset, and demanded that no changes be introduced to the Mass. Karlstadt, who had the support of the city council of Wittenberg, took the fateful decision to defy Frederick. Following a riot on Christmas Eve, Karlstadt presided over the celebration of the first evangelical Mass on Christmas day, 1522. Shortly thereafter, the city council of Wittenberg passed a reforming decree, following Karlstadt's lead: the Mass was to be said in German, communicants were to be given both bread and wine, private Masses for the dead were abolished, and images were to be removed from the churches.

In short order Frederick intervened and overturned the council's decree, and shortly thereafter Martin Luther returned from exile. When Martin Luther returned to Wittenberg in early March of 1522, he preached eight powerful sermons, and "restored old custom." Reform was to take place, but old "customs and practices" should be changed only after preaching of the Word of God had "convinced the weak" (and also the princes). Karlstadt's leading role in Wittenberg was at an end.

In the summer of 1523, Karlstadt took up the post of pastor in the town of Orlamünde, a parish he had held as a sinecure. It was here that he instituted, however briefly, church reforms as he saw fit. At Luther's instigation, however, and in spite of having been elected by the congregation, Karlstadt was removed from the parish of Orlamünde, and also banished from Saxon terrritory in September, 1524. The expulsion order called him a rebellious and satanic spirit.

The story of Andreas Karlstadt illustrates at first hand how the evangelical reforming movement began to fragment from within. No sooner had a consensus begun to emerge among evangelical reformers on the authority of Scripture and the centrality of faith, than differences also began to surface. The issue in Wittenberg appeared to be the speed of reform. But this really was a question of what role princes, kings, and city councils should be allowed to play in dictating the speed of reform. This was a large enough question, but very soon even more fundamental theological questions surfaced. Andreas Karlstadt was one of the first of a small but growing party of reformers who grew away from Luther and the mainline reform, and who have earned the title of radical reformers.

It is true to say that Anabaptism was a child of the Reformation. But it is even truer to say that Anabaptism was a child of the **Radical** Reformation. The Anabaptist story cannot be told apart from the important mediating influences of Andreas Karlstadt, Thomas Müntzer, Caspar Schwenckfeld, and others who had become disillusioned with the mainline reforms of Luther and Zwingli. Tracing some of the ideas and influences of radical reformers, as we will do below, goes a long way toward introducing the Radical Reformation context and critique out of which Anabaptism emerged and of which it formed a part.

Karlstadt's Orlamünde Theology

Scripture Alone

Karlstadt had a different conception of how to interpret and apply Scripture than did Luther, already by 1521.

No Human Traditions

Karlstadt was willing to allow *no* human tradition to remain, and called rather for a reform of the church only according to what had been commanded in Scripture. While Luther was willing to accept the basic structure of the Mass, for instance, and a very sacramental view of the Supper, Karlstadt purged the sanctuary of images and radically undid the sacramental view.

Spirit and Letter

A second crucial difference between Karlstadt and Luther concerned the role of the Spirit in relation to the letter of Scripture. Both Luther and Karlstadt insisted that a literal reading of Scripture was primary, and that Scripture must be read with Christ at the centre. Both insisted that the external word was the means of grace by which faith was born. Nevertheless, Karlstadt insisted further that the external word (whether read or heard) could be *interpreted* properly only through the power of the Holy Spirit. (1) Karlstadt's emphasis on the active role of the Spirit in the interpretation of Scripture would be taken up in the Anabaptist movement, and would remain a feature of the radical appropriation of Scripture alone.

> *(1) Karlstadt, (1521)*
> *"...extensive reading [of Scripture] is not sufficient unless you have the Spirit of God."*
> *(In Sider, 1974, 120-21).*

Common People

Finally, Karlstadt was emphatic that no special theological training was needed in order to interpret Scripture. (2) This seemed dangerous to Johannes Eck in 1519, when he told Karlstadt "One does not say to ordinary illiterate folk what one says to learned theologians." In reply Karlstadt wrote: "Scripture is to be taught not only to the learned, but also to women and illiterates." By 1525 both Luther and Zwingli had modified their earlier optimism about the unlearned and Scripture (and hence agreed with Eck's point). Karlstadt and the radical reformers did not.

> *(2) Karlstadt, "De canonicis," (1520)*   *"Since the proper interpretation of Scripture requires not some special authority, but rather merely the comparison of the various texts which speak of Christ, any Christian can engage in biblical interpretation."*   *(In Sider, 1974, 92-3).*

Salvation by Grace through Faith

Grace

At the heart of Luther's theology was the teaching of justification of sinners before God by grace, through faith in Christ's sacrificial death. Karlstadt agreed, but believed that God's grace would remake and regenerate sinners, leading them to a subsequent life of discipleship and obedience. In Karlstadt's view, grace is efficacious, and faith results in an overcoming of sin.

The differences between Luther and Karlstadt concerning the nature of divine grace were mirrored also in their respective understandings of the human will. Luther said that free will was a fiction. The human will was bound to sin in this life, and was dependent for salvation on God's predestination.

Karlstadt, to the contrary, argued that grace freed the human will to choose or not to choose salvation. For Karlstadt, sin was volitional. To sin was to will other than what God wills. Since sin is of this nature, the conquering of sin must take place by means of *Gelassenheit,* or the active "yielding" of one's will and desires to God's will. (3)

> **(3) Karlstadt, "Tract on the Supreme Virtue of Gelassenheit" (1520)**
> *"If I desire to ... carry a cross for God's sake, I must first deny and forsake myself. I must totally submerge my own will in God's will and drown self-will in all things. Hence, I must will as God wills."*
> *(Furcha, 1995), 38).*

Karlstadt, as would the Anabaptists after him, linked faith to a visibly and consciously "yielded" life. Karlstadt spoke of the "obedience of faith," and demanded a life of visible conformity to Christ. This emphasis hearkened back to late medieval ascetic spiritual ideals, and emphasized a visible church. Luther spoke of an invisible church, known to God alone.

Priesthood of all Believers

Whether or not Luther intended it to sound that way, the "priesthood of all believers" was a slogan that seemed to imply a church of equals. All believers had the right (so it appeared) to interpret Scripture and to judge clergy on the basis of it. But Luther soon made clear that he had not meant to give the laity such power. Luther's position became crystal clear in 1525, during the Peasants' War, when he backed the princes against the peasants. Karlstadt, on the other hand, continued to give a heightened role to the laity.

The question of priesthood was central to sacramental questions. Do physical elements *convey* divine grace and, if so, what role is played by the priesthood in bringing this about? Karlstadt, influenced by the Sacramentarians in the Netherlands, concluded that the physical elements could not transmit grace. Therefore priests could not sacralize material elements. Priests in Karlstadt's understanding would mediate grace by proclaiming the Word, something the laity could do as well as any ordained clergy.

Luther eventually returned to an essentially Roman Catholic sacramental understanding of baptism and the Supper. Karlstadt did not. He turned the elements of baptismal water and eucharistic bread and wine back to the natural world. What really counted was the inner spiritual reality of faith, regeneration by the Holy Spirit, and the new life which resulted.

Karlstadt was able to carry through a consistent priesthood of believers in large part because of the removal of the liturgical and ritualistic function of priests. This view would appear also in the Anabaptist movement, which in its early years emphasized the right of the laity (when informed by the Spirit) to preach, interpret Scripture, and preside over the Lord's Supper, without benefit of ordination, beyond the presence of the Spirit.

The Nature of the Church

> **(4) Karlstadt (1524)**
> *"It is impossible that one love Christ and not live according to his commands." (In Sider, 1974, 286).*

Because of Karlstadt's understanding that regeneration followed faith in Christ, he saw the church as a community of those who had been regenerated, and who gave visible signs of their regeneration. (4) He had little patience with Luther's admonition that reform should proceed slowly to "spare the weak."

Furthermore, it was within the regenerate congregation that baptism and the Supper were to be practiced. Both, said Karlstadt, were external signs of an inner yieldedness and rebirth.

Although Karlstadt did not institute the rebaptism of adults following confession of faith, he did argue against infant baptism and in favour of adult baptism. This followed directly from his conviction that faith and regeneration were both part of the saving process. Likewise the Supper is a memorial to be utilized by those who have been regenerated by grace through faith. In this important way Karlstadt, although never an Anabaptist in a formal sense, nevertheless laid the necessary groundwork for the emergence of Anabaptism.

Finally, Karlstadt held to a radical equality within the church. The priesthood of all believers remained primary for him. He also supported the election of pastors by the congregation, the correction of those pastors by the congregation, and the power of the congregation to "bind and loose." The similarity is striking between Karlstadt's understanding of the church, and what would appear later in the Anabaptist movement.

Conclusion

When Karlstadt's Orlamünde theology is considered from the point of view of spirituality, it is clear that he stood in closer continuity with late medieval piety than did Luther. Karlstadt's emphasis on an efficacious grace that regenerates and sanctifies sinners, leading to a visibly new life, hearkened back to the theme of sanctification in the late medieval framework. So did Karlstadt's understanding of the potentialities of the human person: he believed, as Luther did not, that human beings were capable of being regenerated by the Spirit of God in this life, that they were capable of becoming righteous. Likewise Karlstadt's understanding of sin as essentially volitional, opened the door to an ascetic approach to the Christian life. Walking in obedience was possible for Karlstadt, if one learned to yield to the Spirit and grace of God. This understanding left a place for the spiritual exercise of preparing for grace, with the expectation of real growth in the Christian life as a result. Finally, the church for Karlstadt was a community of the reborn, a kind of ascetic lay order committed to living new lives in community.

On the other hand, Karlstadt went further than did Luther in rejecting other aspects of traditional piety. He was far more anticlerical than was Luther, and rejected any mediatory role for the clergy, save the preaching of the Word. He enhanced the role of the laity far more than would Luther. Karlstadt was willing to subordinate sacraments to faith in a way Luther was not. And Karlstadt's approach to Scripture was at once more biblicistic (only what is commanded is allowed) and spiritualistic (only those with the Spirit can interpret correctly) than was Luther's view.

Karlstadt's differences with Luther played an important role in delineating an alternative stream of reform in the evangelical movement. His influence as a mediator of this alternative stream of reform is undeniable. He has even been called the "father" of the Baptist movement. Although some clear differences are evident between Karlstadt and the Anabaptists–such as the role Karlstadt maintained for Christian rulers–and although crucial historical links are no longer extant–such as Karlstadt's writing on baptism–his influence on at least the Swiss Anabaptist stream no longer is in doubt. Karlstadt blazed an alternative evangelical reforming trail upon which many an Anabaptist would tread subsequently.

Thomas Müntzer and his Theology

THOMAS MUNCER PREDIGER TOT ALSTAT,

TOMAS MVNCER PREDIGER ZV ALSTET IN DVRINGEN.

There was in all likelihood no person more vilified by learned contemporaries than the infamous Thomas Müntzer, the "destroyer of unbelievers" or, alternatively, "the Satan from Allstedt." Müntzer was concerned from the start of his career with the reform of the existing church. He was called a "Lutheran" already in 1519, and thanks to Luther's intervention he was called in May 1520 to fill a vacant post in the church in Zwickau. But Müntzer already differed from Luther at this early stage. He opposed infant baptism and promoted a spiritualist way of reading Scripture. Müntzer also taught a mystical doctrine of spiritual suffering, and soon came to oppose Luther's "salvation by faith alone." It was on the inner birth of the Spirit through suffering that Müntzer pinned his reforming hopes: When the original internal order was restored to human hearts, then the kingdom of this world would be given over to the elect.

Müntzer saw humanity as divided between sheep and goats, the righteous and the unrighteous. The righteous "sheep" are those who have an *experienced* faith, which has come to them through deep suffering. The unrighteous "goats" are those who have stolen their faith. Primary among the godless goats, said Müntzer, were the clergy themselves, and Luther soon became the primary example.

By 1521 Müntzer had become convinced that the End Times had arrived and that "a new apostolic church must gather the elect and separate them from worldly people." In 1525 Müntzer came to identify the peasants' revolt with the end of the "fifth monarchy prophecied in Daniel." Convinced that he was participating in the End Times drama, Müntzer urged the peasants assembled at Frankenhausen to battle against the professional army of the Landgrave, Philip of Hesse. The result was an unholy slaughter in which an estimated 6,000 peasants lost their lives. After the disaster at Frankenhausen, Müntzer was discovered hiding in an attic of the town. He eventually was brought to recantation. Toward the end of May, 1525, he was beheaded in Mühlhausen.

Scripture Alone

Thomas Müntzer became an evangelical reformer because he embraced the authority of Scripture over against the authority of the Roman Catholic hierarchy. But he emphasized the living Spirit even more emphatically than did Karlstadt. His approach to Scripture was mystical and spiritualistic. (5)

---

(5) Müntzer *"If a man in his whole life had neither heard nor seen the Bible, he could none the less have an undeceivable Christian Faith through the teaching of the Spirit–like those who wrote the Scriptures without any books." (In Rupp, 1969, 216).*

Müntzer believed that all reading of Scripture had to be grounded on a living experience of faith. Especially the "false biblical scholars," he said, liked to "dress up in Scripture," but were not ready to have its meaning revealed to them. (6)

---

(6) Müntzer
"The scholar cannot grasp the meaning of Scripture, although the whole of it has been expounded to him in a human way... He has to wait until the key of David has revealed it to him... Then man will be taught by God alone, person to person, and not by any created being." (Matheson, 1988, 224).

Müntzer's strong emphasis on the inner word, on the direct teaching by the Spirit of God as the true Word, solidly separated Müntzer's understanding of "the Word" from Luther's. Although Karlstadt also emphasized the work of the Spirit in the proper interpretation of Scripture, Müntzer's was yet a stronger spiritualism that did not follow Karlstadt's tendency to find laws of behaviour in Scripture. Müntzer's approach, furthermore, opened up the possibilty of direct, non-scriptural revelations.

Karlstadt and Müntzer's respective approaches to Scripture would each find representatives in the Anabaptist movement that followed.

Salvation by grace through faith

Thomas Müntzer assumed that only some would be chosen for salvation, but those who were so chosen would know it, because the process of salvation would include a painful spiritual purging, an uprooting of self, and a re-making of the inner person.

This view stood close to Karlstadt's view of spiritual regeneration, even though it was not identical with it. Müntzer had a stronger emphasis on suffering, and the painful process of coming to faith.

(7) Müntzer "Any one who rejects the bitter CHRIST will gorge himself to death on honey." (Matheson, 1988, 220).

For Müntzer, one's heart must be "ploughed" before faith can be planted. This understanding owed much to the mystical tradition, and much less to Luther. Müntzer's critique of Luther's "salvation by faith alone" was that it was too easy. It was a preaching, he said, of "sweetness alone." (7) True faith, as opposed to the counterfeit variety, would not be learned in books, said

Müntzer, but rather in "poverty of spirit," something akin to what the mystics called the "dark night of the soul."

In a strikingly similar way (and thoroughly in tune with late medieval ascetic expectations) Karlstadt and Müntzer critiqued Luther's understanding of salvation for not demanding more in the way of regeneration of believers. Karlstadt was more disposed to expect particular ethical results from this rebirth; Müntzer concentrated more on the process leading up to the birth of faith. These differences in emphasis would be echoed in the later expressions of Anabaptism.

Priesthood of all Believers and Doctrine of the Church

Because his reforming career was abruptly cut short, it is difficult to say how Thomas Müntzer would have structured his church in subsequent years.

In Allstedt he seemed quite comfortable with a traditional priestly role as a preacher of the Word and presider over the sacraments of the church. His liturgical work retained the traditional form of the Mass, albeit in German. Although he criticized infant baptism, nevertheless he continued to perform the ceremony. All of this drew the criticism of Conrad Grebel who, in his 1524 letter to Müntzer said that putting the Mass into German and translating liturgical songs "cannot be right."

Grebel was influenced by Karlstadt's more radical biblicism, which looked for rules of reform in the New Testament. We cannot know if Thomas Müntzer eventually would have supported a church made up only of committed believers, although his understanding of the elect who are reborn spiritually certainly contained the possible seeds for such a development.

Müntzer was open to accepting spiritualistic authority, no matter on whom it fell. The emphasis on the work of the Spirit in the interpretation of Scripture meant that such interpretation was now open to all who had in turn opened themselves to the Spirit. This radical interpretive equality, common to both Karlstadt and Müntzer, would continue in the Anabaptist tradition, particularly during the earlier more spiritualistic phases of the movement.

Apocalypticism

Müntzer's growing conviction that he was living in the Last Days certainly pushed him in a socially radical direction, although it appears that he was headed there from the start. Granted that even Martin Luther believed that he was living in the Last Days, still Müntzer drew far more radical implications from this than did Luther or Karlstadt.

As the Peasants' War heated up, Müntzer threw caution to the wind, and spoke with anticipation of the purging which was about to be visited upon the ungodly. (8) Just as God must root out the weeds in the believer's heart, so also will He weed out the ungodly from the world before the End.

> *(8) Müntzer to people of Allstedt, April, 1525.*
> *"Go to it, go to it, while the fire is hot! Don't let your sword grow cold, don't let it hang down limply! . . . God goes before you; follow, follow!" (Matheson, 1988, 142).*

Certainly Karlstadt shared none of Müntzer's enthusiasm for "uprooting of the godless." In contrast to Müntzer's revolutionary apocalypticism, Andreas Karlstadt showed little enthusiasm for End Times speculation, nor was he overly fond of the prophetic books of the Bible (e.g., Daniel, Esdras, Revelation). The differences between them were brought out explicitly at the beginning of the Peasants' War, when Karlstadt wrote personally to Müntzer rejecting the latter's invitation to join his league of the elect. (9)

> *(9) Karlstadt to Müntzer , July 1525.*
> *"I can have no dealings with you about that sort of undertaking or league. [You] should rest your hope in the one God who is able to confound your adversaries." (Matheson, 1988, 92).*

Karlstadt and Müntzer took rather different paths leading away from Wittenberg which led them to contrasting social-political conclusions. Their differing tendencies would become evident also in the Anabaptist descendants they inspired. Karlstadt's lack of apocalyptic and revolutionary enthusiasm was seen also in the Swiss Anabaptists, in the same way that Müntzer's apocalypticism came to be reflected in early South German Anabaptism.

Conclusion

Thomas Müntzer's continuation of late medieval themes is evident. In contrast to Luther, Müntzer's understanding of the Word of God owed more to the mystical tradition. Here Müntzer went beyond Karlstadt as well, for although Karlstadt also emphasized the role of the Spirit in the interpretation of Scripture, he did not suggest that extra-biblical revelation was possible or reliable. Thomas Müntzer, to the contrary, was open to both possibilities. What counted most were the inner experiences of the living God.

The tension between spirit and letter, evident here, would remain among the Anabaptists as well. The resolution of this tension gave a definite "shape" to the Anabaptist traditions that were passed on into the seventeenth century.

In the matter of salvation, Müntzer and Karlstadt critiqued Luther in essentially the same manner, and on the basis of the same late medieval presuppositions. Karlstadt and Müntzer shared the language and conception of late medieval mysticism in their use of the concepts of human free will, *Gelassenheit*, the volitional nature of sin, the possibility and necessity of regeneration and a new life. These emphases would re-appear in Anabaptism.

Finally, Thomas Müntzer's apocalyptic convictions influenced all other aspects of his thought. His emphasis on the living Spirit was a reflection of his conviction that in the Last Days, the Spirit would be poured out in new and powerful ways. His reading of Scripture was coloured by the conviction that the events of the Last Days had been predicted in the prophetic books of the Bible. The parallel he drew between the "inner ploughing of the soul" and the historical "winnowing of the godless" was ruled by his apocalyptic conviction as well.

In all these ways Thomas Müntzer went well beyond Luther (and in some cases, beyond Karlstadt as well) and outlined a reform path that was followed by a significant number of influential early Anabaptists.

Caspar Schwenckfeld von Ossig

SCHWENKFELD

Caspar Schwenckfeld von Ossig (1489-1561) was an aristocrat from Silesia who, like Karlstadt and Müntzer, became an early convert to the Lutheran reform. Like them, he also found his reasons to disagree with Luther and also exerted some influence on parts of the Anabaptist movement.

By 1522 this enthusiastic Silesian evangelical had become advisor in church affairs to Duke Frederick II at Liegnitz. By 1529, however, Schwenckfeld had left Silesia in a self-imposed exile. Three events conspired to bring this about: increasing political pressure from Ferdinand of Austria, who had come to rule the duchy of Silesia in 1526; Schwenckfeld's own estrangement from Luther because of Luther's conception of saving faith; and Schwenckfeld's steady movement in a spiritualist direction. In April of 1529, Schwenckfeld made a "discreet withdrawal" from the territory and remained a wanderer and itinerant lay theologian for the rest of his life.

In Strasbourg, where he found refuge from 1529 to 1534, Schwenckfeld came into frequent contact with a wide variety of Anabaptists (Swiss Brethren, Pilgram Marpeck, Melchior Hoffman). During his stay in the city Schwenckfeld influenced Melchior Hoffman's speculations about the nature of Christ (Christology). A decade later he argued extensively, in print, with Pilgram Marpeck. After his stay in Strasbourg, Schwenckfeld found temporary refuge in Ulm and Esslingen. He ended his life in hiding, protected by old friends and benefactors. He died in Ulm in 1561, after a prolonged illness.

Scripture Alone

Caspar Schwenckfeld has been described as a spiritualist because of his continuing and consistent emphasis on the interior action of the Spirit in the hearts of believers. It was the inner Word which brought salvation, not the outer, literal word. (10) Nevertheless, this emphasis on the inner Word did not mean that the outer Word was of no value to Schwenckfeld: he continued to study and exegete Scripture, he encouraged the preaching of the Word in public services, and invariably, he argued his spiritualist points of view scripturally. Still, he maintained that a true exposition of the Word could be done only by those who had been taught by the Spirit.

> **(10) Schwenckfeld**
> *"The word of life is inner spiritual scripture which actually creates faith. . . . Faith is necessary before one can understand the outer word of the Scripture." (Seebass, 1986, 96).*

Schwenckfeld's emphasis on the role of the Holy Spirit in the interpretation of Scripture recalls the critiques of Luther by Andreas Karlstadt and Thomas Müntzer, even though Schwenckfeld expressed his views in stronger and more explicitly spiritualistic tones.

Salvation by Faith

Martin Luther's critique of the Roman Catholic sacramental and penitential understanding of salvation, which he characterized as works righteousness, was replaced by Luther's conviction that human beings are saved from sin solely by faith in Christ's sacrifice. This doctrine Caspar Schwenckfeld embraced wholeheartedly. Nevertheless, Schwenckfeld believed that once faith had come to the human heart through the grace of God and the action of the Holy Spirit, this spiritual reality transformed the natures of the children of Adam.

Schwenckfeld's understanding of salvation thus mirrored in its general outlines (but with no visible lines of dependence) the dissenting evangelical views of Karlstadt and Müntzer: human beings are justified by *becoming* righteous, by the power of God (not by human effort as such), freed and empowered to begin a process of sanctification. He opposed Luther's teaching on bondage of the will and predestination. He was more optimistic about the potential for human regeneration.

Schwenckfeld, like Karlstadt and Müntzer, was concerned with the moral and ethical side of reform. The moral reform of the church, he believed, would come about only as a result of the activity of the Holy Spirit in the hearts of believers. He believed that a true faith born of the Spirit would *necessarily* result in a new life that manifested that faith. Salvation, then, would be a process of progressive sanctification. There could be no "justified and a sinner at the same time" (*simul iustus et peccator*) for Schwenckfeld, as there could not be either for Karlstadt or Müntzer. Faith meant for Schwenckfeld a spiritual bond between Christ and the regenerated believer.

The Supper and Baptism

Building on the view that faith is a spiritual bond between the believer and the risen Christ, Schwenckfeld redefined the Lord's Supper. Already by July 1525 Schwenckfeld was convinced, on his reading of John 6, that Christ was not physically present in the elements of the Supper. He sent a writing to Luther and others which argued this point of view. By October of that same year Schwenckfeld's friend, Valentine Crautwald, had helped him to a further understanding. Concerning the words of institution, "This is my body," Crautwald and Schwenckfeld concluded that the words of institution indicated a "mystical flesh" which could be "eaten" only by those spiritually united with Christ through faith. (11)

In this way Schwenckfeld moved away from the traditional sacramental position in which there was a physical and real presence of Christ's body in or with the elements. At the same time by his formulation Schwenckfeld could retain a real (though spiritual) presence of Christ: believers partook in the mystical body of Christ, because of their inward faith. But on the crucial question of whether the

---

(11) Schwenckfeld

"*Eating means . . . partaking of the nature of Christ through true faith. The bodily food is transferred into our nature, but the spiritual food changes us into itself, that is, the divine nature, so that we become partakers of it.*" (In Maier, 1959, 22).

inner feeding was in any way intrinsically related to the outer eating of earthly elements, Schwenckfeld said emphatically that they were *not* related–even though the two might coincide on occasion.

At about the same time, Schwenckfeld also addressed the question of baptism. As might be expected, Schwenckfeld emphasized the inner, spiritual baptism. Schwenckfeld, like Karlstadt and Müntzer, opposed the baptism of infants because the rite was dependent upon the outward element of water, and not upon inward faith. Water baptism, said Schwenckfeld in 1526, must follow catechetical instruction and an inner baptism of the Spirit. Nevertheless, although he opposed infant baptism as a misuse, Schenckfeld did not commend or practise rebaptism. Since the essential baptism was a spiritual, interior baptism, water baptism could be applied at any point, before or after the baptism of the Spirit.

baptism

The question of how the inner life was related to the outer life of church ordinances was answered in a decisively spiritual mode by Schwenckfeld. Although Schwenckfeld saw a decisive separation between spirit and flesh, inner and outer, and although the salvific accent fell on the activity of the living Word, the inner life, and spiritual regeneration, nevertheless Schwenckfeld still maintained a place for the external life of the church as a testimony to, and a manifestation of the inner rebirth. Outer ceremonies were not bound to the inner life of the Spirit in any essential or mediating way, but they could, when properly used, **point toward** grace and salvation. Schwenckfeld's spiritualist answer would pose a problematic alternative for Anabaptists who shared with him an emphasis on the necessary interior work of the Holy Spirit.

The Nature of Christ (Christology)

Because of Schwenckfeld's fundamental conviction that the spiritual and material realms (divine/creature; spiritual/physical) were distinct and separate from each other, the question of Christ's nature became primary for him. The fact that God had taken on human flesh in the person of Jesus appeared to contradict the dualistic principle that Schwenckfeld accepted as axiomatic. If, as Schwenckfeld believed, the "creaturely" was in fact the "antithesis to the divine," how could one reconcile the human and divine natures of Christ? Could salvation be mediated to humankind by a "creaturely" Jesus?

In explaining the incarnation Schwenckfeld maintained that Jesus was not simply born of God in His divinity, and of Mary in His humanity, but rather owed **both** directly to God. Christ was divine, said Schwenckfeld, because the origin of Christ's human flesh was God the Father, and not a combination of God and the Virgin Mary.

This answer helped Schwenckfeld avoid the conclusion that Jesus was a "creature," and helped explain the unique "divine humanness" of Jesus, but it looked suspiciously like an heretical docetic teaching. (Docetism was the teaching, held especially by the Gnostics, that Jesus's humanity was apparent, not real).

This brief sketch does not begin to do justice to the complexity of Schwenckfeld's theological argument and position, but at least this much of his view must be described in order to place a good part of the Anabaptist movement in perspective.

Andreas Karlstadt influenced the early Swiss Brethren views on baptism and the Supper. Thomas Müntzer passed on some of his mysticism and apocalypticism to South German Anabaptism through Hans Hut. Caspar Schwenckfeld's christological views lived on, in modified form, in North German/Dutch Anabaptism, mediated by Melchior Hoffman to all Melchiorites, including Menno Simons. We will revisit these christological questions again in chapter 18 below.

Conclusion

Caspar Schwenckfeld's dissatisfaction with Luther's understanding of salvation by faith alone paralleled in some important respects the objections of Andreas Karlstadt and Thomas Müntzer. But Schwenckfeld's spiritualist emphasis was built on a strong opposition between the spirit and the flesh in a way not seen in Karlstadt or Müntzer. Schwenckfeld emphasized the spirit side of the spirit/flesh polarity in a way that brought all "creaturely" or created things into question. This spiritualization was simultaneously a radical desacralization of all things physical. Taken to its logical extreme the spiritualist position denied any spiritual relevance to outward observances, seeing in ceremonies only human deformations of spiritual realities.

The Anabaptist movement would struggle long with the spiritualist option. The reason for the attraction of the spiritualist point of view was not that Schwenckfeld himself persuaded so many Anabaptists, but rather because most Anabaptists shared with Schwenckfeld the basic premise that spiritual realities, not physical tokens, were of the essence.

Summary

From the surveys above it should be evident that although Luther's early critique of the medieval church was instrumental in setting into motion an evangelical reform movement, the interpretation of how such a reform was to be carried out varied widely. Rather than seeing these radical interpretations as "deformations," it is truer to the nature and development of the reforming phenomenon of the sixteenth century to say simply that the Reformation included within its scope, all of these tendencies and interpretations, and more.

The three radical reformers surveyed above do not exhaust the early Radical Reformation story, but outlining the views of Karlstadt, Müntzer, and Schwenckfeld is a necessary, if minimal, beginning to telling the Anabaptist story. Anabaptism did not emerge *ex nihilo* (out of nothing) as a result of *simply* a pure and earnest Bible reading, but rather it mirrored and echoed radical critiques of those who had gone before. Early Anabaptism would take those critiques some steps further, abandoning some emphases and developing others.

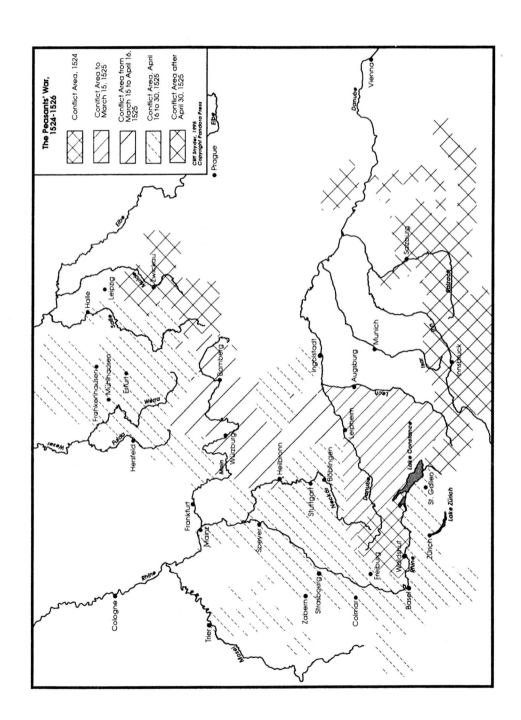

**The Peasants' War,
1524-1526**

▨	Conflict Area, 1524
▨	Conflict Area to March 15, 1525
▨	Conflict Area from March 15 to April 16, 1525
▨	Conflict Area, April 16 to April 30, 1525
▨	Conflict Area after April 30, 1525

Cliff Snyder, 1995
Copyright Pandora Press

• Prague

Chapter 4

The Peasants' War

Testimonies from the Peasants' War

Charges against Hans Fischer, Preacher at Sterzing

"On Palm Sunday there were many peasants ... at Peter Kurssner's ... and they sent for the preacher, who told them that their oath and whatever they had sworn to their territorial prince was not valid before God, and that they should not be at all concerned at not keeping it. And the Mass was of no value–the priests merely practiced sorcery thereby. He also said that the Sacrament, which is kept reserved in the church for consoling the sick, was of no value, and snapped his fingers with great disrespect. ... He abused the king, electors, and princes before the citizens and peasants and called them fools, dolts, braggards, and blind folk ... and related how the Greeks and Swiss had expelled their princes and nobles and they now held and ruled their lands for themselves."

Tom Scott and Bob Scribner, **The German Peasants' War: A History in Documents** (New Jersey: Humanities Press, 1991), 106.

Report on Hans Hasse from Meiningen

"Hans Hasse was one of the first who rebelled... He ... said publicly that one was not obliged to pay your princely grace any corn or market dues; and undertook to provide no services to his [lord] from whom he holds a hereditary tenancy in fee. ... He always declared that one should appoint preachers who will preach [under the inspiration of] the Spirit; moreover, he often said that no authority should be tolerated..."

Ibid., 250.

The Peasants' War: Religious or Political?

Church historians (in particular, Reformation historians) have been accustomed to denying that the Peasants' War had anything essential to do with the Reformation. This attitude can be traced back directly to Martin Luther, who repudiated any such connection with his own reform efforts. (1)

---

(1) Luther replies to the "Twelve Articles" of the Peasants.
"Because you would defend yourselves, and suffer neither violence nor wrong, ... leave the name of Christian out of it; leave out, I say, the name of Christian, and do not make it a cloak for your impatient, disorderly, unchristian undertaking. I shall not let you have that name, but so long as there is a heartbeat in my body, I shall do all I can to take that name from you."
(In Sessions, 1968, 34).

Scholars now have come to a very different conclusion: the Peasants' War clearly did have socio-economic roots (grievances concerning serfdom, forced service to lords, etc.), but it would have been unthinkable without the religious justification provided by Martin Luther and the other evangelical reformers. (2) In fact, "Scripture alone" and church reform had broader social and economic implications than simply matters of inner faith and eternal salvation.

(2) "Without the powerful ideas and emotions generated by the Reformation a commoners' protest ... would simply have been inconceivable." (Stayer, 1991, 43).

The Peasants' War was not a unified movement or uprising. Rather, it was a combined series of regional revolts. But it was a tremendously cataclysmic event, drawing in as many as 300,000 persons, with an estimated 100,000 casualties. Just as the Peasants' War is an integral part of the larger Reformation story, it also is central to the story of Anabaptism, as we will see below.

The Regional Uprisings

It is common to divide the Peasants' War into five phases and regions.

–Stülingen, Upper Swabia, and the Black Forest (1524-25)

–Franconia (1525)

–Thuringia (1524-25)

–Alsace and the Palatinate (1525)

–The Tirol (1525-26)

Stülingen and Upper Swabia

One of the earliest uprisings occured in the summer (May/June) of 1524 in Stülingen and Upper Swabia. The unrest in this region would continue, off and on, until December 1525. It spread into the Black Forest, and drew in the city of Waldshut and its reformer, Balthasar Hubmaier.

By 1523 Hubmaier had taken Zwingli's side on questions of images and the Mass. By Spring of the following year he had prepared a reformation programme for Waldshut, but Hapsburg pressure required him to flee to neighbouring Schaffhausen. He was able to return to Waldshut in October of 1524 and he then instituted evangelical church reforms.

The former pilgrimage preacher now presided over the removal of images and relics from the church, and the Mass was celebrated in German. The Hapsburgs continued to threaten military action, but in response, a troop of armed volunteers from Zurich marched to reinforce Waldshut. Among these volunteers were members of the emerging "radical" evangelical circle in Zurich. (3)

(3) The Austrian Government reports on the situation in Waldshut.

"Those of Waldshut have mingled with the rebels of Stühlingen and with some of the Black Forest peasants, and have sought aid, counsel, and support in their disobedience. [They] have admitted to their town several hundred reinforcements from the Swiss, and especially from Zurich..."
(Scott and Scribner, 1991, 150).

It was in the midst of this tense situation that the Peasants' War broke out in earnest, sweeping Waldshut and Hubmaier into its political and military events. Then in January of 1525 the first "rebaptisms" took place in Zurich. Hubmaier was convinced by the arguments for adult baptism, and he accepted baptism at the hands of Wilhelm Reublin in Easter of 1525. Under his leadership, Waldshut became an Anabaptist city, but at the same time it also actively supported the rebellious peasants with supplies and troops. The peasant armies, in turn, provided military defense for the city against its Austrian lords.

The peasant resistance in southern Germany reached serious proportions when the revolt spread to Upper Swabia in 1525. By the end of February, 1525, the Upper Swabian peasant army had come to number about 30,000 persons. It was carnival time, and many monasteries became the unwilling providers of refreshments (beer and wine) and food.

The town of Memmingen in Upper Swabia was a key centre of unrest. *Twelve Articles* In March, 1525 the famous "Twelve Articles of the Peasants" were composed there by the furrier and lay preacher, Sebastian Lotzer. (4) These articles circulated widely in other regions throughout the revolt.

---

(4) From the **Twelve Articles.**
"(1) In the future we should have power and authority so that each community should choose and appoint a pastor, and that we should have the right to depose him should he conduct himself improperly. The pastor thus chosen should teach us the Gospel, pure and simple, without any addition... (2) From [the tithe] he [the church provost] shall give to the pastor ... a decent and sufficient maintenance for him and his... What remains over shall be given to the poor of the place... (3) We take it for granted that you will release us from serfdom as true Christians, unless it should be shown us from the gospel that we are serfs." (Sessions, 1968, 17-18).

A "Christian Union" was formed at Memmingen on May 7, 1525 combining the forces of the peasant bands of Allgau, Lake Constance and Baltringen. Then the Upper Swabian revolt spread throughout the Black Forest, overtaking many monasteries.

Among the monasteries invaded and plundered by the peasant troops was the Benedictine monastery of St. Peters' of the Black Forest. The prior there was Michael Sattler. He soon left that monastery, eventually joined *Michael Sattler* the Anabaptists, and met a martyr's death in 1527 at the hands of the Hapsburg authorities.

By June of 1525 the peasants were in retreat, responding to news of military defeats elsewhere. On the 4th of November, 1525, Klettgau peasants and their Waldshut allies were defeated at Griessen; the city of Waldshut fell in early December, 1525. One of the few experiments in "civic Anabaptism" had come to an end.

The rebellion in southwest Germany in 1524 and 1525 generated widespread support and exhibited impressive military strength, but it was disorganized politically, and did not follow through on its successes.

Franconia

In March of 1525, revolt broke out in Rothenburg ob der Tauber, and eventually spread throughout Franconia and into Mühlhausen in Central Germany. In Franconia, the peasants put forward more radical demands than they had in Upper Swabia: they asked that the empire be reorganized to include representation from a peasants' parliament.

By happenstance, Andreas Karlstadt was present in Rothenburg, but *Andreas* his role was ambiguous. Eventually he decided that he should serve as *Karlstadt* chaplain to the peasant troops. Unfortunately, the rumour circulated among the peasants that in spite of his simple dress, Karlstadt was not really "one of them," but rather a scholar with a university doctorate. Karlstadt came close to being stabbed by an angry peasant soldier.

Karlstadt subsequently wrote a letter of admonition to the peasants in which he warned that God might punish them for their excesses–thus virtually guaranteeing that the peasants would pay no more attention to him. Having just missed being stabbed by a soldier, Karlstadt now came close to being hanged by angry townsfolk in Rothenburg.

Karlstadt was no Thomas Müntzer when it came to rallying troops for insurrection. When the Peasants' War was over he managed to escape Rothenburg and after years of wandering eventually returned to his first profession: he found a post as a university teacher in Basel, Switzerland.

The Franconian peasant revolt centred around three different armies from the Tauber, Odenwald, and Neckar valleys respectively. They achieved some spectacular military successes, including the capitulation of the city of Heilbronn, but in early June the troops of the Swabian League led by Truchsess Georg von Waldburg defeated peasant armies at Königshofen, then at Sulzdorf and Ingolstadt, and finally at Schwäbisch-Hall in July. With this the Franconian phase of the Peasants' War ended. The defeat of the strong Franconian peasant armies was disastrous for the peasants' uprising as a whole.

Thuringia

Thomas
Müntzer

The uprising in Thuringia has been mentioned briefly above, in recounting the career of Thomas Müntzer.

The revolt in Thuringia was prefaced by an urban uprising in the city of Mühlhausen in 1523. Müntzer arrived in the city after some significant constitutional gains already had been made, but he and Heinrich Pfeiffer, the local pastor, agitated for even more radical reforms. Müntzer and Pfeiffer were expelled, but returned in the Winter of 1525. By March, 1525 their radical programme had prevailed. Citizens elected a new government, dissolved local monasteries, and expelled the Catholic clergy. (5) Thomas Müntzer went further, setting out to organize a regional and military "Eternal League of God."

> **(5) From the Mühlhausen Chronicle**
> *"On 17 March ... the citizens foregathered at the town hall to dismiss the old council from their offices, which were handed over to the preachers [Müntzer and Pfeiffer] and the Eight. They then elected a new council, to be called eternal... Everyone ... was summoned to swear obedience, whereupon a German Mass was celebrated in both churches..."*
> *(Scott and Scribner, 1991, 145-46).*

The Peasants' Revolt as such broke out in Thuringia in April, 1525 in the territory of the prince-abbot of Fulda. A central demand in Fulda was the adoption of the Twelve Articles. When the revolt involved some towns subject to Philip of Hesse, he raised a small army of 350 horse and 1,400 infantrymen. He marched from success to success.

The army gathering at Mühlhausen formed the most serious regional threat. More than 10,000 peasant soldiers assembled there towards the end of April, 1525. Included in this army, as a combatant and troop captain, was the later Anabaptist leader Melchior Rinck. Also present with *Melchior Rinck* this army, supposedly selling books, was Müntzer's follower Hans Hut, *Hans Hut* who would later become one of the most successful Anabaptist missionaries in South German and Austrian lands.

Thomas Müntzer worked hard, although with little success, to form alliances with other towns and peasant bands, but the peasants were more interested in plunder. In the first week of May, more than twenty castles and religious houses were plundered. (6)

---

(6) From the Mühlhausen Chronicle
"On 29 April Pfeiffer, Müntzer, and their followers, together with the Eichsfeld contingent ... marched to Ebeleben, where they sacked the castle, tearing down and smashing whatever they could, drank up the wine, seized the corn in sheaves in the fields, fished out the ponds, then attacked and plundered the nunnery at Marksussra, likewise the castle of Almenhausen and others, and sent back many wagons piled high with booty to the lower parish in Mühlhausen..." (Scott and Scribner, 1991, 147).

The plundering was a fatal error, for the breathing space allowed Ernst von Mansfeld to regroup, and Philip of Hesse was allowed to march unopposed into Thuringia. The bloody battle of Frankenhausen took place on May 15. (7) Frankenhausen brought the Thuringian revolt to a close.

---

(7) Count Philipp von Solms describes the battle at Frankenhausen.
"The peasants had drawn up their battle order before dawn on a high hill on the other side of town... Following good advice, we brought our guns up the slope so that they could fire into them, and attacked the nearest of them with horse and foot. They did not hold firm but ran to seek the safety of the town. We gave pursuit and killed the majority of them between the hill and the town... Over five thousand peasants were slain and left for dead..." (Scott and Scribner, 1991, 290-91).

Alsace and the Palatinate

The Alsatian peasantry had a long history of revolt, dating back to before the middle of the fifteenth century. The uprising that began in April 1525 replayed many of their grievances, this time marked by anticlericalism, insistence on the preaching of the Word of God, and acceptance of the Twelve Articles.

Soldier with crossbow

Early May saw a series of successes, as the peasant armies took monasteries and castles virtually unopposed. Nevertheless the rebellion was short-lived. The Duke of Lorraine besieged the city of Saverne, which capitulated on the 16th of May. One estimate has it that on that one day some 18,000 peasants were slaughtered. This ended the Alsatian revolt.

On the other side of the Rhine, in the Palatinate, the peasant's uprising also began in April, with a gathering of a peasant band near Durlach in Baden. The revolt in the Palatinate was characterized by some limited successes (e.g., the taking of Bruchsal) but the peasants of this area negotiated away their advantages, and disbanded at the earliest opportunity. By May 23, Bruchsal had been taken back by Ludwig, the elector palatine. On the 26th of June he defeated a band of some 8,000 peasants at Pfeddersheim near Worms, marking the end of the Peasants' War in western Germany.

The Alpine Lands

The Tirol, under the governance of Ferdinand of Austria of the house of Hapsburg came close to open revolt in January and February of 1525, when the Swabian peasantry incited revolt among the miners of Schwaz. The full-scale revolt broke out in May, 1525 when angry peasants freed a compatriot who had been sentenced to death for fish poaching. By the 22nd of May, the Tirolean peasants had taken the town of Hall, plundered the Fuggers' residence there, and expelled the bishops of Trent and Bressanone. Michael Gaismair, who was elected captain by the Bressanone troop, soon emerged as undisputed leader of this revolt.

Michael Gaismair

Gaismair was born in 1485 in Tschoefs, Tirol, the son of a mining entepreneur. By 1523 he was serving as state secretary of the vice-regent of Tirol, and by early 1525 he was the secretary of prince-bishop of Brixen. On May 13, the day after he had prevented entry by a peasant troop into the prince-bishop's residence, he was elected by the same peasants as their leader.

The early revolt was characterized by anticlericalism and unconditional trust in the good will of Ferdinand of Austria. Ferdinand called a diet (assembly of the Estates) at which the peasants sat as a separate Estate. Ferdinand proved a skillful negotiator, eventually agreeing to secularize and take control of the prince-bishopric of Brixen. The diet lured Gaismair to Innsbruck, where he was promptly arrested. He managed to escape and fled to Zurich. From there he made plans for an invasion of the Tirol. Ferdinand ignored the negotiated agreements and marched through the region, punishing the peasants for their presumption.

---

(8) From Gaismair's **Landesordnung.**
"You shall promise and swear to pledge body and goods for one another, ...and in all things to seek not self-interest but first and foremost the honor of God, and then the common good...
You should root out and expunge all godless men who persecute the Word of God, burden the common man, and hinder the common good.
You will spare no effort to establish a wholly Christian constitution, which is founded in all things on the Word of God alone...
All privileges shall be abolished, for they are contrary to the Word of God and pervert justice...
All fortifications around towns and all castles and fortresses should be demolished, so that henceforth there should be no more towns, but only villages, in order that all distinctions between men will be abolished, from which disruption, pride, and disturbance may arise in the land, but rather that there will be a complete equality in the land."
(Scott and Scribner, 1991, 265-66).

A second rebellion broke out in Salzburg in March 1526. By this time Michael Gaismair had composed a constitution (the *Landesordnung*) and had raised an army of some 2,000 men. (8) He marched through the heart of the Tirol and joined the revolt in Salzburg.

When that revolt failed, Gaismair took his army on to Padua, in Venetian territory. From there he tried to keep the hopes of revolt alive in the Tirol. Ferdinand made no less than one hundred attempts to assassinate him, and finally succeeded in April, 1532. With that Gaismair's programme of justice for the Tirolean poor came to an end.

Although the visible connections between the Tirolean revolt and Anabaptism are few, the Tirol became a hotbed of Anabaptism in the years immediately following 1526. The region produced Anabaptist leaders like Jakob Hutter, Pilgram Marpeck and Helena of Freiburg, as well as countless recruits and converts who subsequently joined Anabaptist communities in the more tolerant territories of Moravia.

Conclusion

Why have we told the story of the Peasants' War? What do these feudal grievances and violence have to do with the Anabaptist movement?

Although the Peasants' War was most fundamentally a search for social, economic and political redress by people of the lower social orders, evangelical reforming ideas provided crucial catalysts for the revolt. Because the Peasants' War involved people from the lower social order and gave voice to their aspirations, and also because it involved an interpretation of Reformation ideas, it had numerous connections to the emerging Anabaptist movement. In many parts of Germany, Switzerland, and Austria, the Peasants' War provided the context in which Anabaptism emerged.

There are visible direct links between the Peasants' War and Anabaptism. Some important Anabaptists and future Anabaptists participated in, and were committed to many of the social and economic goals of the Peasants' War. We may think here especially of Balthasar Hubmaier in Waldshut, and of Hans Hut's and Melchior Rinck's commitments to Thomas Müntzer's aims. The revolt in the Tirol undoubtedly prepared the way for the Anabaptist movement which followed.

Finally, the Anabaptist stream of reform continued to address moral, social, and economic questions as part of its *religious* reform. The mainline reformers, on the other hand, disassociated reform of the church (theological and structural) from reform of the larger social and economic abuses. Luther's reforming vision did not include social equality as either a means or an end. (9) Peasants and Anabaptists insisted that equality questions could not be avoided for Christians as Christians.

---

(9) Luther replies to the Twelve Articles.
"Did not Abraham and other patriarchs and prophets have slaves? Read what St. Paul teaches about servants... ...a slave can be a Christian, and have Christian liberty... This article [against serfdom] would make all men equal, and turn the spiritual kingdom of Christ into a worldly, external kingdom, and that is impossible. For a worldly kingdom cannot stand unless there is in it inequality of persons, so that some are free, some imprisoned, some lords, some subjects, etc." (Sessions, 1968, 35).

Peasant concerns were echoed especially in the continuing Anabaptist critique of clerical immorality and inferior cure of souls. The peasants' demand that local communities elect their own pastors, that those pastors be supported economically by the communities they served, and that they be morally accountable to those communities (and subject to the discipline of those communities) were all demands made repeatedly by the peasants that were carried forward in Anabaptism, but not within mainline Protestantism.

Likewise the peasants' call for more just economic relationships among Christians, and their opposition to lending money at interest, also was continued within Anabaptism, as will be seen later. And, the more democratic social ideal articulated by the peasants was achieved, in part, in the Anabaptist communities. Particularly in matters of conscience and religious conviction, maintained the Anabaptists, all human beings stood equally before God and would have to answer to God. The social and political radicality of such an attitude was plainly evident to the political authorities. In the sixteenth century, religious dissent was also civil dissent.

Luther's notorious anti-peasant blasts toward the end of the peasants' uprising all but ended the grassroots appeal of his reform programme. (10) By

---

(10) Luther, "Against the Robbing and Murdering Hordes of Peasants"
"Dear lords, here is a place where you can release, rescue, help. . . . Stab, smite, slay, whoever you can.
If you die in doing it, well for you! A more blessed death can never be yours, for you die in obeying the
divine Word and commandment in Romans 13..." (Sessions, 1968, 39).

---

contrast, Anabaptism recruited not only peasants and craftsmen disaffected with social and economic conditions, but also won over religiously motivated common people to a more democratic and radical current of reform, in which they were called upon to appropriate the message of Scripture for themselves, and to reform their lives according to the guidelines of Scripture. The Anabaptist insistence that questions of usury, economic sharing, moral accountability and community discipline were also *spiritual* matters echoed concerns voiced in the peasants' movement. These echoes were not heard with the same intensity in either Wittenberg or Zurich. (11)

---

(11) Hermann Mühlfort, Lutheran Mayor of Zwickau, writes in June, 1525.
"Doctor Martin has fallen into great disfavor with the common people, also with both the learned and
unlearned: his writing is regarded as having been too fickle. . . . In the third tract [Against the Robbing
and Murdering Hordes of Peasants] ... he called for the private and public murder of the peasants... Here
I do not agree. . . . There was enough murdering of peasants, burghers, women, and children taking
place... Martin has not done well in Zwickau and in the countryside and towns; he has written the truth in
condemning rebellion, but the poor have been greatly forgotten." (Scott and Scribner, 1991, 322).

Although persecuted and virtually extinguished in some regions, Anabaptism survived in attenuated form to become an alternative Reformation movement of the common people in the years following 1525.

Chapter 5

The Reformation Context Revisited

The Anabaptist Perspective

Schwytz, Switzerland, November 4, 1525.

"Rudolf Ruotsch Wiss of Wesen confesses that of the three faiths, namely our true old faith [Catholicism], the Lutheran, and the Anabaptist, the Anabaptist faith is the best. He will stay in that faith and will also die in it. He also confesses that there are only four sacraments: baptism, the altar [The Lord's Supper], marriage, and ordination. He also believes there is no purgatory nor (does he believe) in the intercession of the holy saints and the dead. On Saturday following All Saints Day (Nov. 4, 1525) he was executed by drowning."

QGTS, II, #685, 563-64. (Translated by A. Snyder).

"These two, Luther and Zwingli, exposed all the deception and villany of the pope and brought it to the light of day as if they would strike everything to the ground with thunderbolts. But they put nothing better in its place. As soon as they began to cling to worldly power and put their trust in human help, they were just as bad–like someone mending an old kettle and only making a bigger hole. . . . Because God wanted one united people, separated from all other peoples, be brought forth the Morning Star, the light of his truth, to shine with all its radiance in the present age of this world."

The Chronicle of the Hutterian Brethren, Vol. I (Rifton, N.Y.: Plough Publishing House, 1987), 41.

The Historical Place of Radical Reform

Modern

There is much about the radical wing of the evangelical reforming movement that resonates with modern sensibilities. There was, for example, a democratizing instinct among the peasants and common people that occasionally verged into revolutionary political action. This recalls post-colonial liberation struggles in the twentieth century more than lowly medieval peasants keeping to their "place" in the social hierarchy. Among some sixteenth century spiritualists there was an emphasis on the individual and the importance of individual conscience and belief that strikes us as a thoroughly contemporary attitude.

Medieval

While there were elements of radical reform that anticipated the modern period, there were many more that hearkened back to the medieval period that was passing away. The secular attitudes of individualism and the natural rights political theories that emerged after the Enlightenment were thoroughly foreign to the radical reformers. Radical reform was more "medieval" than "modern." One mark of its rootage in the medieval world was the way in which all matters of social, political, and economic concern were immediately also religious questions.

World View

The medieval world view assumed a universe under God's rule, in which a struggle between good and evil was being waged. There was no secular realm in the modern sense. There was an earthly realm, but it was the scene of the supernatural struggle.

Luther

The sixteenth century was witnessing a shift in this world view. Some historians have suggested that Martin Luther helped initiate the modern division between the religious and the secular by separating individuals' inward, personal faith, from their visible life in the world. For Luther, the true church of justified believers was essentially invisible, and known to

God alone. The former visible signs of sanctity, which had defined medieval piety, no longer proved or demonstrated anything significant. An apparent sinner could well be destined to be justified by faith in God's eyes, and an apparent saint could well be a hypocrite, bound for hell.

While the shift to inward faith did not of itself define the modern understanding of secularity–it was, after all, a thoroughly religious point of view–it has been argued that Luther's separation of salvation from a visible life of piety in this world did prepare the way and anticipate post-Enlightenment secularism.

With respect to this shift in world view, the radical reformers remained far more wedded to the medieval understanding, which linked outward action in the world to the inner state of faith. The consequences of this were very significant, because it meant that radical reformed piety continued to insist on a particular way of life in this world as a **necessary** expression of Christian faith, and evidence that such faith existed. Radical reformers still looked for visible "saints" and signs of sanctity on this earth.

Radical Reformers

Political and Social Changes

By the time of the sixteenth century it appeared increasingly doubtful that the medieval political ideal of one Christian empire would ever come to be. The medieval political argument had centred on the question of whether the pope or the emperor was the divinely appointed head of Christendom. Luther was appealing to venerable anti-papal arguments when he called on secular rulers to take control of the churches in their territories.

Luther's appeal to Scripture as the highest authority for church reform assumed the rule of God over all, but "Scripture alone" changed the terms of reference, for some people at least. Since Scripture revealed God's will, shouldn't God's will concerning political and social relationships be sought in Scripture?

Luther

Müntzer

Thomas Müntzer was convinced that the political order should be governed by the fact that the End Times had arrived. The question was not obedience to rulers, or the maintenance of hierarchies, but rather how to prepare the way for the physical reign of Christ and the elect on earth. This apocalyptic context for political and social thought had medieval antecedents in the writings of Joachim of Fiore.

Peasants

For the leaders of the Peasants' War, the Bible spoke not so much about the Elect and the End Times, but rather about equality of human beings, under God. All human beings are God's children, and in the Garden of Eden there was no separation into nobility and commoners. That separation, therefore, must have been a "human invention," rather than a necessary mirror of the heavenly hierarchy. Likewise, God created all the earth (the rivers, woods, and wild animals) for everyone, and not for the exclusive use of the nobility, at their pleasure.

The conclusion seemed a logical one to the peasant reformers: the God-given, biblical order would free the peasants from feudal obligations, and would free woods, rivers, fish and game for use by all.

Martin Luther viewed these appropriations of "Scripture alone" as gross errors and perversions of what he had intended. The Gospel, he said, is about salvation through faith in Jesus Christ. The Gospel does not speak to political situations, except to counsel the obedience of subjects to the political authorities and to support the maintenance of social inequality and hierarchy, even among Christians (Paul's words concerning slaves and masters). In this respect, the peasants were more willing to abandon and revise the medieval social and political structure than was Luther.

Anabaptists

By 1526 the rupture in the evangelical camp was well known. In matters relating to political structure, the Anabaptists were not initially of one mind, as we will see in due course. But in matters relating to social structure, the Anabaptists generally followed the lead of the peasants. They continued to speak the language of equality of human beings before God. And the Anabaptists continued to insist upon the authority of God over all authorities. In cases of conflicts of conscience, when political authorities demanded something that was deemed to be contrary to God's will as expressed in Scripture, the Anabaptists insisted that they were bound to obey the higher Lord. This emphasis had strong medieval roots.

Economic Changes

The economic situation in the sixteenth century was a long way from the early feudal and agrarian reality. The increase in trade and commerce and the growth of towns and cities saw Europe poised on the edge of a capitalist revolution. Money could be made with money, rather than only with land.

Throughout the middle ages, peasants and crafts people had evolved communal associations that were expanded by the guilds and confraternities in the towns and cities. Built upon the ideals of hand labour and the common good, these associations tended to oppose both noble privilege on the one hand, and the unbridled accumulation of profit on the other.

Communal Traditions

The radical wing of the Reformation built on this communal tradition. Even more, the guidance for economic activity was to be sought, said radical reformers, in Scripture. As a result, in economic questions the radical reforming movement tended to echo medieval pronouncements encouraging "honest labour," prohibiting usury and discouraging retailing. One's faith was to have visible economic results. By contrast, Luther and other mainline reformers were far more ready to consider economic activity neutral in matters of salvation.

Religious Changes

It is self-evident that religious changes were underway at the time of the Reformation. But given the prevailing world view and the medieval assumptions about the place of the church in the divine order, it stood to reason that a critique of the existing church authority and power structure was a direct challenge to the status quo. But what was to be put in place of the old was not clear. Radical reform was one answer to the question.

The Theological "Shape" of Radical Reform

Should one describe the forest or the trees in telling the story of this branch of reform? There is no easy equating of Karlstadt, Müntzer, Schwenckfeld, and the peasants, for the particular differences between them all are numerous and in many cases, substantial. But on the other hand, when we step back from individual cases and look to broader issues–to the "shape" of these radical critiques–it also is true that there were remarkable similarities in the radical rejection of Luther and his views. Our survey has emphasized these similarities.

Looked at from this longer range, the radical reformers belong in another theological "forest" than did Luther. Moreover, the radical reformers share a kinship that places them together in the *same* theological forest, apart from Luther. Without negating the value of careful distinction between radical reforming individuals we may also say that there is something important to be learned in noting the broad commonalities between their views.

Scripture Alone

The evangelical movement had an achilles heel. The appeal to the authority of Scripture encouraged a multiplicity of views, not uniformity. The divergent approaches of Luther, Karlstadt, Müntzer, and the peasants provided ample demonstration of this fact.

Nevertheless, the early radical reformers all critiqued Luther's scriptural approach in a very similar way, appealing to the necessity of reading the letter of Scripture in the power of the Holy Spirit. This spiritualistic critique had important consequences because the claim was based on an equality of persons rather than on a sacramental or educational hierarchy. If biblical truth is known only by letter and spirit together, anyone graced with the Holy Spirit will be able to interpret the words of Scripture correctly, even

Holy Spirit

if someone else has to read them aloud. Conversely, anyone who lacks the Holy Spirit simply is not able to interpret Scripture correctly.

The insistence by the radical reformers that spirit *and* letter belonged together (their interpretation of Luther's *sola scriptura*) had radical consequences that drove the thin edge of the wedge between radical and mainline evangelical reformers. The criticism of pastors (anticlericalism)–which had helped form a united evangelical front in the early years–would now be directed not only against Roman Catholic clergy who "denied Scripture" by appealing to traditional church interpretive authority, but also against "evangelical learned scribes" who appealed to the letter of Scripture but "lacked the Spirit."

Spirit and Letter

If the Holy Spirit had to be present to validate a Scriptural interpretation, this meant that scriptural questions were not to be decided automatically by the scholar-theologian-preacher in the employ of a prince or city council. It meant that scriptural questions would not be decided by a definitive reference to Hebrew and Greek texts, available only to a humanist elite.

In fact, if the Holy Spirit was the ultimate authority by which scriptural questions were to be decided, the result was an interpretive anarchy which, the sixteenth century authorities were convinced (and not without reason), was politically dangerous. The radical insistence on Scripture *and* Spirit contained the seeds of Believers' church thinking, and threatened the state church monopoly of scriptural interpretation.

Salvation by Grace through Faith

At the very heart of the joint critiques of Karlstadt, Müntzer and Schwenckfeld was their rejection of Luther's understanding of salvation.

This was no insignificant objection. After all, this was Luther's central theological point: human beings are saved by faith in Christ's sacrifice, through God's grace and election, and not by any human effort or merit.

Grace

The radical reformers embraced the emphasis on grace and faith (against the sacramental structure), but disagreed with Luther's conclusion that saving faith changed one's legal status before God (forensic justification) but *did not* change one's essential human condition as a sinner (at once justified and a sinner).

Transformation The radical reformers argued, rather, that saving grace works in believers to *transform* them in the here and now, and that believers thus transformed will participate in some way in the salvation process. This fundamental point of difference indicated two areas more in which Karlstadt, Müntzer and Schwenckfeld agreed with each other and jointly disagreed with Luther, namely in their understanding of the human potential for regeneration, and their understanding of the transformative power of the Holy Spirit.

The Nature of the Human Person

The radical reformers we have surveyed agreed that human beings are radically sinful beings, in need of redemption. Together they agreed that human beings could, by the power and grace of God and the Holy Spirit, be remade in their human natures so that they would at least be on the path to sanctification in this life. Furthermore, they held that God's grace enabled sinners to choose freely either the path of salvation, or the path to perdition.

Free Will Here the radical reformers decisively parted company with Luther, who denied the possibility of free will, and held to the doctrine of predestination. Luther insisted that believers would live better lives out of gratitude (and Luther's sermons give ample evidence of his concern for such "good works" subsequent to faith), but for Luther no works of any kind could have a bearing on *salvation*, which depended alone on God's gracious election and Christ's sacrifice.

The Holy Spirit

We have already noted the importance of the Holy Spirit to the radical reformers' understanding of the evangelical scriptural principle. In the context of salvation, the Holy Spirit was seen as the power of God which conveyed faith to believers.

The radical reformers agreed with Luther that the grace of God which grants saving faith comes before faith (it is a "prevenient" grace, and cannot be earned by good works). Nevertheless, they insisted that saving grace is also an **efficacious** grace which has the power to remake human nature.

For this reason the radical reformers could speak of rebirth, regeneration by the Spirit, and the new life which emerged as the result of the action of the Holy Spirit. By the power of God, sinners come to repentance and believe the Gospel; by that same power of God they are reborn and regenerated by the Holy Spirit, and become new persons. These new persons then live lives that give witness to the sanctification that God's grace is working in their lives.

Regeneration

Karlstadt, Müntzer, and Schwenckfeld thus expected a reform of the church not simply through a preaching of the Word, but because those convicted by the *living* Word would be regenerated and so live new lives.

Karlstadt, Müntzer and Schwenckfeld alike critiqued the lack of moral and ethical reform in the mainline churches. This perceived deficiency they attributed to, in Müntzer's words, the preaching of a "sweet Christ" who required for salvation only that one have faith. For these three reformers, on the contrary, accepting the good news of salvation through Christ meant also yielding inwardly before God and being remade into a new person.

This fundamental agreement between Karlstadt, Müntzer and Schwenckfeld points to their common rootage in late medieval piety, which allowed for the linkage of grace and regeneration in a continuous process of sanctification *leading to* justification before God. Each of these radical reformers had different points of access to this late medieval tradition, but in terms of their understandings of salvation, the results were essentially the same. And, because of their agreement that God's grace could and would regenerate believers, these reformers also expected the preaching of the Gospel to result in a visibly reformed (i.e. moral) church.

Late Medieval Piety

While these reformers did not agree on how to structure their churches, their agreement and understanding in the matter of salvation provided the essential underpinning for the emergence of a believers' church in the Anabaptist movement.

Baptism and the Supper

Karlstadt and Müntzer were agreed that God's grace opens the possibility of response for the sinner (freedom of the will), and that faith means believing and accepting God's gracious offer of pardon through Christ.

All of this meant, however, that infant baptism was a rite that no longer made sense theologically, for infants do not make personal faith decisions, nor are they visibly regenerated after choosing to live new lives. If *Water no* the water was just water, and no longer a divine sacrament (a visible sign *Sacrament* that conferred invisible grace), then water baptism could be no more than an outer witness to a more essential and inward baptism. That is, the outer baptism was a sign that an individual had in fact consciously yielded inwardly to the working of God–something no infant could possibly do.

And yet further, the New Testament evidence concerning baptism seemed weighted heavily in favour of adult baptism. Although neither Karlstadt, Müntzer or Schwenckfeld took the step of rebaptizing adults on confession of faith, nevertheless they provided the essential logic for the practice of adult baptism by their critique of the practice of infant baptism.

In the matter of the Lord's Supper these radical reformers were in *No Real* close agreement in rejecting a real presence in the elements–although this *Presence* seems to have been less of an issue with Müntzer. But again, their rejection of Roman Catholic sacramentalism, and their emphasis on an inner working of the Holy Spirit leading to rebirth, regeneration and sanctification led them to think of the Supper in a more spiritualist fashion than would Luther.

Priesthood of all Believers

Karlstadt, Müntzer and Schwenckfeld were in agreement with the apparent meaning of Luther's phrase "a priesthood of all believers." That is, they agreed that the Roman Catholic clergy were not especially privileged with regard to the sacraments, and that any Christian could perform priestly functions by virtue of Christian baptism.

Luther, however, soon backed away from the democratizing implications suggested by the provocative phrase. The radical reformers did not. Priests are not "made" by virtue of an "indelible mark on the soul" (ordination), conferred by a clerical hierarchy based on apostolic succession. Rather, pastors are those chosen by the Spirit of God to proclaim the Gospel. There cannot be a centrally controlled priesthood. At best there can perhaps be an election or commissioning by a local congregation–something to which Luther had appealed early on, in his struggle against the medieval church.

Calling of Pastors

The call for congregational election and congregational disciplining of pastors was widespread in the Peasants' War. So also was the call for fiscal reform, and the demand that local tithes be controlled and spent in the parishes which furnished the tithes.

This certainly was one way of interpreting a priesthood of all believers, but it was not the way Luther intended. The spiritual calling of pastors, along with the congregational validation of that call, would survive only in the early Anabaptist movement.

Early Radical Reformers and Anabaptism

It must be said that the radical reformers who were to have the strongest influence on the Anabaptist movement shared significant theological commonalities that placed them in close proximity to one another (in the same theological forest, if one will), and at the same time at some distance from Martin Luther–even though he was their shared point of evangelical theological origin.

This is not to downplay significant differences between Karlstadt, Müntzer, and Schwenckfeld, but rather to suggest that the theological principles they shared were of fundamental significance. These theological commonalitites made them partners in the sixteenth century reforming conversation. They shared and spoke a language which Luther did not speak.

Conversation Partners

The fact that the Anabaptist movement also came to speak that same radical theological language, and encountered problems with the mainline Reformation leaders at exactly the same points as had the earlier radical reformers, means that Anabaptism properly belongs in the radical reforming camp, as a partner in that common conversation.

How did the Anabaptists come to share in that conversation? The fact that Anabaptists spoke radical reforming language can suggest two possible explanations.

One explanation is that there were direct lines of influence from the early radical reformers to Anabaptists. In some individual cases these lines of mediation and influence are clear, as has been noted above and will be noted again. But this explanation leaves a large question unanswered. How are we to explain the appearance of these radical teachings among the masses of people who made up the rank and file of the Anabaptist movement? What explains the appearance of a theology of regeneration in an illiterate peasant of a remote rural village of Switzerland?

Here historians, dependent upon written records, encounter mostly silence. The influence of a Karlstadt or a Müntzer cannot be demonstrated in the absence of documentary evidence. But it seems unlikely that there was any such direct influence on a wide scale.

Literacy

Perhaps the problem lies in the way that historians have conceived of the origination and spread of ideas, and concentrate mostly on documentation left behind by a literate elite. It is evident that radical reforming ideas circulated widely among the common people, usually carried by lesser-known figures who communicated slogans, reform ideas, and interpretations of Scripture by oral means. Furthermore, these ideas, we must conclude, were not written on blank slates but rather either found, or did not find, a corresponding echo in the unlettered hearers.

Looking to literate and published interpreters of reform will tell a partial, though important part of the story. There were influential figures such as Karlstadt, Müntzer and Schwenckfeld who set the basic terms of reference for radical reform.

The other side of the story, however, requires a thesis less easily demonstrated. What led many thousands of common people to accept radical reforming ideas as true and even self-evident?

The answer to this question, suggested by the surprising uniformity in crucial theological presuppositions in all branches of Anabaptism, is that the radical reformers were giving voice to *widely shared* ideas about the meaning of reform, salvation, regeneration, and sanctification. In the second place, these ideas were widely shared because although they may seem radical to us, radical reforming ideas in the sixteenth century were actually more conservative than radical. They expressed long-cherished medieval ideals, tenaciously maintained in a rapidly changing world. Radical reform was more medieval than modern. It resonated easily with the common people because it gave voice to long-familiar notions.

Conservative Radicality

The origins of Anabaptism undoubtedly lie in large measure in the radical reformers who first articulated an alternative view of evangelical reform; but they also lie in the regenerationist and ascetic tradition of late medieval piety which conceived of salvation in terms of sanctification. Perhaps it is for this reason that in spite of the fact that different branches of Anabaptism show different points of contact with the early Radical Reformation, nevertheless the Anabaptist movement has a distinctive theological "shape." It is a "shape" that is rooted in medieval piety and spiritual ideals.

Conclusion

We return in conclusion to the question of piety and spiritual practice. There were options that opened and others that closed thanks to Luther's critique of late medieval doctrine and practice. We may summarize with the following points.

Scripture and Religous Practice

All evangelical reformers accepted the appeal to the authority of Scripture, but in what way would the "Word of God" be expected to inform one's spirituality? A blanket appeal to Scripture opened up a host of new, unanswered, but crucial questions.

–Was the Word essentially an inner word, or an outer, written word? If it was the former, then "hearing the Word of God" would indicate a process of inward discernment; if the latter, a process of understanding the written text of Scripture.

–If the "living Word of God" was seen as an inner, spiritual word, were extra-biblical revelations (dreams, visions, prophecies) to be sought and valued on par with written Scripture?

–If the "Word of God" was understood to be the written biblical word, should the written Scripture be combed for a concrete rule of life for believers, which should then be followed literally?

–If the "Word of God" was seen to be the written Scripture, should one seek to discover the esoteric secrets of the Last Days within its prophetic books?

–If the Word was the written text which came to life when it was preached, did it have to be exegeted by linguistic and theological experts who had access to the most reliable versions in the original languages?

All of these possibilities, and more, were opened by the apparently simple expedient of appealing to the authority of Scripture alone. The emergence of alternative evangelical views, we can see in retrospect, should have been a foregone conclusion. The historical process of development demonstrates that it was possible to be in the evangelical reforming camp by one's acceptance of the authority of Scripture, and yet differ widely concerning its interpretation and meaning for one's spiritual life.

Penance and Salvation

The most obvious late medieval spiritual practices that evangelicals repudiated had to do with the sacrament of penance and the mediation of the saints. A huge field of popular piety was removed at one stroke. But how was "salvation by faith alone" supposed to be lived out practice?

On this score the radical reformers turned out to be more conservative than Luther, and retained the ascetic, late medieval piety of a life of penance and renunciation, based on a doctrine of regeneration. A new life is to be lived in the here and now. God's grace is efficacious. True faith leads to moral reform. External behaviour is a good sign of the presence or absence of faith.

The Radical Reformation re-composed medieval themes in a Reformation key. But the context was new and many questions needed to be answered.

–Granted that one must yield to the work of God in one's life, what are the particular external marks of a "yielded heart"?

–Are there necessary marks of humility demanded of believers?

–Are there necessary marks of regeneration demanded of believers?

–In cases of manifest moral failure, what church practice takes the place of the previous practice of confession and penance?

For the Anabaptists, the practical answers to these questions would be worked out in a painful process of dialogue, disagreement, and excommunication over a period of years.

The nature and function of the sacraments

The sacraments had played a central role in medieval piety and practice. They were now in the process of being redefined, and it raised a host of questions.

–If all Christians are priests, do all Christians then have the power to "make" sacraments?

–If, on the contrary, *no one* has the power to "make" a grace-conveying sacrament out of a physical object, then what principles explain what happens in the actions of corporate worship?

–If physical objects always remain just that, is it the faith of the recipient that makes a sacrament out of a physical celebration?

–Is Christ made physically present *at all* in this world? How?

–Should baptism and the Supper simply be celebrated as inward events, in which spiritual realities are experienced individually?

More questions of this kind could be listed. Given the centrality of corporate worship to Christian spirituality, the answers to these questions were extremely important. The sacramental edifice had been challenged, but what was to be put in its place, on what theological basis, and with what results for Christian spiritual practice and piety?

It was in the midst of this historical, intellectual, and religious upheaval that Anabaptism emerged. It answered some of the questions posed above, drew some specific conclusions, and set a particular theological and reforming path that set it apart from other reforming streams.

B.
The Setting of
Initial Boundaries:
1525-1540

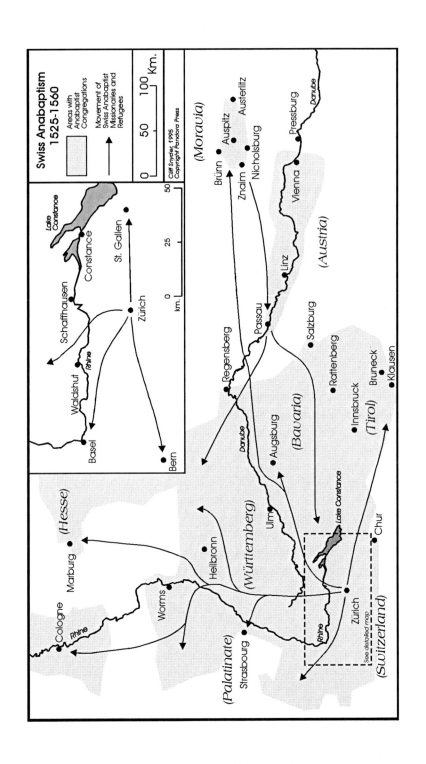

Swiss Anabaptism
1525-1560

Areas with Anabaptist Congregations

Movement of Swiss Anabaptist Missionaries and Refugees

Cliff Snyder, 1995
Copyright Pandora Press

0   50   100 Km.

Lake Constance
Schaffhausen
Constance
St. Gallen
Waldshut
Rhine
Basel
Zürich
Bern

0   25   50
km.

(Moravia)
Brünn · Auspitz · Austerlitz
Znaim · Nicholsburg
Pressburg
Vienna
(Austria)
Linz
Passau
Salzburg
Regensberg
Rattenberg
Bruneck
Klausen
Innsbruck
(Tirol)
Danube
Augsburg
(Bavaria)
Lake Constance
Chur
Ulm
(Württemberg)
Heilbronn
Worms
Cologne
Marburg · (Hesse)
Rhine
Strasbourg
(Palatinate)
Zürich
See detailed map
Rhine
(Switzerland)

Chapter 6

The Origins of Swiss Anabaptism

Margret Hottinger of Zollikon

On November 18, 1525–just a few months after the first baptisms in Zurich– a group of prisoners was brought before the judges of that city. Heading up the list were people whose names many have come to recognize: Conrad Grebel, Felix Mantz, George Blaurock, and Michael Sattler were among the prisoners. Most people don't know that Margret Hottinger of Zollikon, daughter of Jakob Hottinger, was also in that group of Anabaptist prisoners.

The court pronounced against the defendants that same day, saying that either they accepted infant baptism as correct church practice, or they would be imprisoned until they recanted or died. Three men from the group of prisoners, when faced with this option, recanted and left town. One of those who recanted was Michael Sattler. In November of 1525 Michael Sattler was not yet ready to be imprisoned for his faith, let alone be martyred. We may suppose that he had not yet been baptized, but the records do not say one way or the other.

Margret Hottinger was among those who refused to recant. The judges said concerning Margret that "if she persists, she should be placed in the Wellenberg." The Wellenberg was a damp prison tower, built in the middle of the Limmat river. It has since been torn down. Being locked up in this unheated tower, in the middle of a river in November, with a Swiss winter coming on, was nothing to be taken lightly.

Margret had been raised in an unusual family. Barely a year and a half before her own arrest, her uncle Klaus had been executed by beheading in

Lucerne as an evangelical heretic. Two of her brothers, and several cousins were active in the reforming movement of their village even before adult baptism began. The young evangelical radical, Conrad Grebel, was a family friend. It came as no surprise when Margret's father Jakob, whom we have already met arguing with a doctor of theology, was among the first to be baptized in Zollikon. And it was no surprise when shortly thereafter, two of Margret's brothers, and Margret herself, were baptized and in trouble with the law.

After being held in the Wellenberg for four months, Margret was questioned again and urged to recant. The court scribe wrote down her answer: "Margret Hottinger ... will stay with her baptism, which she holds to be right and good; whoever is baptised will be saved, and whoever does not believe in it and opposes it, such a one is a child of the devil." Apparently, spending the winter in the Wellenberg prison, and getting mostly bread and water to eat, had not dampened Margret's resolve.

But finally, after six months of this harsh imprisonment Margaret, along with a large group of other Anabaptists, agreed to sign a general recantation written by a court official. But in spite of her recantation, Margret did not desist. Some time later in 1526 Margret travelled to the neighbouring city of St. Gall, in the company of her brother Jakob Hottinger (the younger). There she attracted the attention of a local historian, who was no friend of the Anabaptists. Johannes Kessler of St. Gall described Margaret in his chronicle, the *Sabbata*. It reads as follows:

> There arose a wild and arrogant error through the women of the Anabaptists, particularly one young woman from Zollikon in the canton of Zurich named Margret Hottinger ... [She] lived a disciplined way of life, so that she was deeply loved and respected by the Anabaptists.

So far, except for the "wild and arrogant" part, Kessler could have been writing Margret a letter of recommendation. But he then accuses Margret of claiming that she was God, and of forgiving sins, and some other dubious things. But he concludes by saying that Margret "lived an austere life and overcame many obstacles," and that the Anabaptists held her to be "devout and immersed in God."

In spite of Kessler's exaggerations, there can be no doubt that Margret exercised significant influence and leadership among the early Swiss Anabaptists of Zollikon and St. Gall. Her leadership was based on her spiritual gifts and her pious way of life–as even Kessler had to admit. In 1525 and 1526, it seemed evident that God had granted the Spirit to all of God's servants, both men and women, as Joel had prophecied.

The Zurich police were very efficient. By 1527, most of the Anabaptist inhabitants of Zollikon had been forced to recant, and the few Anabaptists left there had to live very hidden lives. Most of Margret's relatives fell away from Anabaptism, but she did not. She was arrested in 1530 for being an Anabaptist, along with her father Jakob and a young brother, Felix. They were arrested just north of Lake Constance, while attempting to flee to Moravia (now the Czech Republic), the land of religious free-dom. Her young brother Felix was released, because of his tender age. However, her father Jakob was put to death, and Margret was sentenced to be drowned.

One account of her execution relates some of the effort that went into getting her to renounce her Anabaptist beliefs. The account says that after the executioners had begun to carry out the sentence of drowning,

> She was pulled out of the water and asked again to recant, but in no way did she wish to do that. Rather she said: "Why did you pull me out? The flesh was almost defeated." With that the judgement was carried out [i.e., she was drowned].

With this testimony ends the story of Margret Hottinger, early Swiss Anabaptist, prophetic witness, leader, and martyr.

*(For the full story, see **Profiles of Anabaptist Women: Sixteenth Century Reforming Pioneers**, C. Arnold Snyder and Linda A. Huebert Hecht, eds. [Waterloo, WLU Press, 1996], 43-53).*

The Ambiguity of Swiss Anabaptist Beginnings

The story of the emergence of Swiss Anabaptism has often been told beginning with Zwingli's reformation of Zurich, passing to the eventual disaffection of Conrad Grebel and Felix Mantz, and leading inexorably to the separated pacifism of the Schleitheim Articles. But as the story of Margret Hottinger suggests, early Swiss Anabaptism contained within itself ambiguities that needed to be clarified not only by the Swiss Anabaptists, but by all Anabaptists.

–**Spirit and Letter**. What role was to be played by prophets in relation to the letter of Scripture? Margret Hottinger and other "inspired" exegetes brought this question to the forefront.

–**Leadership and the role of women**. Were Swiss Anabaptist communities to be composed of people who were considered spiritual equals? Were prophetically inspired women to be given leadership in the fledgling movement?

–**Territorial and civic reform**. Should Anabaptism compete with, and possibly replace, reforms like Zwingli's in Zurich? Swiss Anabaptism's ambiguous beginnings include Hubmaier's reform of the city of Waldshut, and the military alliance struck between Anabaptist Waldshut and the Black Forest Peasant troops in 1525. Was this a possible Anabaptist model of reform?

–**Participation in governing functions**. Governing meant administering and swearing oaths and wielding the sword of government to reward good and punish evil. Was this to be allowed?

Zurich and Zwingli

The first rebaptism of adults in the Reformation period occurred in Zurich in January, 1525. It was carried out by former followers of Ulrich Zwingli, the reformer of that city. The story of Swiss Anabaptism, then, is closely tied to the reform of Zurich under Zwingli, although the influence of Karlstadt is discernible, and the Zurich radical group also read Thomas Müntzer's tracts.

Ulrich Zwingli had been a Roman Catholic priest in the Swiss town of Glarus from 1506 to 1516. Like Balthasar Hubmaier, he accepted a post as a pilgrimage preacher in the town of Einsiedeln, a post he occupied from 1516 to 1518. He was a scholar, part of the humanist current of reform, and dedicated himself to the study of Greek and Hebrew. Erasmus' views had some influence on his thought.

In 1518 Zwingli accepted a post as people's preacher at the cathedral in Zürich. It is clear that he owed some debt to Martin Luther, in a general sense, but his path to reform was distinct from Luther's, owing much more to humanism, sacramentarian influences from the Netherlands, and Andreas Karlstadt.

By 1522, Zwingli was speaking the new language of the Reformation, and had begun to preach sermons that were expositions of Gospel texts. Some of his ideas resulted in the breaking of the Lenten fast of 1522 by a group of Zwingli's followers–they gathered together and defiantly ate some ceremonial sausages. Zwingli also preached against images (idolatry) and clerical celibacy (as a Catholic priest he had been living with a concubine). By the end of 1522, Zwingli had resigned his post as priest, and had accepted the post of preacher under the direct control of the city council. He was well on his way to winning over the city council in favour of his reform ideas, but his position required some political skill.

Zwingli's reform proceeded by means of civic conciliar action, urged on by Zwingli's encouragement of the laity. In the early years Zwingli recommended lay Bible reading, and fostered Bible study groups. (1)

---

(1) Zwingli, Archeteles, (1522)
"The more unskilled a man is in human devices and at the same time devoted to the divine, the more clearly that spirit informs him, as is shown by the apostles and by the foolish things of this world which God has chosen. . . . It is not the function of one or two to expound passages of Scripture, but of all who believe in Christ." (Harder, 1985, 185).

His sermons were calculated to incite unrest from the grass roots, pressuring the council for change. A pattern emerged. Once an issue had become disruptive, a conciliar disputation would be held, under Zwingli's direction, and the council would prudently decide what would be made law in Zurich.

Zwingli skillfully played the man in the middle, but something was bound to break. Eventually it did, when Zwingli's more radical followers disagreed with him over the slow pace of reform. This break recalls, not without reason, the similar rupture between Karlstadt and Luther in 1522 at the base of which was the question of the speed and extent of reform, and the "sparing of the weak."

The Zurich Radicals to 1524

The followers of Zwingli that came to be labelled radicals took Zwingli at his word, in particular concerning the study of Scripture. Many of the radicals who later became Anabaptists had been meeting together to study the Bible since 1522. Following the sausage incident, the radical movement turned attention to the question of the tithe, images, and the Mass.

Among the Zurich followers of Zwingli were Conrad Grebel and Felix Mantz, both educated urbanites. Wilhelm Reublin came to the area after a turbulent time of reform preaching in Basel, and took up a pastorate in the neighbouring Swiss town of Witikon late in 1522. He was aided by Simon

Stumpf of Höngg. There was a large cast of lesser players, both within the city and in the countryside, including the Hottingers from Zollikon.

Serious radical agitation for church reform began outside of the city itself, in the countryside governed by Zurich. The focus was the tithe, an issue taken up later by the peasants in 1525. Early in 1523, both Reublin and Stumpf began preaching in their country churches that the local congregations should stop paying the tithe, because the income was going to support "good for nothing monks, who have stolen their living from the people long enough." But the Zurich council ruled that the tithe should continue to be paid. The city council would not allow the basic economic structure to be tampered with, and it had no intention of letting church incomes slip out of its grasp.

Tithe

The radicals in the countryside did not give up, however. The next issue was the question of images. Simon Stumpf preached openly concerning the "idolatry" of images in his country church (a theme also preached by Zwingli) and his congregation took matters into their own hands, "purifying" their sanctuary in unruly fashion by smashing images. Similar incidents began to occur in and around Zurich. The Zurich council decided to hold a public disputation in October 1523, concerning images and the Mass, following this radical challenge in the churches of Stumpf and Reublin.

Images

Balthasar Hubmaier's reform of Waldshut proceeded at first very much in step with Zwingli's in Zurich. He took part in the October disputation in Zurich, defending a Zwinglian position on the Mass. Hubmaier also understood the Supper as a memorial, called for the Mass to be said in the vernacular, and called for it to be celebrated "in both kinds."

Waldshut

Hubmaier later broke with Zwingli on the question of infant baptism, but he may have been misled. He wrote later that Zwingli had once agreed that infants should not be baptized. (2)

> **(2) Hubmaier recalls a conversation with Zwingli, ca. 1523.**
> "I conferred with you personally on the Zurich Graben about the Scriptures concerning baptism. There you said to me, rightly, that one should not baptize children before they have been instructed in the faith."
> (Pipkin and Yoder, 1989, 194-95).

Following the Zurich disputation on the Mass of October 1523, Zwingli prudently decided to implement reforms according to the rather conservative wishes of the city council. The council had decreed that the time for radical changes in church reform had not yet arrived. Zwingli's reluctance caused some of his radical followers to begin an even more serious critique of the pace of Zurich reform. It was at this point that the critiques of Karlstadt and Müntzer concerning Luther's "sparing of the weak" caught the attention of Conrad Grebel and his compatriots.(3)

---

(3) Grebel and friends to Müntzer, September, 1524.
"After we took the Scripture in hand ... we gained some insight and became aware of the great and harmful shortcomings of the shepherds... [A] false forbearance is what leads to the suppression of God's Word... [Your] writing against false faith was brought out here to us and we ... were wonderfully happy to have found someone who is of a common Christian mind with us and ventures to show the evangelical preachers their shortcomings..." (Harder, 1985, 286).

The tensions were palpable within the evangelical camp. The next point of attack of the radicals was a logical one, prepared as it had been by the critiques of Karlstadt and Müntzer, namely the question of baptism.

Baptism

In 1524 the issue of baptism had not yet been resolved in the evangelical camp. In particular it was not clear why Zwingli, with his spiritualized view of the sacraments, would insist on infant baptism. The water itself, he said, was only a sign of an inner change, just as the elements of the Supper were only memorials of Christ's sacrifice and a testimony to an inner faith. The logic of the case would seem to have been pushing Zwingli away from infant baptism, towards adult baptism.

In any case, the radicals again forced Zurich's hand. Early in 1524, the inhabitants of Witikon and Zollikon refused to allow their newborn infants to be baptized, following the preaching of Wilhelm Reublin and

Johannes Brötli. Within Zurich itself, the issue of baptism was taken up by Grebel and Mantz.

Private talks were held between the radicals and their former teacher Zwingli, who published a book he hoped would end the matter. His main argument there was that the New Testament neither commanded nor forbade infant baptism; therefore, the testimony of the Old Testament had to be considered decisive. Zwingli then argued that baptism should be seen as the covenant sign equivalent to Old Testament circumcision: infants who were to be educated into the faith were baptized as the symbol of their incorporation into the covenant community.

circumcision

The disruptions of the radicals continued: some sermons were interrupted, and some infants–notably Grebel's daughter–remained unbaptized. Zurich's response was to call a public disputation on baptism for January, 1525. This was held, and the result was predictable. The council decreed that Grebel and Mantz were to desist from any more agitation in the city, and that all infants were to be baptized. Foreigners were expelled from the territory and had eight days in which to leave. Among those exiled were Reublin and Brötli.

Soon after the council mandate (dated January 21, 1525) a group of the Zurich radicals gathered at house of Felix Mantz's mother. According to a contemporary account, Grebel, Mantz, Blaurock and others were present. After a discussion of the events of the day, they decided to perform baptism on one another. (4) In this way the first "rebaptisms" took place. Of course, they were

> **(4) The first adult baptisms in Zurich.**
> *"After fear lay greatly upon them, they called upon God in heaven, that he should show mercy to them. Then George arose and asked Conrad for God's sake to baptize him; and this he did. After that he baptized the others also."*
> *(In Snyder, 1984, 70).*

not understood as rebaptisms at all, but rather as the only true baptism. A definitive break with the Zwinglian reform had taken place.

Although further nuances in baptismal theology would become evident, the essential argument oppposing infant baptism and arguing for adult baptism was presented at the first disputation on baptism in Zurich. According to Heinrich Bullinger's report, Mantz, Grebel and Reublin argued that biblical baptism required receiving instruction, having faith, and pledging commitment, and no infant could do these things. (5) Bullinger did not give the specific biblical citations used in the public disputation, but from Grebel's published concordance (1525) on the subjects of faith and baptism and later Swiss Brethren argumentation, it is safe to assume that among the central passages were Matthew 28:18-20, Mark 16:15-16, Acts 2:38, Acts 9:17-19, Acts 16:17-34, and Acts 19:1-5.

---

(5) Bullinger describes Anabaptist arguments at the first baptismal disputation.

"[They said] baptism should be given to believers to whom the gospel had previously been preached, who have understood it, and who thereupon requested baptism for themselves, and killing the old Adam, desired to live a new life. Because infants knew nothing of this, baptism did not apply to them. For this they drew on Scripture from the Gospels and the Acts of the Apostles and pointed out that the apostles had not baptized infants but only adult discerning people." (Harder, 1985, 335).

The passages from Matthew and Mark outline a particular order in Christ's great commission: Go forth and teach, then baptize those who believe, following which, have them obey my commandments. This sequence of events, argued the earliest Anabaptists, outlined the proper biblical order concerning baptism. It was this line of argumentation that would reappear in virtually all branches of the Anabaptist movement.

Less often noted is the emphasis in Grebel's concordance on the necessary work of the Spirit of God in bringing about faith–the fact that faith "comes from heaven" is a central theme for Grebel. The passages from Acts provide examples of the apostolic practice of baptism, including the notable case of rebaptism in Acts 19:5. These passages emphasized not only the necessary conjunction of profession of faith and baptism, but also the role of the Holy Spirit in the process.

Implicit in the earliest Swiss statements on baptism, then, was the inner baptism of the Spirit which produced faith, and resulted in the witness of an outer baptism of water. Hubmaier's detailed biblical defence of adult baptism and his description of a three-fold baptism of spirit, water, and blood, soon to appear in print, repeated and built upon many of these earlier passages and interpretations.

The Spread of Anabaptism from Zurich

The baptizing movement spread rather quickly to neighbouring towns and cities. In part this seems to have been a deliberate attempt on the part of the Zurich radicals to win adherents to an alternative vision of reform: they were hoping their vision of reform would supplant Zwingli's. In part the spread of Anabaptism also was a result of the deportation orders handed down to all Anabaptist non-citizens.

The first town to be evangelized by the Anabaptists was the neighbouring village of Zollikon, home to the Hottinger clan, where a democratic, communal baptizing movement flourished in spite of mass arrests by the Zurich authorities. The movement also spread west towards Basel and Bern, and east to St. Gall and Appenzell. More significant in the context of 1525 was the spread of the movement to the north of Zurich, to Schaffhausen, Hallau and Waldshut, where the Anabaptists encountered the growing movement of peasant unrest.

Zollikon

In spite of the early leadership of Conrad Grebel, Felix Mantz, and George Blaurock, none of them wrote or published significant works in defence of adult baptism. This task fell to Balthasar Hubmaier, an early Swiss Anabaptist leader of surpassing importance who has been unfairly marginalized by modern historians. Hubmaier did more to define an early theological and biblical core of Anabaptist teaching than did any one else. (6) His writings on baptism continued to be cited verbatim by Swiss Brethren into the seventeenth century. But Hubmaier presents one of the great ambiguities of Swiss Anabaptist beginnings. What attitude did other Anabaptists take towards Hubmaier and his political involvements?

Hubmaier

Balthasar Hubmaier

> *(6) Hubmaier,* **On the Christian Baptism of Believers,** *July, 1525.* "Baptism in the Spirit and fire is to make alive and whole again the confessing sinner with the fire of the divine Word by the Spirit of God. ... Baptism in water in the name of the Father, and the Son, and the Holy Spirit, or in the name of our Lord Jesus Christ, is nothing other than a public confession and testimony of internal faith and commitment... Now, so that the kingdom of Christ might increase, the person breaks out into word and deed. ... From these descriptions ... anyone can see and recognize that the word or teaching should precede the outward baptism, along with the determination to change one's life by the help of God."
> *(Pipkin and Yoder, 1989, 100-101).*

Waldshut already was in a political alliance with the rebellious Black Forest peasants when Reublin and Grebel made several trips to that city in March, 1525. They were attempting to convince Hubmaier to accept the Anabaptist position on biblical church reform, and eventually they succeeded.

On Easter Sunday, 1525, Reublin baptized Hubmaier, who in turn baptized around three hundred Waldshut citizens during the Easter season alone. In time the majority of Waldshut citizens accepted rebaptism, including most of the city council. Clearly neither Hubmaier's involvement in the Peasants' War nor his post as a civic reformer in Waldshut were obstacles to his baptism. There were other similar cases as well. The city of Schaffhausen also came very close to accepting adult baptism as its official position.

Early Swiss Anabaptism was not a sectarian movement of separation from the world. The Swiss Anabaptist movement began as a grass roots, alternative movement of popular reform, not as a separatist and thoroughly pacifist movement. A close examination of the question of the sword of government in the first two years of the Swiss movement demonstrates the fact.

Swiss Anabaptism and the Sword

Conrad Grebel and Felix Mantz were personally committed to a nonresistant (pacifist) position. On this the documentation leaves no room for doubt.

In Conrad Grebel's 1524 letter to Thomas Müntzer he argued that Christians "must reach the fatherland of eternal rest not by slaying the physical but the spiritual. They use neither worldly sword nor war, since killing has ceased with them entirely."

Felix Mantz's writings also give witness to an equally committed pacifism, rooted in obedience to the commandments of Scripture. But Mantz's writings give evidence of a deeper Christocentrism.

In the farewell hymn he wrote just before being drowned in the Limmat, Felix Mantz insisted that the true servants of Christ do not hate or murder. (7) Those who take the sword demonstrate that they are Satan's children, and they will receive their just reward, if they do not repent.

Grebel's statements and Mantz's farewell foreshadow Schleitheim's later statement on the sword. There can be no doubt that a strong personal rejection of the sword was present among some of the first Anabaptists in Zurich.

> *(7) Felix Mantz' Farewell Letter*
> *"The true love of Christ shall not destroy the enemy; he that would be an heir with Christ is taught that he must be merciful, as the Father in heaven is merciful. . . . Christ also never hated any one; neither did his true servants, but they continued to follow Christ in the true way, as He went before them." (Martyrs Mirror, 415).*

But not all the Swiss Anabaptists were moving in lock-step with Grebel and Mantz on this question, nor does nonresistance seem to have been a requirement for membership in the Swiss movement prior to Schleitheim, as the case of Hubmaier demonstrates. And Hubmaier's case was not the only one.

Two Swiss Anabaptist pastors who directly benefitted from peasant protection were Wilhelm Reublin and Johannes Brötli, both co-workers with Grebel and Mantz. Reublin and Brötli centred their activity in the town

Hallau

of Hallau, located between Zurich and Waldshut. At Hallau the peasants' revolt and Anabaptism merged. Most of the citizenry accepted baptism (performed in the local church), and troops from Hallau joined the Black Forest peasants as well as participating in a variety of local armed conflicts–including the armed defence of their Anabaptist pastors.

The conclusion is inescapable that along with preaching baptism following confession of faith, Reublin and Brötli also were allowing those they baptized to use the sword in a "just cause."

Krüsi

In the area of St. Gall, Hans Krüsi led a similar movement that merged Anabaptism and peasant aspirations. Krüsi also had worked closely with Conrad Grebel, in the St. Gall district, and at the time of his arrest had in his possession the concordance put together by Conrad Grebel listing Bible passages on faith and baptism–later printed in Augsburg under Krüsi's name.

But in spite of this pedigree, Krüsi was not a consistent pacifist. The peasants in the Anabaptist villages where he preached organized themselves for armed defence, and also pledged themselves to defend their preacher with arms–a pledge they failed to carry out when Krüsi was apprehended in the middle of the night, much to Krüsi's vocal disappointment. As he was being taken away by the authorities, Krüsi is said to have shouted at the top of his lungs, "Where are you now, you who promised to help me?!" Hans Krüsi was burned at the stake in the Catholic Canton of Lucerne on July 27, 1525.

The Grüningen area, south-west of Zurich, also saw the blending of peasant unrest with Anabaptist concerns. It was in the Grüningen district that Conrad Grebel, Felix Mantz and George Blaurock carried out an extensive missionizing activity following the first rebaptisms. Nevertheless, Grüningen Anabaptism was closely related to the social, political, and economic concerns of the peasantry.

In April of 1525 the Grüningen peasantry sacked three religious establishments, including the monastery at Rüti. A recent detailed historical study has demonstrated that the ringleaders of that movement subsequently became central leaders in the stubborn Grüningen Anabaptist movement. Many of the grievances articulated by the peasants survived in Anabaptist form in Grüningen.

Swiss Anabaptism in 1525 was far from being uniformly pacifist, apolitical, or separatist, even among the Grebel circle. Furthermore, there is evidence from Zollikon and other places that this early Swiss Anabaptism was radically democratic in its organization, leadership, and economic structure, recalling again some of these same impulses among the peasants.

A significant document that appears to have been composed during this early stage of Swiss Anabaptism is a "Congregational Order" that may well have originated in Zollikon. The "Order" contained seven points on which members of the congregation should agree. (10)

---

(10) From the "Congregational Order."
"1. The brothers and sisters should meet at least three or four times a week... 2. When the brothers and sisters are together, they shall take up something to read together. The one to whom God has given understanding shall explain it... 3. Let none be frivolous in the church of God... 4. When a brother sees his brother erring, he shall warn him... 5. ...none shall have anything of his own... 6. All gluttony shall be avoided [at the meetings]... 7. The Lord's Supper shall be held, as often as the brothers are together..." (Yoder, 1973, 44-45).

The Congregational Order was a sober, practical document. Its reflects a time when rather public and frequent meetings were possible. Its democratic tone is noteworthy. The meetings were under the control of the "brothers and sisters," who also were responsible for the Spirit-led exegesis of the Word. Clearly there were frequent communal meals, as well as frequent celebrations of the Supper. Notable as well was the institution of a rudimentary "community of goods." In fact, the sharing of goods among the believers would become one of the common Anabaptist emphases in all branches of the movement.

When we recreate the Anabaptism of the first congregations in Switzerland, and try to imagine that participation in these early congregations must have been like for Jakob and Margret Hottinger, the "Congregational Order" helps us set an important part of the picture. Early Swiss Anabaptism was democratic, open to the Spirit, hopeful of reforming church and society. It was an Anabaptism that had yet to resolve many questions.

After the Peasants' War

Things changed radically with the failure of the Peasants' War. By the end of 1525, Waldshut had fallen to the Swabian League, as had all the territory north of Zurich. Anabaptism was left with no political support anywhere in the Swiss territories. In this hostile environment, many abandoned the movement. For those who stayed, there was a growing emphasis on separation from the affairs of the world.

The reality of the matter was that the local authorities in Zurich, St. Gall, Bern and Basel began to take stronger and stronger legal measures against the baptizing dissenters. Zurich published a mandate which decreed death by drowning for those who rebaptized others, and imprisonment and fines for those who accepted baptism.

By January 1527, Protestant Zurich had executed its first heretic: Felix Mantz, former student and friend of Zwingli, learned in Greek and Hebrew, had rebaptized contrary to the Council's mandate. He was arrested, tried, and drowned in the Limmat river on January 5, 1527. If Anabaptism was going to survive, it would do so not as a widespread reform, but as a persecuted, underground movement.

Michael Sattler

It was within this tense setting that Michael Sattler emerged as a leader of the Swiss Anabaptists in the summer of 1526. His pilgrimage had begun in the Benedictine monastery of St. Peter's of the Black Forest, near the city of Freiburg. He had reached the rank of prior, second in command of the monastery. The monastery had begun a process of strict observant reform by 1519 or 1520, and it is likely–although by no means certain–that Sattler, as prior, was in favour of that reform.

Black Forest

In 1525, the Black Forest troop of peasants–containing, as we have noted, volunteer fighters from Anabaptist Waldshut and Hallau–took the monastery of St. Peter's of the Black Forest, on their way to a successful siege of the city of Freiburg. Unfortunately, we can only conjecture about Sattler's whereabouts at that time, or his movements subsequent to the taking of St. Peter's, but the next time we find Sattler in the historical record, he appears in Zurich on a list of prisoners that included Margret Hottinger of Zollikon as well as Anabaptists from the Waldshut area. As we noted in telling Margret Hottinger's story, Michael Sattler swore an oath at this time that he would have nothing to do with Anabaptism in the future, and was released.

Did Sattler leave the monastery in the midst of the peasant unrest, and was he first introduced to Anabaptism by brethren in the Black Forest troop? We will probably never know for certain, even though the circumstantial evidence suggests that it was so.

Whether it was Michael Sattler or Michael Wüst who came to reside in the Swiss village of Klingnau, in the house of Hans Kuenzi, learning how to weave, remains a disputed question. But it is certain that by the summer of 1526 Michael Sattler had committed himself fully to the Anabaptist cause, and began to preach, teach and baptize in the same Swiss villages where the peasants had earlier taken up arms.

His work took him then into the Strasbourg area, where he preached and baptized in the neighbouring city of Lahr, and into Strasbourg itself, where he pleaded for the release of imprisoned Anabaptists (among them, Jakob Groß) and held talks with Martin Bucer and Wolfgang Capito, reformers of that city. Sattler's emphatic separatism is already evident in a letter he wrote to Bucer and Capito, following their meeting. (8)

(8) Sattler to Bucer and Capito. "Believers are chosen out of the world, therefore the world hates them. The devil is prince over the whole world, in whom all the children of darkness rule. Christ is the Prince of the Spirit, in whom all who walk in the light live. . . . The flesh is against the spirit and the spirit against the flesh." (Yoder, 1973, 22).

It was this radical separatism, which rejected as "worldly" all manner of armed resistance or governmental involvement ("the sword"), that soon came to define the Swiss Brethren position.

The Schleitheim Gathering and Articles

On February 24, 1527, an important meeting took place in the small Swiss border village of Schleitheim. It was at this meeting that many of the initial ambiguities within Swiss Anabaptism were resolved.

We wish we knew more about the participants at this meeting, but no list has survived. The literary evidence that remains, in the form of seven articles of "Brotherly Union," allows us to say with certainty that Michael Sattler was there and provided the basic draft of the articles that were adopted.

The resulting document has come to be called the Schleitheim Articles. These articles were the first systematic detailing of Swiss Anabaptist views. They mark a "crystallization point" for the Swiss movement. (9) The changed political circumstances meant that Anabaptism now had to organize for survival, rather than offer competing reform models.

---

(9) From the **Schleitheim Articles.**

1. **Baptism:** *"Baptism shall be given to all those who have been taught repentance and the amendment of life...and to those who desire to walk in the resurrection of Jesus Christ..."*

2. **Ban:** *"The ban shall be employed with all those who have given themselves over to the Lord, to walk after [Him]...according to the command of Christ [Matthew 18]."*

3. **Lord's Supper:** *"All those who desire to break the one bread in remembrance ...[and] drink of one drink of remembrance...must beforehand be united in the one body of Christ..."*

4. **Separation from the world and all evil:** *"All who have not entered into the obedience of faith ... are a great abomination before God... [The Lord] orders us to be and to become separated from the evil one..."*

5. **Election of shepherds by the congregation:** *"The shepherd in the church shall be a person ... who has a good report of those who are outside the faith. . . . He shall be supported, wherein he has need, by the congregation which has chosen him... If they sin they shall be publicly reprimanded..."*

6. **Sword:** *"The sword is an ordering of God outside the perfection of Christ. . . . But within the perfection of Christ only the ban is used..."*

7. **Oath:** *"Christ ... forbids His [followers] all swearing..."*

(Yoder, 1973, 36-41).

Of these articles, the first three were held in common with the Anabaptists who had gone before, from Grebel, to Reublin, to Hubmaier. These three articles would be held in common with Anabaptists in other regions as well.

New defining elements were introduced, however, with articles four through seven. The strong stress on separation from the world set the tone for the last four articles. They were a clear contribution from the ex-monk Sattler and picked up common themes from his known writings. He called for a church that knowingly and purposefully distanced itself from society, rejecting society's values. He expected judgement to fall soon on the sinful world, and would not partake of either the sin or the punishment.

The upshot of articles four through seven was that those who accepted baptism in the Schleitheim mould also were separating themselves totally from involvement in society at large. They were establishing an alternative society, in the world, but not of it. Unlike the peasants and militant Swiss Anabaptists of 1525, the Schleitheim group did not hope to reform the world according to a utopian pattern. They had given up on the world and were withdrawing from it, awaiting the divine judgement of the Last Days which they believed was imminent. But articles four through seven were **not** universally accepted in the Anabaptism that emerged elsewhere, as will be seen in the chapters which follow.

Conclusion

We can return in conclusion to Margret Hottinger, and the ambiguities we identified at the beginning.

> *(10) From Kessler's* **Sabbata.** *"There were also some [in St. Gall] ... who had earlier learned and heard from Protestant preachers that the New Testament was a matter of the spirit and not of the letter... [They] threw their Testaments into the stove ... saying, 'The letter is dead, the spirit gives life.'"* (Harder, 1985, 455).

Margret Hottinger had prophetic gifts that she exercised in the Anabaptist community. There were also many other cases where early Swiss Anabaptists appealed to the direct guidance of the Holy Spirit and experienced emotional conversions. But there also had been some cases of excessive spiritual enthusiasm, particularly in St. Gall. (10)

Besides reacting to a changed political situation, the Schleitheim Articles also reacted against a "great offense" that some "false brothers" had introduced, "thinking to practice and observe the freedom of the Spirit and of Christ." In place of this "spiritual license," Schleitheim insisted upon a sober, ascetic life: "They who are Christ's have crucified their flesh with all its lusts and desires."

There had been some ambiguity on questions of spirit and letter in early Swiss Anabaptism, but Schleitheim resolved the question for the

Letter

Swiss. Baptism in the Schleitheim mode meant that the letter, not the spirit, outlined the rule of life. It meant, more concretely, that the life of Christ was the ethical measure of one's own life.

We can only conjecture what the Scheitheim decision might have meant for Margret Hottinger and others who, at an earlier stage, clearly operated in a more spiritualistic way. To the extent that Schleitheim was followed,

Margret's prophetic functions were marginalized. Nevertheless, she continued as an Anabaptist, even unto death.

The democratic leadership style seen in the early Anabaptism of the "Congregational Order" was narrowed by Schleitheim. It appears that the role of women in the movement was reduced, dependent as it had been on the exercise of spiritual gifts. In contrast to the "brother and sisterly" leadership of the Congregational Order, Schleitheim provided guidelines for the election of a male shepherd. Nevertheless, later Swiss Anabaptist writings continued to criticize the state churches for silencing rank and file members, suggesting a significant continuation of democratic practice among the Swiss Anabaptists.

Schleitheim pronounced decisively against the civic Anabaptism carried out by Hubmaier in Waldshut, as well as against any use of the sword or the swearing of oaths. As far as the Swiss territories were concerned, the Anabaptism that predominated after 1527 was the separatist, apolitical, pacifist and non-swearing Anabaptism of Schleitheim. This variety of Anabaptism managed to survive in isolated pockets of resistance in remote Swiss mountians and valleys.

Sword

Nevertheless the debate on the relationship of Anabaptism to the world was not yet settled outside of Switzerland. As we will see below, Balthasar Hubmaier established yet another experiment in civic Anabaptism in Moravia, in the city of Nicholsburg. The debate among the Swiss Anabaptists on the questions of government simply moved East with the Anabaptist refugees from Switzerland.

Many hundreds of Swiss Anabaptists, like Balthasar Hubmaier and Jakob, Margret, and Felix Hottinger, migrated eastwards to Moravia. Others fled to the Palatinate, down the Rhine and eventually even into Hesse and the Netherlands. The later Swiss Brethren, then, were not geographically "Swiss," but rather were described as "Swiss Brethren" in a doctrinal sense.

The origins of Swiss Anabaptism were unique within Anabaptism as a whole. The theological influences of Zwingli and Karlstadt are visible among the early Zurich radicals; some distant influence from Thomas Müntzer also is evident. Like other branches of radical reform, Swiss Anabaptism was rooted in the demand for church reform based on Scripture alone. Zwingli initially encouraged lay Bible reading, but soon backed away from the interpretive consequences. In the canton of Zurich two distinct interpretive communities emerged, both appealing to Scripture alone. The issue of water baptism finally sealed their separation.

Local political and religious pressures meant that Swiss Anabaptism moved quickly from being a movement aspiring to territorial reform, to a movement defining itself as separatist–all within the space of two and a half short years. But the initial ambiguities would remain debated issues in the *larger* Anabaptist movement for several decades more.

Swiss Anabaptism was unique in that it moved to a sectarian position in a very short time. All surviving Anabaptist groups eventually arrived at similar affirmations, but the path leading there was filled with inter-Anabaptist discussion, testing, and dissension as the concrete implications of Anabaptist beliefs were defined.

As for Michael Sattler, framer of the Schletheim Articles, he was arrested in Austrian territory shortly following the Schleitheim meeting and tried by Austrian authorities in the town of Rottenburg on the Neckar river, in Württemberg. He was sentenced to a horrible death: he was to have part of his tongue cut off, be forged to a cart, have his flesh ripped from him eight times with red hot tongs, following which he was to be burned at the stake. This was carried out on May 20, 1527. His wife Margareta, who had been arrested with him, was drowned two days later after refusing to recant.

Title page from the earliest Swiss Brethren hymnal,
the *Ausbund* (1564)

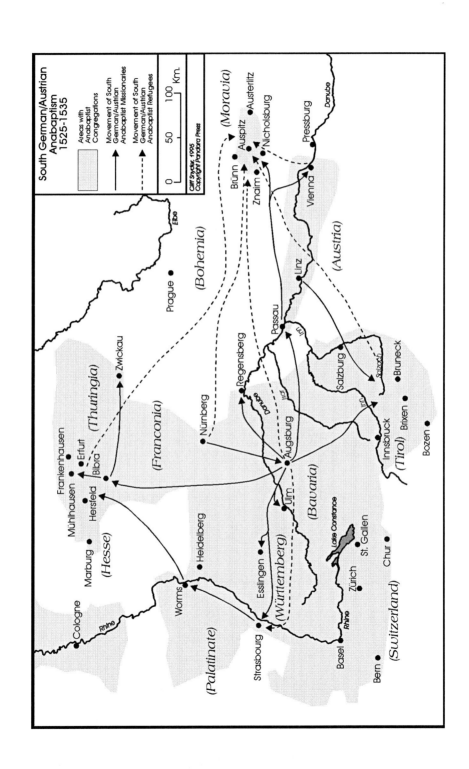

South German/Austrian
Anabaptism
1525-1535

Areas with
Anabaptist
Congregations

Movement of South
German/Austrian
Anabaptist Missionaries

Movement of South
German/Austrian
Anabaptist Refugees

0   50   100   Km.

Cliff Snyder, 1995
Copyright Pandora Press

Chapter 7

The Origins of
South German/Austrian Anabaptism

***Warrant for the arrest of Hans Hut,
city of Nuremberg.***
*Description: "a very learned, clever fellow, a
fair length of a man [i.e., tall], a rustic person
with cropped brown hair, a pale yellow mous-
tache, dressed in gray woolen pants, a broad
gray hat, and at times a black riding coat."
(Seebass, 1982, 54).*

We already have met Hans Hut briefly, at the disastrous battle of Frankenhausen. In beginning to tell the story of South German/Austrian Anabaptism we can do no better than to recall the rest of Hans Hut's story. He was, without a doubt, the person most responsible for the emergence and the character of this branch of Anabaptism.

Hans Hut was born around 1490 in Haina, in Central Germany. We know nothing about his early life and education. He was literate in German, but he may well have been self-taught. His religious interests are evident in the fact that he filled the office of church sexton in the town of Bibra for four years.

By trade Hans Hut was a bookbinder and a bookpeddler. This was an exciting career in the 1520s for anyone interested in religious matters.

Thanks to the newly-invented printing press, books were becoming a desireable and affordable commodity. Book production increased radically in the beginning of the sixteenth century, urged on by the religious debates. Religious pamphlets literally poured out of the German presses beginning in that decade. We have no inventory lists, but it is virtually certain, given his later contacts and activities, that Hans Hut dealt in popular religious books.

Hans Hut was in touch with printers and buyers of books throughout all of central and south Germany. From 1521 on he sold books in Würzburg, Bamberg, Nuremberg, Passau and into Austria. He also travelled to Wittenberg, where he showed a preference for Karlstadt's and Müntzer's views.

He got to know Thomas Müntzer very well. When Müntzer had to flee Mühlhausen in September of 1524, he spent a night and a day at Hut's house. Furthermore, he entrusted Hut with the task of having his latest book, the *Vindication and Refutation* printed in Nuremberg. Among Hut's contacts there was the humanist schoolteacher Hans Denck, the man who would later baptize him.

We have no way of tracing the development of Hut's thought on reform questions, but we do know that Hut absorbed the early radical critique of infant baptism, perhaps from Müntzer. In 1524, before the first baptisms in Zurich, Hut refused to have his third and youngest child baptized in Bibra. Given the choice of having the infant baptized or being exiled, he chose exile.

The Peasants' War was now well underway in Central Germany, and by Hut's presence at the fateful battle of Frankenhausen, it is evident that he was a follower of Müntzer. Although the authorities bought his story, that the battle was just a bookselling opportunity, we know from other evidence that Hans Hut was a signed member of Thomas Müntzer's "Eternal Covenant."

After the defeat of the peasant forces at Frankenhausen Hut returned briefly to Bibra and preached there, castigating the clergy for celebrating the Mass only for pay. He promised his hearers that God would punish the ungodly priests. Some claimed that he had said that power was now in the hands of the little people, and that the authorities should be killed.

Whether or not Hut actually said the latter thing, he had said and done enough that he had to leave Bibra on the run. He appears to have resumed his bookselling travels. By May of 1526 he had accepted baptism in Augsburg, at the hands of Hans Denck. Immediately he began an amazing missionary activity on behalf of the baptizing movement.

Among the documented places where Hans Hut founded Anabaptist congregations are: Haina, Coburg, Königsberg (Franconia), Ostheim, Bamberg, Erlangen, Nuremberg, Uttenreuth, Augsburg, Passau, Steyer, Freistadt, Eisenstadt, Vienna, Melk, Linz, Laufen, and Salzburg. There were in addition numerous smaller villages and rural locations where Hut won and baptized converts. He baptized many hundreds of people and they, in turn, baptized many hundreds more, taking the movement into the Tirol and Moravia.

Hans Hut shared some basic Anabaptist principles with the Swiss. (1) He taught that baptism in water was an outward response to a baptism by the Spirit, that baptized believers bound themselves to the discipline of the congregation of believers, and that they were to celebrate a memorial Supper. Nevertheless, Hut's Anabaptism was pitched in another key. It gave stronger emphasis to the work of the Spirit, it expected suffering on the way to a true faith, and it was explicit in its apocalyptic predictions. The urgent and intense missionary activity in Hut's circle was fueled by the need to baptize the 144,000 elect of the Last Days.

> *(1) Hans Hut, "Of the Mystery of Baptism."*
>
> *"[Baptism is] a willing resolve (to put oneself) under the obedience of Christ, with an exhibiting of divine Love towards all brothers and sisters in the Lord with body, life, goods and honour..."* (Rupp, 1969, 389).

Hans Hut accomplished his founding work in less than a year and a half of Anabaptist activity. He was arrested in Augsburg in September, 1527. After being racked severely, he died under mysterious circumstances, asphyxiating as the result of a fire in his cell. Frustrated judges publicly condemned his lifeless body to death and burned it at the stake.

*(For a concise biography, see Gottfried Seebass, "Hans Hut: The Suffering Avenger," in H-J Goertz, ed., **Profiles of Radical Reformers** (Scottdale, Pa.: Herald Press, 1982), 54-61).*

The Mixed Beginnings of South German/Austrian Anabaptism

There was a time in Anabaptist studies when it was assumed that the baptizing movement had to have one point of origin and one essential "nature." Polygenesis historians have pointed to a variety of intellectual and historical currents that contributed to Anabaptist beginnings in different regions. As the story of Hans Hut demonstrates, the varied roots of South German/Austrian Anabaptism are found in the ashes of the Peasant's War, the apocalyptic theology of Thomas Müntzer, and the mystical spiritualism of Hans Denck. To this mix must be added interaction with the Swiss Anabaptism that had come before. All this meant that South German/Austrian Anabaptism also had its share of internal tensions that needed resolution.

–**Spirit and Letter**. Contrasting approaches emerged between a spiritualist emphasis on an experience of the inner Word (Denck), and an emphasis on an interpretation of apoclayptic, prophetic Scripture (Hut). What role, if any, should inspired prophets play in the interpretation of Scripture?

–**Last Days**. Virtually everyone agreed that the End Times had arrived. But was it possible to outline a calendar of people and events of the Last Days? Could the date of Christ's return be calculated? Hans Hut thought so.

–**Church and Government**. What role may baptized adult Christians play in the affairs of the world? For apocalyptic Anabaptists, "the world" was just at the point of disappearing forever, and the question was not a pressing one. For spiritualist Anabaptists, questions of church and government were determined by the need to retain spiritual integrity.

The Beginnings: Müntzer, Denck, and Hut

The story of South German Anabaptism is complex because it must describe the birth and spread of a grass roots movement over a large territory. One way to give an impression of this process is to tell the stories of some of the central people involved. The story of South German Anabaptism must begin with Thomas Müntzer, even though he never practiced adult baptism.

Thomas Müntzer

Two central and related themes had emerged in Thomas Müntzer's life and writings: an emphasis on the necessary work of the Spirit of God in believers (the work of the "inner word"), and a conviction that since the End Times had arrived, believers had an active role to play in bringing in the Kingdom.

On the first point, Müntzer thought that when genuine believers came to faith, they had to experience the "bitter Christ" in their own hearts. Coming to faith would be a painful experience in which sinners had to "yield" to the sharp ploughshare of the Spirit in their hearts. The mystical roots of this teaching are evident. | *Yieldedness*

The crucial point that led Müntzer from contemplation and inward suffering to a support of social revolt was his conviction that these were the Last Days, that judgement was at hand, and that God would purge the world by a painful revolution, in the same way that He spiritually purged the Elect. | *Revolution*

Müntzer understood the church to be the visible bride of Christ (a small band of elect) containing only the saved. As we have seen, Müntzer eventually cast his lot with the peasants, in the belief that they were God's agents, beginning the purging process of the Last Days. This was mysticism with a hammer, as Hans-Jürgen Goertz has so aptly said, and it appealed to Hans Hut in particular. Hans Denck, by contrast, was more in tune with a personal, mystical spirituality.

Hans Denck

Hans Denck was born sometime around 1500 in Bavaria and attended the University of Ingolstadt from 1517 to 1520. He was a humanist scholar, well versed in Latin, Greek and Hebrew. He came to Basel in 1522, worked as a proofreader in various print shops, and identified with the evangelical reform movement led by Johannes Oecolampadius, upon whose recommendation Denck received a teaching appointment in 1523 at the St. Sebald school in Nuremberg.

Once in Nuremberg, Denck began to associate with the circle of mystical humanists and to identify with the radical currents of reform that had found a strong resonance in those circles. The writings of both Müntzer and Karlstadt were well known in Nuremberg. Denck, who had been strongly influenced by the Rhenish mysticism of John Tauler and Heinrich Suso, shared many theolgical and spiritual roots with them.

Mysticism

Hans Denck probably came to know both Thomas Müntzer and Heinrich Pfeiffer in Nuremberg when they visited that city in 1524. Hans Hut, at this time an active member of Müntzer's circle, came to Nuremberg on at least two occassions to have some of Müntzer's writings printed. He testified later that he had stayed with Denck at least once in 1524.

By January of 1525 Hans Denck had been expelled from Nuremberg. He appeared next in the Swiss city of Schwyz, where he was imprisoned briefly for preaching against infant baptism. Coming next to St. Gall, he consorted with the Anabaptists gathered around Johannes Krüsi, the "not-so-pacifist" Anabaptist preacher. Denck, however, had probably not yet accepted adult baptism, even though he was visibly leaning in that direction.

Baptism

By September of 1525, Denck was in the South German city of Augsburg, where he would remain for a year and a month. At some point—whether in Augsburg or at some point prior to his arrival there—he accepted baptism, and became an active Anabaptist leader. It was during his stay in Augsburg that Denck wrote three important works: *Whether God is the Cause of Evil*, *Of the Law of God*, and *He Who Truly Loves the Truth*.

In Augsburg Denck also met Balthasar Hubmaier, who was passing though the city on his way to Nicholsburg, Moravia, following his imprisonment and expulsion from Zurich. And, in the spring of 1526, in a watershed event for the history of South German Anabaptism, Hans Denck baptized Hans Hut into the movement. Augsburg was an important early focal point for the beginnings of South German Anabaptism.

By late summer of 1526 Denck had fled Augsburg, and by November of 1526 was in Strasbourg. Martin Bucer and Denck carried out a public debate before several hundred citizens on December 22 and 23, 1526 with the result that the council, at Bucer's urging, expelled Denck from the city. He fled to the imperial city of Worms where he collaborated with Ludwig Hätzer on a translation of the Old Testament prophets and also joined forces with Melchior Rinck in promoting Anabaptist reform in the city. They succeeded in converting Jacob Kautz and Hilarius, both young Lutheran preachers, to the Anabaptist cause. It was also in Worms that Denck composed his most Anabaptist writing, *Concerning True Love*. But by July 1, Kautz and Hilarius had been banished, as had also Melchior Rinck; Denck and Hätzer then left the city.

In August of 1527, Hans Denck took part in some meetings of the "Martyrs' Synod" in and around Augsburg, as will be detailed further below, following which he withdrew to Basel. By this time he had become disillusioned by Anabaptist divisions and, at the urging of his old friend Oecolampadius, he composed an apology which came to be called (posthumously and misleadingly) his *Recantation*. He died in Basel in mid-November of 1527, a victim of the plague.

Primary among Denck's reforming ideas was his insistence that the inner Word was more important than the outer word, an emphasis he shared with Müntzer and Hut. Consequently, he shared the radical reformed critique of Luther's understanding of salvation, and insisted on a visible life of discipleship. (2) This inner, mystical emphasis, combined with a demand for a new life, would remain a constant for Denck throughout all his travels and changes.

> *(2) Hans Denck defines baptism.*
> "[The] sign of the Covenant, [which] is to be given and not to be denied to any of those who by the power of God have been invited to it through the knowledge of genuine Love and who desire such Love and agree to be followers." *(Furcha, 1975, 109).*

Of all early Anabaptist leaders, Hans Denck was one of the least

Inner Piety

dogmatic. He called for religious toleration, since he considered outward ceremonies to be largely secondary. What truly counted was the inner life of the spirit and faith. As Werner Packull has noted, this interior emphasis was democratic and anticlerical. The Spirit could and did speak to all, not just to the literate doctors of theology. Although there are no demonstrated connections between Denck and the Peasants' War, he agreed with Müntzer and Karlstadt in the appeal to mystical roots, the call for spiritual self-surrender, the democratic stress on the Spirit, as well as in his

Baptism

anticlericalism.

It was Hans Denck's acceptance of water baptism as the outer sign of inner repentance and commitment that defined him as an Anabaptist, although he did move away from a firm commitment to the "ceremonies" of water baptism and the Lord's Supper just before his death. During his Anabaptist phase, however, Denck maintained that for those who inwardly accepted God's gracious offer of a new life in Christ, the next step was water baptism. Thus the outer sign of baptism indicated publicly that one had made an inner commitment thenceforth to live a new life in Christ. (3)

(3) Denck on baptism. *"...whoever is baptized into the death of Christ is baptized in order that he might die to the old Adam as (Christ) has died and that he may walk in a new life with Christ as He (Christ) was raised." (Furcha, 1975, 19).*

Here the ethical emphasis emerged as strongly in Denck's thought as in that of other Anabaptists. Salvation is not dependent on "imputed righteousness" on the basis of faith in Christ alone, but rather salvation involves living a sanctified life, in the power of Christ's Spirit. (4) Hans Denck joined other Anabaptists in opposing the Protestant understanding of being justified simply on the basis of one's faith in Christ's sacrifice alone, without a corresponding walk of discipleship.

(4) Hans Denck, "The Law of God." *"[Christ] has fulfilled the Law, not to place us above it, but to give us an example to follow Him." (Furcha, 1975, 49).*

Hans Hut

Hans Hut was baptized by Hans Denck, and he shared Denck's mystical emphasis. Nevertheless, Hut's teaching as an Anabaptist retained much of Thomas Müntzer, and much less of Denck.

Like Müntzer, Hut emphasised God's grace as a purging of the soul, the necessity of suffering while this purging was taking place, the reception of a living Spirit in all believers, and a preaching about the imminent End Times. (5) So close are the parallels that Hans Hut's major writing on baptism was for some time thought to be a writing by Thomas Müntzer. There is some justice to Seebass's judgement that Hut's theology represents "a cruder version of Müntzer's basic assumptions."

> *(5) Hans Hut, "Of the Mystery of Baptism."*
> "*No man may come to the truth, unless he follow in the footsteps of Christ and his elect in the school of all tribulation, or have at least in some small part pledged himself to follow the will of God in the justifying of the Cross of Christ.*" *(Rupp, 1969, 381).*

In particular, Müntzer's emphasis on the necessity of suffering was taken up by Hut's interesting teaching on the "Gospel of all Creatures." (6) According to Hut, God had revealed in all creation the fundamental "gospel" that lower orders of creation must suffer the will of the higher orders of creation. Just as animals must suffer at the hands of human beings, so also human beings must be subject to, and suffer, at the hands of God. This call to *Gelassenheit*, or giving place to God's will, and the call to accept the suffering that such yielding would entail, was thoroughly Müntzerian. It was central to Hut's preaching and teaching.

> *(6) Hans Hut on the "Gospel of all Creatures."*
> "*In the 'Gospel of all creatures' is nothing else signified and preached than simply Christ crucified, but not Christ alone as Head, but the whole Christ with all members, this is the Christ which all creatures preach and teach.*"
> "*As the peasant does with his field, before he sows seed in it, so does God also with us, before he plants his Word in us...*"
> "*...no man can come to salvation, save through suffering and tribulation which God works in him, as also the whole Scripture and all the creatures show nothing else but the suffering Christ in all his members.*" *(Rupp, 1969, 383; 385; 386).*

The Angel from the East seals the 144,000 Elect with the mark of TAU on the forehead. Revelation 7:3.

Hut's understanding of baptism illustrates his unique blending of Anabaptist emphases with Müntzer's views. Hut's defence of water baptism restated the Anabaptist themes that the Gospel is to be preached, after which, when faith results, baptism is to be given. Baptism is a covenant sign that incorporates believers into the fellowship of the Christian Church; the outer baptism "follows preaching and faith," and is a sign or covenant of the "true reality."

This formulation recalls the three successive baptismal steps, seen already in the earliest Swiss Anabaptism: First comes the preaching of the Word, then faith results, and only then is water baptism administered. Like Hubmaier, Hut also spoke of a three-fold baptism of spirit, water, and blood, thus echoing previously articulated Anabaptist understandings of baptism. Nevertheless, Hut also introduced new emphases that recall his previous allegiance to Thomas Müntzer.

Although the spiritualist emphasis was present in Swiss understandings of baptism, Hut developed the concept of the inner baptism further.

For Hut the essential or true baptism begins with knowledge of God, deepens in a process of suffering and doubt, and is fulfilled through the work of the Spirit. Hut's understanding, drawn from Müntzer and perhaps also from Denck, points to roots in German mysticism and concentrates on the spiritual process of yielding one's will when coming to true faith. (7)

> **(7) Hans Hut, "On the Mystery of Baptism."**
> *"Whoso will do the will of God must renounce his own, whoso will find somewhat in God must by so much lose himself." (Rupp, 1969, 392).*

A second original theme that emerged in Hut's baptismal practice was his linking of water baptism with the sealing of the 144,000 elect of the Last Days (Revelation 7:3). Hut typically baptized followers on the forehead with this mark of the elect of the Last Days. With this practice, Hut's blending of Müntzer's apocalyptic convictions with Anabaptism is most evident.

In both teaching and practice, Hans Hut gave Anabaptist baptism, mystical and apocalyptic emphases not seen previously, which point to his own theological origins as a follower of Thomas Müntzer.

Melchior Rinck

In tracing the story of Melchior Rinck we look to Central Germany–to Hesse, Saxony, and Thuringia–and to a person who was in close contact with both Thomas Müntzer and Hans Denck. Melchior Rinck was born in 1492 or 1493, apparently of peasant parents from Hesse.

He received a good education at the Universities of Leipzig and Erfurt, where he excelled in classical languages. His nickname was "the Greek," an allusion to his linguistic skill. Rinck was an early convert to evangelical reform: already in 1523, as chaplain in Hersfeld, Rinck had begun to preach in a reformed mode, following the lead of the Hersfeld pastor Heinrich Fuchs, who had been in the evangelical camp since 1521. Their preaching eventually brought about a confrontation with the abbot and the city council, a small revolt in the city, and an order by Philip of Hesse that the two pastors be arrested and expelled from Hessian territory. Their supporters in Hersfeld saw that they were released from prison, given money, and escorted safely across the border. Early in 1524, through the intervention of Jakob Strauss, Melchior Rinck did find a post as a Lutheran preacher first in Oberhausen, and then in Eckhardshausen, near Eisenach.

Later that same year or early in 1525 Rinck married Anna, daughter of the Lutheran supporter Hans Eckhart. Given Rinck's later accusation that Anna had married him not out of love or free choice, but in order to find a "quiet life," it seems a safe assumption that at the time of his marriage

Müntzer

Rinck was not yet a follower of Müntzer, for Müntzer's life was anything but quiet already by 1524. Thomas Müntzer returned to Mühlhausen in late February 1525, and Rinck was on the battlefield in Frankenhausen by May 1525. As Erich Geldbach notes, Rinck "must have fallen very suddenly under Müntzer's influence."

Unfortunately, details are lacking concerning Rinck's involvement with Müntzer and the Peasants' War. Rinck later did not deny that he had been involved in the Peasants' War, although he did deny any leadership role. His opponents claimed, to the contrary, that he had been a leader more zealous than either Müntzer or Pfeiffer. Although later opponents may have exaggerated, Rinck's involvement in the Peasants' War was not innocent or inciden-

Frankenhausen

tal. He was a leading combatant (a troop captain) at Frankenhausen.

Rinck (perhaps understandably) never clarified his own relationship to Thomas Müntzer during the years 1523 to 1525. From the few surviving writings from Rinck's hand–all from a later date–no real influence from Müntzer is discernible. Certainly Müntzer left a far stronger theological imprint on Hans Hut than he did on Melchior Rinck.

Rinck's whereabouts and activities after the defeat of the peasants are unknown until January 1527, when he appeared in Landau in conversation with the Reformed pastor Johannes Bader. Bader had been leaning in an Anabaptist direction, but then changed his mind and supported infant baptism. Hans Denck passed through Landau on his way from Strasbourg to Worms. Denck and Bader held a disputation on January 20, the proceedings of which Bader published; in reply, Melchior Rinck wrote a "Refutation."

Hans Denck

What evidence there is suggests that Hans Denck baptized Melchior Rinck, probably sometime in January 1527. In any case, Denck and Rinck now made their way to Worms and worked there together for the Anabaptist cause, as noted above.

Rinck surfaced again as an Anabaptist evangelist in and around Hersfeld (in Hesse) in the summer of 1528, where he had formerly worked as chaplain. When he presented a written petition to be allowed to preach publicly in the parish church in Hersfeld, word reached the Margrave Philip of Hesse. He summoned Rinck to his hunting lodge and interviewed him personally. Given the option of expulsion or an examination by Philip's theologians at the University of Marburg, Rinck chose the latter. The articles discussed at that August, 1528 debate are still extant, and provide us with a little insight into Rinck's Anabaptist teachings.

Erich Geldbach has shown convincingly that the general argument and structure of Rinck's articles closely parallels that seen in Hans Denck's booklet "Concerning True Love," published in the previous year at Worms. Nevertheless, Rinck's writing displays none of Denck's emphasis on the inner Word, nor is there any trace of Müntzer's revolutionary apocalypticism in Rinck's 1528 writing. Melchior Rinck may have been influenced by Müntzer in 1525, and he was probably baptized and clearly influenced by Denck in 1527, but he remained very much his own person theologically.

As a result of the debate, Rinck was expelled from Hessian territory in the summer of 1528, but he came back again. He was arrested again in Hessian territory in April of 1529 and, with characteristic leniency, Philip of Hesse had him held in the monastery of Haina until May, 1531, when he was released without any penalty except the condition that he remain out of Hessian and Saxon territories. (8) This condition Rinck violated immediately, returning to the same general area near Hersfeld. He was arrested for the last time while preaching on a favourite baptismal text, Mark 16:16.

(8) Letter from Melchior Rinck, from prism. "Just as one cannot damn children on account of unbelief, likewise one cannot declare them saved on the grounds of faith, since one cannot preach and they cannot hear. Just as they neither know nor hate evil, so are they without knowledge and love of the good." *(Yoder, 1973, 135).*

Philip of Hesse now pronounced a sentence of life imprisonment for Rinck. For the next twenty years Melchior Rinck heroically resisted all attempts to dissuade him from his Anabaptist belief–he was visited by Peter Tasch after the latter's recantation of Anabaptism, as well as by Martin Bucer, but all to no avail. He was still living in prison in 1553 at sixty years of age. There is no further notice of him in the historical record. It is assumed that he died in prison, probably before 1560.

The origins of Melchior Rinck's Anabaptism are in the Müntzer/Denck tradition. Nevertheless, one could hardly arrive at such a conclusion by an analysis of his writings or the testimonies of those whom he instructed in Anabaptism.

We find in Rinck a strong anticlericalism, but nothing beyond what was commonly seen among Anabaptists. Like all Anabaptists, Rinck rejected Luther's understanding of salvation by faith, and upheld the standard Anabaptist view that emphasized the necessity of good works. The historical records indicate that Rinck was concerned above all with baptism, and that his teaching resembled most of all that of the Swiss Brethren in its biblically literal foundation–although no dependence is suggested by this. Although he taught that baptism in water had to follow one's "having been taught of God," he showed no tendency to depreciate water baptism in favour of an inner, spiritual baptism. There is no evidence that Rinck shared Denck's mystical and spiritualist bent; his tendency was more literalistic.

Likewise, Rinck did not emphasize baptism as an apocalyptic sign of the 144,000 elect, as did Hut, although he appears to have baptized by making a sign of the cross on the forehead. While there is some sporatic evidence that he may have preached that the End Times were near, this was no pronounced emphasis in his teaching as it had been with Müntzer and with Hut.

The testimonies of those whom he taught identify the core of his teaching as very basic Anabaptist teachings: One comes to faith by hearing the Word preached (that is, being taught by God), then comes repentance, water baptism, and living a new life.

South German Anabaptism after Hut and Denck

In spite of the true generalization that at its origins it was a more mystical, spiritualistic, and apocalyptic Anabaptism, the South German movement showed little uniformity in its development after 1527. Divergent Anabaptist expressions within South German Anabaptism multiplied, partly because of a loss of leadership. Just as Swiss Anabaptism lost its original leaders very quickly (Grebel in 1526, Mantz and Sattler in 1527, Hubmaier in 1528, Blaurock in 1529), so also the founding South German Anabaptist leaders disappeared quickly from the scene (Denck and Hut both perished in 1527).

Werner Packull has spoken of the "devolution" of Hut's movement, especially following the failure of his End Times prophecies and his own death, and the "evolution" of a more sectarian, congregational Anabaptism. In fact this process seems to have been underway from the very start.

Four primary groupings have been identified that emerged from the Hut-Denck beginnings.

–those who developed Hut's militant apocalypticism a few steps further (e.g., Augustine Bader).

–direct heirs of Hans Denck's mystical and spiritualist tendencies (Bünderlin, Entfelder, and eventually, Kautz).

–transitional figures who synthesized mysticism, apocalypticism, and a separated congregationalism (Schiemer, Schlaffer) who went on to influence the Anabaptism of Pilgram Marpeck, on the one hand, and the communitarian Hutterite movement, on the other.

–and finally, the "Central German" stream that had begun after its own fashion along separatist lines, in spite of its Denck-Hut lineage (Melchior Rinck).

In what follows we will give a brief overview of these various groupings and developments.

Augustine Bader

Augustine Bader and his wife Sabina were baptized by the sober Swiss Anabaptist leader, Jakob Gross, in Augsburg. Nevertheless, Augustine was influenced far more by Hans Hut's apocalyptic hopes.

Augustine and Sabina were arrested in Augsburg in September 1527, in the same police sweep that rounded up Hans Hut and Jakob Gross. Hut died in that prison, and Gross languished there for years. But Sabina was released to look after her small children, and Augustine was released following a recantation. They soon were back with the Anabaptists, with Augustine functioning as an elder in the Augburg congregation.

After some close escapes, Augustine left Augsburg early in 1528 and visited Anabaptist congregations from Strasbourg to Moravia. He began

Prophecy

to receive visions, and became convinced that he was a prophet of the Last Days. He had trouble convincing others, but did end up with four devoted followers. In November of 1529 the small band set up a community of goods in a village near Ulm. Bader predicted the End for Easter, 1530. After an invasion by the Turks, he said, his infant son would be the messiah and ruler over all. In the meantime, Augustine would rule in his stead.

None of this ended well. Suspicious authorities arrested them all, and Augustine Bader was beheaded in March, 1530. Sabina Bader, who had managed to escape arrest, eventually gathered her children together again in Augsburg, where she lived until at least 1547.

There was an openness by Hut and some of his followers to direct visions, revelations and prophecies such as inspired Augustine Bader. In spite of Bader's demise, and the relatively small number of persons involved in his movement, individual prophets in the Hut tradition remained active. Some migrated to Strasbourg, where they would play important roles in Melchiorite Anabaptism after 1530.

However, the prophetic, apocalyptic strand of Anabaptism very quickly moved to the margins of the South German movement. After 1530 it played an insignificant role. Nevertheless, prophetic apocalypticism did continue to play an important role in North German/Dutch Anabaptism, reaching a climax at Münster. With the fall of the city in 1535, apocalyptic expectation progressively decreased in importance in the north as well.

Hans Bünderlin and Christian Entfelder

Hans Bünderlin and Christian Entfelder, both representatives of the mystical spiritualist Anabaptist stream, were described by Werner Packull as "homeless minds." As did Hans Denck himself, these individuals passed through an Anabaptist phase, but eventually came to embrace a spiritualized Christianity that had little use for the "external ceremonies" of baptism and the Lord's Supper, or for an emphasis on the written Word. The tension between the spirit and the letter and the inner and outer realms was brought into particular focus by these Anabaptists.

Spiritualism

The theological issues raised by the spiritualists were among some of the most important to be faced by the Anabaptist movement. We will return to Bünderlin and Entfelder when we look at Anabaptism in Strasbourg.

Leonhard Schiemer and Hans Schlaffer

Leonhard Schiemer fit well into the South German Anabaptist context, for his writings give evidence of his having received much from late medieval mystical thought. He had been a Franciscan monk for six years, left the monastery and became a tailor, witnessed the debate between Hut and Hubmaier in Nicholsburg, was baptized by Hut in Vienna, participated in the Martyrs' Synod in Augsburg, and soon was captured in the Tirol and martyred in January, 1528. He had been an Anabaptist all of six months.

Schiemer's writings emphasized the cleansing nature of suffering and the presence of the divine Spirit in human beings. He also assimilated Hut's teaching on the Gospel of all Creatures and Hut's concern for the things of the End Times. Nevertheless, Schiemer did not set dates, or focus on a coming time of vengeance, when the righteous would finally get the chance to use their swords, nor on the suffering of inner purgation.

Suffering

Rather, Schiemer's response to the events of the End Times, which he was sure he was witnessing, was to call for separated communities of believers who would be willing to suffer the ultimate consequences, just as Christ their Head had suffered. Schiemer also emphasized strong community discipline (an element not emphasized to the same degree by Hut himself) and in general called for stringent ethical standards. In these matters, and in the matter of the sword, he stood closer to Denck and the Swiss than to Hut. There is some limited evidence of Swiss contact in Schiemer's case.

Separated Communities

Like Hut and Schiemer, Hans Schlaffer also emphasized suffering and the Gospel of All Creatures, and he expected the return of Christ very soon. Hans Schlaffer had been a parish priest who had moved in an evangelical direction already by 1526. It is not known when he was baptized but like Schiemer, he would have been an Anabaptist for only a short time prior to his martyrdom. He was martyred shortly after Leonhard Schiemer, in January of 1528.

Schlaffer, like Schiemer, had moved beyond Hut and closer to the Swiss understanding, particularly in his conception of a separated, suffering fellowship. In his doctrine of the sword Hans Schlaffer gave no evidence of Hut's expectation of participation in divine vengeance.

Schiemer and Schlaffer represent transitional figures in South German and Austrian Anabaptism. They were baptized by Hut, but moved in a more sectarian direction. This is evident in the way they interpreted suffering. The mystical theme of internal suffering seen in Müntzer and Hut was reinterpreted by Schiemer and Schlaffer and became a martyr theology of external suffering. A similar theology of martyrdom was appropriated by virtually all the surviving Anabaptist groups, but especially by the Hutterites and the followers of Pilgram Marpeck who remembered Schiemer and Schlaffer as martyrs.

Transition

Just as importantly, Schiemer and Schlaffer demonstrate how quickly Hut's Anabaptism could and did move into a separated congregational mode. The Anabaptism of Schiemer and Schlaffer was transitional in the fact that their apocalypticism and mysticism (already toned down from Hut's accustomed levels) would be toned down even further in the communities of Pilgram Marpeck and the Hutterites. Llikewise, the beginning outlines of a separated church would emerge with even more strength in the majority of South German groups.

Pilgram Marpeck

Pilgram Marpeck was born around 1495 into a family of wealth and influence in the Tirol. His father Heinrich had been a city and mining magistrate in Rattenberg. Pilgram himself became a member of Rattenberg's city council, served as Mayor in 1522, and occupied the powerful position of mining magistrate from 1525 until his resignation from that post in 1528. Even after his conversion to Anabaptism and his departure from the Tirol, Marpeck remained willing to participate in civil service posts, as long as his conscience was not compromised.

It appears that Marpeck was won over to evangelical views through contact with Jakob Strauß and Stephan Castenbaur (Agricola). From 1520 on Marpeck had many opportunities to hear the new views defended. However Marpeck became an Anabaptist in the end. He reported later that he was unhappy with the "fleshly freedom" of the evangelicals, and was won over by the "obedience of faith" of the Anabaptists. While details are missing, it appears that Leonard Schiemer and Hans Schlaffer helped shape Marpeck's Anabaptist views. Leonhard Schiemer's arrest, torture, trial and death by fire in Rattenberg finally led to Marpeck's resignation from his governmental post in Rattenburg in January 1528.

Obedience of Faith

On leaving the Tirol, Pilgram and his wife Anna travelled first to the Bohemian mining town of Krumau, where there was a substantial Anabaptist congregation, and they appear also to have spent some time in Austerlitz, Moravia. According to one report, an Anabaptist congregation there commissioned Marpeck an elder, and sent him to Strasbourg. By late summer of 1528, Pilgram and Anna had moved to Strasbourg where Pilgram worked as an engineer in the employ of the city, and functioned also as an Anabaptist leader (1528-1532). He was forced into exile following a dispute with the city's preachers. After a period of wandering that took him from Switzerland to Moravia (1533-1544), Marpeck found employment in Augsburg where he ended his days, quietly leading a small Anabaptist group in that city (1544-1556).

Marpeck's thought was more indebted to German mysticism and Hans Denck than to the Swiss or Schleitheim. Nevertheless, his path led between the spiritualist descendants of Hans Denck, such as Bünderlin, Kautz and Entfelder, on the one hand, and the Swiss and the Hutterites on the other, as we will detail in chapters to follow. He was in direct conversation with virtually all Anabaptist parties (except for the Dutch, where little evidence exists of direct contact).

Middle Way

Against the spiritualists Marpeck stressed the incarnate Christ and the necessity of visible church ordinances, while against the more literal-minded Swiss and Hutterites, he stressed the freedom of the Spirit and the centrality of love. Thus although Marpeck argued for a visible and separated church against the spiritualists, he opposed a legalistic use of the ban and the insistence on external ordinances of separation such as the Swiss followers of Schleitheim were elaborating.

Because of Marpeck's mediating position between spiritualist Anabaptists on the one hand, and the more literalistic and separatist Swiss and Hutterites on the other, his writings provide a particularly clear window into inter-Anabaptist dialogues. Although the groups led by Marpeck did not, as far as we know, survive much past the sixteenth century, in his person Marpeck represented a pivotal dialogue partner in the Swiss/South German Anabaptist context up to the middle of the sixteenth century.

Conclusion

We may note in conclusion some emphases that were unique to South German Anabaptism, in comparison to Swiss Anabaptism. South German Anabaptism was marked by:

—**Strong mystical roots.** These were seen in Thomas Müntzer, Hans Denck and Hans Hut, all of whom stressed the inner work of the Holy Spirit in believers.

—**A lively apocalyptic expectation.** This expectation of the End was most evident in Hans Hut, but by contrast was far less conspicuous in Denck and Rinck. The apocalyptic strand, although it was spectacularly present in Hut and in some of his followers, actually had a limited reach and life span in South German Anabaptism. This undoubtedly was due to Hut's early demise in 1527 and the failure of his prediction that Christ would return by 1528. The mystical strand of South German Anabaptist thought proved to be the longer-lived and, in many ways, more influential than Hut's initial apocalypticism.

—**A marked stress on suffering.** Suffering was emphasized in South German Anabaptism as a way of conforming to the way of Christ, initially in the painful coming to faith, but also in the later Christian walk.

—**An emphasis on community of goods.** This emphasis was notable in Hut's Anabaptism and among his followers—although such a tendency was not unique to the South German movement, and was shared to a lesser degree by the Swiss.

—**Identification with the social upheaval of the Peasants' War.** The identification of many South German Anabaptists with the peasants' movement was reflected in Hut's doctrine of the sword (to be reviewed in a later chapter) and in a stronger anticlericalism than seen elsewhere.

In the end persecution, the failure of Hut's End Times predictions, and continuing contact with other Anabaptist streams moved South German Anabaptism movement very close to Schleitheim's separatism.

The Core Teachings of Anabaptism

Anabaptist Views shared with Other Christian Confessions

The Creed: The Twelve Articles of the Christian Faith

Views shared with Evangelical/Protestant groups

Anti-Sacramentalism: Critique of Catholic Sacraments

Anticlericalism: Critique of the Catholic Clergy

Authority of Scripture: Critique of Papal Authority

Salvation by Grace through Faith: Critique of Catholic view

Anabaptist Doctrinal Emphases

Holy Spirit: The Active Power of God

Spirit and Letter: Scripture Interpreted by Spirit

Salvation: Faith and Works Together (Discipleship)

Human Person: Yieldedness to the Spirit; Free Will; Human Effort

Eschatology: Expectation of the Last Days

The Anabaptist Doctrine of the Church (Ecclesiology)

Baptism of Adults: Teaching, Faith, then Water Baptism

The Ban: Fraternal Admonition and Discipline

Memorial Lord's Supper: Closed to non-Baptized; a Remembrance

Mutual Aid: No Ultimate Claims to Earthly Goods

A Visible Church, Willing to Suffer: Perseverance to the End

Chapter 8

The Core Teachings of Anabaptism

Hubmaier's catechism is a very early and unusually comprehensive Anabaptist expression of the core teachings of the movement. Although there is no evidence that the catechism was used outside Nicholsburg, Hubmaier's catechism is useful because the Anabaptist essentials he described systematically were echoed (less systematically) by Anabaptists elsewhere. In the early Anabaptist context, Hubmaier's catechism was unusual because it was systematic, but it was unexceptional in its content.

Hubmaier said he composed his catechism with a view to educating new church members. The catechism is written in dialogue form between "Leonhart" and "Hans," and is structured in two main sections. The first deals primarily with dogmatic questions. The second teaches distinctive features of Anabaptist practice and belief, often drawn in contrast to prevailing belief and practice. The outline of the order of topics taken up in the catechism is as follows.

Part I
God; Christ; Sin
Ten Commandments; Repentance; Prayer
Promise and Gospel; Faith (The Apostles' Creed)
Baptism (Spirit, Water, and Blood)
Church (Universal and Particular)
Ban (Fraternal Admonition)

Part II

Lord's Supper (a memorial); Confession of Sin

Fasting; Restraint of Tongue; Sabbath Observance

Against the Veneration of Saints, Miracles, Images

Hearing God's Word in Church

Love

Sin, Redemption, Works and Grace

Outward and Inward Call of God

Genuine Good Works

Judgement Day; Eternal Life

Persecution; Hell

Hubmaier's catechism was so comprehensive that it should probably be read as a summary of the Anabaptist faith, written in the genre of a catechetical dialogue. One can hardly conceive of new believers or young people committing it to memory.

In what follows we will use Hubmaier's catechism as a springboard or point of departure. It will enable us to highlight elements of belief and practice that were common to all branches of the Anabaptist movement. Points that were peculiar to Hubmaier we will leave for later chapters.

Anabaptist Views shared with Other Christian Confessions

Hubmaier's catechism reminds us again that the Anabaptists considered themselves to be a part of the larger Christian tradition.

The Creed

Hubmaier included in his catechism instruction on the universal or ecumenical foundations of the faith, in particular the teaching of the Apostles' Creed, commonly called the "Twelve Articles." In addressing the second generation believers to be raised within the church, Hubmaier recognized the need for the youth of the church to learn these basics of the Christian faith.

Hubmaier was not alone in his appeal to the Creed as the grounding of Christian faith. Acceptance of the historical Christian teachings, as summarized in the ecumenical Creeds and symbols, was common to all Anabaptist movements, even though the Apostles' Creed did not form a central part of Anabaptist worship, as far as we know. The Anabaptists were predominantly orthodox in their understanding of the central elements of the faith, but with one major and one minor exception.

One glaring exception to the general doctrinal orthodoxy of Anabaptism was Melchior Hoffman's understanding of the nature of Christ (Christology). Since Menno Simons and his followers accepted Melchior's view, this was a significant exception. Even so, Menno considered himself to be an adherent of the Apostles' Creed. (1) We will examine Melchior Hoffman's Christology further in chapter 18 below.

> *(1) Menno Simons to Gellius Faber.* "I trust also that we ... agree not only as to the twelve articles [of the Creed] ... but also as to all the articles of the Scriptures." (CWMS, 761).

The "minor" heterodox exception that could be named in addition was be a tendency towards anti-trinitarianism in Silesia and by some individuals in the Netherlands. This tendency was not widespread, and tended to be taken up in more isolated cases.

These caveats aside, it can be said that the accusations of Anabaptist "heresy" were almost never doctrinally based. Charges of heresy were virtually always directed against Anabaptist church practices such as believers' baptism, the ban, and an exclusive, memorial Lord's Supper. They were not usually accusations that the Anabaptists had abandoned the common Christian doctrines of faith.

Toward the end of the sixteenth century the Anabaptists followed the lead of the Protestant denominations and began elaborating confessions of faith which outlined distinctive Anabaptist interpretations and church practices in more detail.

Views shared with Evangelical/Protestant groups

Just as Hubmaier's catechism reminds us that the Anabaptists were adherents of the ecumenical Christian Creeds, so also it reminds us that the Anabaptists were a part of the wider evangelical reform movement.

Anti-Sacramentalism

Hubmaier's catechism expressed a thorough rejection of Roman Catholic sacramentalism.

Lord's Supper   Hubmaier composed the following catechetical exchange concerning the Lord's Supper:

> *Leonhart*: Is the bread not the body of Christ and the wine his crimson blood, as the Maoz-priests have been telling us?

> *Hans*: By no means; the bread and wine are nothing but memorial symbols of Christ's suffering and death for the forgiveness of our sins. (Pipkin and Yoder, 1989, 354-55).

Even more strongly, in answer to the question "what is the Mass," Hubmaier, the former priest, has "Hans" reply: "It is the very idol and abomination, spoken of by the Prophet Daniel..."

Baptism   Likewise concerning baptism, Hubmaier wrote the following:

> *Leonhart*: What is your opinion of the infant baptism which the water-priests use?

> *Hans*: Nothing other than that the adult child gives a bath to the young child, thereby depriving it of the real water baptism of Christ. (Pipkin and Yoder, 1989, 350).

Anabaptists everywhere were agreed that neither priests nor sacraments were capable of conveying God's grace. In holding to this, Anabaptists were following the Protestant critique. The rejection of priests and sacraments was the first step towards Anabaptist baptism, for if the water could not convey grace or confer salvation, on what basis was infant baptism to be defended? Said in terms of Luther's understanding of salvation, the question was: "If we are saved by grace through faith, and not by sacramental mediation, how then can infant baptism be continued, since infants do not have faith?"

Although different answers to this question came from Lutherans to Reformed to Anabaptists, the posing of the question was common to all evangelical groups, because they all questioned the medieval sacramental structure. As we have seen, a crucial step in the direction of the eventual Anabaptist answer was provided by radical evangelical reformers who first questioned the validity of infant baptism.

Sacraments questioned

On the question of the Lord's Supper, that later would split apart the Protestant Reformation, the Anabaptists were united in holding that the Lord's Supper was a memorial. This points to their theological kinship to the Reformed branch of Protestantism on this particular issue (Karlstadt and Zwingli). There were no Anabaptists who took up the Lutheran view of the Supper, although Pilgram Marpeck–apparently influenced by Luther– came the closest to retaining a more sacramental view.

Virtually all of the first generation Anabaptist leaders were inspired by the evangelical critique of the sacraments, even though they came to part company with the mainline reformers in their understanding of what would take the place of the sacramental view.

Anticlericalism

Hubmaier and virtually all Anabaptists shared in the anticlericalism of the early Protestant reformers. Their language could be just as intemperate (although probably not as inventive) as that of the more famous reformers.(2)

(2) Hubmaier, Catechism. "*Indeed, it is in many cases manifest what incompetent shepherds and pastors have been forced upon us by popes, bishops, provosts, abbots, and also by secular emperors, kings, princes, and nobles, by their bulls and mandates, such as courtisans, donkey curriers, fornicators, adulterers, procurers, gamblers, drunkards, and foolish rouges, whom we would in truth not have trusted to herd our pigs and goats, but still we had to accept them as our souls' shepherds. They have become nothing but thieves and murderers...*" *(Pipkin and Yoder, 1989, 342)*

Anticlericalism was common within the Anabaptist movement generally, although the focus of Anabaptist anticlericalism very soon included the Protestant clerics as well as the Catholic.

The Authority of Scripture

The Anabaptists followed Luther and the Protestant reformers and insisted upon the authority of Scripture in all matters of faith. Hubmaier called for a testing and trying of all teachings "by the plumb line of the Bible." (3) In accepting scriptural authority over against papal authority the Anabaptists showed themselves to be part of the sixteenth century evangelical movement.

> *(3) Hubmaier, Catechism.*
> *"[God's] saving, living, and eternal Word admonished and instructed us and so clearly taught us that we henceforth know thoroughly how to navigate only by the glow and star of his holy Word."*
> *(Pipkin and Yoder, 1989, 340)*

It would become evident soon enough that this "scriptural principle" was not a simple way to answer all questions of faith and practice. The Anabaptist path away from the mainline Protestant position was first marked out by radical reformers who were the first to diverge from Luther's understanding of the scriptural principle.

Salvation by Grace through Faith

In their understanding of salvation (soteriology) the Anabaptists took their point of departure from the Protestant, rather than the medieval church. Luther had insisted that salvation depends only on God's grace and the human response of faith, and not on any sacramental or penitential mediation.

Hubmaier's catechism expresses this reforming insight in the following way:

> *Leonhart*: Show me ... a message of the gospel.
>
> *Hans*: Christ died for the sake of our sins, and arose for the sake of our justification, Rom. 4:25.
>
> *Leonhart*: What follows from this message?
> *Hans*: Faith.

Leonhart: What is faith?

Hans: Faith is the realization of the unspeakable mercy of God, his gracious favor and goodwill, which he bears to us through his most beloved Son Jesus Christ, whom he did not spare and delivered him to death for our sakes that sin might be paid for, and we might be reconciled to him and with the assurance of our hearts cry to him: Abba, Father, our Father who are (sic) in heaven. (Pipkin and Yoder, 1989, 348).

In accepting the principle of salvation by grace through faith, the Anabaptists again gave evidence of their evangelical point of departure.

Nevertheless, this point of departure could be developed in different ways. The full Anabaptist understanding of salvation was distinct from the mainline evangelical position, as well as from that of the late medieval church. The closest similarity is found among the earliest radical reformers who differed with Luther.

Anabaptist Doctrinal Emphases

It is evident that Anabaptists shared important fundamental positions with the evangelical (Protestant) reforming stream. Nevertheless the Anabaptists formed part of the Radical Reformation stream when they also criticized Luther and Zwingli at the same points as had the radical reformers who had preceded them.

In matters of doctrine, as we will see below, Anabaptism was not very unique. Anabaptists tended to repeat what the early radical reformers had already said. The crucial doctrinal point perhaps was the one that insisted upon linking faith and practice. If faith must express itself in a particular practice of obedience, then a particular visible form of church is required of believers.

Anabaptism became a separate, identifiable movement within radical reform when it developed radical reform teachings in practical directions. But first to the doctrines underlying the practice.

The work of the Holy Spirit

Anabaptism of all kinds was based on the expectation that God's Spirit would work in the hearts of human beings to initiate and sustain a life of faith. This emphasis is visible even in Hubmaier, who was among the least "spiritual" Anabaptist leaders. For Hubmaier the necessary working of the Spirit was expressed as the first of three baptisms, namely the baptism of the Spirit, which is "an inner illumination of our hearts that takes place by the Holy Spirit, through the living Word of God." (Pipkin and Yoder, 1989, 362).

Hubmaier linked the work of the Holy Spirit to the hearing of the Word in a way not always seen among other early Anabaptists. Nevertheless he sounded a thoroughly Anabaptist note when he insisted that a spiritual rebirth and regeneration was the first step in the process of salvation.

Spirit and Letter

Bible

The Anabaptist emphasis on the active working of the Spirit of God meant that Anabaptist biblicism always was mediated by the expectation that the Holy Spirit would illuminate and provide the proper understanding of Scripture. So although the Anabaptists accepted the scriptural principle as a point of departure for church reform, it is more accurate to say that in their view, divine authority needed to be based on ***Scripture and Spirit together***, rather than the "Scripture alone" of Luther.

Hubmaier expressed this understanding in the following way:

Leonhart: How does God draw or call a person?

Hans: In two forms, outwardly and inwardly. The outward drawing occurs through the public proclamation of his holy gospel... The inward drawing is this, that God also illuminates the person's soul inwardly, so that it understands the incontrovertible truth, convinced by the Spirit and the preached Word in such a way that one must in one's own conscience confess that this is the case and it cannot be otherwise. (Pipkin and Yoder, 1989, 362).

It was here, in the Anabaptist connection between the Bible and the Spirit as the highest authorities, that we need to speak of a spirit/letter linkage that was shared by Anabaptists of all kinds. As we have seen above, this linkage was first articulated in the evangelical camp by the early radical reformers.

Doctrine of Salvation (Soteriology)

Although Anabaptists always maintained that believers are saved by grace through faith, here the similarity to mainline Protestant teaching ended.

For Hubmaier as for other Anabaptists, the faith that leads to salvation is a faith that bears *visible fruit* in repentance, conversion, regeneration, obedience, and a new life dedicated to the love of God and the neighbour, by the power of the Holy Spirit. In other words, true faith leads to discipleship. Righteousness was not simply imputed to the sinner for Christ's sake, as Luther had maintained. Rather, being saved meant *becoming righteous* by the power of the risen Christ.

Fruit of Faith

In many ways this understanding of salvation stood closer to the late medieval tradition. It denied the radical depravity of all humankind. It insisted on the necessary unity of the inner life of the spirit with the outer life of obedience and discipleship.

Medieval piety

The important Anabaptist linkage between the life of faith and the life of obedience, that is, between the inner and the outer lives of believers, was not original to the Anabaptists, but was first articulated in an evangelical reforming context by the radical reformers.

Faith and Works: Discipleship

The active working of the Spirit of God was the crucial first step without which there could be no life of discipleship. The spiritual emphasis in all of early Anabaptism points not only to the importance of the spirit/letter linkage for Anabaptists, but also to the necessary connection they made between the inner life of the spirit (faith, rebirth, regeneration) and the outer life of discipleship (obedience).

This is seen clearly in Hubmaier's discussion of faith.

> *Leonhard*: How many kinds of faith are there?
>
> *Hans*: Two kinds, namely a dead one and a living one.
>
> *Leonhart*: What is a dead faith?
>
> *Hans*: One that is unfruitful and without the works of love, James 2:17.
>
> *Leonhart*: What is a living faith?
>
> *Hans*: One that produces the fruits of the Spirit and works through love, Gal. 5. (Pipkin and Yoder, 1989, 348).

This inner/outer connection, basing discipleship on a living faith, typified the Anabaptist theological approach. It was prefigured by the radical reformers.

The Human Person (Anthropology)

The Anabaptists understood the human person in a way most like late medieval Christians. That is, they believed that human beings had the *capacity* to be reborn, regenerated, and re-made by the Holy Spirit.

Gelassenheit.

The principle of yieldedness (*Gelassenheit)* was rooted in late medieval mysticism and piety, and was central to the radical reformers who diverged from Luther. Although the word *Gelassenheit* is not found in all Anabaptist testimonies, the concept was central to Anabaptist theology and sprituality.

Anabaptists believed that human beings had to respond to God's call. They had to yield inwardly to the Spirit of God, outwardly to the community and to outward discipline, and finally, in the face of a hostile world, believers might have to "yield" by accepting a martyr's death. The necessary unity between the inner life of believers and their outer lives of discipleship and community life is seen here again.

Doctrines of Sin and Free Will.

In order for human beings to be able to respond and yield to God's call in Christ to repentance and a new life, they must be free to respond. All Anabaptists held (more often implicitly than explicitly) that human beings were made free, by God's grace, to accept or not accept the call of God in Christ. In this respect also, Anabaptist theology stood closer to late medieval teaching than it did to mainstream Protestantism.

Hubmaier broached the subject of the free versus the bound will in his catechism, arguing that the human will was bound in sin following Adam's fall, but the fallen will was restored again through Christ, even though it was held prisoner in a sinful body. (4) Hubmaier's point was that there is something of good in human beings, but that it needs a further step of rebirth in order to be truly good. (5)

> **(4) Hubmaier, Catechism.** *"...the image or inbreathing of God is still in us all, although captive and as a live spark covered with cold ashes is still alive and will steam if heavenly water is poured on it."* *(Pipkin and Yoder, 1989, 360)*

> **(5) Hubmaier, Catechism.** *"If we are now again to become free in the spirit and healthy in the soul ... then this must take place through a rebirth."* *(Pipkin and Yoder, 1989, 361).*

The heavenly rebirth is a double gift of grace, first through Christ's sacrifice which restores Adam's Fall, and then through the offer of rebirth to the sinner who is still captive. The sinner, however, is "free" to refuse this second grace, to condemnation, or accept it to salvation.

While most Anabaptists did not discuss the fine points of the Fall, nor did any others elaborate a theological anthropology as did Hubmaier, still all Anabaptists assumed a doctrine of free will, while at the same time insisting that salvation was a gift of grace, not a payment for meritorious works. The basic logic of Hubmaier's position was repeated throughout the movement. The same basic position had been argued by the radical reformers, against Luther.

Eschatology

Virtually all Christians in the sixteenth century, Anabaptists included, were convinced that they were living in the Last Days, and that Christ was about to return. In his catechism, Hubmaier limits himself to speaking generally about judgement day, with no particular anticipation that it was near at hand.

Other Anabaptists were less restrained on the subject. A popular understanding (with roots in the medieval Joachite tradition) conceived of the Last Days as the time when Christ's Spirit would be poured out on humankind, resulting in dreams, visions and direct revelations, just as it had been in the time of the Old Testament prophets. Likewise, a strong conviction that these were the Last Days led many Anabaptists to scrutinize the prophetic books of Scripture in order to discover there the "signs of the times."

Dreams and Visions

As is well known, there were differences among the Anabaptists on the question of the genuineness of direct "revelations" such as dreams and visions, and a scriptural approach that attempted to discover the secrets of God's timetable in the biblical prophetic books.

Nevertheless, it is important to note that because of the strong emphasis on the presence and activity of the Holy Spirit that underlay Anabaptism, virtually *all* Anabaptists were open to some measure of the revelatory power of the Holy Spirit. Because of the strong stress on the authority of Scripture, all Anabaptists took the biblical words of prophecy seriously as well.

The differences that arose later in the movement can best be understood as differences of degree, not differences in kind, along a spirit/letter *continuum*. Anabaptist apocalyptic expectation, at one level at least, can be seen as a natural working out of the necessary conjunction of spirit and letter. But even more, Anabaptists saw themselves occupying a period in history that was radically new, that stood close to the end of all time.

The Anabaptist Doctrine of the Church (Ecclesiology)

The majority of the **doctrinal** emphases noted above could be found outside the Anabaptist movement as well as within it, as for instance with Karlstadt and Müntzer. It was when it put its doctrine of the church into **practice** that Anabaptism defined itself as a distinct reforming movement. Adult baptism was central in establishing the distinction. Hubmaier's catechism says:

>*Leonhard*: After faith what do you desire?

>*Hans*: Water baptism. (Pipkin and Yoder, 1989, 349).

For the Anabaptists, the response of faith led immediately to the community of believers, through water baptism.

The doctrine of the church was central to Anabaptist theology. The church was to be the visible Body of Christ. For Hubmaier and other Anabaptists the biblical model of Christian community was the congregation of yielded, regenerated, faithful, baptized, committed and obedient believers–a community of saints. The anchor of Anabaptist theology and spirituality was this community, formed first by the spiritual, and then the water baptism of believers, maintained by fraternal admonition, and nurtured by the Supper of the Lord, by communal worship and visible expressions of love among the members of the body. *Church of Believers*

There were four marks of this "visible community of saints" that were accepted by all Anabaptists, regardless of origin. They were: *Shared Practices*

–**baptism**

–**the ban**

–**the Lord's Supper**

–**mutual aid**

The first three of these Anabaptist marks of the church had been outlined in a programatic way already in the first three of the Schleitheim Articles of 1527. Mutual aid, while not explicitly mentioned at Schleitheim, was practiced in the earliest Anabaptist communities.

Water Baptism

The inner call of God's Spirit, or the baptism of the Spirit as Hubmaier and others called it, demanded an outward and visible response from those who had been inwardly called and who had freely accepted the call.

It was by public water baptism that one confessed one's sins before the congregation of God's people, testified to one's faith in the forgiveness of sins through Christ, and was incorporated into the fellowship of the church, accepting the fraternal responsibilities that went along with membership in the church.

Water baptism signified that the inner yieldedness to Christ had already taken place (the water was the "covenant of a good conscience"). It signified that the believer was now yielding to the Body of Christ on earth, the church. It signified a willingness to suffer all for Christ and the brother and sister. Baptism meant moving from "the world" to "the Body of Christ," the church. All of this was articulated coherently for the first time in Hubmaier's important booklet, published in 1525, "On the Christian Baptism of Believers." (See Pipkin and Yoder, 1989, 95-149).

Although it is true that the term Anabaptism was used to denigrate the movement by its opponents, and also that the Anabaptists themselves preferred to be called Brethren, nevertheless contemporary critics of the movement were close to the mark when they emphasized baptism on confession of faith as a central teaching by which to identify the Brethren.

If the Brethren had been content to emphasize the baptism of the Spirit, and had abandoned the outer baptism of water there would have been no Anabaptist movement. The spiritualizing solution of suspending the outer sign remained a temptation for Anabaptists in the sixteenth century, as we will see below. It was the stubborn maintenance of the visible, outward pledge of baptism in water, before God and the church, that formed a significant church boundary for all so called Anabaptists.

Why, if the water contained no saving power as water, did the Brethren continue to insist on water baptism? The answer is not simply that they were being true to the biblical command to believe and be baptised, in that order–although this was the most common answer given by Anabaptists questioned in prison. Just as fundamentally, water baptism was a pledge, promise, or vow to the believing community, the true church of believers. One's subsequent Christian life was based on that pledge. The obedience of faith required not simply inward assent to the Spirit, but also an outward witness and commitment to a regenerated life *in community* with others who also had made the same pledge. In this way the visible church, the true church, the Body of Christ on earth, was built on the basis of outward signs of an inner change. The Anabaptist movement became a reforming movement because of a conviction that the inner and the outer realities of faith and obedience could not be separated or severed from one another.

Community

The Ban

For Hubmaier and the Anabaptists generally, the reform of the church would never be complete until members of the church committed themselves to that church freely by their public baptism, and by that baptism also committed themselves to the discipline of the community. (6)

> *(6) Hubmaier, Catechism.* *"[Through baptism one] publicly and orally vows to God and agrees in the strength of God the Father, Son, and Holy Spirit that he will henceforth believe and live according to his divine Word. And if he should trespass herein he will accept brotherly admonition, according to Christ's order, Matt. 18:15ff."* *(Pipkin and Yoder, 1989, 349).*

According to the central Scripture passage, Matthew 18:15ff., the church had the power to discipline, admonish, and correct. But even more than that, Christ had given it the power to bind and to loose, on earth and in heaven. The extreme of discipline–excommunication–was to be performed only for "refusal to be reconciled to the brother or to desist from sin." Ideally, of course, the aim was not to exclude, but to win back the sinner and be able to accept such a person back "with joy, as the father did his prodigal son..." (Pipkin and Yoder, 1989, 353-54)

In order for such community discipline to function, there had to be a prior theological understanding that one's outer life closely reflects the state of one's inner life. If saving faith is, as Luther said, known only to God and therefore invisible, the ban is not only unnecessary, it is the height of presumption. But if, as the Anabaptists believed, the inner and the outer lives are two sides of the same coin, so to speak (and the church is conceived as the Body of Christ on earth, with the power to bind and to loose, Matt. 18), then the ban becomes fundamental both to salvation *and* church reform.

The ban in Anabaptism took the place of the Roman Catholic rite of confession and absolution. By means of the ban, the church loosed the penalty for sin. Seen from another perspective, the Anabaptist ban was an answer to how the church might be reformed "in head and members."

The Lord's Supper

(7) Hubmaier, Catechism. "[The Lord's Supper is] a public sign and testimonial of the love in which one brother obligates himself to another before the congregation that just as they now break and eat the bread with each other and share and drink the cup, likewise they wish now to sacrifice and shed their body and blood for one another..." (Pipkin and Yoder, 1989, 354).

As noted above, for Hubmaier and all Anabaptists the Lord's Supper was understood as a memorial of Christ's death and sacrifice. But more concretely, the Supper is a sign of binding oneself to the love of the brother and the sister. (7) Just as water baptism testifies that one is serious about the demand to love God above all–that one has died to self and risen in Christ–so the Supper testifies to one's seriousness in loving the neighbour as oneself. This "horizontal" understanding of the Supper as a public *response* and a *pledge* to the community of faith is typically Anabaptist.

From the start, membership in the Body of Christ meant ultimate allegiance to that body in economic, social, and political matters. Within this Body of Christ a new life had begun. New commitments were made to one another that included mutual accountability in spiritual and temporal matters. This mutual solidarity was commemorated with the celebration of the Lord's Supper, along with the remembrance of Christ's death.

Mutual Aid

Because of the new life that had begun, governed by the Spirit of Christ and modeled on the example of His life and that of the apostles, economic relationships within the church were no longer to proceed as they did "in the world." Likewise hierarchical relationships based on social class were challenged. Submission to the Anabaptist community of saints had a democratic, levelling effect. We will see in later sections of this study how these initial Anabaptist convictions came into concrete expression in different groups, over time.

The emphasis on a *visible* church, which was understood to be a part of God's kingdom incarnate, underlined the importance of the outward expressions of belief. Baptism, the ban, the Supper, and renewed social and economic relationships served as signs and seals of that commitment to the visible "members of Christ's body."

Thus for Anabaptists the church and the world remained in a tension that was not present in quite the same way in the Protestant and Catholic churches. It was within the tension of this church/world polarity that the concrete working out of Anabaptist eschatology also would take shape.

Consequences of Faith: Suffering and Martyrdom

To the four marks of the Anabaptist church listed above one would like to add suffering and martyrdom. But in this case we are dealing first with an historical reality for the Anabaptists that very soon came to be explained theologically. The historical reality came first.

Anabaptists were not the only Christians to suffer persecution and martyrdom in the sixteenth century. Nevertheless, because of the swift and near-universal condemnation of Anabaptism in western Europe, the movement soon faced more systematic persecution, with its accompanying physical suffering and martyrdom, than was the case for most other Christian groups. Anabaptists faced the reality of suffering and death.

Torture of Geleyn the Shoemaker

In facing the historical reality of persecution, the Anabaptists had at their disposal a theology that was able to place that suffering in perspective.

Hubmaier reflected theologically on suffering by including it in his baptismal theology. Following inward regeneration and the outward witness in water, Hubmaier said, the baptism of blood could be expected to take place.

The phrase baptism of blood rightly evokes images of martyrdom; Hubmaier meant to evoke such images, for he insisted that suffering and persecution would necessarily be the lot of true believers. But it is important to note that when Hubmaier speaks of the baptism of blood he is not referring in the first instance to a martyr's death. He is speaking of the continuing path of yielding one's desires daily to the will of God.

The baptism of blood is a daily practice in the disciplines of yielding and obedience. The late medieval ascetic roots of Anabaptism prepared the way for a theology of martyrdom. (8)

---

(8) Hubmaier, "On the Christian Baptism of Believers." *"The flesh must daily be killed since it wants only to live and reign according to its own lusts. Here the Spirit of Christ prevails and gains the victory. Then the person brings forth good fruits which give testimony of a good tree. Day and night he practices all those things which concern the praise of God and brotherly love. By this the old Adam is martyred, killed, and carried to the grave. This is a summary and right order of a whole Christian life which begins in the Word of God." (Pipkin and Yoder, 1989, 147).*

In the sixteenth century the "baptism of blood" could be much more than simply a mortification of the flesh, or an ascetic exercise–it could be a call to accept the fact that one's own blood would be shed. If a believer were called to witness to the truth by accepting death–as was Hubmaier himself–the way to the greatest test of faith and obedience would have been prepared by daily practice in the third baptism, the "mortification of the flesh" that was supposed to occur daily.

The existence of a deep and common theological rationale for the ultimate outer testimony of the flesh in suffering and martyrdom can easily be discerned in the records documenting the martyrdom of thousands of Anabaptists in all parts of Europe.

The "Shape" of Anabaptist Theology

Readers may well be struck by the strong similarities between the Radical Reformation positions of Karlstadt, Müntzer and Schwenckfeld, and the Anabaptist doctrinal positions described above. In fact, the basic "shape" of Anabaptist theology was outlined by the early radical reformers and mediated directly to significant leaders of the Anabaptist movement. The radical reformers provided an alternative interpretation of evangelical reform that set key terms of reference also for the Anabaptist movement.

The emphasis of the radical reformers on the interpretive and regenerating activity of the Holy Spirit (efficacious grace) marked out a significant theological path also followed by the Anabaptists. It was this active presence of the Spirit that called for a life of discipleship–an emphasis not original to the Anabaptists, but one that they did embrace heartily.

Because of this efficacious grace, the radical reformers and the Anabaptists alike expected visible and external signs of the inner working of grace. They shared a vision of church reform based on regenerationist principles.

Regeneration

The most significant point of coincidence between Karlstadt and Müntzer, on the one hand, and the Anabaptists on the other can be summarized as a common vision of salvation which took its point of departure from Luther's critique of the Roman Catholic view, but which rejected Luther's understanding of forensic justification and called instead for an inner/outer transformation and a process of sanctification of believers.

The insistence on freedom of the will also reappeared in Anabaptism, with a corresponding difference in how Anabaptists and mainline reformers would conceive of human participation in the matter of salvation. For the radical reformers and Anabaptists alike, God's grace frees human beings to choose either salvation or damnation.

This principle was important from a church reforming perspective: believers were *responsible* for the lives they came to lead. Following Christ was a conscious choice, not a matter of predestination. Believers willingly subjected themselves to discipline. The church was a visible community of saints.

In sum, Anabaptism was not so much "Protestantism taken to its proper ends" as it was *Radical* Protestantism taken some practical steps further.

Radical Protestantism

Seen from the Anabaptist perspective, the critique and alternative theological outline of the early radical reformers provided a crucial transitional framework of reforming principles. What the Anabaptists elaborated further, on the basis of the radical evangelical critique, was a doctrine of the church, an *ecclesiology,* that set Anabaptism apart from reformers and radical reformers alike.

The radical reformers also had prepared the way for distinctive Anabaptist church practices with their critique of infant baptism, their calls for church discipline, and their sacramentarian view of the Lord's Supper. But it was Anabaptism as such that came to insist that the only proper, biblical understanding of church reform was the establishment of freely chosen adult baptism on confession of faith, by which believers pledged themselves to community discipline and solidarity with the other members of the Body of Christ on earth.

Conclusion

The general doctrinal and ecclesiological principles outlined in this chapter were universally held by adult baptizers in the sixteenth century. They can be said to constitute the most generally accepted "core" teachings of the Anabaptist movement as it was taking shape from Switzerland to Moravia to Friesland.

On the basis of these common teachings alone there is reason to retain the descriptive term "Anabaptist" for all of the baptizing groups, in spite of differing origins and regional and individual differences. It was the shared core of teachings, with adult baptism at the centre, that provided guidelines for Anabaptist communities as they attempted to put their beliefs into practice in their various historical situations.

The Anabaptists themselves recognized that they were neither Roman Catholics *nor* Evangelicals (later called Protestants), but rather were brethren of yet another movement. The disagreements that took place subsequently between the Anabaptists themselves, while they were strongly held and often led to schism, nevertheless took place between people who agreed on the above essentials, even while they disagreed on the *implications* of these essentials for the life of faith.

It must be said further that it is only when we look *within* the boundaries of this body of belief and practice, *within* the limits of this field of agreement, that we can begin to understand the development of Anabaptism over the course of the sixteenth century and into the seventeenth. The disagreements Anabaptists came to have with one another were hammered out on this common anvil of shared belief. The working out of those differences led eventually to denominational expressions of Anabaptism, namely the continuing Swiss Brethren, Hutterite, and Mennonite traditions.

It is important to note what is *not* present in the outline presented above, in contrast to earlier descriptions. If the Schleitheim Articles are taken as one of the earliest outlines of Anabaptist distinctives, we must note that only Schleitheim's articles concerning baptism, the ban, and the

<u>Separation</u>

Supper were universally Anabaptist. Separation from the world, enjoined in Schleitheim's article 4, was being settled in the Swiss context by 1527, but the relationship between church, world, and government was still being worked out in the South German and North German/Dutch movements until well into the last half of the sixteenth century. Schleitheim's injunctions against sword bearing and oath taking (articles 6 and 7) remained contentious issues in the wider Anabaptist circle. We will document some of the discussion and disagreement among the Anabaptist groups on these questions below, when we examine "Anabaptism and Political

<u>Pastors</u>

Reality." Likewise the recommendations for the election of pastors from the congregation (article 5 of Schleitheim) were not universally accepted, and in fact were ignored altogether in the Melchiorite stream.

In spite of the fact that the Schleitheim Articles, then, do not qualify as a pan-Anabaptist confession of faith, nevertheless we see in early Anabaptism a movement with significant internal agreement and coherence. The shape of that "theological forest" was first outlined by the radical reformers, Karlstadt and Müntzer. Building on this common radical reforming approach to church reform, the Anabaptist movement established a new branch of radical reform because of its insistence on the distinctive signs of adult baptism, the ban, a memorial Supper closed to all who had not taken the previous two steps of commitment, all of which was to lead to new social and economic relationships.

Nevertheless, an Anabaptist doctrine of the church (*ecclesiology*) did not arrive complete and full-blown with believers' baptism, the ban, a closed Supper, and mutual aid. In early stages of its development Anabaptists could and did overlook numerous practical problems which later would become divisive issues. In other words, in spite of the significant shared core at the heart of the movement, identifying the broadest of shared boundaries tells only the beginning part of the Anabaptist story.

The full Anabaptist story must be told in a framework that highlights not only diverse historical origins, but also deeply significant commonalities, differing rates of community self-definition within different regions (with attention paid to the inevitable pressures of social, political and economic realities in those regions), the fluidity of movement between various Anabaptist groups during the various developmental phases, and the significance of cross fertilization, as ideas from various Anabaptist currents came into dialogue. It is this complex of intramural conversations that stands behind the development of later Anabaptist theological and ecclesiological *traditions*.

Perhaps in light of the evolutionary historical development of Anabaptism it would be best to say that what is needed is a "recovery of Anabaptist conversations," rather than a "recovery of *the* Anabaptist Vision."

Anabaptist Conversations

Of course, conversations about faith essentials are going on at present among the Believers' Church descendants of the Anabaptists. These conversations have been going on non-stop since the sixteenth century. My proposal as a Believers' Church historian is simply to suggest that the historical dialogue that shaped this faith tradition be allowed to inform contemporary Believers' Church conversations. There is much food for thought not only in the origins of Anabaptism, nor only in the eventual traditions that emerged, but perhaps especially in the developmental period in between.

Historically speaking, it was only at the end of a dynamic period of development that the rigid definition of boundaries for Anabaptist groups emerged. In spite of historical commonalities of belief and shared experiences of persecution and martyrdom, the surviving Anabaptist communities came to the conclusion that salvation was to be denied even to the Anabaptist brethren outside their own groups. When we reach this final stage we have in a significant way reached the end of the Anabaptist story. It is at this point that we begin to tell the stories of the groups we call Swiss Brethren, Hutterites, and Mennonites.

Chapter 9

The Communication of Anabaptist Ideas

Evangelization in Thuringia

Heinz Kestener of Schwerstedt was arrested in December of 1527 on suspicion of being an Anabaptist. In his testimony he described his meeting with some of Hans Hut's apostles. Heinz had taken onions to a neighbouring town, he said, and on his return trip he met three men walking on the road. They walked together and "talked about many things." As they were about to part company, one of the men asked his name and asked further if they could stay with him on their return. He agreed, and two weeks later they appeared, in the evening. This time they told him that they had been sent to him by God, and that the world would end in eleven months. Then they spoke of the Word of God and the Holy Gospel, and finally one of them asked Heinz what he believed concerning baptism.

Heinz Kestener of Schwerstedt

Heinz said that he was not interested in rebaptism, and they all went to bed. The next day the men left, warning about the cataclysm to come and blessing him as they departed. (Testimony in Wappler, 1913, 254-56).

Anstad Kemmerer of Halle reported in detail about his meeting with some of Hans Hut's followers, and his subsequent baptism.

Anstad Kemmerer of Halle

He was away from home, having breakfast with a friend at an inn, when he noticed a short man going about here and there in the room. This man finally sat next to him and read from a book. The little man (*mennelein*) then asked him what he believed about baptism, and started a conversation on the subject. As Anstad remembered it, the small man read from Jeremiah about baptism and then told Anstad that there were those who had been chosen by God to gain salvation by this baptism. Furthermore, he told Anstad that he knew who the elect were, and that there was very little time left for the elect to come to God. Those who received this baptism were not to worry about food, drink or clothing for there was enough for everyone. He then offered to include Anstad in the company of the elect, through baptism.

Anstad said that in view of the short time left, he did not want to run away from God's grace and so he requested baptism. This was done forthwith. Someone brought a "little mustard pot" of pure water, and in the presence of three or more men and the same number of women (people Anstad did not know), they read from books that they carried, they prayed, and then asked him to kneel. Anstad did, and recited the Creed out loud, after which they poured water on him and made the sign of the cross on his forehead.

After the baptism, they admonished him to be faithful, to treat others in the fellowship kindly, and not to be involved with usury (lending money and charging interest). They told him further that the Lord would return in eleven months, that there were some 16,000 already in the company of the elect including "great and honourable people, margraves and others." After Hut's apostles left, however, Anstad fell into doubt, repented of his baptism and returned to his old faith. (Wappler, 1913, 258-61).

Ambrosius Spittelmaier describes his method of evangelization. (*"Reply to Questioning," Oct. 25, 1527, Nuremberg*).

"When I or another came to someone, who was not of this faith, I would ask him first whether he was a Christian, what his Christian walk was, how he acted toward his brothers, whether they had all things in common, whether any among them had need of food or clothing, whether they practiced brotherly admonishment, how they practiced the using of all creatures before God and how they understood God and Christ (in the creatures) etc.

If it happened that one or more didn't know these things, and if one desired to know, then we would show the will of God clearly through all the creatures to each one, through the craft each one knew, through his tools (Job 12, John 15, Math. 4, Luke 9, Math. 21), just as Christ taught, so that he learn God's will through his handicraft just as though it were a book.

Likewise a woman through the flax she spins, or other housework which she performs daily. In sum, our teaching is nothing other than making God's will clear to all people through the creature, since invisible things are made known through visible things, and for this reason has God put them before people's eyes. The apostles likewise taught in this same way, for all of history is nothing other than a creature." (Schornbaum, 1934, 48).

Communication in the Sixteenth Century

Communication has been defined as an interaction that takes place between persons, utilizing verbal and nonverbal symbols, usually aimed at influencing *Persuasion* the behaviour of others. The element of influence or persuasion is central to religious communication in the sixteenth century. People who were convinced of the truth attempted to communicate that truth to others, in order to convince them as well. The Anabaptist evangelists who communicated with Heinz Kestener and Anstad Kemmerer were engaged in a mission that concerned the ultimate truth, as they understood it.

There is much to be learned by studying the way in which communication takes place in specific historical settings. A useful formula for the study of communication processes is the following: "Who says what in what channel to whom with what effect?" (Lasswell, 1948, 37). The formula is a useful guide for us, particularly if we make it clear that our interest is not in the routine communication of daily life, but rather in the communication that aims to persuade.

Persuasive communication is closely related to power. The more one is *Power* able to control the messenger, the message and the media (the who, the what, and the channels), the more influence one can wield over the recipients of the message (the effects upon whom).

The debate over whether the Reformation was medieval or modern has preoccupied historians for some time. The debate remains equally intense when communication becomes the focus. It is undeniably true that the Reformation was made possible by the widespread use of Gutenberg's invention, *Print* the printing press. The use of print to promote Reformation ideas has been said to be the first time a modern medium of communication was used to persuade masses of people. On the other hand, older and more traditional forms of communication did not suddenly or miraculously disappear because of the invention of movable type. Spoken and heard words (the oral/

An early print shop

aural communication system) were at least as crucial as was print in the communication of the original reform message to the *masses* of people. The reason for this was that the vast majority of people in the sixteenth century were illiterate, and could not personally read the newly-printed pamphlets, broadsheets and vernacular Bibles that had begun to circulate.

In the sixteenth century, ideas were being spread primarily in non-literate ways, even if writing and print were undeniably crucial intermediate steps in the rapid diffusion of new ideas. The masses of people still were stirred by popular preachers, excited by the news read aloud from broadsheets at the market, informed and entertained by news songs (and slanderous ditties) sung in taverns, and introduced to new ideas by radical craftspeople in their places of work. And, rather than being read in silence, Reformation texts (and vernacular Bibles) also were most commonly read aloud to listeners. There is good evidence that many Reformation pamphlets were deliberately composed with public reading in mind. Printed words were mediated by spoken words.

Social conflict was sharpened by the evangelical reform because the Bible was cited as the source of ultimate authority. This was a brilliant way of undermining the interpretive privileges of the old guard, but the interpretation of the Bible, in the vernacular, by the masses could not help but sharpen social and political conflict. The revolutionary nature of the appeal to Scripture alone in a predominantly oral culture was intensified by one further, crucial Ref-

Spoken Word

ormation slogan: all Christians are in fact priests. From this second affirmation people deduced the right–even the duty–to interpret Scripture for themselves.

Commoners who were literate in the vernacular were pivotal in bringing together Scripture alone and the priesthood of all believers for the illiterate majority. Clerical and upper-class literacy in the sixteenth century remained the preserve of those who had had access to a Latin school and university education. Such people were to be found in important pulpits and council chambers in the cities. But the commoner who had learned to read in a vernacular tongue related to the oral world of the lower classes, and exercised his or her literacy in that social context–among the craftspeople in the cities and villages and the peasants in the countryside. (1)

(1) What the common people were saying: testimony collected by the city council of St. Gall, 1524.
"If he [the witness] ate some bread or a slice of radish it would do him as much good [as the host]."
Another witness: "When a priest says a Mass, he has performed a mortal sin, and in fact, when the sacrament is lifted up, it is no different from lifting up a slice of radish."
Another witness: "When a priest goes to the altar, it is like a thief going to the gallows." Another witness: "When we have faith in our hearts, then everything is good." QGTS, II, #411, 342-44.

Thanks to print, vernacular reforming texts and Bibles could be bought and read aloud, and in this process the literate commoners played a crucial mediating role in bringing new ideas to, and promoting radical dissent among the people at the grass roots.

Was the True Word a written word, or a spiritual Word? Appeals to the higher authority of the Spirit over the letter turned out to be impossibly democratic. Some said that those who had the Spirit could claim to have true access to God's Word *even without being able to read the letter*. By hearing the letter of Scripture read aloud, remembering central passages, and living in accordance with its prescriptions, even the illiterate or semi-literate could claim to be true interpreters of the Word. Even further, truly yielded and spiritual people might well receive a direct Word from God in dreams or visions, and clearly literacy played no role in this.

The struggle over the nature of the Word in some cases reflected a very deep societal struggle between those in possession of the skill of *learned* literacy, who controlled the traditional rights of interpretation of the Book, and those without the skill of letters (or with a mere vernacular literacy) who claimed a spiritual right to interpret the Book.

Stages in Popular Reformation Communication

Examining the communication processes at work in the Reformation is revealing, particularly for the light it sheds on the emergence and survival of a dissident grass roots reforming movement such as Anabaptism. Looked at from a communications point of view we can see two distinct stages in the reform process we have outlined to this point.

Popular Pressure

1. Against Rome. The first stage corresponds to the broad evangelical reforming movement that focussed its collective energies against Rome from 1517 to ca. 1525. At this initial stage the reformers happily utilized all available channels of communication, formal and informal, to convince political authorities to adopt a Reformation programme. Part of the early strategy was to involve all levels of society in pressuring governments to reform. Vernacular print communication as well as popular preaching played central roles here.

Political Alliances

2. Power Consolidated. The second phase in this process emerged when key reformers made successful alliances with the politically powerful, and gained control of the official communications channels–the church pulpits and the local presses. The broader evangelical coalition had begun to unravel already by 1521, when some reformers chose to remain with the papacy following Luther's excommunication. By 1522, as we have noted in the cases of Andreas Karlstadt and Thomas Müntzer, serious evangelical dissent also had emerged. By 1525 and the failure of the Peasants' War, the cleavage between the official or magisterial reform movements and the dissident grass roots movements was undeniable.

As we have seen, Anabaptism grew out of the general Reformation pro-test of the first phase, but more specifically, Anabaptism's roots lie firmly in the radical evangelical protest movement of the second phase. The first adult baptisms in Zurich took place just as the Peasants' War erupted, and owed crucial ideological debts to the radical reformers, Andreas Karlstadt and Tho-mas Müntzer. But as soon as the peasants' movement collapsed the Anabaptists also found themselves (with rare exceptions) on the margins of power, limited for the most part to the informal, oral/aural channels of communication. As we have see, this did not mean that evangelization could not take place. To the contrary, Anabaptists simply utilized traditional, medieval communications systems, and used them very effectively indeed.

3. Elimination of Dissent. At this point we can identify the emergence of a third stage in the Reformation communication process. The consolidation of the Reformation was synonymous, in the sixteenth century, with the progres-sive elimination of religious dissent. An alliance of reforming clergy with politi-cal power, and control of the official channels of communication, were huge advantages in gaining religious and political control in a given territory. But sixteenth century society–especially in the rural districts and villages, but also in the cities–still relied heavily on the traditional oral/aural means of communi-cation.

Control of
Communication

Locked out of the official channels of communication, the Anabaptists and other religious dissidents continued to win adherents in the old oral/aural ways. What shaped up in some territories, then, was a virtual propaganda war to win the hearts and minds of the common people. Reformers and govern-ments continued to worry that they might lose the war because alternative communication was undermining them at the grass roots and in the country-side, where 90 percent of the population still lived.

The majority of Anabaptist members and leaders after 1527 were drawn from the working classes. The fact that the Anabaptists often were mobile craftspeople and were operating in their own social milieu gave them an ad-vantage over learned preachers employed by the powerful, all of whom often were viewed with suspicion by those in the lower social orders.

Anabaptist Communication and Evangelization

If we return to the formulaic question posed earlier, namely "Who says what in what channel to whom with what effect?" we already can sketch a preliminary answer for the majority of Anabaptists throughout most of the sixteenth century.

Persons drawn primarily from the lower social orders called upon others (primarily from the same social orders) to repent, be reborn, accept water baptism and church discipline, and henceforth to live regenerated lives unto death, even though they would be persecuted by the world. The channel of communication was predominantly oral/aural, and the aim was the conversion of the hearers and their joining the "saints of God," "the elect," the "Body of Christ on earth" through water baptism.

In what follows we will try to convey an impression of some of the ways in which this Anabaptist evangelization took place. The evidence is drawn from the court records of the time.

Evangelization in Daily Life

Anabaptist evangelization most often took place in the midst of the common round of daily activities. The first to be evangelized were kinship groups and friendship circles. The workplace often seems to have functioned as an informal Bible school. Crafts such as weaving and spinning, for instance, often were carried out in large common rooms with a group of people present and occupied. Anabaptist craftspeople/evangelists thus had a good cover for their religious activities. Anabaptist women also proselytized and taught in such settings.

Jacob Groß

Jacob Groß, the travelling furrier and evangelist from Waldshut, was arrested early in 1526 in Aarau while present with a group of people who were spinning and working together in a large room. The authorities claimed, with some reason it appears, that these people were having an illegal religious gathering. Groß's defender claimed that it was no such a thing "since there was no reading or singing, either by the men or the women."

But it turned out on further examination that Groß had celebrated the Lord's Supper with some of these people, and also had baptized one person, whether at the workplace or elsewhere is not said in the record. It is clear that Groß was doing more than just spinning and working.

Some crafts and vocations lent themselves extremely well to itinerant evangelism. Hans Hut, for example, was a travelling book salesman who was on the road constantly, and so constantly was in conversation with people. His profession lent itself to evangelism, and he applied himself to the task. His followers likewise were constantly on the move, as we have seen already, evangelizing as they went. It is no surprise that some of the liveliest accounts of early Anabaptist evangelism come from the South German movement.

Hans Hut

Hut's predictions concerning the imminent return of Christ lent a special urgency to early South German Anabaptist proselytizing. Many who were baptized by Hut took to the road immediately on evangelistic missions and baptized many converts after only the most rudimentary instruction. The historical records have preserved interesting accounts of some of these encounters that provide us a glimpse into this early evangelistic activity.

One of Hut's apostles, Hans Nadler, has left a fascinating record of his evangelistic method. Nadler's profession also lent itself to itinerant evangelism, for he was a travelling salesman, making his living selling needles to cobblers and tailors in various cities. He was on the move constantly, he met very many people and, as he said, "whenever he met good-hearted persons in inns or on the street during his travels, he would give instruction from the Word of God."

Hans Nadler

This testimony is all the more remarkable because Nadler was illiterate; nevertheless, this handicap did not stop him from being able to defend himself with Scripture in debate, nor did it stop him from persuading people to join the Anabaptist movement.

After his arrest Nadler provided a detailed description of his *modus operandi*. Once he had struck up a conversation with someone he would begin teaching with a series of statements about the heavy consequences of faith, inquiring whether the hearer was disposed to suffer persecution and loss, and to "abstain from the joys of the world."

If the hearer answered yes, Nadler said, then he would outline what the hearer had to do to enter the kingdom of God: "Yes, my brother or sister, you must receive the Word of God like a child and must be born anew," which Nadler then would proceed to demonstrate by citing various Scripture passages on the subject which he had memorized in concordance-fashion.

Secondly, Nadler warned that "as a new child of God, you must submit to the will of God and give your body as a sacrifice to God."

In the third place, Nadler warned that "the world will hate you and be opposed to you–which you must suffer patiently."

If the hearer had not changed his or her mind after all of this, then Nadler proceeded to the teaching, which consisted of an exposition of the Lord's Prayer. In a simple way which unlettered hearers could easily remember, Nadler reinterpreted for his listeners what each phrase of the prayer meant in an Anabaptist sense. (2) After this followed a simple exposition of the Creed.

---

(2) Illiterate evangelism: Hans Nadler teaches the Lord's Prayer.
"After that I began teaching, starting with the Lord's prayer, and said: 'You say, "Our Father in heaven." So you must learn, my brother or sister, and consider that you will now be a child of God when you say "Father." You must live according to his divine will and must do as the word of God and the holy gospel teaches... Secondly you say: "May your name be made holy." ... Look at your prayer. How did you pray? You have chattered a great deal but have not considered in your heart where it goes. Then you continue: "May your kingdom come." ... if God comes with his kingdom and wants to come to you, he does not come to his own unless he brings the cross... Now whenever God laid something upon you as a punishment, you fled to the devil and cried to one saint here and to another one there. My brother, this you must forsake and now live like a child of God. ... "May your will be done." If God's will is now to happen, we must become completely and wholly yielded and rely upon the Lord, that his will may be done in us on earth as in heaven.'"
(Snyder-Penner, 1991, 405).

Nadler's personal, direct and simple approach seems to have been the norm in Anabaptist evangelization of people who were not part of one's own circle of friends and family. Notable in Nadler's method was the way that it was geared to the unlettered. The Lord's Prayer was known by virtually everyone. On this well-known structure Nadler built his Anabaptist teaching. Such memory aids were important in the evangelization of people who relied on memory rather than writing.

Preserving the Faith within the Group

It would seem to be the case that the oral/aural medium was well suited to evangelization, but not so well suited to the preservation of a tradition over several generations. The Anabaptists utilized a variety of means to overcome this difficulty, and to pass on their faith tradition to subsequent generations.

In the first place, given the importance of the Bible to their tradition, Anabaptist teaching subsequent to conversion and baptism seems to have consisted primarily in the teaching of key Bible passages that supported central Anabaptist teachings. This concordance approach to Anabaptist doctrine is evident in testimony after testimony in the court records, in which literate and illiterate Anabaptists alike cite virtually the same passages to defend adult baptism, the ban, etc.

Bible

Many of the booklets carried by Anabaptist leaders, sometimes referred to in Anabaptist testimonies, were in fact small concordances–Hans Hut always carried one. Some of these concordances eventually got into print. They read almost like Anabaptist testimonies, minus the connecting sentences and phrases. Or said the other way, Anabaptist writings and testimonies most often read like prose concordances.

Concordances

More than one inquisitor was astounded by the biblical knowledge of the simple Anabaptists, including the illiterate, women, and peasants. Part of the explanation for this phenomenon was the topical approach to Scripture which made it possible for the unlettered and uneducated to remember impressive amounts of Scripture. The mnemonic structure was provided by the central Anabaptist theological topics: baptism, ban, Supper, discipleship, suffering, martyrdom, apostasy, etc. Continuing biblical education easily added further passages and topics as time and opportunity permitted. (3)

---

(3) Selection from a Swiss Brethren Concordance, ca. 1550
Rebirth

"Ps 87 [:2-6] The Lord loves the gates of Zion over all the dwelling places of Jacob. ... Jer 4; Ezek 36 [:24-27] Thus says the Lord, I want to take you from among the heathens, and gather you together out of all countries... I also want to give you a new heart, and I want to give you a new spirit. I want to take the stone heart out of your bodies and give you a heart of flesh. I want to put my spirit in you, so you will walk in my ways and keep and do my law. Mt 9, 18; Mk 2, 6; Lk 5 [:37-38] No one puts wine in old skins, for then the wine tears the skins and will be spoiled... Jn 1 [:11-13] He came to his property, and his own did not accept him. But as many as accepted him, to them he gave power to become children of God, to those who believed in his name. Who were not born of blood, nor of the will of the flesh, nor of the will of a man, but of God. [Jn] 3 [:1-15] But there was a person among the Pharisees, with the name of Nicodemus... Jesus answered and said to him: Truly, truly I say to you, unless someone be born anew, he cannot see the kingdom of God. ... Rom 1, 6, 7, 12; 1 Cor 14 [:20] ... Gal 6 [:15] In Christ Jesus neither circumcision nor foreskin counts for anything, but rather a new creature..." (Concordantz und Zeiger, n.d., trans. Gilbert Fast).

Songs

In the second place, the importance of song as a carrier and communicator of Anabaptist teaching has not been properly appreciated. The composition and singing of songs was a part of daily life in the sixteenth century. The Anabaptists applied the common sixteenth century tavern technique of composing rhyme to be sung to popular tunes–except that their rhymes encapsulated central Anabaptist teachings, kept alive the stories of Anabaptist martyrs, and taught such things as the Creed and the Lord's Prayer. Eventually these songs also were written down and eventually some of them were printed. The best known of these is the *Ausbund*, which still functions as a hymnal among the Old Order Amish in North America. (4)

Manuscripts

In the third place, the Anabaptists composed a certain number of writings for edification, clarification and defense. In some cases we know of several manuscript copies of such writings that have survived in archives, never having been printed. The multiple manuscript copies that survive indicate that these writings were considered important by the Anabaptists. They were copied by hand and circulated in the communities.

The production of manuscripts and codices was a natural technological alternative to print, which was expensive and out of reach in any case in the earlier years of the movement. Copying by hand was an older technique that served a small underground church perfectly well. There are many instances of earlier Anabaptist printed works being copied by hand, in whole or in part. In time some manuscripts were brought to print; others were not. But communication by handwritten epistle, confessions, accounts of martyrdom, and exhortation was common among the early Anabaptists, whose leaders at least generally were literate in the vernacular. It was with this combination of topical biblical teaching, oral communication, musical composition, manuscript production, and print that Anabaptist teachings were preserved and passed on within the group itself.

---

(4) Ausbund, Hymn 36.
Another Song of Annelein of Freiburg, who was drowned and then burned, 1529.
"1. Everlasting Father in heaven,
I call on you so ardently,
Do not let me turn from you.
Keep me in your truth
Until my final end.
7. They have imprisoned me.
I wait, O God, with all my heart,
With very great longing,
When finally you will awake
And set your prisoners free.
8. O God, Father, make us like
The five virgins of your kingdom,
Who were prudently careful
To wait for the bridegroom,
With his chosen flock."
(Snyder and Hecht, 1996, 199-200).

An Underground Church in Augsburg, 1527-1528

Events in Augsburg will be recounted in the following chapter. Here we will outline the way in which the Anabaptists organized their fellowship in that city in 1527 and 1528. This sketch is possible because of the relatively rich records available in Augsburg for this period. John Oyer's study of Anabaptist women in Augsburg illustrates the way in which informal communication networks operated, making use of men and women in various social positions. Notable is the prominent role of women, often hidden from view in other documentation. Although Anabaptist women did not usually preach publicly or baptize, they were crucial to the functioning of the underground church that operated in Augsburg and elsewhere. The Anabaptist congregation in Augsburg was a large and thriving congregation by September of 1527, at the time of the first mass arrests in the city. Between that time and the second crackdown in April of 1528 Anabaptist women helped hold the movement together through a variety of covert activities.

Meetings

Several women in Augsburg were instrumental in housing Anabaptists and hosting meetings. Susanna Doucher, wife of a prominent sculptor, testified to having been baptized in 1527 and to having attended several secret Anabaptist meetings, one of them in a forest outside the city walls. In spite of her husband's opposition, it turned out that she had housed and fed Anabaptist refugees and had contributed money and goods to the common Anabaptist treasury.

Scolastica Stierpaur also came from the upper ranks of Augsburg society; her husband was the diplomat Crispin Stierpaur, who also joined the Anabaptists. Several Anabaptist ministers found lodging at their house, as did other Anabaptists, and several meetings were held there as well. She reported that "only" three people had been baptized in her house, including the grocerwoman Els Hegenmiller. Dorothea Frölich also was prominent among the Augsburg Anabaptists, present at many meetings and generous to the needy; she hosted and fed Anabaptists in her home.

At the other end of the social spectrum stood Katharina Wiedenmann, whose house was "almost constantly open to Anabaptist visitors." Katharina's husband Simprecht was a cobbler by trade. Their shop and home became "a veritable center of clandestine Anabaptist activity," with people coming and going under the guise of having their shoes repaired. Many women also came

Sewing Circle

together at the Wiedenmann house to sew and "assemble around the distaff"– one of several subversive "sewing circles" that have come to light.

Of course, under questioning both Katharina and her husband tried to make all this sound as innocent as possible, but besides providing a frequent meeting place, the Wiedenmann home also was an alms distribution centre– Simprecht had been elected one of the deacons or purse keepers for the congregation. Katharina distributed many of these alms personally and also served as a messenger to many other Anabaptists in the city, under the guise of routine business.

Two women grocers also were active in the Anabaptist congregation. Barbara Schleiffer was at the centre of Anabaptist coming and going, hosting at least one meeting and greeting and redirecting a steady stream of Anabaptist refugees from elsewhere. Oyer notes that "her steadfastness was a major factor in keeping the Anabaptist movement alive."

Grocers

Els Hegenmiller also was a grocer–it appears that the grocers' guild was uncommonly Anabaptist-minded. Needless to say, a grocer's shop provided a perfect foil for covert communication. Els's testimony revealed the existence of a network of word of mouth communication by which Anabaptists informed each other about upcoming meetings and passed on other news. Els was generous to other Anabaptists, although she and her husband were of modest means. She routinely gave food to Anabaptists in need. For this–and because she shouted to the butchers who ran the neighbouring stall that the Catholic host was a "slimy idol"–the Augsburg authorities cut out her tongue and banished her for life.

There is no doubt that the Anabaptist women of Augsburg were the mainstay of their underground church. They hosted meetings and subversive sewing circles, provided a communications network, evangelized among their peers, housed and fed refugees and travelling Anabaptists, and provided support for the families of those in prison. Oyer suggests that the women were particularly active because they could move about less conspicuously than could the men. And finally these women–like so many other Anabaptist women we come to know in the martyrologies–were amazingly steadfast when they were arrested and subjected to torture. Besides being routinely questioned while being tortured with thumbscrews, several recalcitrant women were branded on either cheek before being banished.

John Oyer has extracted the following four "rules for operating an underground church" from his study of the Augsburg records, based on the techniques utilized by that congregation.

1. Do not ask or learn the name of your baptizer or of any traveling minister. Do not learn the name of the man or woman who provides free housing and food if you are a refugee. Then you will be unable to disclose their names if you are caught and hauled into court and tortured.

2. Hide the leaders at different places, and even disguise them. Have them remain anonymous or use pseudonyms. Move them out of town and on their itinerant ways when it becomes dangerous to keep them longer.

3. Meet secretly. Meet in a forest, a gravel pit, or some isolated building at the edge of a village where the group can sing hymns without being heard. Within the city, meet in the more isolated houses which ought to be hung about with blankets on the inside to block spying eyes. Or meet in the city in very small groups in normal houses where people gather anyway for routine social purposes.

4. Greet each other simply so as to allay suspicion. But in some environments, greet each other with an exchange that indicates to each party the Anabaptist inclination of the other. In this way strangers may recognize the Anabaptist in each other. One says "God greet thee, brother in the Lord." The other answers, "God thank thee, brother in the Lord." Some greetings were less elaborate, but very particular. (Some Anabaptists denied there was any special greeting, others declared that there was).

The techniques described above were widely used within the Anabaptist movement; they recall similar techniques at work among the medieval heretical movements. In both cases the dissident religious communities relied heavily on personal contacts and oral/aural communication to win converts and to carry out their own religious activities.

Conclusion

The study of the process of communication in the Anabaptist movement is just beginning, and many questions are left to be answered. Nevertheless the dynamics of communication outlined above held true, in a general way, for the movement as a whole, even though print played a larger role in the Netherlands than it did for the Swiss Brethren and the South German movements.

Since Anabaptist communication was most often carried on as invisibly as possible, under the cover of normal daily activity, the historian may catch a glimpse of the process only occasionally, when the authorities managed to detect, arrest, and question the participants. Through those occasional windows, however, we see the stubborn resistance of common, everyday people, intent on living out their faith against heavy odds, and zealous in their efforts to convert others to that faith.

The heavy-handed response of the authorities to this grass roots religious dissent–which involved only a small percentage of the total population of any given territory–is explained in good measure by the fact that the oral/aural channels of communication lay mostly outside political and ecclesiastical control. The frightening prospect for civil authorities was that in this still predominantly oral/aural culture there were as many potential dissenting missionaries as there were speakers. For rulers intent on enforcing religious uniformity in order to consolidate political power, securing the pulpits and the presses was only a necessary first step. Religious control would not be achieved until the more extensive oral/aural medium also came under control, for "the spoken word was power in the sixteenth century."

The fact that Anabaptism managed to survive in such a hostile context demonstrates the fact that although outlawed and persecuted, the Anabaptists were not silenced, and hence were not powerless.

Jan Wouterss and Adriaenken Jans moments before being burned at the stake

Anabaptist martyrs often used the occasion of their executions to proclaim their faith to the crowds assembled to watch the spectacle, and to exhort both spectators and their captors to repentance. Steadfastness in the face of torture, and a public, oral witness in the face of an imminent and horrible death (in this case, by fire) were powerful instruments of communication at the popular level. Rather than discrediting the movement, public executions only served to lend it credence. Authorities soon began silencing Anabaptist martyrs with gags, tongue screws, and other means to prevent their public witness. Anabaptists appealed to examples of heroic steadfastness as providing evidence for the genuineness of their movement.

Chapter 10

The Spread and Development
of Early Anabaptism

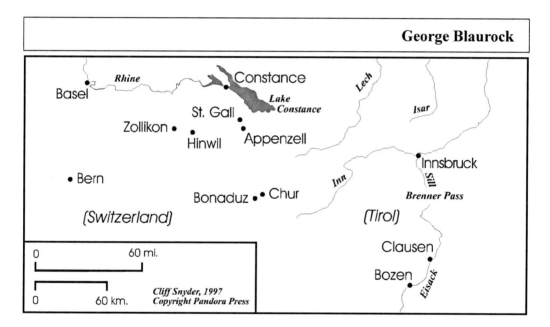

George Blaurock

George Cajacob, better known as George Blaurock, was from Bonaduz, a village in Grisons in eastern Switzerland. He studied at the University of Leipzig in 1513, and served as vicar in the diocese of Chur from 1516 to 1518. He came to Zurich in 1525 and soon joined the circle that had formed around Conrad Grebel and Felix Mantz.

According to the account in the Hutterite Chronicle, and by his own testimony, Blaurock was the first to be baptized in January 1525. Soon he was active in establishing an Anabaptist congregation in the village of

Zollikon, leading in preaching, Bible reading, baptism and celebrations of the Lord's Supper. According to Margret Hottinger, Grebel and Mantz began reading Scripture and preaching in Zollikon, but the baptizing began when George Blaurock arrived.

Blaurock preached that baptism was a sign of conversion and repentance from sin. He taught that the Lord's Supper was a sign that one had accepted Christ's sacrifice and forgiveness of sins. There were emotional scenes in Zollikon at his baptisms, with many witnesses testifying that they came weeping to ask for baptism at Blaurock's hands. Blaurock emphasized conversion and the living of a new life. He also was strongly anticlerical. He told listeners in Zollikon that Zwingli, Luther and the Pope were all thieves and murderers of human souls for baptizing infants.

By all accounts he was a fiery and passionate individual, and a powerful preacher. At one point he preached to 200 people assembled in a large room in Zollikon. Again there was weeping, repentance, and requests for baptism. He also was a notorious disturber of the public peace. During a sermon in the village church in Zollikon, he began banging on the pews with a stout stick, and shouted out to the pastor, Nicolas Billeter, "Not you, but I am sent to preach." He did the same thing again later, in the parish church in the village of Hinwil. According to the pastor Johannes Brennwald, Blaurock called him an antichrist and a seducer for defending infant baptism.

Not surprisingly, Blaurock ended up in prison many times. On his second arrest by the Zurich authorities he was deported back to Chur by boat. After his release from that prison, he worked to establish Anabaptism in Grisons. There he and Felix Mantz were imprisoned again. They returned to the Zurich area, and worked especially in the Grüningen district until yet another arrest in October, 1525.

After a second disputation on baptism in Zurich Blaurock was sentenced to life imprisonment (March 7, 1526), to be held in the Zurich tower until he either recanted or died. Two weeks later he and the other prisoners managed to escape. Mantz and Blaurock returned again to Grüningen, where they were arrested yet again in December, 1526. This time Felix Mantz was sentenced to death, and George Blaurock was beaten out of the city with rods.

Blaurock's movements are difficult to trace after this final expulsion from Zurich. He made a trip to South Tirol in 1527, then appeared briefly in Bern, and then Basel and Appenzell in 1528 and 1529, after which he returned to the Tirol. It is safe to assume much itinerant pastoral activity, now hidden to us, during this period. By May 1529, Blaurock was active further east in the Tirol, primarily in Clausen, Guffidaun, Ritten, and towns near Bozen.

In August of 1529, George Blaurock was captured in Guffidaun along with Hans Langegger, subjected to extensive torture, and then burned at the stake along with his companion. The sentence was carried out in Clausen, Tirol, on September 6, 1529.

It was through Blaurock's activity, and that of others like him, that Swiss Anabaptism spread out from Zurich and encountered the Anabaptism of Hans Hut and Hans Denck.

*(For a fuller biography, see the **Mennonite Encyclopedia**, I, 354-56).*

Swiss and South German Anabaptism in Exile and Conversation

It is not possible to detail the ebb and flow of early Anabaptism across southwestern Europe in the space of one chapter. The German portion alone of the Holy Roman Empire comprised more than three hundred principalities of varying size and importance, all of which could adopt their own practical approaches towards religious dissenters. There remained the various Swiss cantons, the particular cases of Moravia, Alsace, and a variety of free imperial cities. Every territory deserves to have its own story told in order to identify important changes in policy, as well as to detail particular events relevant to the development of the Anabaptist story in that city or region.

In this chapter we will attempt to provide only the very broadest overview of the spread and some developments of the early Swiss and South German Anabaptist movement from 1525 to ca. 1540. We will sketch this development by means of a very general geographical description, some representative biographical sketches, and occasional concentration on crucial cities and territories. Of particular interest is the formative period of interaction between the Swiss and South German Anabaptist movements.

Persecution, Survival, and Exile

The political reality faced in the first decade of the movement (1525-1535) in Switzerland and the Holy Roman Empire was a swift narrowing of official tolerance for Anabaptism. The official persecution of Anabaptists reached a climax of sorts with the events in Münster (1534-35), a story that will be told in more detail in a subsequent chapter.

The Anabaptist kingdom of Münster was used particularly by Archduke Ferdinand of Habsburg to justify repression against Anabaptists in some territories that previously had been tolerant–such as in Moravia, for example. But early in the first decade of the movement, although some political authorities had moved decisively against Anabaptists with imprisonment, torture and death sentences, there remained places where, for a variety of reasons, Anabaptists were tolerated in practice.

In the Swiss areas of origin, the best chance for long-term Anabaptist survival lay in the countryside, where kinship networks and a general distrust of city-based magistrates made detection and enforcement difficult. Swiss Anabaptism would survive in small pockets of rural resistance in the northern cantons of Zurich, Appenzell, Bern and Basel well into the seventeeth century, and beyond. This same general pattern would be seen elsewhere: Anabaptism would come to survive more and more in village and rural settings, where detection and enforcement were difficult for the authorities.

Increased persecution also resulted in significant migrations of Anabaptists from areas where there was active persecution, to those places where they were tolerated outright or where legal enforcement was less severe. The relatively simple story of Anabaptist origins, then, very soon becomes a complicated story of Anabaptist migrations. One may say that after "genesis" came "exodus." *Migration*

The Anabaptism that began in Zurich spread quickly west to Bern, Basel, Strasbourg and Alsace, into Baden and Swabia, along the Neckar river in Württemberg, to eastern Switzerland (Appenzell, St. Gall, Chur), and into the Tirol. But of all the places of refuge, Moravia provided the best opportunities for freedom in the late 1520s, even though the distance and the difficulty of travel were daunting. Several cities, such as Strasbourg, Augsburg, and Esslingen also offered possibilities early on, and these cities in particular became early Anabaptist centres of refuge. The story of Jakob Groß, like that of George Blaurock, illustrates the larger pattern of movement among the Swiss Brethren in this first decade and a half of the movement.

Jakob Groß, whom we have already met in our narrative, was a furrier from Waldshut who was introduced to Anabaptism by Conrad Grebel and baptized by Balthasar Hubmaier in Waldshut, sometime after April 1525. He was married to Veronica, also from Waldshut, who was baptized in that city by Wilhelm Reublin. Although Jakob was from the Anabaptist city of Waldshut, and was baptized by Hubmaier, he nevertheless was a pacifist. He was expelled from Waldshut at the height of the Peasants' War for refusing to take arms in defense of the city. He immediately took up an itinerant ministry in Switzerland. It is not known if Veronica accompanied him on these trips. *Jakob and Veronica Groß*

Jakob Groß worked in the Grüningen district in the late summer of 1525. Here he baptized 35 people in one day before being arrested and expelled. He moved next to western Switzerland, to the Aargau, where he was active especially in and around the city of Aarau. We have already met him, leading Bible studies and religious discussions in work rooms, and baptizing Agnes Zender of Aarau, for which he was arrested in Brugg in late February of 1526.

After Groß was released from that prison, he worked next in the city of Lahr, across the river from Strasbourg. There he was arrested and expelled, and then suffered the same fate in Strasbourg. He went on trial in

Sattler

Strasbourg at the end of 1526. Michael Sattler came to Strasbourg and pleaded with Bucer and Capito for the imprisoned Groß and three more compatriots. There are documented connections between Sattler and Groß, and it is likely that Jakob Groß was present at the Schleitheim gathering in February, 1527.

Jakob Groß soon emerged as a leading Swiss Anabaptist leader in

Hut

Augsburg, where he worked alongside Hans Hut and South German Anabaptists who had been baptized by Hut. Veronica did accompany Jakob to Augsburg, and was active in the Anabaptist congregation there.

Jakob Groß began baptizing soon after Easter of 1527. He is known to

Veronica Groß

have baptized at least 22 persons in Augsburg. Veronica was involved in organizing Anabaptist meetings and admitted, when questioned in prison, that on occasion she also had instructed some of the Anabaptist women. She took up the trade of seamstress, a form of employment that allowed her to "instruct" while working with other women.

The period of toleration in Augsburg was short-lived. Shortly after the Martyrs' Synod in Augsburg (the end of August, 1527), Jakob Groß was arrested at a large Anabaptist gathering in the city. Veronica was arrested with him. She refused to recant or to swear an oath to remain outside the city, and so was beaten out of Augsburg with rods. Jakob was kept in prison indefinitely. After suffering behind bars for some four years, he finally made a public recantation on June 22, 1531 in order to gain release from prison.

Persecution and emigration very quickly brought together Anabaptists of differing convictions in the Tirol, in the South German cities, but especially in the territory of Moravia. In the city of Nicholsburg, Moravia where he fled after being imprisoned in Zurich, Balthasar Hubmaier managed once again to establish an Anabaptist state church. Hubmaier continued to maintain that a Christian government should be allowed to wield the sword, and that Christians were allowed to participate fully in all governing functions.

Hubmaier

Hubmaier gained a considerable following, but also present in Nicholsburg were Swiss Anabaptist refugees who had accepted Schleitheim separatism and nonresistance. As might be expected, the "sword bearers" and the "staff bearers"–both strictly speaking part of the same Swiss Anabaptist movement and origin–eventually came into conflict, although for some time the two views coexisted peacefully.

While differences concerning the sword of government may have simmered just below the surface among the Swiss refugees in Nicholsburg, the first overt division there occurred between the Swiss Anabaptist leader Balthasar Hubmaier and the South German Anabaptist leader Hans Hut.

Nicholsburg

By far the best possiblities of refuge for Anabaptists on the run between 1526 and 1528 lay in the city of Nicholsburg, under the lordship of Leonard of Liechtenstein. By the time Balthasar Hubmaier sought refuge there (ca. July, 1526) Nicholsburg had already moved in a Zwinglian evangelical direction thanks to the efforts of local pastors Hans Spittelmaier and Oswald Glaidt.

Leonard von Liechtenstein

Within a few months of his arrival, Hubmaier had managed to turn Nicholsburg in an officially Anabaptist direction, baptizing Spittlemaier and Glaidt, as well as the city's lord, Leonhard von Liechtenstein. Within a short time the city had become an Anabaptist centre, with the number of baptized estimated at around 2,000. Although many Anabaptists with "differing shades of belief" from Switzerland, Germany and Austria came to Nicholsburg, nevertheless there was no initial trouble in the fall and winter of 1526-1527, such as would develop in the spring of 1527.

Tension

There is indirect evidence that there were underlying tensions–as one might expect–between the Anabaptist followers of Hubmaier and more radically-minded Anabaptist refugees. From later events, it appears that a separatist faction was led by "the one-eyed Swabian," Jakob Wiedemann, which gathered in the village of Bergen, outside the city walls. Into this mix

Hut

came Hans Hut in May, 1527, and won support not only among the more radical faction, but also among some important supporters of Hubmaier in the city. The central point of contention seems to have been Hut's End Times calendar and preaching. Some teaching on community of goods may have been involved as well, but this is not well documented.

Following a private meeting between Hut and Hubmaier, a public disputation was held between them (The Nicholsburg Disputation of 1527) in the church of the city, which was followed in turn by a private disputation at the castle, before Lord Leonard. The main points of contention appear to have been Hut's End Times calculations, opposed by Hubmaier,

End Times

and Hut's accusation of Hubmaier's laxity in allowing too many unprepared people into the church. Hut was thrown into prison by Lord Leonard–who himself was a baptized member of the Anabaptist community–and in spite of Hut's successful escape, the division of the Anabaptist community in Moravia was a foregone conclusion.

On June 24, 1527 Hubmaier published his last work, *On the Sword*.

Sword

The evidence is persuasive that Hubmaier directed his writing on the sword to Swiss Brethren followers of Schleitheim, and against Schleitheim's article 6 specifically. This long-simmering issue had dogged Hubmaier since Waldshut, as Jakob Groß's expulsion from Waldshut recalls, and continued to bother Hubmaier in Nicholsburg. The remarkable fact is not that open opposition emerged on this question, but rather that "sword bearing" and "staff bearing" Anabaptists managed to coexist for so long in Nicholsburg without first resolving this difference. The immediate objects of Hubmaier's *On the Sword* probably were the brethren gathered around Jakob Wiedemann in the village of Bergen.

Just one month after the publication of *On the Sword*, Hubmaier was arrested by Austrian authorities, and subsequently burned at the stake in Vienna on March 10, 1528. His wife Elsbeth was drowned three days later in the Danube.

Back in Nicholsburg, the Jakob Wiedemann group continued its separatist opposition to Lord Lietchenstein's Anabaptist state church, led by Hans Spittelmaier after Hubmaier's arrest. Early in 1528 a debate was held in Bergen between Spittelmaier on the one hand, and Wiedemann and Philip Jäger on the other. The Wiedemann group insisted on nonresistance in the manner of the Swiss followers of Schleitheim; Wiedemann and Jäger also seem to have incorporated some of Hut's End Times teaching–although obviously not Hut's views on the sword. Lord Leonard eventually asked the dissidents to leave, which they did in late winter, 1528. This particular crisis seems to have been precipitated because Liechtenstein had mobilized armed defence in the face of a threat by the Austrian provost.

Nonresistance

The "staff-bearing" group of 200 plus refugees from Nicholsburg found a political space in the Moravian city of Austerlitz where the local lords promised them freedom of worship. In the course of their journey there they established a common purse, based upon a seven point constitution which established community of goods in an eschatalogical context. It was to this group that Jacob Hutter came in 1529 from the Tirol.

Division and Migration

Jakob Hutter

Nicholsburg brought three distinct early varieties of Anabaptism into close contact: the state Anabaptism of Hubmaier that had emerged in the context of Swiss Anabaptism, the separatist Swiss Anabaptism of Schleitheim, and the South German apocalyptic Anabaptism of Hut. Nicholsburg well illustrates the unity and the diversity of early Anabaptism.

In terms of origins, Hubmaier and Hut represented two geographically and ideologically distinct points of beginning. Nevertheless, the disagreement between Hubmaier and Hut did not concern Anabaptist theological essentials regarding the nature of faith, repentance, regeneration, baptism, and a new life (in a word, soteriology), or the memorial Supper and the place of the ban in the congregation. They disagreed rather on the further interpretation of their shared Anabaptist distinctives.

Hubmaier and Hut agreed on the centrality of Mark 16:16 in providing the biblical order pertaining to baptism, for example. But Hut also understood baptism as the eschatological "mark of TAU" that sealed the 144,000 elect of the Last Days–and this further interpretation of baptism Hubmaier could not abide. Conversely, Hubmaier insisted upon church discipline, but supporters of Hut who had been in Nicholsburg testified later that in Hubmaier's church there had been no strict application of the ban or "proper" church order, by their definition.

| Co-existence | The evidence from Nicholsburg suggests that on the basis of their shared beliefs, Anabaptist refugees of all sorts lived together peacefully as brethren for quite some time before variant interpretations of their shared Anabaptist principles led them to schism, in some cases, and to compromise in others.

To take another case in point, it would appear in retrospect that Hubmaier's sword bearing Anabaptism and the pacifist and separatist Anabaptism of Schleitheim were fundamentally incompatible from the start. It has been assumed that Schleitheim marks an immediate and thorough consolidation. But pacifist brethren in Nicholsburg were still working out the full implications of their "two kingdoms" Schleitheim position. The specific problem for the nonresistant Anabaptists in Nicholsburg was that an Anabaptist ruler had granted them asylum and was protecting them with the sword against their enemies. Had Lord Leonard been a "nonbeliever" such protection undoubtedly would have been accepted, as it was later in other parts of Moravia, and presumably Lord Leonard could then have been comfortably (though quietly) consigned to hell along with all other members of "the world." But Lord Leonard was a "baptized brother." Thus the clash between "faithfulness to Christ" in nonresistance, and responsible governance (legitimate defence) could not be avoided by Anabaptists in Nicholsburg, in spite of an extended period of coexistence. In Nicholsburg, Schleitheim's separatist nonresistance proved ultimately divisive, but was not so initially.

The various Anabaptist tendencies that met at Nicholsburg did not	*New Fusion*
emerge unchanged from that setting. The pacifist "staff bearers" who went on to form communal settlements in other parts of Moravia demonstrated a fusion of the Swiss teaching of absolute separatist nonresistance with Hans Hut's apocalyptic expectations, to which eventually was added the distinctive of a legislated sharing of goods. This was a further refinement of the Anabaptist position which had not existed exactly in this form before, either in Hubmaier, the Schleitheim Swiss Anabaptists, or in Hut.

Hubmaier's state church Anabaptism did not long outlive him, and Hut's apocalyptic excitement waned quickly following his death in 1527. The separatist (but non-communitarian) Anabaptism of the Swiss Anabaptists and the separatist communitarian Anabaptism that emerged from the Nicholsburg experience, on the other hand, were interpretations and expressions of Anabaptism that would survive to the end of the sixteenth century and beyond.

The Tirol

The general area of the Tirol provided another primary setting in which early Swiss and South German teachings also met and combined for a time. The Swiss Anabaptist understanding was carried to the Tirol by George Blaurock, as already noted above. Hut's Anabaptism was brought to the Tirol by followers such as Leonhard Schiemer, Hans Schlaffer, and Jakob Hutter.

With the coming of strong Austrian repression in the Tirol in the late 1520s, there were mass migrations of Anabaptist refugees out of the territory. The majority of these emigres would flee to the communal Anabaptist groups in Moravia. But it also was out of the Tirolean setting that Pilgram Marpeck and Helena von Freyberg, among others, emerged to carry their particular (non-communal) Anabaptist views to the Swiss and German territories north and west of the Tirol. But it was Moravia that would remain a focal point for a variety of Anabaptist groups until almost the end of the century. In Moravia would be found later not only communal Anabaptists (Hutterites), but also communities of immigrant Swiss Brethren (often living in the same towns and villages as the Hutterites) as well as a few smaller groups of Marpeckites.

Augsburg and the Martyrs' Synod, August, 1527

A view of Augsburg in the late Fifteenth Century

Until the mass arrests in April 1528, Augsburg was an important Anabaptist centre in southern Germany. Along with Nicholsburg, it provides us a second window through which to view the interaction of various early Anabaptist tendencies.

Hans Denck came to Augsburg in September, 1525, as a teacher of Latin and Greek. It does not appear that Denck was yet baptized, for the issue of baptism did not emerge in Augsburg until 1526, and may well have been brought there in the person of Balthasar Hubmaier. The one piece of evidence pertaining to Hubmaier's activity in Augsburg points to contacts between Hubmaier and Denck. It is possible, although by no means certain, that Hans Denck was baptized by Hubmaier. In any case, on May 20, 1526 Denck baptized Hans Hut in Augsburg. It is therefore possible that for a brief time in the late spring and early summer of 1526, Hubmaier, Denck and Hut may have been together in that city. By late summer, all three had moved on, although Denck and Hut would return: Denck moved on to Strasbourg for a time, Hut began his missionary journeys, and Hubmaier continued on to Nicholsburg.

Denck

Early in 1527 Hans Hut returned and baptized a large group of important Anabaptist leaders: the patrician Eitelhans Langenmantel, the former clergymen Jakob Dachser and Sigmund Salminger, the weavers Gall Fischer and Peter Scheppach, and many others. At about the same time (ca. February, 1527) the Swiss Anabaptist leader and refugee, Jakob Groß, arrived in the city, and began baptizing as well.

Rather than there being evidence of contrary "Anabaptisms" colliding at this point in Augsburg, the records show that Hut established a rudimentary church organization among the Augsburg Anabaptists which featured a common chest for relief of the poor, and which integrated the Swiss Anabaptist missionary Jakob Groß into the leadership structure. Sigmund Salminger was chosen first minister by lot, with Jakob Groß and Jakob Dachser as his assistants.

Cooperation

The evidence from Augsburg suggests strongly that Hans Hut was working (in some places at least) for a broader Anabaptist movement without overtly linking adult baptism to his particular chronology of End Times events or his related understanding of the sword. The appointment of the Swiss Brethren pacifist Jakob Groß to a leadership position suggests as much. More striking still is the fact that Jakob Dachser, baptized by Hut himself, would become one of Hut's foremost opponents at the Martyrs' Synod later in 1527. The Swiss Brethren/South German distinctions (biblicist vs. mystical/non-apocalyptic vs. apocalyptic) which supposedly divided these two Anabaptist movements at their origins were present, but not yet divisive in early Augsburg Anabaptism.

Martyrs'
Synod

The "Martyrs' Synod" took place in Augsburg from August 20 to 24, 1527. The gathering has been given this name because very many of its participants would shortly suffer martyrdom. There were at least 22 Anabaptist missionaries from outside the city in attendance at three successive meetings. The first and the last meetings had more than 60 people present. Hut and his End Times agenda dominated the meetings, and Hut was forced to agree that he would be less forward in presenting his End Times convictions and predictions. Among those who opposed him was Jakob Dachser of Augsburg, who had been baptized by Hut. Once the contentious apocalyptic question had been settled by means of compromise, the assembled brethren also commissioned apostles and missioners to various areas. They were drawn from both the Swiss and South German groups, although South German Anabaptists present at these meetings far outnumbered the Swiss.

Central German Anabaptism

Central German Anabaptism took on various shades and forms, as different Anabaptist groups flourished and waned. The first Central German Anabaptist converts were baptized directly by Hans Hut in northern Franconia, and mirrored his enthusiastic apocalyptic expectation. This more militant and apocalyptic Anabaptist strand was subjected to some key arrests early in 1527. It came to a head in Hans Römer's aborted plans for an attack on Erfurt in January, 1528. By the summer of 1528, Melchior Rinck was establishing a different kind of Anabaptism in western Thuringia, centred in the village of Sorga and in the vicinity of Hersfeld. The Anabaptist congregations he founded in this area survived his own incarceration and some mass arrests in 1533. Many Anabaptists from this area also fled to Moravia. Hans Bott, a follower of Rinck who led a group of refugees to Moravia, got involved in some disputes between communal groups there.

Rinck

By 1534 Münsterite sympathizers and Melchiorite Anabaptists were making their presence felt in Hessian territory. After the collapse of Münster many refugees fled to Hesse, an area more notably tolerant than many others.

Hesse

In May of 1536 some thirty Melchiorites were arrested in Hesse, among them Georg Schnabel. As a result of this arrest and subsequent discussions with Martin Bucer, the Hessian state church instituted the practice of confirmation (in place of adult baptism) and introduced church discipline. In return the former Anabaptist leaders Georg Schnabel and Peter Tasch recanted their Anabaptist beliefs and led a general exodus of former Melchiorite Anabaptists into the Hessian state church under Bucer's tutelage.

By 1540, notes John Oyer, Anabaptism as a wide spread movement had disappeared from Central Germany. After this time, Swiss Brethren did maintain small communities and Hutterite missionaries also recruited actively in the area, but the number of Anabaptist adherents remained small.

*A view of
Strasbourg in
the late
Fifteenth
Century*

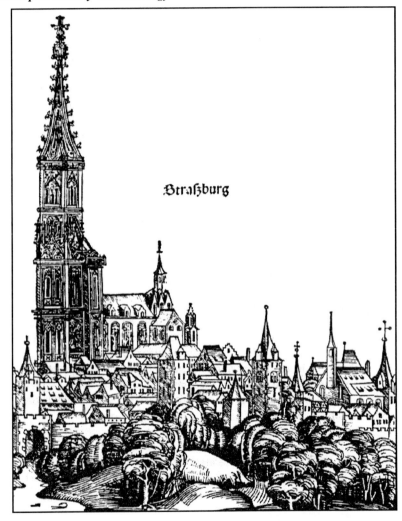

Straßburg

The city of Strasbourg occupied a unique and central place in the development of the Anabaptist movement. The reasons are not hard to find: strategically located for trade and commerce on the Rhine–the central transportation link between north and south–in 1482 Strasbourg acquired considerable latitude when it became a free imperial city, under the jurisdiction of the Holy Roman Emperor alone. In 1524 it had a population of around 20,000, making it one of the largest cities in the Empire.

Already in the late medieval period Strasbourg had a well deserved reputation for toleration, and as a free imperial city it continued that tradition into the sixteenth century. Sebastian Franck, who as a religious dissenter experienced his share of difficulties with political authorities, wrote in his encyclopedic *Chronicle*: "Those who are hanged elsewhere are drived out of Strasbourg with rods." In fact, Franck himself was expelled from Strasbourg (not hanged or beaten with rods, but nevertheless expelled) in December of 1531 for having published the *Chronicle* there.

Sebastian Franck

Sebastian Franck was one of a large group of religious dissenters, famous and not so famous, who resided in Strasbourg for varying lengths of time in the 1520s and 30s. Among the Anabaptist leaders who, at one time or another, were present in the city we may name Hans Denck, Michael Sattler, Jakob Groß, Wilhelm Reublin, Jakob Kautz, Pilgram Marpeck, Melchior Hoffman, Johannes Bünderlin, and Christian Entfelder. The list of non-Anabaptist radicals who were in Strasbourg for varying lengths of time is equally impressive: Andreas Karlstadt, Otto Brunfels, Martin Cellarius, Louis Hätzer, Caspar Schwenckfeld, Sebastian Franck, Michael Servetus, and John Campanus. When we add to this list representatives of an indigenous radical movement (Clement Ziegler and Fridolin Meyger, for example), an unusually tolerant group of city clergy (Zell, Capito, Bucer), and a tolerant and deliberate city council we begin to appreciate why such an unusual breadth of reforming views was represented in Strasbourg, at all levels of the social and political spectrum.

Dissenters

The beginnings of Anabaptism in Strasbourg no longer can be identified in the sources, although it is supposed that there were small groups of Anabaptists in the city already by late summer of 1525. With the fall of Waldshut in December and increased persecution in Zurich and elsewhere, refugees began to arrive in earnest. Among the first to be noted in the record was Wilhelm Reublin–former preacher in Basel, then radical

Reublin

preacher to the peasants in the Zurich district and Hallau, part of the Grebel circle, baptizer of Balthasar Hubmaier, and later involved (for a time) in communal Anabaptism in Moravia. Reublin stayed in the home of Jörg Ziegler, a tailor whose house would remain an important meeting place for Anabaptists. Reublin was not the originator of this small group, but rather came to visit a group already functioning.

Although there was a report in July 1526 that preachers were subjected to insults when they baptized infants, the preachers were hopeful that the Anabaptist movement was on the wane. But in November Hans

Denck

Denck arrived, followed by Ludwig Hätzer, Jakob Groß and Michael Sattler in quick succession. Of these Hans Denck was the most active, and disturbed the city's preachers the most. He quickly gained a significant gathering in the city to the point that the reformers felt directly threatened. Following a private disputation in Capito's home with Cellarius, a public disputation was held on December 22, 1526 with the city's clergy, in front of 400 interested citizens. Martin Bucer carried the debate for the Strasbourg preachers. Denck was both irenic and evasive. The result was that Denck was banished from the city and left December 25.

Radical Variety

There were emerging Swiss Anabaptist conventicles in Strasbourg just prior to the composition of the Schleitheim Articles (February 24, 1527). They operated primarily among the craftspeople of the city. There were furriers, tailors, tanners, coopers, weavers and cobblers involved. Michael Sattler associated with this group of people. There were, in addition, persons who had associated more closely with Hans Denck and Ludwig Hätzer, such as the notary Fridolin Meyger, who continued to organize meetings in the city. And finally, local grass roots reformers like Clemens Ziegler continued their activity. But the lines of division between the grass roots radicals still were not firmly established. Clemens Ziegler (who never became an Anabaptist) was present at one Anabaptist meeting where a baptism took place, and continued to host Anabaptist meetings; Jörg Ziegler claimed that he had been asked to lodge Anabaptists by Capito and Hans

Denck. One would have to agree with Müsing's observation that "the boundaries between the various groups were fluid" and probably not clearly visible to the participants themselves in early 1527. Likewise the clergy were not of one mind as to how to deal with the various dissenting groups and individuals. Capito's vacillation and Bucer's growing determination point to either end of the spectrum.

The city council, while not yet declaring itself on doctrinal questions, based its actions on the principle that civic order and peace were to be maintained. On July 27, 1527, half a year after Zurich had drowned Felix Mantz for being an Anabaptist, the Strasbourg authorities promulgated their *first* decree against any who might reject a Christian government and destroy the unity of the community. With characteristic leniency, the penalties for disobedience to the mandate were not specified, but were to be applied in each particular case. In light of increasingly harsh measures being taken elsewhere, this mandate encouraged, rather than discouraged the arrival of even more religious refugees.

Toleration

The boundaries and lines of division between the various radical groups in Strasbourg, including those between Anabaptists of differing tendencies, became increasingly visible from 1527 to 1533. Likewise by 1533, with the convening of the territorial synod, the city had consolidated its position doctrinally and with respect to the dissident groups in Strasbourg.

The year 1527 saw a continuation of Anabaptist meetings in the city, the most notable of which revolved around Fridolin Meyger. Meyger, closely associated with Denck and Hätzer, was baptized by Jakob Kautz most probably in the latter half of 1527. The meetings involving Meyger and many others took place at the two syphilis hospitals and in Meyger's own home, and resulted in some expulsions. In the summer several hundred Anabaptist refugees from Augsburg came to Strasbourg, responding to

Fridolin Meyger

the increasing repression there. Among these refugees were followers of Hans Hut.

Michel Ecker

An interesting mix of the visionary "Hutian" element and more sober Swiss emphases is represented by the Anabaptist Michel Ecker, a cutler who had been exiled from Sterzing in South Tirol and resufaced in Strasbourg. He professed nonresistance and refused to swear oaths, but also offered to share his visions with the Strasbourg preachers and the council. They were not particularly interested in his revelations. He testified that every Sunday he and some 250 others would gather for worship at Fridolin Meyger's house.

Pilgram Marpeck

In September 1528 Pilgram Marpeck became a citizen of Strasbourg through the purchase of citizenship. His Anabaptist convictions and concerns for social justice led him to associate with Fridolin Meyger and Lukas Hackfurt, the latter of whom was responsible for poor relief.

These interests led to Marpeck's arrest in October 1528 for having allowed a meeting of Anabaptists in his house. Arrested along with him were Meyger, Reublin, and Kautz, the latter two of whom had returned to Strasbourg in spite of having been banned earlier. Meyger recanted and swore an oath at this time. Reublin and Kautz would not, and remained in prison.

The record is silent concerning Marpeck's fate. Perhaps he was pardoned, for in his defense he argued that the meeting had taken place in order to help the many poor refugees that were to be found in the city, and there is no record of further hearings with him concerning this arrest. In any case he soon was in the employ of the city, supervising the purchase of forest land, the cutting of trees, and the construction of dams to transport the wood to Strasbourg. Perhaps his usefulness as a city engineer kept him out of prison.

Reublin and Kautz

The arrest of Reublin and Kautz sheds some interesting light on how these two Anabaptists, representing the Swiss and Denckian streams respectively, understood each other in late 1528. In spite of some recognized differences–Reublin said that he did not agree with all of Kautz's points–nevertheless in January 1529, after some two and a half months spent in prison together, they composed a joint confession, written in the first person plural.

It would not be long, however, until the lines of division between the more literal Swiss Anabaptists and the more spiritualist group–implicit already in Sattler and Denck and visible, though not divisive, in Reublin and Kautz–would be drawn clearly in Strasbourg. The year 1529 saw the arrival of Hans Bünderlin, Christian Entfelder, Sebastian Franck, and Caspar Schwenckfeld. All of them were, or soon became, defenders of a more spiritualized Christianity.

Spiritualism

The move away from external Anabaptism to spiritualism by Bünderlin and Entfelder echoed Hans Denck's repudiation of divisive external ceremonies just before his death in Basel. Bünderlin and Entfelder, both former Anabaptist leaders of some repute, brought to light a fundamental tension present in the theological underpinning of Anabaptism as a whole.

Tension

Simply put, if the essential baptism is spiritual, to which the water is only a witness, and if the essential Supper is also spiritual and the physical elements are incidental, why should mere ceremonies be observed–particularly since they are non-essentials that only serve to divide believers from one another? To this challenge Pilgram Marpeck responded with two booklets written in 1531: *A Clear Refutation* and *A Clear and Useful Instruction.*

Lending weight to these spiritualist defections from Anabaptism in Strasbourg were Sebastian Franck and Caspar Schwenckfeld, both of whom were influential radical leaders and prolific writers. The spiritualist option was presented in a variety of appealing ways in the year 1529 and following. It was made all the more attractive by unrelenting persecution, growing division within Anabaptism, and the spiritualist root at the heart of Anabaptism itself.

It was into this rich and volatile setting that Melchior Hoffman came in the summer of 1529. Hoffman developed yet a third expression of Anabaptism which, although it incorporated adult baptism, the ban, and a memorial Supper, nevertheless placed these church ordinances in a visionary, apocalyptic context. From Hoffman would originate all of the Anabaptism of North Germany and the Netherlands, as will be described in the chapter to follow.

Strasbourg after 1533

By 1533 the Strasbourg council and preachers set out to define their reformation in the face of the varied challenges posed by the religious dissidents in their midst. The end result of several synodal sessions in 1533

was the emergence of Martin Bucer as the pre-eminent pastor in Strasbourg– "the bishop of our church" in the words of Capito–and the consolidation of the civic reformation in the city. The council now had the mandate to regulate not only law and order in the city, but also matters of church doctrine and discipline.

By 1533 the boundaries dividing Anabaptist groups from each other also were increasingly visible. The Anabaptist Hans Frisch, who lived in the city from 1529 to 1534, described the Anabaptists in Strasbourg as divided into three distinct groupings:
    –those following the teachings of Hoffman (Melchiorites)
    –those following the teachings of Kautz (spiritualists), and
    –those following the teachings of Reublin (Swiss Brethren).
He added that the Hoffman and Kautz groups were "a little mixed together."

Strasbourg remained a tolerant city, and remained an Anabaptist centre that was important especially to small numbers of Swiss Brethren in the 1540s, after Bucer managed to win over the Melchiorite leaders Georg Schnabel and Peter Tasch, and most of their following, in 1538 and 1539.

Conclusion

In spite of distinct Swiss and South German origins, the story of early Anabaptism is a story of mutual influence and interaction. Swiss Anabaptism, given its stronger emphasis on the literal word of Scripture, proved less susceptible to divergent interpretations than did South German Anabaptism. South German Anabaptism, in spite of its rootage in late medieval mysticism, certainly did not develop in any one predictable direction. The continuation of a militant Hutian line and a spiritualist Denckian line points us back to ideological differences in emphasis between Denck and Hut. The emergence of a moralistic, sectarian, and communitarian stream points us to Swiss Anabaptist influences on the South German movement. The biblicistic and ethically oriented Anabaptism of Rinck reminds us that strong leaders shaped Anabaptist essentials according to their own understanding and predispositions, regardless of who baptized them.

This not to deny differences among early Anabaptists, but to say that in actual practice many differences were overlooked in the early communities. In Nicholsburg differences led to schism. In Augsburg they led to compromise. In Strasbourg they led from peaceful cohabitation to the eventual separation of Anabaptist groups from each other. But in all these cases the initial Anabaptist communities had fluid boundaries and were composed of brethren of different Anabaptist orientation and origins.

These tensions did not last. By 1530 Anabaptists were defining their borders more and more strictly in their relationships with one another, according to increasingly specific criteria. In 1530 yet another powerful voice would be added to the divisive chorus when Melchior Hoffman began preaching his Anabaptist message.

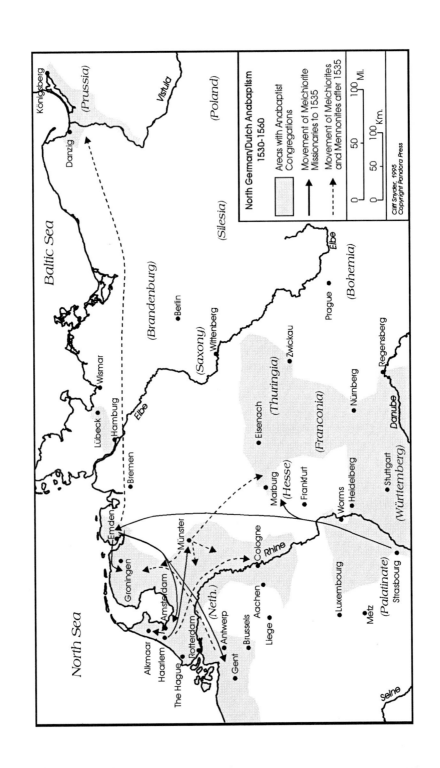

North German/Dutch Anabaptism
1530-1560

Areas with Anabaptist
Congregations

Movement of Melchiorite
Missionaries to 1535

Movement of Melchiorites
and Mennonites after 1535

Mi.
0   50   100

Km.
0   50   100

Cliff Snyder, 1995
Copyright Pandora Press

Baltic Sea

North Sea

(Prussia)

Königsberg
Danzig
Vistula

(Poland)

(Silesia)

(Brandenburg)

Berlin
Wittenberg
(Saxony)

Prague
(Bohemia)
Elbe

Wismar
Lübeck
Hamburg
Elbe
Bremen

Emden
Groningen
Alkmaar
Haarlem
The Hague
Rotterdam
Amsterdam
(Neth.)
Antwerp
Gent
Brussels
Aachen
Liège
Luxembourg
Metz
Strasbourg
(Palatinate)

Münster
Cologne
Rhine

Marburg
(Hesse)
Frankfurt
Worms
Heidelberg
Stuttgart
(Württemberg)

Eisenach
(Thuringia)
Zwickau

(Franconia)
Nürnberg

Regensberg
Danube

Seine

Chapter 11

The Origin and Spread of
North German/Dutch Anabaptism

The Anabaptism of North Germany and the Netherlands can be traced to the overwhelming influence of one man, who stamped the northern movement with very discernible features. That man was Melchior Hoffman, and his brand of Anabaptism proved to be both fruitful and unstable. His conversion to Anabaptism in 1530 and his evangelistic work up to his imprisonment in May 1533 mark the first phase of North German/Dutch Anabaptism.

Melchior Hoffman was born between 1495 and 1500 in Schwäbisch Hall. He became a furrier by trade, but he was also literate in German, enthusiastic about religious issues, and a persuasive and powerful speaker. (1)

By 1523 Hoffman was active as a Lutheran lay missionary in Livonia (1523-26). The work of the Holy Spirit was centrally important to Hoffman already in his early years as a Lutheran lay reformer, and it appears that Karlstadt was more influential for him than was Luther. His ministry concentrated on the poor, and had strong anticlerical tones, with resulting social unrest and violence in the city of Dorpat.

> *(1) Obbe Philips describes Melchior Hoffman.*
> "This Melchior was a very fiery and zealous man, a very smooth-tongued speaker who was celebrated for his great calling and commission..." *(SAW, 208).*

Hoffman's attraction to apocalypticism also was evident in his early work. He preached that the Holy Spirit was being poured out on all people. The two witnesses of the Last Days (Elijah and Enoch) were already present in the world, he believed. Nevertheless, he taught that the sword was to be used only against evil doers, and not in the church.

Hoffman also came to believe in the progressive divinization of human beings: the spiritual battle was an inner one. What was needed was spiritual yieldedness (*Gelassenheit*), so that God could do what God willed, and so re-make the human being.

Salvation

It is clear, in retrospect, that Hoffman would have problems remaining in the Lutheran camp. "At once justified and a sinner" did not fit Hoffman's understanding of regeneration and salvation, nor did predestination fit very well either. The background to Hoffman's teaching on *Gelassenheit* was the medieval mystical tradition, the Theologia Deutsch, and Andreas Karlstadt.

Hoffman's career as a "Lutheran" was a rocky one. He missionized for a time in Stockholm, and then moved on to Schleswig-Holstein (1527-29). His open break with the Lutheran reformers came in the matter of the Lord's Supper. Hoffman finally denied a real presence of Christ in the elements. Following a disputation in April, 1529, after which Hoffman was banished, his break with the Lutheran stream was complete. Lutheran clergy now were added to the list of false prophets. Henceforth for Hoffman, Lutheranism was a "new popery."

Following a brief work in East Frisia in the Spring of 1529, Hoffman moved south to Strasbourg, where he came into contact with several varieties of Anabaptism and spiritualism. As noted above, present in the city were groups of Swiss Brethren, spiritualist followers of Hans Denck, followers of Pilgram Marpeck, the spiritualist Caspar Schwenckfeld, and a group of enthusiastic disciples of Hans Hut. Hoffman felt an affinity for the Anabaptist prophets and visionaries. (2)

Prophecy

Visible in the writings Hoffman published in Strasbourg in 1530 was a preoccupation with prophetic Scripture and contemporary prophecy. Hoffman later would be responsible for publishing the visions of Ursula Jost, which dealt with the End Times. These visions were destined to have a large impact in North Germany and Holland. Hoffman was convinced that God was speaking directly through such contemporary prophets, and his congregations always included numerous prophets and visionaries, with roughly an equal number of both men and women.

It is particularly difficult to identify specific Anabaptist influences on Hoffman, for he seems to have appropriated elements from different theological streams, as they suited him. We do not know who baptized him, but it is clear that he joined no existing group in Strasbourg.

> **(2) Barbara Rebstock's vision, confirming that Hoffman was the prophet Elijah, returned for the Last Days.**
>
> *"She saw a white swan swimming in a beautiful river or watercourse, which swan sung beautifully and wonderfully. And that, she interpreted to apply to Melchior as the true Elijah. She had also seen a vision of many death heads on the walls around Strasbourg. When she wondered whether Melchior's head was among them, and she tried to see, she became aware of Melchior's head, and as she gazed upon it the head laughed and looked at her in a friendly way. Thereafter she saw that all the other heads came alive, one after the other, and they all began to laugh..." (Snyder and Hecht, 1996, 278).*

Rather, he formed his own. Nevertheless his first Anabaptist writing, *The Ordinance of God* (1530), emphasizes the same Anabaptist distinctives noted elsewhere in the movement:

Anabaptist

–sinners are called to unite with Christ through repentance and water baptism

–baptized believers celebrate the Supper of unity (understood in a memorial sense)

–believers submit to and practise discipline within the community of the covenant.

Hoffman's teachings on the sword and government, so crucial to later developments in Münster, are hard to unravel, since he blended together elements that tended to fly apart. Hoffman's reading of biblical prophecy led him to the view that the ungodly clergy would be done away with before Christ's return. On the other hand, along with this lively expectation of the imminent destruction of the ungodly mob, Hoffman also taught that the saints (individual Christians) were *not* to take up the sword. Apparently God would find other means of destroying the ungodly than

Sword

through the direct participation of the elect. On still another front, when it came to political authority, Hoffman taught that there would be pious political rulers who would be God's instruments in bringing about the final victory of the saints. Hoffman maintained this view of political authority to the end.

Ambivalence

The ambivalence visible in Hoffman's drastic anticlericalism, his rejection of the sword for individual saints, his prediction of the extermination of the ungodly before the second coming, and his expectation of holy intervention on the part of godly authorites proved to be problematic later. Hoffman's Anabaptist followers resolved the ambiguities in his views in a variety of ways, not all of them peaceful.

By April of 1530 the authorities in Strasbourg had heard enough and decided to arrest Hoffman, but he managed to leave town one step ahead of the police and re-surfaced in the north, in the city of Emden. He is said to have baptized 300 in the church in Emden. Much as did Hans Hut earlier, Hoffman baptized persons who became zealous evangelists and baptizers of others. In both cases the expectation that Christ's return was imminent seems to have provided a special impetus for evangelism.

The way for Anabaptism in the Lowlands had been prepared by the sacramentarian movement, and Anabaptism very quickly became a mass movement of religious resistance. From the Emden beginnings, Hoffman's

Netherlands

version of Anabaptism spread into the Netherlands, where it was to have its greatest success. Among those baptized as a consequence of Hoffman's journeys to the north were Jan Volkerts Trijpmaker, Sikke Snijder, Obbe Philips, Dirk Philips, Bartholomeus Boekbinder and Pieter de Houtzager.

But in December 1531, disaster struck when the Melchiorite apostle, Jan Volkerts Trijpmaker, was put to death along with nine others. Hoffman was shaken, and he suspended water baptism. The Melchiorite movement in North Germany and the Netherlands went underground.

Hoffman himself remained at large, working both in Strasbourg and in the north, until May of 1533, when he allowed himself to be arrested in

Strasbourg. In effect, he turned himself in. He believed the prophecy of a Frisian man, who predicted that Hoffman's arrest would trigger the events of the Last Days. Melchior Hoffman died in the Strasbourg prison some ten years later, still waiting.

Along with Melchior Hoffman's Anabaptist spiritualism and apocalypticism, his turn to Anabaptism in 1529 also resulted in a novel Christology that remained a discernible feature for almost a century among the Anabaptists of the Netherlands. As we noted above, the spiritualist Caspar Schwenckfeld appears to have provided Hoffman with the basic elements of this Christology, although Hoffman and Schwenckfeld differed on some details.

Christology

Hoffman's Christology remained the most visible heterodox Anabaptist teaching. It remained a point of contention inside and outside of the Anabaptist movement for many decades. Menno Simons defended Hoffman's view to his dying day. We will return to Melchiorite Christology in some detail in chapter 18 below.

The Melchiorite Anabaptist movement took strong root, particularly in the cities of Amsterdam, Leeuwarden and Groningen; the East Friesland region in the far north was strongly Anabaptist from the start. The province of North Holland, directly north of Amsterdam, was soon evangelized (the cities of Alkmaar, Hoorn, and Enkhuisen) and Anabaptist conventicles and martyrs appear in this region beginning in 1534. Anabaptism also moved south to Zeeland, Flanders and Brabant (with the city of Antwerp as an important Anabaptist centre) around 1534. And of course, outside the Netherlands proper, in nearby Westphalia, the city of Münster grew to become the Anabaptist focal point in the north in the years 1534 and 1535.

Jan Matthijs of Haarlem

Soon after Melchior Hoffman was imprisoned in Strasbourg in 1533, the Melchiorite baker Jan Matthijs began his prophetic activity in Amsterdam, initiating a second distinct phase of development in Melchiorite Anabaptism.

Led by direct dreams and visions, Matthijs reinstated baptism. He claimed the authority to do this because he believed himself to be the prophet Enoch of the Last Days.

The baptism which Matthijs resumed was reminiscent of Hans Hut's conception. Hut, Hoffman and Matthijs interpreted Anabaptist baptism in the sense of the TAU, following Revelation 7:3: a mark of the 144,000 elect.

Matthijs's message had three central components:

–This is the time of the working of the Spirit

–God is about to return and judge

–those who are baptized will be spared.

Among those baptized by Matthijs and sent out as apostles was Jan van Leiden, later to become the proclaimed "King of Münster and the world."

Jan Matthijs disagreed with Melchior Hoffman on some basic issues. On the question of the measure of obedience due the authorities (especially tyrants) and the role of outside "godly authorities" generally,

Matthijs leaned toward action on the part of the saints, as opposed to waiting for God or pious magistrates to act. Matthijs became convinced that God had given the sword to the elect, particularly after the Anabaptists won a political victory in the city of Münster.

Matthijs's conviction that he was the Enoch of the End Times also ran counter to the view in Strasbourg. Both Hoffman and Barbara Rebstock were convinced that Cornelis Poldermann was Enoch. (3)

---

(3) Barbara Rebstock has a vision confirming Cornelius Polderman as Enoch.
"She also saw a vision that occurred in this manner. She saw in the vision a great drawing room or beautiful salon, grand and stately, and full of brethren and sisters all sitting properly around the room in a row. And there stood a youth in the middle with a white garment draped about him. And he had in his hand a golden chalice full of strong drink and he went along the row from one to the other offering each the chalice, but no one could touch the drink, so strong was it. At last he came to one brother named Cornelius Polterman, who was Melchior's disciple. He took the chalice from the youth's hand and drank from it before all. This ... was interpreted to mean that Cornelius Polterman would be Enoch." (Snyder and Hecht, 1996, 278-79).

Finally, Matthijs was convinced that Münster, not Strasbourg, was the true New Jerusalem to which Christ would return. With Hoffman held increasingly incommunicado in the Strasbourg jail, Matthijs' interpretations came to be more and more accepted in the north.

To all accounts, Jan Matthijs possessed impressive persuasive and dramatic powers. Obbe Philips recalled that the brethren needed to be convinced and "became obedient" to Matthijs after "much negotiation." (4) Matthijs soon became prominently involved in the reform of the city of Münster.

(4) Obbe Philips recalls how Matthijs convinced the brethren that he was Enoch.
"He carried on with much emotion and terrifying alarm, and with great and desperate curses cast all into hell and to the devils to eternity who would not hear his voice and who would not recognize and accept him as the true Enoch." (SAW, 214).

Bernhard Rothmann and Münster

Parallel to events in the Netherlands were the reforming activities in the city of Münster in Westphalia. The leader of the reforming party there was Bernhard Rothmann.

Rothmann was born around 1495 in Stadtlohn, received a master's degree from the University of Mainz, and by 1529 had begun to preach the evangelical gospel just outside Münster. By 1531 there were acts of iconoclasm in his church which caused problems for the Münster city

| *Conflict*

council. The situation in Münster was not unlike that of many other Reformation cities. There were three social groups at odds: the ruling class of patricians who controlled the city council; the Guilds (popularly based) who wielded increasing power; and the clergy (headed by the Catholic bishop).

The first effects of the Reformation were anticlericalism and iconoclasm. Attempts to silence Rothmann did not work, primarily because the city council found such pressure advantageous in its struggle against the privileges of the Catholic clergy. The Bishop was forced to acknowledge the Reformation (the Treaty of Dülmen, 1533) and the laity came to exercise authority in the city. But it was not yet clear which party of the laity would gain control, that is, the privileged patricians, or the guilds. This situation gave Rothmann the power of leverage. In general, Rothmann leaned more in the direction of the guilds. With the arrival of Heinrich Rol, he had also received a Zwinglian conception of the Supper.

| *Heinrich Rol*

Heinrich Rol was an ex-Carmelite who came to Münster as an evangelical preacher following the council decision to make Münster an evangelical city. In his view, the sacraments were to function as the instruments for building the Christian community, not as the means for dispensing grace.

When Rothmann also began leaning in this "Zwinglian" direction it posed a political problem for the city of Münster, for being located in northern Germany, and with Lutheran neighbours, Münster needed

Lutheran allies against the Catholic bishop. Futhermore, Rothmann and his fellow evangelical preachers began questioning infant baptism and recommending adult baptism, although they had yet to take the step of instituting the practice.

The city council saw clearly that this Reformed/Anabaptist theology-in-the-making was severely limiting the political options open to the city. By 1533 there was an open struggle among three groups: the remaining Catholics (now outnumbered), the Lutherans (supported by council), and the reformed followers of Rothmann (backed by the guilds). Observing this situation in May of 1533 was an interested onlooker and visitor to the city, Jan van Leiden, who had been baptized by Jan Matthijs earlier in the year.

By January of 1534 the situation had become a tense stalemate, exacerbated when Rothmann, Rol and other leading figures accepted rebaptism from Bartholomaeus Boeckbinder and Willem de Kuyper. Anabaptism already was an imperial crime punishable by death, and the effect was to isolate the city even more within the broader political context.   *Baptism*

By the time Jan van Leiden arrived in January of 1534, sent as an apostle of Jan Matthijs, some 1,400 people already had accepted rebaptism in the city, including nuns who had left their cloister and accepted baptism. The tide within the city had shifted in favour of the Anabaptist faction. Those within the city who were most concerned to maintain the city's independence from the prince-bishop came to support the Anabaptist party as the best option under the circumstances.

The elections for city councillors of February 23 fell to the Anabaptists—Bernhard Knipperdolling was one of two burgomasters elected. Many political opponents already had left the city, and the die was already cast, since the bishop had set up military headquarters in the nearby town of Telgte in preparation for a siege. On February 24, Jan Matthijs himself entered Münster, claiming prophetic authority, and three days later the bishop began the siege of Münster. On that same day, Feb-   *Elections* ruary 27, 1534, all non-baptized inhabitants of Münster were forced either to leave, or to accept rebaptism.

It is estimated that out of a population of 7,000 to 8,000 people in Anabaptist Münster, approximately 5,000 were from the city itself, with about 2,400 immigrants, plus a few hundred professional soldiers fighting for the city. Around 300 men and 2,000 women were forced into accepting adult baptism against their will. The Anabaptists were to hold the city for sixteen months.

| Sword |

On the question of the sword, historians have asked when and how Melchior Hoffman's teaching of peace for individual believers was abandoned. Karl-Heinz Kirchhoff has demonstrated that a key historical eyewitness to the Münster events falsified his account in defence of the bishop's military actions, positing the existence of a violent Anabaptist group in Münster already in early January 1534.

Kirchhoff has demonstrated that the original Anabaptist group in Münster was predominantly pacifist in the Melchiorite sense, and that an aggressive crusading mentality was brought into the city by Jan Matthijs. It was Matthijs who, first of all, wished to slay the "ungodly" still left in Münster; it was Knipperdolling who voted for the more moderate course of explusion. It also was Matthijs who insisted on the forced baptism of all who were to remain. As for the Münsterites themselves, political and End Times motives combined to lead them to the "militant theocracy" they came to support. (Kirchhoff, 1970).

| Matthijs |

Following Jan Matthijs' arrival in Anabaptist Münster, Bernhard Rothmann's role within the city diminished. He now assumed the role of propagandist for the New Jerusalem under the leadership first of "Enoch" (Jan Matthijs), and then under "King" Jan van Leiden, defending the taking of the sword of righteousness and, in a later phase, polygamy.

The tragic result of the Münsterite establishment of the New Jerusalem is too well known to need much elaboration here. The city soon was established according to the guidelines seen in Acts, including the forcible institution of community of goods, with deacons appointed for the care of the poor. Those who would not listen to the prophet Jan Matthijs were to be expelled from the city. He preached with confidence that the second coming of Christ would take place, at the latest, by Easter 1534. On the fifth of April, Easter Day, citizens lined the city walls in expectation of viewing the spectacle of God destroying the heathen. In what was perhaps an act of desperation, Jan Matthijs eventually decided to sally forth with a few companions, confident that God would come to their aid. He was quickly hacked to pieces and his head paraded on a lance by the besieging soldiers.

With the death of Jan Matthijs the way was clear for Jan van Leiden *Jan van Leiden* to assume power within the city. His credentials were not impressive: he was a tailor, a salesman, and an amateur actor, all of 24 years of age. Nevertheless, he claimed that God had told him in a dream that he was to be Jan Matthijs' successor, and such was his personal charisma and ability that he managed to assume that role.

In July of 1534 he married Matthijs' widow Divara, and began instituting other changes in the city's organization, primarily along Old Testament lines. By the end of that month he had instituted polygamy within *polygamy* the city (in which women now outnumbered men by a good margin). There was some resistance on the part of women who were not willing to participate in the arrangement, and some resistors were put to death. Jan van Leiden himself eventually took sixteen "concubines" as well as his "leading wife," Divara. In September of 1534 a prophet in the city proclaimed Jan to be "King over the New Israel and over the whole world." King Jan now took on the role of the "new David," King of the righteous and castigator of the unrighteous.

The persistent call from Münster in 1534 and 1535 for other Anabaptists to come and be a part of the New Jerusalem had a profound effect on the Melchiorite movement in the Low Countries. It appears that the majority of Anabaptists in the north in fact supported the Münsterites, with a minority dissenting from the violent turn of affairs. Added to the difficult economic conditions of the time, persecution of Anabaptists had begun in earnest in the Netherlands in 1534. One can only imagine the strong appeal of the Münsterite message "Flee out of Babylon ... for this is the time of the Lord's vengeance"–a message directed precisely to persecuted folk living in difficult economic conditions.

| *Migration to Münster* |

In March of 1534, many thousands of people from North and South Holland answered the call to assemble near Hasselt in the province of Overijssel, where a prophet of God was supposed to be present to guide them to the New Jerusalem of Münster. Many travelled by land, and more by sea. Some twenty-seven boats with 3,000 men, women and children arrived at the designated place on March 24. The unfortunate pilgrims were met by officers and soldiers, who had been forewarned. There was no armed resistance, although some of the pilgrims had arms and far outnumbered the government officers. The majority of the pilgrims were sent home. There also were a few executions.

Other Melchiorites in the Netherlands became more aggressive, especially as the siege of Münster wore on and agents from Münster participated more actively in mustering armed resistance. Some three hundred Anabaptists managed to take over the monastery of Oldeklooster in Friesland in March of 1535 and held it for a week, finally succumbing to an all-out military attack. At least half lost their lives.

| *Menno Simons* |

This episode strongly affected Menno Simons, who was a priest in neighbouring Witmarsum at the time. It is possible that Peter Simons, who perished in the Oldeklooster attack, may have been Menno's brother. Jan van Geelen, the Münster emissary responsible for leading the Oldeklooster adventure, planned an attack on the Amsterdam city hall for May 10, 1535. Only forty local Anabaptist supporters participated in the abortive attack, the end result of which was increased persecution by the authorities and, back in Deventer, the arrest and martyrdom of Fenneke, van Geelen's wife.

Back in Westphalia, after two failed assaults on the city, the Bishop decided on the more expensive expedient of a total blockade. This was

successfully accomplished, and by April of 1535 the situation inside the city was desperate. There was so much hunger that is was said that some people were eating grass. It is not known how many men, women and children died of starvation and disease in the beleaguered city, but it is estimated that in the three months prior to the taking of Münster, between 600-700 men lost their lives attempting to flee.

The final taking of the city began June 25, 1535. It was made possible through the betrayal of the city by two of its citizens, and initiated a two day bloodbath. The stench in the city was said to be overwhelming, and the thousands of dead eventually were buried by neighbouring peasants. Rothmann's body never was identified, and he may have managed to escape the slaughter. If so, he never re-appeared in the historical record. Jan van Leiden was paraded around the countryside for show, and finally in January 1536 he, Bernhard Knipperdolling, and Bernd Krechting were publicly tortured for hours with red-hot tongs and eventually executed before the cathedral. Their remains were hung from the tower of St. Lamberti Church in three iron cages.

*The three cages still hang from
the tower of St. Lamberti Church*

Melchioritism after Münster

After the fall of Münster, the Melchiorite movement in the north entered a third phase of its development. This phase began with the disintegration of the Melchiorites into several factions, identified by James Stayer as follows:

1. The pacifist group, critical of Münster, gathered around Dirk and Obbe Philips and David Joris.

2. Followers of Jan van Batenburg in the Netherlands, who continued to wield the "sword of righteousness."

3. Münsterite refugees in Westphalia grouped around Heinrich Krechting.

4. Rhineland and Hessian Melchiorites led by Georg Schnabel and Peter Tasch.

5. The remnants of the Melchiorites in Strasbourg, gathered around Lienhart Jost.

The first attempt to gather these groups together was undertaken by David Joris, who emerged as the most important Melchiorite leader in the days immediately following Münster's collapse.

For the purposes of this survey we will first trace three post-Münster Melchiorite tendencies through their leaders, namely the Münsterite continuation led by Jan van Batenburg, the spiritualist solution offered by David Joris, and the "Obbenite" group that gathered eventually around Menno Simons. We will conclude with an overview of the geographical spread and theological development of Dutch Anabaptism in the period from 1535 to ca. 1600.

Jan van Batenburg

Jan van Batenburg joined the Melchiorite movement in April, 1535, while Münster was still under seige. Following the collapse of the New Jerusalem, he gathered around him frustrated Münsterites who still cherished the hope of punishing the ungodly with the sword of vengeance.

The Batenburgers lived a secret existence, no longer baptizing converts but plundering churches, burning crops, and occassionally executing the "ungodly." Although van Batenburg was arrested and executed in 1538, unrest of this type continued sporadically in Westphalia and the Netherlands. Some held the hope that in 1540, God would intervene and re-establish Münster again as the New Jerusalem, raising all the dead Münsterites from the grave and destroying the godless with heavenly fire.

Banditry

As late as 1580 Jan Willems, a follower of Batenburg's disciple Cornelis Appelman, was burned at the stake. He had led a band of terrorists, reprinted Rothmann's *Restitution*, and had taken twenty-one wives. The crusading ideals expressed at Münster, while no longer at the centre of the Melchiorite movement, lingered on here and there for a surprisingly long time.

David Joris

David Joris, along with Dirk and Obbe Philips, had been one of the few Melchiorite leaders opposed to the crusading interpretation of the Münsterites during the height of excitement in 1535.

In the summer of 1536 at a meeting of Melchiorite leaders at Bocholt, Westphalia, David Joris emerged as the most important leader of the post-Münster Melchiorites. His approach was conciliatory, emphasizing points of unity rather than points of difference. In fact, as Gary Waite has demonstrated, a listing of active Anabaptist leaders from 1536 to 1540 shows Davidjorist leaders far outnumbering competing groups. In the years immediately following the collapse of Münster, Davidjorist leaders outnumbered "Obbenite" leaders five to one.

Leadership

Joris' mediating approach stressed the message that the visible kingdom would come into being sometime in the future, as a result of God's action, rather than there being a visible kingdom established in the here and now by human agency, as had been attempted by the Münsterites and was being continued by the Batenburgers. Joris' spiritualized pacifism allowed that Christians could be government authorities although, like Hoffman, he held that the authorities should be tolerant of religious differences and not interfere in the affairs of the church.

Joris' preeminence in post-Münsterite Anabaptism up to 1539 is undeniable. However, although Joris won a leadership victory at Bocholt in 1536, in 1538 he failed to convince the Strasbourg Melchiorites of his spiritual authority. This marked the beginning of the end of his dream to unite actual and erstwhile Melchiorites under his prophetic leadership.

Spiritualizing

David Joris continued to spiritualize his message to the point that eventually he was content to drop all external signs of Anabaptism. By 1544 he had disappeared from the Netherlands, re-appearing in Basel under a pseudonym. He died there in 1556, in complete anonymity, although his movement continued in his absence into the next century.

Menno Simons

Menno Simons became an Anabaptist leader in the wake of the disastrous events of Münster. Menno (b. 1496) had been ordained a Catholic priest in 1524 at Utrecht and served in the parish of Pingjum near Witmarsum. His path to reform began with doubts about the sacramental

Sacramentarian doubts

claims relating to the Lord's Supper. According to his later account his doubts had begun almost immediately, but it took him twelve more years to move first to a sacramentarian position, then to the evangelical position, and finally to Melchiorite Anabaptism. He did not leave the Catholic priesthood until 1536.

Two of the most important leaders of the non-Münsterite branch of Melchioritism were the brothers Obbe and Dirk Philips. It was this pacifist Melchiorite wing that Menno eventually would join. Menno says that he had begun questioning the biblical basis for infant baptism following the martyrdom of the Anabaptist Sicke Freerks Snijder in 1530.

He said later that he had found no word in Scripture concerning infant baptism. Nevertheless, he preached against the Münsterite kingdom during 1535, but in January 1536, he suddenly left the priesthood and "sought out the pious," either in Leeuwarden or Groningen.

He received baptism at the hands of Obbe Philips, and married   *Baptism* Gertrude, who would accompany him until his death in 1561. They became parents to two daughters and one son. He was ordained an elder sometime early in 1537, again by Obbe Philips, and began a tireless mission of reorganizing the scattered Melchiorites. By 1542 the authorities had put a price of 100 guilders on his head but miraculously, in spite of constant travel and a life spent underground, Menno never was betrayed or apprehended.

Menno Simons clearly was not a Münsterite, but he was just as clearly a *Melchiorite* Anabaptist. The most visible evidence of this was Menno's adoption of Melchior Hoffman's "celestial flesh" Christology–a position he   *Christology* defended (with growing reluctance) until his death (see chapter 18 below). Menno also stood well within the Melchiorite tradition in his view concerning political authority. Menno died a natural death at Wüstenfelde in January, 1561.

Dirk Philips and Leenaert Bouwens

Two younger leaders were to play central roles in the development of Dutch Anabaptism, beginning around 1550. Dirk Philips and Leenaert Bouwens were particularly instrumental in promoting a strict church discipline–an emphasis which resulted in a series of church splits and divisions among the Anabaptists of the north.

Dirk Philips, younger brother of Obbe Philips, was born in 1504. One source identifies him with the Franciscan Order prior to his joining the Anabaptists. He was baptized at the height of the Münster episode, in December 1534 or January 1535, by Jan Matthijs' emisary, Pieter Houtsagher.

Soon after Dirk's baptism, Houtsagher participated in a spectacular event: he and several others ran through the city of Amsterdam with unsheathed swords, proclaiming the day of the Lord. Houtsagher was arrested and then executed in Haarlem.

Not much is known of Dirk's activities following the fall of Münster, but he clearly had sided with his brother Obbe and formed part of the non-Münsterite, pacifist Melchiorites. He probably was active in and around Emden.

Leadership

Beginning in the mid-1540s, Dirk took on a more prominent leadership position. He was present at the debate with the Davidjorist, Nicolaas van Blesdijk in 1546 and soon emerged as a central figure in the controversies surrounding the elder Adam Pastor and the question of the proper form of maintaining church discipline (chapter 16 below).

Leenaert Bouwens (1515-1582) became an Anabaptist at an unknown time. He first appears in the historical record as a minister who attended the Lübeck conference in 1546. He was ordained an elder by Menno Simons in 1551. He was present at the conference that adopted the "Wismar Articles" in 1554.

Evangelism

Although he lived near Emden, Bouwens developed an amazing itinerant ministry stretching from Antwerp to Danzig. He kept a detailed record of his activities from 1551 to 1582 which is still extant. It records an astounding number of baptisms–10,386 individuals baptized by Bouwens alone, in 182 different locations, in the space of 31 years.

In spite of the valuable leadership qualities of both Dirk and Leenaert, both men were strict disciplinarians, which contributed to dissension and division among the Anabaptists in the Netherlands.

The Development and Spread of Dutch Anabaptism

As was also the case in Swiss and South German Anabaptism, there were evident differences in emphasis and practice among the North German/ Dutch Anabaptists before, during, and after the Münster episode, particularly regarding the matter of the sword, and the question of the spirit and the letter.

Nevertheless, there were also evident similarities and fundamental points of coincidence. It was on the basis of these commonalities that David Joris managed to forge a temporary pan-Melchiorite agreement at the Bocholt conference of 1536. The militantly Münsterite faction (Batenburgers, followers of Bernd Krechting) represented a minority grouping that faded slowly but surely from the scene, especially after the death of Batenburg in 1538.

The followers of David Joris, on the other hand, were more numerous and influential immediately following Münster, and remained a strong Anabaptist force until at least mid-century. Joris' move to Basel under a pseudonym weakened his movement in the Netherlands, however, and after 1540 the "Mennist" party gained ground steadily. After 1550 the followers of Menno comprised the undeniable majority of North German and Dutch Anabaptists, with the competing factions in decline.

The geographical spread of Anabaptism in the Netherlands can only be described in cursory fashion. In spite of the Münsterite experience, there continued to be a hidden Anabaptist presence in Westphalia. In neighbouring Hesse, a Melchiorite faction led by Peter Tasch and Georg Schnabel gathered followers alongside the original Anabaptist followers of Melchior Rinck. East Friesland (especially the city of Emden and its vicinity) and Groningen remained strong centres of Anabaptism throughout the sixteenth century. Not only did leaders like Menno, Dirk Philips, and Leenaert Bouwens find refuge in these northern territories, but many thousands of Anabaptist refugees also fled there when persecution became intense in other areas. In spite of persecution, Amsterdam remained an Anabaptist centre throughout some difficult years of persecution. These ended in 1578 with the taking of Amsterdam by Prince William I. He extended toleration, and the Anabaptists there entered a "golden age." Many Anabaptists also lived in North Holland throughout the sixteenth century.

South Holland

The situation in South Holland, or what is present-day Belgium, followed a different pattern thanks to the political situation there. In Flanders and especially in the city of Antwerp, Anabaptism grew very rapidly in the 1530s and 40s. It was countered by edicts enforced by the imperial government resident at Brussels. There was a constant flow of emigration from Flanders not only to the northern Netherlands, but also to London.

From 1553 to 1565, Leenaert Bouwens' remarkable ministry also reached Flanders, where he baptized many hundreds. The increased repression in the south that began in the 1550s resulted in the emigration of many Flemish Anabaptists, and the relocation of many more to other parts of Flanders. The eventual takeover of the southern provinces by a Catholic regime (1585) led to much more emigration, especially to the northern Netherlands, and the virtual extinction of Anabaptism in Flanders. Some of the cultural differences between the Flemish Anabaptist refugees and their Frisian Anabaptist hosts contributed later to the stubborn Flemish/Frisian Anabaptist schism.

Lower Rhine

In the area of the lower Rhine, in Cologne and the surrounding territory, there had been Anabaptists since the early 1530s. Menno Simons himself missionized in this area beginning in 1544, as did Dirk Philips. It was especially along the Rhine that Swiss Anabaptists moved north and met North German/Dutch Anabaptists moving south. Beginning in the 1550s there was increased interaction between these two groups. In 1555 a meeting took place in Strasbourg between Swiss and Dutch representatives in an effort to resolve the christological differences between them. In 1557 Swiss leaders met again in Strasbourg and this time the main topic under discussion was the ban.

It remains to mention the steady spread of Dutch Anabaptism in the far north, along the Baltic coast to the east into Schleswig-Holstein, Mecklenburg, and into the Vistula Delta and the city of Danzig. The Hanseatic cities, located as they were along well-travelled trade routes, also came to have Anabaptist congregations. Hamburg, Lübeck, Wismar and Rostock all had a documented Anabaptist presence by the 1530s.

Baltic Coast

Further east, estimates are that some 3,000 Dutch refugees, the majority of whom were Mennonites, came to Danzig and East and West Prussia from 1527 to 1578. The link with the Netherlands was provided by Dutch shipping that connected the cities of the Baltic coast with the port cities of the Netherlands. This general eastern migration of Dutch Anabaptists would continue into the next century, culminating in the settlement of Mennonite emigres in Russia late in the 18th century.

Conclusion

North German/Dutch Anabaptism, as this survey shows, was grounded in the Anabaptism of Melchior Hoffman. Swiss Anabaptism played no discernible role in its origins. South German Anabaptism played a role only insofar as it was mediated through Melchior Hoffman himself.

Melchior Hoffman's teaching included a strong preaching of repentance, rebirth, and a new life, an emphasis on the End Times, the possibility of direct revelations in dreams and visions, and the expectation of the physical punishment of the ungodly. His spiritualist emphasis and concern with the atonement resulted in his holding an unorthodox, docetic Christology which was passed on and accepted in Dutch Anabaptism.

Like Hans Hut, Hoffman expected suffering to be the lot of true believers, until God brought about the restoration, soon to occur. Unlike

Hans Hut (who had no great hopes in the magistracy, and hoped rather that the Turks would execute vengeance on the powerful), Hoffman expected godly rulers to be God's instrument of vengeance. Hoffman's radical followers soon went beyond both Hut and Hoffman and embraced an aggressive, crusading activity on behalf of God's restoration.

Much as was the case in South German Anabaptism, the discernible point of origin of the North German/Dutch Anabaptist movement is not in doubt. Nevertheless, Melchior Hoffman's Anabaptism proved amenable to wide interpretation, variation, and change, depending upon individuals and circumstances. The story of North German/Dutch Anabaptism after the fall of Münster is a story of competing Melchiorite points of view and emphases, vying for the support of the same group of people. It also is a story of increasing interaction, as the century wore on, with other Anabaptist groups.

Chapter 12

Anabaptists and Scripture:
An Overview

Anabaptist Testimonies Concerning Scripture

Balthasar Hubmaier, Zurich Disputation concerning the Mass (1523)
"If they are commanded, show us the Scripture and there will be no more question. If they are not commanded, then they should not exist. For everything which God has not taught us either with words or deeds should not be and is in vain." (Harder, 1985, 241).

Balthasar Hubmaier, *On the Christian Baptism of Believers* (1525)
"Although I also do not reject tongues or languages for the exposition of dark passages, still for the sun-clear words one needs neither tongues nor lungs." (Pipkin and Yoder, 1989, 99).

Balthasar Hubmaier, *Theses ... concerning the instruction of the Mass*
"The Spirit makes us alive, and the Spirit comes with the Word." (Pipkin and Yoder, 1989, 75).

Hans Denck, *The Law of God* (1526).
"The one who has received God's new covenant, i.e., in whose heart through the Holy Spirit the Law was written, is truly just. Whoever thinks he can keep the Law by following the good Book ascribes to the dead letter what belongs to the living spirit. He who does not have the Spirit and presumes to find it in Scripture, looks for light and finds darkness, seeks life and finds utter death, not only in the Old Testament but also in the New..." (Furcha, 1975, 59-60).

Hans Denck, *The Law of God* (1526)
"He who honors Scripture but lacks divine love must take heed not to turn Scripture into an idol as do all scribes who are not 'learned' for the kingdom of God." (Furcha, 1975, 63).

Hans Hut, "Of the Mystery of Baptism"
"No man can come to salvation, save through suffering and tribulation which God works in him, as also the whole Scripture and all the creatures show nothing else but the suffering Christ in all his members." (Rupp, 1969, 386).

Hans Hut, "Of the Mystery of Baptism"
"God's commandment does not consist in the letter but in the power which the Spirit gives..." (Rupp, 1969, 386).

Melchior Hoffman, *Weissagung usz heiliger götlicher geschrifft...* (1530)
"God the almighty does nothing that he has not revealed beforehand and given in secret through his prophets."

Melchior Hoffman, *Ordinance of God* (1530)
"For all words of God are of equal weight, also just and free, to him who acquired the right understanding of God and the Key of David. The cloven claws and horns (only) the true apostolic heralds can bear, because (to explicate) the Scripture is not a matter for everybody–to unravel all such involved snarls and cables, to untie such knots–but only for those to whom God has given (the power)." (SAW, 202-03).

Melchior Hoffman, *Prophetische Gesicht und Offenbarung der goetlichen würckung zu dieser letsten zeit...* (1530).
"Discerning the spirits is not something for anyone, but rather a particular office of God and his Holy Spirit."

| **Consensus, Difference, and Development** |

Was there a specifically Anabaptist way of reading and interpreting Scripture (an Anabaptist hermeneutics)? Based upon the survey of Anabaptist origins above, the answer will have to be "yes and no." There were both commonalities, and differences, in the way the earliest Anabaptists read and interpreted the Bible. And, there were changes and developments over time. We can mark three distinct phases in the development of Anabaptist hermeneutics.

1. A common core. Anabaptism became a movement because of *agreement* on the meaning and centrality of a core of biblical texts relating to church reform. These common texts and interpretations defined the movement as Anabaptist. We will review this scriptural core briefly below.

2. Disagreement and development. The common core of biblical texts provided a point of departure for church reform, but there were differences in approach *from the start*. The collected citations above demonstrate the fact. These interpretive differences became increasingly divisive as Anabaptists tried to work out practical answers to real life problems.

Anabaptist differences were worked out in the period from 1525 to ca. 1560. We will detail those various views, disagreements, and developments in the next major section of this study. Although Anabaptists agreed on the importance of some foundational texts, it is also true to say that Anabaptism became a movement *in spite of* significantly different interpretive approaches.

3. Consensus and agreement. On the far side of interpretive differences lay a narrower consensus and eventual agreement on an interpretive approach, as well as agreement on practical questions relating to discipleship and church practice. We will outline this interpretive and practical tradition in the chapter 19 below.

A Common Core

It is possible to overemphasize difference in telling the Anabaptist story, particularly if one concentrates on the second, developmental phase of Anabaptism. It bears repeating that the baptizing movement became a movement because there was a core of *agreement* concerning what the Bible required of believers. The core of Anabaptist beliefs surveyed in chapter 8 above reflects Anabaptist agreement concerning what were the essential biblical texts defining a reformed church.

Salvation

First, the early Anabaptists maintained that the biblical order concerning salvation was that teaching (hearing the Gospel), repentance, and faith (all the work of the Holy Spirit) *must* precede water baptism, and that water baptism and a commitment to a new life *must* follow hearing, repentance, and faith.

(1) "Much Scripture even in the New Testament called for evangelical obedience and if God called for it, Anabaptists argued, it must be his will and it must be possible to do it. Works were the outward expression of faith and not simply the fruit of faith as Luther had said." (Klaassen, 1982, 42).

The Anabaptist understanding of salvation, as entailing both faith and obedience, was not limited to one Anabaptist tendency or region, but can be seen clearly in all Anabaptists, from Hubmaier, to Sattler, Denck, Hut, Hoffman, Rothmann, and Menno. A variety of scriptural texts were used to argue the point, but a text commonly cited was James 2:17: faith without works is dead. (1)

Along with the insistence on the principle that faith would lead to visible works came also agreement concerning the biblical works that would mark the true, reformed church.

Baptism

In the first instance, the fundamental biblical texts concerning adult water baptism were those relating the Great Commission of Jesus to the disciples, first to teach, and then baptize all nations (Matthew 28:18ff.; Mark 16:15ff.).

In the second place, the Anabaptists agreed that in Matthew 18 they had found the biblical church polity that would lead to a properly reformed, disciplined church. They believed that sin must be admonished and corrected, leading either to repentance and readmittance, or expulsion of the unrepentant. The church had to be a visibly reformed and visibly "pure body."

Ban

Third, Anabaptists agreed that those who had repented, believed, and been baptized on their confession of faith, and who thereby submitted to the community discipline of the ban, were to celebrate a memorial Supper together, symbolizing and pledging again their commitment to each other and to God. I Corinthians 11:23, with its warning about celebrating "unworthily," was an especially significant Bible verse for the Anabaptists.

Supper

Fourth, baptized believers would share generously of their earthly goods with other members of the Body of Christ (the church), according to the general pattern described in the Acts 2 and 4.

Mutual Aid

There was widespread agreement among Anabaptists of all kinds (implicit if not explicit) that at least on these points the Spirit had illuminated the letter of Scripture and had outlined the proper order of salvation and structure for a reformed church. Agreement on these biblical boundaries of belief and church practice marked all Anabaptists.

However, as we will see in more detail below, there were also interpretive differences from the start that continued to cause the Anabaptists trouble. Granted that the Spirit had to inform the reading of the letter, just how was that Spirit *interpreting* the letter in specific cases? There was, it is fair to say, considerable dissension on this question until later in the sixteenth century.

A crucial developmental aspect of the Anabaptist story is the working out of more precise scriptural interpretive principles. We will trace some of these developments in the sections that follow.

The Spirit and the Letter

Anabaptist testimonies from all regions emphasized that without the baptism of the Spirit there could be no understanding of the letter of Scripture.

In this important sense there were no strict literalists among the Anabaptists. The democratic tendencies and the anticlericalism seen in Anabaptism were rooted in the expectation that the Holy Spirit would inform the reading of the letter of Scripture. The first mark of an Anabaptist approach to Scripture, then, was an emphasis on the activity of the Spirit in any true reading of Scripture. Although there was agreement that all true biblical interpretation had to be led by the Holy Spirit, there was no consensus on how far the influence and activity of the Holy Spirit extended in the interpretive process.

Pure Life

In the second place, the Anabaptists believed that a true interpreter of Scripture is known by the outward witness of that interpreter's life. Anabaptists sounded a late medieval reforming note when they critiqued pastors who claimed to be preaching the truth, but nevertheless continued to live dissolute and undisciplined lives.

Negatively expressed, this attitude could be called anticlerical. Positively expressed, the same attitude pointed to the Anabaptist insistence that inner regeneration and the presence of the Holy Spirit must produce visible, outward fruit. In the absence of such good fruit there was reason to question the presence of the Spirit. And without the Spirit, there could be no true interpretation of the Bible.

Thus there were visible demonstrations of the presence of the Spirit that had to be manifested by those who were interpreting the letter of Scripture.

These spirit/letter and inner/outer tensions marked the outer boundaries of the Anabaptist approach to Scripture. But tremendous questions remained within those boundaries.

–Does the letter of Scripture stand in judgment over the spirit, or should the order be reversed?

–How is Law related to Gospel; the Old Testament to the New?

–Does the Holy Spirit of the Last Days speak extra-biblically?

–Who is competent to decide the truth of spiritual and scriptural revelation: illumined "apostles," biblically learned teachers, congregations?

–Are there specific good fruits that give reliable evidence of the presence of the Spirit, and thus of a trustworthy interpreter of Scripture?

These interpretive questions were debated within Anabaptism as the movement struggled to define its spiritual and biblical path of reform.

When leading Anabaptist representatives are plotted along a spirit/letter continuum, three positions emerge which in some ways do, and in other ways do not parallel the regional differences noted by polygenesis historiography: the more literally oriented approach; the more spiritualistic (mystically oriented) approach; and the prophetic apocalyptic approach.

Letter over Spirit

From the start there were Anabaptists who emphasized the priority of letter over spirit–although they always affirmed the need for the spirit. Representative leaders who held this position included first generation Swiss Anabaptists (e.g., Conrad Grebel, Michael Sattler, Balthasar Hubmaier), first generation South German Anabaptists (e.g., Melchior Rinck), second generation South German Anabaptists, specifically from the Hutterite group (e.g., Jakob Hutter, Peter Riedeman), and later Melchiorite Anabaptists in the Netherlands (e.g., Menno Simons).

Developmentally speaking it is significant that the Swiss maintained an early literal emphasis throughout, while the Hutterites and Melchiorites grew into that view out of spiritualist and prophetic apocalyptic origins. By the late sixteenth century there would be a strong congruence between the Swiss, Mennonite, and Hutterite approaches to Scripture, but the paths that led there were not the same.

It must be noted further that among these more literal-minded Anabaptists the work of the Holy Spirit was not rejected. Rather, these Anabaptists tended to limit the working of the Spirit to what was verifiable (or sometimes, communicable) in and through Scripture.

Literalist Principles

Some basic principles of interpretation were outlined by the Swiss Anabaptists at an early stage. One central exegetical principle, seen already in 1524 in Conrad Grebel's writings and visible also in Hubmaier, was that the reform of the church and the Christian life had to be ruled by what Scripture had *commanded*. The principle that "whatever has not been expressly commanded in Scripture is forbidden," led to a closely literal exegesis of biblical texts which in the end came to define the Swiss Anabaptists.

However, it is important not to lose sight of the fact that among the early Swiss Anabaptists there was a *progression* toward a more literal exegesis that began with appeals to the direct working of the Spirit. The Anabaptist sources from the Zurich area reveal that many of the first Swiss Anabaptists, some of them baptized by Grebel, appealed to direct revelations of the Spirit.

A second interpretive principle that played a central role in the Swiss Anabaptist movement was an emphasis on the New Testament over the

New Testament Old. The words of Scripture were all words of God, but they did not carry the same weight or significance in guiding the life of believers. The Bible was not thought to be "flat." The Old Testament had been superseded by the New, and within the New Testament Christ's words and example were definitive.

This principle also emerged eventually in the Hutterite and Mennonite traditions, as will be noted later.

In the question of the spirit and the letter, Balthasar Hubmaier stood very much in the Swiss Anabaptist tradition, emphasizing strongly the letter of Scripture, although he too appealed to the working of the Spirit in the believer. In fact, Hubmaier held together the working of the Spirit to the hearing of the outer word. Although he taught that the working of the Spirit was necessary for regeneration, "the Spirit comes with the Word." For Hubmaier, the external word, written and preached, was the means by which the internal Word chose to work.

Hubmaier

Although Hubmaier disagreed with some other Swiss Anabaptists concerning the sword of government, as we will see in more detail in a later chapter, he had no basic disagreement with other Swiss Anabaptists on questions of how to interpret Scripture. Along with other Swiss Anabaptists, Hubmaier rejected all practices not explicitly commanded in the Bible (but especially in the New Testament), primary among which was the baptism of infants.

It must be noted that the more literal reading of Scripture was simply an interpretive *approach* that provided no guarantee of particular ethical results. If we take the question of the sword as an example, we see that the literal interpretive emphasis had a variety of historical results among the Anabaptists:

Sword

(a) a defence of Christians taking the sword (Hubmaier)

(b) a moderate acceptance of the possibility of rulers also being Christian (Menno)

(c) a strict division between nonresistant followers of Jesus and all others (Sattler, Riedeman)

(d) a rigorous biblicistic ethic of following New Testament commands (Grebel).

It is not historically accurate to say that the central *Anabaptist* hermeneutical principle was the priority of the New Testament over the Old. This principle did emerge early in the Swiss Anabaptist movement, but took considerably more time to be accepted in other regions, where other principles of scriptural harmonization were applied.

Spirit over Letter

Among the earliest Anabaptists there were also individuals who stood at the other end of the spirit/letter continuum, who emphasized the higher importance of the Spirit (the inner Word) over the letter (the outer word)—although as long as they remained in the Anabaptist camp they never denied the need for the letter of Scripture.

In this "spiritualist" grouping we find Margret Hottinger, Hans Denck, Leonard Schiemer, Hans Schlaffer, Jakob Kautz, Hans Bünderlin, and Christian Entfelder. All of them were baptizers in a more spiritualistic, mystical mode.

Margret Hottinger, Leonard Schiemer and Hans Schlaffer died as Anabaptist martyrs. Hans Denck, Jakob Kautz, Hans Bünderlin, and Christian Entfelder, on the other hand, abandoned the outward ceremonies of Anabaptism and moved on to a more inward, personal religion. Hans Denck is a particularly good representative of this latter group of spiritualist Anabaptists.

Hans Denck

The Testaments On the question of the relationship of the Testaments, Hans Denck set the tone for this group of Anabaptists. On his own testimony, Denck valued the "inner Word" above the "outer word." On the spirit-letter continuum, Hans Denck stood at the opposite extreme from Grebel, Sattler, and Hubmaier.

For Hans Denck and those in the spiritualist stream, the harmonization of the Old and New Testaments was resolved, in the first instance, by a higher spiritual unity beyond the letter. The spiritualist Anabaptists thus appeared to hold to a "flat" Bible, in which the Old and New Testaments were of equal value. Nevertheless, for Denck and the others there was a higher spiritual law which led them to value the New Testament over the Old in practical matters relating to the Christian life. It is *Christ*, said Denck, who has revealed the fundamental spiritual principle that underlies both Testaments, and this principle is the divine spirit of love.

There was to be a visible separation from the world for Denck and the spiritualistic Anabaptists in their baptizing periods. This separation was marked by water baptism and maintained by the ban, and so marked a division between "the children of God and the children of the world." But the temptation was always strong for the spiritualist Anabaptists to simply emphasize the "essential" inner life, sometimes to the exclusion of the outer symbolic marks of the church.

Separation

Hans Denck's fundamental principle was not obedience to visible ordinances commanded in Scripture, but rather obedience to the inner working of the spirit of Christ within each human being. Denck's hermeneutics was oriented to the principle of Christocentric love, not to a literal "following after Christ" (*Nachfolge Christi*).

Love

Hans Denck's well-known saying, that "the medium is Christ whom no one can truly know unless he follows him in his life," demonstrates the interrelationship he maintained between the inner Word and ethical behaviour. But in the end, when it appeared that the outward signs separating the church from the world were leading to legalism, and hindering more than helping, Hans Denck and other spiritualist Anabaptists simply left the baptizing movement behind.

Pilgram Marpeck

One is tempted to create a further category for Pilgram Marpeck, for he fit somewhere between the literalist and spiritualist poles described above, and shared important emphases with each. Marpeck was influenced initially by the "transitional" South German Anabaptists, Schiemer and

Schlaffer. He continued to share with them an appreciation for the ultimate nature of the inner, spiritual life. In his criticisms of the more literalistic and legalistic Anabaptists, Marpeck would have recourse to the spiritualistic principle. On the other hand, he vigorously opposed a spiritualism that wished to abandon the symbolic, outer marks of the church.

Pilgram Marpeck always worked to maintain a balance between spirit and letter, and carried out vigorous disagreements with more extreme representatives of both of the above tendencies, as we will note in more detail in chapters to follow.

Prophetic Spirit and Prophetic Letter

Virtually all of the early Anabaptists, including the earliest Swiss Anabaptists, were convinced that they were living at the very end of history, and that Christ was about to return. Nevertheless, for some of the early Anabaptists, this conviction provided the interpretive framework for reading all of Scripture. Scripture, as Melchior Hoffman put it, contains the secrets of history encoded in and behind its words.

Visions

Since the Last Days were to take place in the age of the Spirit, these Anabaptists expected to receive spiritual revelations (dreams, visions) and considered them to be complementary to prophetic scriptural revelation. Among Anabaptists of this tendency are found the important Anabaptist leaders Hans Hut, Melchior Hoffman, Jan Matthijs, Bernhard Rothmann, and David Joris. We will look in more detail at Hut and Hoffman here, as representatives of this interpretive tendency.

Hans Hut

Hans Hut's own writings contain few examples of his full exegetical method, primarily because he met his death after finishing only his book on baptism, the first of seven detailed writings that he had planned. But we find direct evidence of Hut's approach to Scripture in the testimonies of his

followers. Hut derived what he called "seven judgments" from Scripture,
which he taught only to full initiates. The seven judgments were:

> 1) The Covenant of God: (Gospel, faith and baptism)
> 2) The Body of Christ (Supper)
> 3) The End of the World
> 4) Concerning judgment and the future of God
> 5) The resurrection of the dead
> 6) The Kingdom of God
> 7) Eternal judgment (punishment of the damned).

These judgments were considered to be a summary of all biblical teaching
in both Testaments, apparently revealed directly by the Spirit of God to
Hut.

According to Hut's own testimony, the Christian of these Last Days
was to act in accordance with the divinely revealed prophetic calendar and
a prophetic (Spirit-led) reading of the "signs of the times." And, according
to Hut's biblical calculations, Christ would return sometime before Easter,
1528.

Although the Swiss Anabaptists also believed that they were living in
the Last Days, Hut's prophetic spiritualism played an interpretive role in
his reading of Scripture that is not seen in the Swiss stream. Although Hut
at times sounded much like a Swiss Anabaptist, emphasizing the union of
believers into one body with Christ at its head, his primary emphasis was
not on a separated church following strict biblical guidelines, such as many
of his followers would soon develop. Rather, Hut was primarily concerned
to gather together the elect who would be the Bride of Christ when the
Lord returned within a few months. His ethics was governed by his understanding of the End Times calendar.

The seventh seal is opened, four trumpets sound, and an angel announces "woe, woe, woe" to the inhabitants of the earth.
Revelation chapter 8.

Melchior Hoffman

Melchior Hoffman's approach to Scripture, like Hut's, focused on the prophetic books of the Bible and a setting of dates for the return of Christ. Hoffman also put the spirit/letter question in an apocalyptic context, and he also emphasized the activity of the Holy Spirit in the Last Days. After 1530, probably under the influence of Hut's followers in Strasbourg, Hoffman also accepted extra-biblical prophetic revelation as authoritative.

The most notable feature of Melchior Hoffman's interpretation of Scripture is, without a doubt, his allegorical and figurative method of interpreting biblical texts in relation to the signs of his times. Klaus Deppermann observed that Hoffman's figurative reading could mean either a typological or an allegorical reading. In a typological reading, certain pairs are bound together in meaning, e.g., Melchisedek and Christ. In an allegorical reading, the spiritual meaning of a past event is linked to a present reality, e.g., the Exodus is linked with the salvation of the soul, or the Temple of Solomon with the Church. Hoffman was not very precise in his application of such distinctions, but the figurative method allowed Hoffman and his followers to range widely beyond the strictly literal text, and then to apply the resulting "biblical" insights to contemporary events.

Interesting as Hoffman's figurative reading of Scripture was, it must be noted that he was in essence a preacher of repentance. At the heart of Hoffman's preaching of repentance stood the Gospel message of Christ's atonement for human sin, which all apostolic messengers were to preach. Through Christ's perfect satisfaction, and by means of the proclamation of the Gospel by "apostolic messengers," God's grace and forgiveness was extended to all human beings. It remained for them only to accept that grace, repent, yield to God and enter into a new life.

Repentance

A scriptural theme to which Hoffman returned often was the "pure fear of God" which he saw as the necessary first step–and a necessary continuing step–in the saving process. Hoffman effortlessly collated scriptural references on this theme, from Isaiah to Malachi, Maccabees, and Matthew, and also made reference to numerous biblical characters as both positive and negative examples. Opposed to the pure fear of God was fear of the world, which was no more than idolatry, or the elevation of created things above the Creator.

Fear of God

By 1530, Hoffman had associated God's grace in Christ, the preaching of the Gospel, repentance, *Gelassenheit*, and the acceptance of Christ's sacrifice, with the baptism of believers. Even though Hoffman's debt to the late medieval mystical tradition is evident, his treatment of the scriptural themes of the two kingdoms, free will, repentance, regeneration, baptism, and salvation was straightforward, in no way peculiar, and thoroughly Anabaptist.

Baptism

Nevertheless, the way in which Hoffman set out to discover the "hidden" prophetic messages which, he was convinced, were to be found in Scripture, was less predictable. Building on his conviction that all the past, present, and future secrets of history were coded in the Bible, Hoffman set out to unlock "the door of the divine Word through the key of David."

Hoffman thought that since the future course of history had been hidden in prophetic Scripture, a figurative interpretation of all of Scripture–Old Testament as well as New–was possible for those who had been granted the spiritual "key" of interpretation. Those who held this "key of David" would be able to apply the principle of the "cloven hoof," which was the spiritual ability to explain and harmonize apparent contradictions and difficulties in Scripture.

The presuppositions behind Hoffman's interpretive method certainly were not foreign to the Anabaptism that preceded him. Anabaptists of all persuasions were convinced that they were living in the End Times. Hans Hut also had assumed that the secrets of history, particularly the events of the Last Days, were hidden in prophetic Scripture and waiting to be uncovered by those in possession of the Spirit. Likewise the view that the Spirit would be poured out in the Last Days was a common theme, as was the view that those led by the Spirit would be the true interpreters of Scripture.

What set Hoffman's scriptural approach apart was not the premise that the Spirit was directing his interpretive activity, but rather his amazing capacity to apply a figurative method of interpretation to Scripture passages that appeared, on the surface, to have no inherent relationship.

Typical of Hoffman's treatment of End Times texts is his exegesis of Revelation 16:17: "And the seventh angel poured out his vial into the air." Hoffman begins his exegesis of this passage by noting that "the Spirit of God" divides all peoples into four parts, like the elements, into parts that correspond to the Sea, the Earth, the Air, and Fire (or "Heaven").

This four-fold division corresponds, said Hoffman, to the different comparison that Christ made in Matthew 13(3ff.), in the parable of the sower. The "figure" for the rich and the proud is the earth covered in thorns, or in the book of Revelation, the sea; the figure for the ungodly or impious is the path, or the way side, which corresponds to the earth; the figure for the careless is the stony ground, which corresponds to the air;

and the figure for the children of God is the good ground, which corresponds to fire or heaven.

Having established all of this, Hoffman then exegetes the passage: the messenger of the Lord (the "angel" signifies a preacher of the Gospel in the last days) pours out God's Word (the vial that is poured out is the Gospel) into the air. This means that "the teaching of God's Word out of God's Spirit and through the spirit and courage of the teacher is poured into the hearts of the careless ones, and becomes air, or is compared to the birds in the air."

Hoffman's point, in the end, was far simpler than the path by which he chose to make it: those who are careless and not mindful of God will miss the last proclamation of the Gospel and the Spirit of God, to their condemnation. Examples of this kind of "figurative" exegesis in Hoffman's writings could be multiplied many times over, with little difficulty.

Also crucial to Hoffman's figurative interpretive framework was

The great winepress of God's wrath.
Revelation 14:19-20.
Images of impending judgment were powerful motivators in the sixteenth century.

his understanding of the different roles to be played by different members of the church. Since Hoffman expected the Spirit of God to be active in all believers, one might have expected him to support a church in which all members would have equal interpretive opportunity. But although earlier in his reforming career Hoffman had held such a view, in Strasbourg he

came to the conclusion that there were different spiritual offices within the church, each with its particular function. In descending order, these offices were: apostles, prophets, pastors, and regular members.

The apostles were the overall leaders, for they possessed the greatest spiritual gifts of interpretation and leadership. To the apostles was granted the power to "unravel" the mysteries of Scripture and the mysteries contained in contemporary dreams and visions. Concerning the interpretation of Scripture, Hoffman wrote:

> The cloven claws and horns [only] the true apostolic heralds can bear, because [to explicate] the Scripture is not a matter for everybody–to unravel all such involved snarls and cables, to untie such knots–but only for those to whom God has given [the power]. (SAW, 202-203).

Hoffman considered himself to be an "apostolic messenger," rather than a prophet. Nevertheless, the prophets served an extremely important function in his movement, since they directly conveyed the living words of God.

The Dreams and Visions of Ursula Jost

It is important to remember that Melchior Hoffman was convinced that he was standing *in continuity* with the biblical prophetic tradition, informed by the same Spirit of God that had informed the biblical prophets. It is therefore not surprising that prophetic dreams and visions came to play a role in the Melchiorite movement. The Strasbourg prophets were extremely influential, particularly the prophetesses Ursula Jost and Barbara Rebstock.

The visions of Ursula Jost were published by Hoffman in 1530. Besides the visions themselves, they do contain some interpretation of the visions by Ursula herself, and were prefaced and concluded by Hoffman.

They give us some insight into how visions functioned and were understood in the first phase of Hoffman's Anabaptist movement.

There is no good way, first of all, of conveying an adequate second-hand impression of the visual richness of Ursula Jost's visions, for they are panoramic, colourful, and full of exotic imagery in the manner of the book of Revelation. One reads of great wars, clouds dripping blood, rainbows, wreaths, toads, snakes, bishops, knights and virgins.

Nevertheless, the basic dramatic and narrative framework is easily grasped by the modern reader. Two kingdoms are at war with one another–the one clear, light, and good, the other murky, dark and evil. The recurring images of wreaths and rainbows (on the side of good) and dark warriors, fearsome creatures, and black pits (on the side of evil) have obvious symbolic meaning. Even when the exact interpretation of specific visions is hidden from us, taken as a whole Ursula's visions powerfully convey images of a titanic struggle between the Kingdom of God and the Kingdom of Satan, images of the impending judgment from God, and images of hope for the elect after times of suffering and persecution.

Two Kingdoms

Many of Ursula's visions are easily recognizable as elaborations on biblical themes. The power and providence of God reappear throughout, most often revealed in visions of God's ultimate judgment.

Judgment

In her fifty-seventh vision, for example, Ursula saw a powerful hand, holding a great rod. Although she asked what it might mean, no answer was given to her at the time. In her following vision, however, "the clarity of the Lord" asked her if she knew what the hand meant. "Then I answered and said: 'Oh Lord, how can I know if it was not explained to me?'" Then the Lord explained that the hand was "the strong hand of the almighty, the God of Israel, and He will wreak vengeance on all people, and if they do not better themselves, he will punish them severely."

Along with the themes of judgment and repentance, the images of the narrow way leading to salvation, and the broad road leading to destruction also appear several times, as does the theme of resurrection. The cross, needless to say, appears in numerous visions throughout.

Along with the biblical themes present in Ursula Jost's visions are particular emphases which also appear in Melchior Hoffman's own writings. There are at least two visions rejecting a sacramental understanding of the Supper and images, and several strongly anticlerical visions. The poor play prominent roles in several visions, sometimes as victims of clerical greed.

Anticlericalism   In her fourteenth vision, for example, Ursula saw a huge crowd of people hacking away at the earth, in heavy labour, with hoes. She then saw a huge crowd of "bishops and spiritual prelates and scribes (*Schriftgelehrten*)" all coupled together, standing and watching the workers work.

And there is judgment against the ungodly and idle clergy. In her twenty-first vision, Ursula saw a bishop brought along on a great chair, but then his head was split open and he was thrown into a dark pit.

As in Hoffman's writings, the Turks also make an appearance as the instruments of God's vengeance, as do the apostolic messengers who proclaim divine justice.

In short, the conceptual structure, biblical themes, and Melchiorite thematic emphases of Ursula Jost's visions place her solidly within the Anabaptist (and specifically Melchiorite) tradition. While the visual imagery is rich and sometimes overwhelming, the theological grammar standing behind the imagery can be read in Hoffman's own works.

There is no doubt that Melchior Hoffman and Ursula Jost both believed that these visions were directly revealed by God in the manner of biblical prophecies. Ursula, who appeared to have some doubts at one point, was reassured–in a vision of course–that she was not being deceived and that she would see great wonders and "the clarity of God." The Holy Spirit, they believed, had never closed the canon of Scripture. But what is striking, both in Hoffman's figurative exegesis and in the interpretations of

Ursula Jost's visions, is not that new revelations were added to Scripture, but rather the reverse. The "figures" extracted by Hoffman and the visons of Ursula Jost are often incredible, but the *meaning* extracted from them was surprisingly commonplace, in essential *continuity* with, and in reinforcement of, the biblical prophetic tradition.

What may we conclude about Melchior Hoffman's manner of interpreting Scripture? In the first place, Melchior Hoffman's exegetical method was not always figurative. The core of Hoffman's Anabaptist repentance theology was based on a straightforward, literal exegesis. Hoffman clearly placed the redemption of humanity through Christ at the centre of his concern.

Conclusions

In the second place, Hoffman's emphasis concerning the End Times needs to be read in the context of his preaching of two kingdoms, sin, grace, repentance, baptism and salvation. The nearness of Christ's return lent increased urgency to the message of salvation.

In the third place, for all its flights of fancy, Hoffman's figurative exegesis was not a pure spiritualism divorced from the letter of Scripture. To the contrary, Hoffman referred to Scripture at every turn, in bewildering profusion. The objection to Hoffman's figurative method of interpretation cannot be that he ignored the text of the Bible in favour of direct spiritual revelations, for he fairly devoured biblical texts.

What would cause trouble in the Melchiorite movement later were some key interpretive assumptions:

Problematic Assumptions

–The same Holy Spirit that coded prophetic Scripture, has now decoded it accurately for those in possession of the "Key of David."

–Decoded prophetic Scripture yields precise information about contemporary people and events.

–The Holy Spirit reveals God's will through the dreams and visions of contemporary prophets.

The first assumption led to an undeniable concentration on the prophetic books of Scripture (those in which the hidden could be brought to light); the second gave a sharp social, economic, and political relevancy to the prophetic secrets thus revealed; the third opened the door to all manner of prophecy, much of which proved to be mistaken.

Prophetic Spiritualism

If we return to the spirit/letter continuum, we see that in an important sense Hut, Hoffman, Matthijs, Rothmann and Joris must be classed with the spiritualists, while in another sense they also belong with the literalists.

On the side of the spirit, room was made for direct, extra-biblical prophecy. On the side of the letter, there was a marked preference for interpreting the prophetic and apocalyptic books of Scripture.

For Hut, Matthijs and Rothman, the acceptance of both extrabiblical prophecy and a preference for exegeting apocalyptic Scripture (Daniel, Esdras, Revelation) opened the door to varieties of acceptance of the sword of righteousness in the hands of the elect, as End Times events unfolded. Rothmann, as we will see in due course, came to locate more authority in the five books of Moses and the Prophets than in the New Testament. In this way he defended not only a holy crusade, but also polygamy in Münster.

Hut, Hoffman, Matthijs, Rothmann and Joris were radical spiritualists, but after their own fashion they also emphasized, read, and scrutinized the written letter of Scripture. This combination of prophetic spiritualism and prophetic biblicism was not "foreign" to the core of Anabaptist theology. It grew out of the combined biblical and spiritual emphases found there.

The core of Anabaptist beliefs, with its strong emphasis on the activity of the Holy Spirit, and the generally shared conviction that the Last Days had arrived, encouraged the growth of the prophetic/apocalyptic interpretation of Scripture. Hut, Hoffman, Matthijs and Rothmann (less so Joris) did not reject the letter in favour of spirit, but rather held spirit and letter together in their own particular ways.

<hr>

Conclusion

<hr>

The three Anabaptist interpretive tendencies and groups identified above interpenetrated at many levels and developed in different ways, over time, in different historical settings.

The Swiss Anabaptists happen to have reached an early consensus on a more literalistic, ethical interpretation of Scripture, with a decided emphasis on the New Testament witness to the life and words of Christ and the apostles. The spiritualistic and apocalyptic frames of interpretation did not become live issues for Swiss Anabaptist *hermeneutics*. This does not mean, however, that "Anabaptism" had settled interpretive questions at this early date. The South German/Moravian and North German/Dutch streams, for example, had to grapple with the spiritualist and apocalyptic interpretive tendencies for the better part of the century.

The major sections which follow will examine Anabaptist discussions and differences concerning political reality, socio-economic reality, and religious reform. These Anabaptist discussions had to do with Scripture, its spiritual interpretation, and its practical application.

We will see that the various positions we have noted above were subject to change over time, across the Swiss/South German-Austrian/North German-Dutch lines established by the polygenesis description. As the Anabaptist movement progressed along the road to self-definition some interpretive positions gained strength, while others faded from view. The apocalyptic and prophetic readings of Scripture and the signs of the times that characterized so much of the movement in the 1530s had faded to minority positions by the 1550s, and had virtually died out by the end of the century.

The most widely accepted Anabaptist interpretive position by the end of the century among all surviving Anabaptist groups, including the former Melchiorites, concluded that the letter must be the measure of the spirit.

C.
The Development of Anabaptism: 1525-ca. 1600

1.
Anabaptism
and
Political Reality

Chapter 13

The Sword and the Oath in Swiss and South German/Austrian Anabaptism

Hans Büchel, Aubsund hymn 46

"A new Christian song concerning these last frightening times, in which so many and various sects and false prophets are revealed, together with the bloody tyranny."

(7) ... A book was published at Worms in 1557 where highpriests and scribes gathered together and finally decided

(8) that those who taught anything against them should be judged by the sword and their blood should be shed.
Also those who would not go to their churches should be arrested...
Is this not a tyranny,
that one is made to confess
that the truth is a lie?

(9) Who has ever heard of such a thing, that one would convert Christians to God's Kingdom
with the sword? . . .

(10) . . . The Lord taught his disciples...
'They will bring you before the judges,
you will be slandered as I was
because of my name...'

(11) O pious Christian, in this battle
Faith and Love are what is needed,
and also Patience.
Give yourself over to God with wife and child,
from the heart, body and soul
and you truly will be granted
spiritual fruit...
You should meekly feed
the enemy who is doing you wrong.
Show mercy, oh my brother
to everyone,
just as your Father [in heaven] does."

Sebastian Franck's impression from Strasbourg, 1536.

"Some among them, but a very few, hold that if one is to be Christian, one should really not swear concerning anything, for whatever reason: neither for God's sake, nor concerning faith, nor for the sake of the neighbour out of love. They also maintain that no Christian can be a magistrate, to whom belongs the power of capital punishment or war, for Christians only use the ban and not the sword. They also hold that a Christian may not go to war or kill anyone, for any reason whatsoever. Michael Sattler, who was burned at the stake, was of this opinion and also those who followed him, but very few others.

The others, almost all of them, maintain that one may testify to the truth with an oath, if it furthers love or has to do with faith, and they draw on many examples from both Testaments. Hans Denck was of this opinion. This group grants that magistrates may be Christian, as long as they conduct themselves according to God's command, and that magistrates rightly use coercion and war, as long as they do not use it wilfully, but take it up out of need and obedience." Franck, 1536, cxcvii.

Testimony of Nikolaus Guldin at his trial, Esslingen, 1529

Guldin admitted that in the Anabaptist groups of his acquaintance, some had joined (infiltrated) who were against government authority. However, "when they noted that such people were among them, they had not stood for it, but rather they disciplined them with the ban, and excluded them. For their belief was to be obedient to the authorities in all things that were not against God." QGTS, II, #541, 439-40.

Hans Marquart, July, 1532

"The reign of the world is heathenish. Whoever wishes to come to the reign of God must climb down from the throne and humble himself, die to the old, heathen pride, and give himself over to God."
QGTS, II, #561, 466.

Felix Mantz, prison testimony, Zurich, 1525.
"Concerning civil authority he said that no Christian would kill with the sword or would resist evil."
QGTS, I, #124, 128.

Recantation Formula for Anabaptists, city of Basel (no date: 1520s?).
Anabaptists must confess under oath, first before the magistrates and then before the entire church community where they live, that it is proper "that the authorities wield the sword against evildoers, either against heretics (seducers) or for the protection of the holy faith."
STAZ, EI 7-2, #67 .

Government Mandate, Appenzell, April 4, 1548. TA,
"[All Anabaptists must swear an oath that they will] keep armour and weapons [in order to] defend the praise, honour and need of the land, and to turn away harm." QGTS, II, #313, 232-33.

Joerg Maler, second hearing, Augsburg, April 1550.
He returned to Augsburg (against his previous promise to stay out) because the Swiss were enlisting people as soldiers. He was expelled from Appenzell when he refused to be enlisted. He came to Augsburg in 1548.

   He was not in agreement with the Swiss Brethren concerning the oath: "Some brothers held that absolutely no oaths should be sworn or taken. He believed then, and does still, that a Christian may swear or take an oath, when it maintained justice or furthered the truth or served the needs and love of the brother."
QGTS, II, #323, 237-39.

Anabaptism and Political Reality

The potential relationship of Anabaptists to the political powers of the day was dependent upon factors both internal and external to the movement.

The core doctrines of Anabaptism did introduce real limits and challenges to the political status quo. A church composed of those who had freely chosen baptism as adults would not be a territorial church in any conventional, sixteenth century sense. So there was the corresponding external factor of government reactions to Anabaptism. What kind of political space, if any, would be made available for the practice of Anabaptism?

Internal Factors: Toward an Anabaptist Political Ethic

Looking first at Anabaptist teachings that impacted on potential relationships with governments, we can trace the development of a succession of doctrines and practices that increasingly moved toward a principled separatism.

There was first of all the requirement, universally shared by all so called Anabaptists, that baptism should be administered only to adults. This in itself, it turned out, was reason enough for sixteenth century political authorities to outlaw the baptizing movement. There would be those in any given political territory, perhaps many, who might choose not to be baptized, and no one knew what chaos or anarchy might result from such a situation. As long as Anabaptists were unwilling to abandon their defining principle of adult baptism on confession of faith they were in effect calling for uncoerced, voluntarily gathered believers' churches.

This internal, theologically limiting factor thus came face to face with the external reality of political life in the sixteenth century. If Anabaptism was going to occupy a legitimate political space, there had to be rulers who accepted the existence of such believers' churches in their territories.

Insofar as the core principles were upheld as necessary marks of the true church, the Anabaptist reform placed itself on the margins of what was acceptable politically in the sixteenth century, although that fact became increasingly apparent only over time. But there remained further internal points of clarification. Would Anabaptism move in a direction of *accomodation* with civil society and governments, or would it move in a direction of *separation* from them? Movement in either direction was possible. We know this because there were Anabaptists who did, in fact, propose adjustments in both directions.

Because of the almost uniformly negative reaction by political authorities to the core principles of Anabaptist reform, it appears in hindsight that a strong separatism was implied in Anabaptism from the start. But in fact, it is truer to say that Anabaptism as a whole *developed into* separatism. There were other roads taken and tried on the way to what eventually became a separatist tradition. The movement towards an Anabaptist tradition concerning church and government is the story that will concern us in this chapter and the next.

External Factors: Anabaptism and Political Reality

The largest political territory into which Anabaptism spread, if it may be called a territory, was the Holy Roman Empire, which in the sixteenth century included in its scope a good third of western Europe. But the Holy Roman Empire was not a centralized or coherent political territory. It was ruled by an Emperor who was chosen by seven electors. The so-called empire encompassed hundreds of territories, principalities, and cities of varying sizes, with a wide variety of freedoms and privileges.

With the election of Charles of the house of Hapsburg as the fifth Holy Roman Emperor (Charles V, emperor from 1519 to 1558), the Holy Roman Empire was added to Hapsburg holdings elsewhere. Seen on a map of western Europe, the political area controlled by the Hapsburgs has the appearance of a large sandwich, with strength on the outside, but

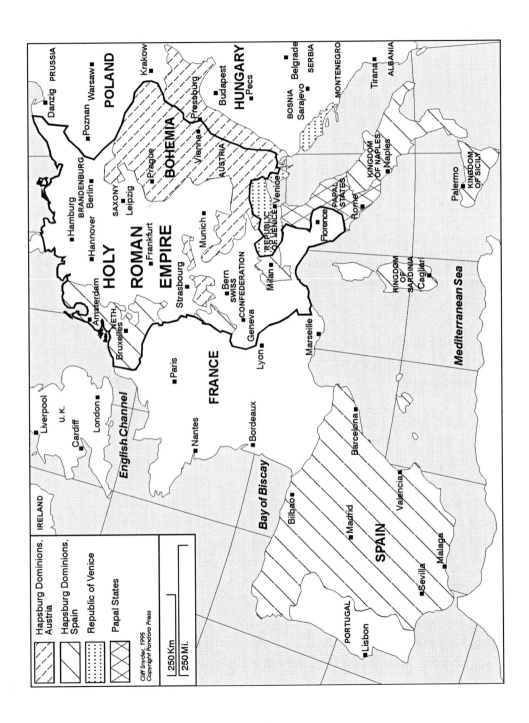

weakness in the middle, precisely in the Holy Roman Empire. Hapsburg political strength rested not in the Empire, but rather in Austria and Spain, the hereditary lands ruled directly by the royal house.

To the east lay the traditional Hapsburg Austrian lands. They were ruled by Archduke Ferdinand, brother of Charles V and later to succeed Charles as Holy Roman Emperor (1558-64). These lands had grown to include Moravia and Bohemia in the sixteenth century (over which the Hapsburgs worked to establish tighter political control).

The Austrian territories marked the eastern frontier of Christian Europe, for the Ottoman Turks had marched up the Danube and were threatening Vienna and the borders of Austria itself. The "Turkish threat" kept the emperor and his brother quite occupied militarily and strained financially. Hapsburg preoccupation with the Turks, in fact, provided crucial political breathing space for princes and cities intent on establishing Protestant reforms. As long as the Hapsburgs were occupied to the East, they couldn't enforce Catholic practice in dependent territories.

Further to the west were scattered Austrian territories and dependencies that included the Tirol and isolated territories located here and there in areas as far west as Württemberg and Alsace. Anabaptists could fall into Hapsburg hands (and be tried in Austrian courts) in places as diverse as Rottenberg on the Neckar, the Tirol, Austrian territory proper, Moravia, Bohemia, and of course, the Netherlands.

Far to the west lay the Spanish dominions of the Hapsburgs. They were ruled directly by Charles (known to the Spanish as Charles I). These territories included the southern part of Italy (the Kingdom of Naples) and the Kingdoms of Sicily and Sardinia in the Mediterranean.

Slightly further afield, the Spanish administration of the Hapsburgs also ruled over the Netherlands, including Luxembourg and what today is Belgium. This territory was politically more vulnerable, isolated as it was from other Hapsburg holdings. It was separated from Spanish dominions by France, and from Austrian lands by German territories. And, of course, beginning in 1492, Charles (as king of Spain) became the ruler of most of the American continents, whose vast size and wealth became known only gradually.

Looked at from the Hapsburg perspective, Anabaptism was virtually unknown in the Spanish territories proper. It made a strong appearance, as we have seen, in the Netherlands, which not coincidentally was making a bid for independence from Hapsburg control in the sixteenth century.

In the east, Anabaptism was initially strong in the Tirol, where the peasantry had risen in revolt against Hapsburg rule in 1525-26. Anabaptism then spread up and down the Danube in Austria proper. Resolute Hapsburg persecution soon forced Anabaptists to flee from those areas to the toleration of nearby Moravia, where strong local lords resisted Hapsburg pressure, with decreasing success, throughout the sixteenth century.

Hapsburg resistance to all "evangelical heresy" (which included Anabaptism in its scope) was legendary for its cruelty and thoroughness. Of the executions that can be documented in Swiss, German, and Austrian territories (not counting Spain and the Netherlands), about seventy occurred in Switzerland, about 360 in German territories of the Empire, and more than 400 in Hapsburg territories proper.

Archduke Ferdinand in particular "distinguished himself by the amount of blood he shed in suppressing Anabaptism." The inquisitorial process had been perfected in Spain in the late fifteenth century, and it was applied consistently (in direct proportion to local Hapsburg influence) in all Hapsburg lands. It included routine torture and the most painful forms of inflicting death that could be imagined. All this is amply documented not only in martyrologies like the *Martyrs Mirror*, but also in official court records.

Not surprisingly, these methods achieved their end. Anabaptism managed to survive long-term only in lands that were under more marginal imperial control, such as Moravia and the northern Netherlands. Swiss territories, Protestant and Catholic alike, also came to be uncompromisingly hostile to Anabaptists (although they executed fewer people).

The natural result of high levels of political persecution in Swiss and Hapsburg territories was that the more persistent among the Anabaptists migrated to other areas. The political problem was not removed, but simply displaced elsewhere. Cities and territories in Moravia, Alsace, the Palatinate, Württemberg, Hesse, and increasingly in the northern Netherlands and along the Baltic coast, became destinations for Anabaptist refugees and their communities. The pattern of migration in search of religious toleration, which has continued into the twentieth century among Mennonites, Amish, and Hutterites, is a phenomenon that began almost immediately following the first adult baptisms in Zurich.

The economic motive underlying Moravian toleration would come into play prominently in subsequent centuries. It came to define Mennonite, Hutterite and Amish migrations into the twentieth century. Rulers of underdeveloped lands in search of industrious settlers would offer privileges to the descendants of the Anabaptists, all too often revoking those privileges once lands had been improved and were productive again.

In this way beleaguered Swiss Anabaptists would find political space in the Palatinate after 1648, where they were invited to settle after the Thirty Years' War devastated the territory. Dutch Anabaptists were welcomed in the Vistula Delta, where their ability to reclaim land from the sea was valued. Mennonites in Prussia would be invited to settle in the Ukraine by Catherine II, who valued their agricultural skills. The British crown would offer generous land grants to Mennonites and Amish in Pennsylvania, and to Mennonites and Amish in Upper Canada following the American Revolution, for the same reason. In the sixteenth century, however, political space such as Moravia offered was rare indeed, and by the end of the sixteenth century, Moravia also proved inhospitable.

With almost negligible exceptions, Anabaptism was forced to develop in an openly hostile political environment. Even in the exceptional settings of Waldshut, Nicholsburg, Münster and Moravia, where some kind of official arrangement existed, the reality still was that in the sixteenth century climate, those political arrangements themselves virtually guaranteed political intervention from the outside.

There was no escaping the fact that to be an Anabaptist in the sixteenth century meant that one had placed oneself on the margins of acceptable society. It is thus not surprising that internally, a separatist interpretation of Anabaptism came to prevail, and that the biblical themes of the righteous having to suffer at the hands of the unrighteous, the persecution and exile of God's chosen people, and the final reward of the faithful remnant, would become increasingly important in defining the movement. In this chapter we will trace some of the internal biblical and theological debates that accompanied the Swiss and South German/Austrian Anabaptist move towards a separatist *tradition*.

The variety of positions that was taken up by different Anabaptists on questions of the sword and the oath (we will outline six different views in this chapter alone) reflects the uncertain, exploratory nature of the time, when all things seemed possible and little was certain. In the context of early Swiss and South German/Austrian Anabaptism, the Schleitheim Articles loomed large because they were a very early articulation of a clear political ethic. Anabaptists elsewhere had to elaborate their own views in dialogue with the defenders of the Schleitheim position.

Without a doubt the importance of the Schleitheim Articles has been overrated by modern Mennonite interpreters: they *do not* represent the defining moment for Anabaptism as a whole. But it is also true that Schleitheim represented a strong articulation of an Anabaptist political ethic that needed to be countered by Anabaptists who were proposing alternative models.

Sattler, Denck, and Marpeck: Law or Love?

One point of tension in the development of an Anabaptist political ethic lay between the more literal reading of the New Testament, represented early in the Swiss tradition by Michael Sattler's Schleitheim Articles, and the spiritualist reading of Scripture as a whole, represented by Hans Denck. Pilgram Marpeck presented a mediating voice between the two tendencies.

Michael Sattler

Beginning at the letter side of the spirit/letter continuum, Michael Sattler's writings emphasized a Christocentric, New Testament measure of behaviour. The backdrop against which this ethic was formulated was that there were two separate kingdoms ruled by two separate "princes" (Christ and Satan). Individual believers and the church as a collective must separate from the world, and follow the biblical ordering which Christ had outlined for his followers. Both the example of Jesus's life, and the commands Jesus gave his followers in New Testament Scripture set the norms of conduct for the church.

The central point concerning the oath (article 7 of Schleitheim) made reference to Matthew 5:33-37, where Jesus requires no swearing at all by way of command. Believers simply are to affirm "yea" or "nay." Christ has commanded us not to swear, and we should therefore obey. The results of this "simple" conclusion were catastrophic in the sixteenth century political context. Those who refused to swear any and all oaths were placing themselves outside the margins of acceptable civil society. (1)

(1) "For early modern Europeans, oaths defined and legitimated the relationships between governing authorities and their constituents or subjects, ... and served as the glue that held both urban and rural sociopolitical structures in place. The existence of a community without an oath was unthinkable. Thus the refusal of the oath seemed like a repudiation of society." (Pries, "Oath Refusal," 65).

Sword

Schleitheim's well-known arguments against sword bearing (articles 4 and 6) cited Scripture in the following way.

a) Matthew 5:39. "You shall not resist evil." This first mention of the sword comes at the end of Article 4, concerning separation. Members of the perfection of Christ are to yield before the world, and trust in God. The descriptive name of nonresistance has been given to this position primarily because of the centrality of Matthew 5:39.

b) Romans 13:1ff. "The sword is an ordering of God outside the perfection of Christ." Article 6 on the sword immediately makes clear that the sword of government stands outside of the perfection demanded by Christ. Reference to John 8 clarifies what this means for the church.

(2) Schleitheim. "The rule of the government is according to the flesh, that of the Christians according to the spirit. . . . In sum: as Christ our Head is minded, so also must be minded the members of the body of Christ through Him..." *(Yoder, 1973, 40)*

c) John 8:11. "But within the perfection of Christ only the ban is used..." The ban is to be used within the Body of Christ; the sword outside the Body. Further, these two means of discipline are not related to each other in any way (Article 6), for what is outside Christ is "nothing but an abomination which we should shun."

The remainder of Article 6 clarifies how Romans 13 is to be interpreted in the setting of the two opposed kingdoms. The basic response is that Christ is the example from whom we are to learn. (2)

The result of this emphasis on the New Testament Christocentric letter was a thoroughgoing separatism: the letter of Scripture read in this way provided a literal, objective rule of life and political ethic for believers, members as they were of the "Kingdom of Heaven and of Christ."

Hans Denck

Hans Denck did not accept the literalist interpretive framework that underlay Schleitheim's views on sword and oath, even though in many respects Denck arrived at ethical conclusions that closely resembled those of Schleitheim. Hans Denck followed the mystical tradition in asserting that an inner spiritual change would result in a life in conformity with God's will, as revealed in Christ's life.

Denck's treatment of the oath points to clear differences between his reading of Scripture and that of Schleitheim, as Sebastian Franck recognized. Where Schleitheim makes yea and nay into an ordinance to be obeyed by those who have "the mind of Christ," in *Concerning True Love* Denck argues that even saying yea or nay when one cannot fulfill what one promises amounts to perjury. Denck argued further that calling God to witness for events that have occurred in the past is of a different order than promising something for the future. He permitted the former. When people swear oaths, said Denck, it corresponds to the Apostle Paul's calling God as a witness (2 Corinthians 1:23). Hans Denck had little interest in an ordinance or biblicistic prohibition concerning oaths, but rather was concerned with the spirit of the text, which he believed had to do with truth telling.

Oath

Denck's position on the spiritualist side of the continuum also led him to assert nonviolence as the norm for the Christian. His understanding was that there exists a progressive revelation of God's will in Scripture, but that this progressive revelation is a spiritual one, not a literal one. Old Testament guidelines "may have been good" in their time, but it is the higher law of love in Christ, written on human hearts, that provides the spiritual, hermeneutical, and ethical guideline for Christians. (3)

Sword

---

(3) Denck "The zeal of Moses in killing the Egyptian who had harmed an Israelite was in some sense good in that he was zealous for the right against the wrong (Ex. 2:11ff). But if Moses had known perfect Love or indeed possessed her, he would have allowed himself to be killed in place of the Israelite, his brother, rather than strangle the Egyptian, his brother's enemy." (Furcha, 1975, 105-6).

Denck was resolutely nonresistant, but the foundation for his stand was a spiritualistic emphasis on following Christ *in love*, and not the more literally biblicist argument deriving from Christ's commands and behaviour. His political ethic was more flexible as a result.

(4) Denck *"It is the nature of love not to will or desire the hurt of anyone, but as much as is possible to serve for the betterment of everyone. . . . Insofar as it were possible for a government to act [in love] it could well be Christian in its office. Since however the world will not tolerate it, a friend of God should not be in the government but out of it, that is if he desires to keep Christ as a Lord and master. Whoever loves the Lord loves him regardless of his station. But he should not forget what characterizes a true lover [of God], namely that for the Lord's sake he renounce all power and to be subject to no one but the Lord." (Klaassen, 1982, 250-51).*

Denck doubted that the world would tolerate Christ-like behaviour in a ruler. But his nonresistance emphasized not an ordinance legislating absolute separation, but rather the more flexible biblical norm of "the love of Christ." (4)

On the basis of the Schleitheim consensus, the Swiss Brethren very quickly moved to a legislative (not to say legalistic) attitude concerning the outward ordinances of oath, sword, separation, dress and conduct. Denck's legacy was continued by, on the one hand, outright spiritualists such as Bünderlin and Entfelder, but on the other by the Marpeck circle, whose members struck a middle course between the legislative approach of the Swiss and Denck's spiritualist approach.

Pilgram Marpeck

There is one striking similarity between Marpeck's approach and that of the Swiss Brethren. Marpeck argued strongly for the existence of two kingdoms with contrasting modes of behaviour pertaining to each. He argued for the separation of the heavenly and earthly kingdoms, and called for the Christian to affirm citizenship in the heavenly kingdom, to the exclusion of all other loyalties. This was a very Sattlerian language and argument, but in fact the differences in approach between Sattler and Marpeck were substantial.

Sword

According to Marpeck, what prevents a magistrate from being saved is not (as Schleitheim argued) that simply being a magistrate violates a law of discipleship (Jesus refused this, and therefore we must refuse it as well).

What prevents a Christian from being a magistrate, Marpeck insisted, are any acts required by the office that go contrary to God's will and the rule of Christ's Spirit.

Pilgram Marpeck's conclusion, like Hans Denck's, was that insofar as a Christian would be able to govern according to the law of Christian love (something he thought was probably impossible, given what he knew of governing), serving as a magistrate was allowed to Christians. (5) Marpeck's own employment as a civil servant, as well as his acceptance of exile when his principles were violated, demonstrated concretely how he understood benign, limited government service to be possible.

> **(5) Marpeck** *"For Christian wisdom is not suited to [worldly rulers] nor will it serve them since it brings about only grace, mercy, love for the enemy, spiritual supernatural things, cross, tribulation, patience and faith in Christ without coercion, killing of the body and the external sword, but only through the Word of God." (Klassen and Klaassen, 1978, 558).*

Pilgram Marpeck argued christocentrically, as did the Swiss Brethren and as would Menno Simons, but in effect he admonished the more literalistic Brethren to deepen their understanding of Christ's life and example, and to apply this deeper understanding both to the question of the world with its sword, and the church with its ban. According to Christ's example, evil is to be resisted and overcome by means of good, by means of loving patience. (6) Insofar as the love of Christ dwells in the heart, Marpeck

> **(6) Marpeck** *"...revenge is no longer permitted in the New Testament for, through patience, the Spirit can now more powerfully overcome enemies than it could in the Old Testament. Therefore, Christ forbade such vengeance and resistance, and commanded the children who possessed the Spirit of the New Testament to love, to bless their enemies, persecutors, and opponents, and to overcome them with patience." (Klassen and Klaassen, 1978, 63).*

said, that love maps out a new manner of "overcoming evil" in this life, be that evil inside or outside the church community.

Thus the most fundamental reason Christians forego violence and coercion, both inside and outside the church, is that they are ruled by Christ's law of love, a gift of grace which bears good fruit, in season and out. This "loving resistance," first articulated by Hans Denck in the Anabaptist movement, played a role in Anabaptist discussions in the middle of the sixteenth century. But the centrality of love as the measure which was to guide the use of *both* the sword and the ban was not a position that was destined to survive as a practical community guideline.

Oath

There is less textual evidence than one might wish for determining Marpeck's position on the oath, but the evidence is consistent. It appears that sometimes Marpeck swore oaths, but at other times refused to take the civic oath and counselled others not to take it. Marpeck's position appears to have been that there should be no rule either for or against oath-taking, other than the rule of love.

In conclusion, there are significant differences between Michael Sattler's foundation for a political ethic for Christians, and those of Hans Denck and Pilgram Marpeck. In a significant point of unity, however, all three looked to Jesus as the example, model, and foundation for political ethics.

Christ at the centre

Perhaps because of his monastic background, Sattler looked to the New Testament words by and about Jesus, and His way of life, as providing a literal and concrete rule of life for the Christian. Denck and Marpeck, on the other hand, emphasized the more flexible norm of the law of love in the hearts of believers as the foundation for Christian ethics. Here the influence of the late medieval mystical tradition (as represented, for example, by the *Theologia Deutsch*) is evident.

The problem for Christian ethics as outlined by these two distinct interpretive traditions remains with us today. Is the image of two kingdoms the appropriate context in which to understand Christian ethics? If so, are those "kingdoms" to be distinguished from one another by law or by love?

Sattler and Hubmaier: Lordship of Christ, or Lordship of God?

A second point of tension in the early Anabaptist movement emerged within the literalist Swiss Anabaptist camp itself. Michael Sattler and Balthasar Hubmaier agreed on basic interpretive principles. But they came to disagree in their respective biblical understandings of how God had ordained church and government to fit together. A crucial point of difference between them was that Sattler's political ethic was Christocentric, whereas Hubmaier's was theocentric.

Michael Sattler

In the Schleitheim Articles, Michael Sattler argued that there are two op-   *Two Kingdoms*
posed kingdoms, and that the Christian belongs under the lordship of Christ. Once the two kingdoms were identified, the remaining argument flowed logically. Christians are no more to participate in the governmental order than they are to participate in any other works of the kingdom of darkness. Schleitheim's position can quite properly be called separatist nonresistance.

Balthasar Hubmaier

Hubmaier's last booklet, *On the Sword* (Pipkin and Yoder, 1989, 492-523)   *Sword*
was directed against Schleitheim's strict ethic of "doing what Jesus did." Hubmaier made three central points. First, he argued that at best we are Christians, not Christ. Insofar as we remain human, our kingdom is still of *this* world. (7) Christ's followers and disciples "are stuck in [this world] right up to our ears, and we will not be able to be free from it here on earth."

> *(7) Hubmaier* "Christ alone can say in truth 'My kingdom is not of this world.'" (Pipkin and Yoder, 1989, 497).

   Certainly this was one crucial point of the argument, for if Christians are considered fundamentally *incapable* of "living as Christ lived," then the appeal to His life loses its ethical force, and is relativized.

Likewise if Christians are firmly lodged "in this world," and cannot appeal to an alternative "citizenship in heaven" (as Christ alone could), then separation from the "kingdom of this world" is not only ill-advised, it is impossible. Hubmaier would develop these points in more detail throughout the tract.

> **(8) Hubmaier** *"Just as Christ wanted to do justice to his office on earth, likewise we should fulfill our office and calling, be it in government or in obedience." (Pipkin and Yoder, 1989, 500).*

Hubmaier's second argument against Schleitheim's view stated that Christ's role (or "office") was that of Saviour. Jesus Christ, Son of God sent on a mission of salvation, assumed one human body and one earthly function, and so could not possibly play all social roles (e.g., that of judge or magistrate). Therefore the example of His life cannot be universally binding on all persons in every conceivable social station and situation. Everyone, concluded Hubmaier, should thus continue in their proper offices, performing the duties appropriate to those offices. (8)

To these arguments Hubmaier added a third: God, said Hubmaier, did not ordain two opposed kingdoms, but rather a harmony between them. Hubmaier harmonized the command not to kill (Matthew 5) and the divine "ordering" of the sword of government (Romans 13), by insisting on the *personal* focus of the first command and the *social* focus of the second. (9) Those who refuse to mete out justice through government are themselves guilty of killing, said Hubmaier, for by failing to defend the innocent one, they are guilty of that death.

> **(9) Hubmaier** *"...the judges, governments, and executors of justice are called servants of God in the Scripture and not murderers, Rom. 13:4. God judges, sentences, and kills through them, and not they themselves." (Pipkin and Yoder, 1989, 500).*

Against an ethic based exclusively on the measure of Christ's life (a "Lordship of Christ" ethic), Hubmaier insisted on "the Lordship of God," who had ordained both nonresistance and the "legitimate" use of force, each in its proper sphere.

Not surprisingly, Hubmaier nowhere addresses the question of oath refusal. It is clear that in no way did he oppose the swearing of civil oaths. Such oaths belonged to the sphere of civil authority ordained by God for human governance and peace.

Oath

The dilemma for Christian political ethics posed by the contrasting approaches of Sattler and Hubmaier remains pressing in our own day. There is no doubt that Jesus calls for a perfectionist ethic in the Gospels, but to what extent is even a "regenerated" human being capable of being a citizen of heaven? Do all mechanisms of human governance therefore fall into the realm of Satan? Did God not also ordain government for good? To what extent can or should the ethic of Jesus influence and limit the public ethic of God's governance of the world?

Sattler and Hut: Ordinances or Prophetic Calendar?

A third point of tension in the early Anbaptist movement emerged between the literalist and Christocentric Swiss reading of Scripture and the prophetic-apocalyptic interpretation. These divergent interpretive approaches led to differences on questions of the oath and the sword, as a review of Hans Hut's position makes clear.

Hans Hut

From Hans Hut's early following of Thomas Müntzer we know that he was no pacifist in his pre-Anabaptist career, nor did he become much of a "nonresistant" after his adult baptism.

At his interrogation, Hut stated that he had opposed the pacifist brethren, who had maintained that a Christian was not to bear the sword when the authorities so demanded it. Likewise he had opposed those who did not wish to swear civil oaths. Hut testified more specifically that he had opposed some Swiss brothers who had "made an ordinance" forbidding the participation of Christians in war–a clear reference to Schleitheim and to those who were following its ordinances. He, on the other hand, had argued that "this was not contrary to God, nor was it forbidden."

Hans Hut had faced a dilemma after 1525: the Peasants' War had failed. The ungodly had not been rooted out, but rather the peasants had been thoroughly defeated and Müntzer and Pfeiffer put to death. How were these facts to be interpreted?

Hut came to admit that the peasants had been mistaken, but even as an Anabaptist he did not abandon Müntzer's hope that the righteous would, in the end, be able to punish the ungodly by the sword. The essential adjustment had to to with timing, motivation, and personnel. (10)

---

(10) Hut's testimony from prison. "They now see that the peasants were not right about their uprising, for they had sought their own and not God's honour. ...A Christian may well have a sword but ... it must remain in the scabbard until God tells him to take it out. Before then they would all be scattered and tried. Finally the Lord would gather them all together again and himself return. Then the saints would punish the others, namely, the sinners who had not repented." (Klaassen, 1982, 273).

Hut's understanding of the sword emerged in the context of his eschatological and prophetic calendar. According to his own testimony and that of his followers, Hut continued to identify Müntzer and Pfeiffer as the

| Vengeance |

Elijah and Enoch of the Last Days. He eagerly awaited God's vengeance on the ungodly at the hand of the invading Turks, after which the elect would complete God's work of just vengeance, sword in hand.

Hut's understanding of the proper use of the sword was not in harmony with Schleitheim, Denck, Marpeck, or Hubmaier. It was given shape by his previous commitment to Thomas Müntzer's apocalyptic hopes, the cause of the peasants, and his reading of prophetic Scripture. His interrogation statement, that he had taught obedience to governmental authority, has to be interpreted in light of his expectation that Christ would come again very soon, after which the believers who had obeyed governments, and held their swords in their sheaths, would be called upon to wield them against the impious.

Hans Hut own position could best be described as "provisional pacifism," based on a dispensationalist reading of history and Scripture. There would be different ethical requirements depending upon the particular period of history one happened to inhabit. And, the identification of a particular dispensation would be revealed to those in possession of an interpretive key, revealed by the Spirit of Christ. The dispensationalist manner of interpreting Scripture would appear again later in the Anabaptist movement, in the Kingdom of Münster.

The historical results of the prophetic-apocalyptic interpretive approach are clear enough in the history of the Anabaptist movement. For some Anabaptists, End Times ethics came to include not only Hut's provisional pacifism, but also Münster's "godly crusade" of aggression against the ungodly, coerced religious conformity, and legislated polygamy. Contemporary disasters following much the same interpretive approach are evident still in the last decade of the twentieth century, as the tragic, fiery end of the Branch Davidians in Waco, Texas illustrates. The historical specifics vary, but the interpretive paths leading there are strikingly similar.

Hutter and Riedemann: Return to Separatist Nonresistance

The emergence and development of communitarian Anabaptism in Moravia manifested a pattern that would be evident elsewhere in the Anabaptism movement: from spiritualistic and apocalyptic beginnings there evolved increasingly separated communities, defined by ethical boundaries set by external rules of conduct or *Ordnungen*.

On reading later Hutterite statements on the sword and the oath, one would be hard-pressed to identify Hans Hut as the progenitor of this movement, even though it was Hut's missionary activity that was primarily responsible for bringing it into existence.

As we have seen, in 1527 Hut disagreed with pacifist brethren who were legislating external prohibitions concerning the sword, the oath, clothing, and behaviour in general. Still, in less than five years his followers in Moravia had themselves become pacifist brethren who became, if anything, even more zealous legislators of external ordinances than had been the Swiss whom Hut had criticized. No doubt the failure of Hut's predictions for Christ's return, and the necessity of maintaining a disciplined community life in a threatening political environment played important roles in Hutterite development in this direction.

The communitarian movement in Moravia within which Jacob Hutter worked, although still showing some faint signs of the apocalyptic hope that was Hut's legacy, was strongly separatist and thoroughly nonresistant in the manner of Schleitheim and the Swiss. There was no hint of Hut's "provisional pacifism." (11)

---

(11) Jacob Hutter, writing in 1535.
"We desire to molest no one; nor to prejudice our foes, not even King Ferdinand. Our manner of life, our customs and conversation, are known everywhere to all. Rather than wrong any man a single penny, we would suffer the loss of a hundred gulden; and sooner than strike our enemy with the hand, much less with the spear, or sword, or halbert, as the world does, we would die and surrender life." (Klaassen, 1982, 275).

Hutter's nonresistant emphasis remained in Peter Riedemann's extremely influential later writing and teaching, with an even more marked emphasis on a legislated separation and absolute nonresistance. (12) Riedemann elaborated further when he addressed biblical counter-arguments, in particular the citing of Romans 13 in a "theocratic" sense, such as Hubmaier had done.

(12) Peter Riedemann, "Account." *"No Christian is a ruler and no ruler is a Christian, for the child of blessing cannot be the servant of wrath." (Klaassen, 1982, 261).*

How can it be that Paul calls government authorities "servants of God," and yet it is claimed (by Schleitheim as well as by Riedemann) that they are not true Christians?

Riedemann answered that not all "servants of God" are God's chosen people, citing the Old Testament examples of Nebuchadnezzar and the king of Assyria. Rulers, Riedemann concluded, are as free to "come to Christ" as are subjects (although rulers will find it "more difficult" to do so, he says), but when they do come to Christ they must surrender to Christ. This means that rulers who become Christians will cease to rule, in imitation of Christ.

This very Schleitheimian two kingdoms polarity would remain a hallmark of the Hutterite community. Included in this polarity was the requirement that Christians were to follow the higher truth revealed by Christ concerning the swearing of oaths. (13) Riedemann's understanding of the church was militantly separatist.

> *(13) Riedemann, "Account."* *"Weigh up the words of Christ carefully. He said, 'To men of old was said: Ye shall not swear falsely, but I say unto you: Swear not at all.'"* *(Klaassen, 1982, 201).*

Conclusion

The earliest baptizing movements in Switzerland, South Germany, and Austria were not of one mind in their interpretive approaches to Scripture, nor were they of one mind concerning the proper relationship of church to government. Their differences on the issues of the oath and the sword illustrate these points clearly enough. By 1530, however, some earlier questions had been settled.

–The separatist nonresistant ethic of Schleitheim soon became the accepted position of the Swiss Brethren, although the text of Schleitheim itself was cited only sporatically as the century wore on. Nevertheless, the Christocentric and separatist two kingdoms foundation of Schleitheim's position on sword and oath did survive and came to define the political ethics of the Swiss Anabaptists.

Schleitheim

–Denck's spiritualist emphasis on the love of Christ in the hearts of believers led some Anabaptists to leave the baptizing movement, because of its emphasis on external rites and rules. They defended instead an inner, largely invisible religion of the heart. The individualist thrust of this ethic allowed for "loving" political service.

Spiritualism

The spiritualist stream, while not representing an articulated political ethic, remained a very live option for Anabaptists weary of battling the world. An appeal to an inner religion of the spirit opened the door to various degrees of Nicodemism, namely the public appearance of conformity with outward religious practice while believers inwardly and secretly continued to practise their true convictions.

| Marpeck |

–Pilgram Marpeck's emphasis on an ethic based on the love of Christ in believers' hearts, as well as the public and visible practice of a new life based on the New Testament, outlined a flexible political ethic that allowed for limited, benign government service. The documentation is sparce, but apparently this moderately separatist social and political ethic was the norm in the scattered communities of Pilgramites in Switzerland, South Germany, and Moravia. The Pilgramites were never numerous, and all trace of them is lost in the seventeenth century. Nevertheless, there is growing evidence that they influenced the Swiss Brethren later in the sixteenth century.

| Hubmaier |

–Hubmaier's option, which closely resembled the church polity of the Reformed churches, did not survive as an Anabaptist option. Anabaptism found no legitimate political defenders anywhere in western Europe who wished to make Anabaptism the religion of their states.

| Hut |

–Hut's option of provisional pacifism faded away quickly after the prophecies on which it was based proved to be mistaken. This view soon was transmuted by the majority of Hut's followers into a separatist ethic closely resembling the one articulated in the Schleitheim Articles.

| Hutterites |

–The Hutterite separatist political ethic, with its emphasis on nonresistance and the non-swearing of oaths, sprang from South German/Austrian beginnings (Denck and Hut), but soon came to resemble most closely the views expressed at Schleitheim. There is good reason to assume some direct influence from the Swiss Anabaptists in this development. George Blaurock had brought Swiss Anabaptism to the eastern Tirol (1527-1529), and the text of Schleitheim was copied repeatedly by the Hutterites. Seven separate copies of the Articles have survived in various Hutterite codices.

Chapter 14

Melchior Hoffman and
the Melchiorite Tradition:
Sword and Oath

Melchior Hoffman

Melchior Hoffman's statements to the Strasbourg authorities, following his arrest in 1533.

"According to the Scripture there would be insurrection and unrest in the whole world, indeed, the time for it was there. The whole mob of the clergy would be destroyed. The true Jerusalem could not come into being or be built up until Babylon with all her mob and support would collapse and brought to ruin."

"God says, that they should supply themselves with food and other necessities, for the city [Strasbourg] would suffer hunger and need. Weapons should also be stocked. In the third year of his, Melchior Hoffman's imprisonment, God would come. The city need not be afraid of the Anabaptists, and those Anabaptists who will not take the sword should be ordered to the moats, for they will do no harm. . . . He would not take a sword into his hands, for he, Hoffman, would alone pray to God for us all. He has also warned his brothers about it."

(Klaassen, 1982, 328-29).

With very few exceptions, Anabaptist scholars are agreed that Melchior Hoffman represents a unique Anabaptist tradition, independent of the Swiss Anabaptists, with some visible links to the South German Anabaptism of Denck and Hut. In fact, later Mennonite understandings concerning separation from the world, the sword, and the oath appear to have developed directly from Hoffman and his teachings, and in response to historical developments, with no visible connection to either the Swiss or South German Anabaptist groups.

By 1529 and Melchior Hoffman's conversion to Anabaptism in Strasbourg the question of "legitimate state Anabaptism," such as Hubmaier had attempted, had been resolved in the Swiss and South German/Austrian movements. Uniformly negative political reaction to Anabaptism meant that there would be no politically legitimate Anabaptism, unless some cataclysmic event were to change the nature of politics altogether. There still remained four live options among Anabaptists of Strasbourg in 1529.

| Four Options |

–the separatist option (Swiss Anabaptists)

–Marpeck's moderate separatism

–the spiritualist option (followers of Denck)

–the apocalyptic option (Hut's followers).

The latter two appealed most to Hoffman.

Hoffman, like Hut, had an overwhelming concern with the End Times. It governed his reading of Scripture. Apocalyptic expectation, although increasingly abandoned by the majority of Hans Hut's followers in Austria and Moravia, still remained a live option for those who continued to hope for the reform of society as a whole. Hoffman firmly believed that there would be political rulers who would be converted and then help prepare the way for Christ's return. They would make a political space available to the saints. After that, the return of Christ as ruler over all the earth would change the rest of the political map. At the time of his arrest, Hoffman was convinced that Strasbourg was the site of the New Jerusalem.

There is no way to gauge the degree of apocalyptic expectation within the Anabaptist movement as a whole around 1530, but certainly many Anabaptists (perhaps most Anabaptists) continued to hope and wait expectantly for Christ's return. Christ's coming finally would establish the Anabaptist communities as the faithful Bride of Christ who would rule with Him in the New Jerusalem.

So it was that the political "miracle" of the Anabaptist takeover of the city of Münster, prepared for as it had been by Melchior Hoffman's apocalyptic Anabaptism, seemed to many thousands to indicate that political reality had been altered decisively, and that the End Times had definitely arrived.

Hoffman and the Sword

The tension that arises when Matthew 5 and Romans 13 are read literally, so significant in the early Anabaptist debates concerning the sword of government, was less pressing for

"And I John saw the holy city, new Jerusalem, coming down from God out of heaven, prepared as a bride adorned for her husband." Revelation 21:2

The image of the church as the Bride of Christ, a foretaste of the New Jerusalem, was a powerful and defining image in all branches of the Anabaptist movement.

Melchior Hoffman. He tended to read all Scripture through apocalyptically tinted glasses.

Hoffman did not agree with the Swiss Brethren way of harmonizing Matthew 5 and Romans 13. In his exegesis of the first five verses of Romans 13, Hoffman emphasized above all that "the authorities are ordained of God." Hoffman qualified the statement by saying that the earthly magistracy has no real authority over the spiritual Adam or the spiritual Mount of Zion. Nevertheless, since order among the beasts of the earth must be kept, God had ordained that everyone be obedient to the authorities "in all that is not contrary to God." As an example Hoffman noted that one must be obedient even if the Antichrist himself is set up as a king, so long as God gives the Antichrist this power. But the limits of obedience are reached when, as in the case of Daniel, the Antichrist demands idolatry.

Rulers

Are rulers then to be considered "antichrists" or "outside the perfection of Christ"? Hoffman answered with a definite "no." In a passage that recalls Hubmaier's more theocratic interpretation, Hoffman argued that the political authorities were ordained of God to punish evil and protect the good, and those who perform this function are "always God's servants and friends." (1)

> *(1) Hoffman comments on Romans 13:4.* "Some today do not wish to acknowledge the authorities as Christians... [This] is a blindness such that they cannot tell the difference between offices, therefore we must bear their blindness for a time yet, until the true light dawns." Hoffman, 1533, T8b.

Hoffman considered Schleitheim's relegation of political authorities to "the world" and hell as a misguided "blindness." The political sword was central to his conception of the events of the Last Days. (2)

Not only did Hoffman reserve a legitimate place for Christian authorities in the time before Christ's return, he reserved a special, God-

> *(2) Hoffman* "Although priests and Israelites in the New Testament were to use no other sword than the sword of the spirit, this was not a command that men should not trim an animal's claws, nor kill according to God's command or not take the sword, but rather such use of the sword is God's good will..." Hoffman, 1533, T8b ff.

ordained role for them in the calendar of End Times events. Hoffman insisted that the political authorities were not to coerce in the church itself, which was to be governed only by the ban. Nevertheless once the final events had begun to unfold, the "godly rulers" would take the sword in defence of the true faith. The sword would prepare the way for the coming of Christ.

Here Hoffman's conclusion brings Hans Hut to mind: the role of the political authorities would be determined by the particular point (or "dispensation") that had been reached in the calendar of End Times events. Hoffman's direct appeal to various rulers, that they carry out their God-ordained functions now that the final trumpets had sounded, owed nothing to Schleitheim's radical two kingdoms view which placed political authorities "outside the perfection of Christ."

On the question of the two kingdoms and of church and government, *Two Kingdoms* Hoffman resolved the tension between Matthew 5 and Romans 13 in a unique manner. The office of the ruler or governor was ordained of God and thus open to Christians (here one thinks of Hubmaier), but governments and individual rulers needed to *choose* to work on the side of the light, particularly in these dangerous Last Days. If they did not choose the light they were working on the side of darkness and the Antichrist. Into which "kingdom" individual rulers belonged would not be decided automatically by virtue of their governing office, as Schleitheim had said, but rather by the convictions, choices, and deeds of the rulers themselves.

There was thus a crucial ambiguity in Hoffman's political ethic that *Ambiguity* allowed for both pacifist and crusading interpretations. While Hoffman himself emphasized divine initiative, and denied that the elect would "take" the sword themselves prior to the collapse of the forces of Hell and the establishment of the New Jerusalem, nevertheless, he allowed that Christians could be "given" the sword legitimately as rulers. The ambiguities in his view of the sword in the Last Days proved to be a volatile mix. (3)

(3) Klaus Deppermann describes Hoffman's legacy.
"With the idea that the extermination of the godless must precede the day of final judgement, and with the conception of an earthly reign of saints in a theocratic intermediate kingdom until the return of Christ, Hoffman had created the most important ideological presuppositions for the Anabaptist kingdom of Münster." (Deppermann, 1982, 187).

In the end Hoffman stood at quite a distance from the Schleitheim Articles. Although he stood much closer to Hubmaier in one respect, and to Hans Hut in others, nevertheless Melchior Hoffman conceived of a unique Anabaptist biblical interpretation and political ethic that was irretrievably linked to prophesied events of the Last Days.

Hoffman and the Oath

In his commentary on Daniel 12 Hoffman did maintain that oaths should not be sworn. Hoffman held this position already in 1526, prior to the composition of the Schleitheim Articles. His line of argumentation does not parallel in any way Schleitheim's article 7.

The strongest parallel between Schleitheim's article 7 and Hoffman's argument lies in the fact that both positions were based on Matthew 5:33-36. Following this, however, the respective discussions diverged. Hoffman, objected to to three arguments.

Oath

–that swearing is allowed "because of love of neighbour"

–that the nobility are bound to swear oaths of loyalty

–that the swearing of oaths maintains civil order, since evil persons would feel free to do evil if they were not sworn to the good.

To these objections Hoffman replied, first, that "love of neighbour" is not a sufficient cause for going against the clear commands of Christ. Such logic, he said, might also lead one to sleep with the neighbour's wife, or even to commit murder out of "love for one's neighbour." Hoffman's literal exegesis here is striking: there can be no relativizing of this command by an appeal to love. To the nobility, Hoffman argued that one cannot promise obedience to two masters (Matthew 7). And concerning the prospect of civil chaos if oaths were not sworn, Hoffman maintained that evil persons were not restrained by oaths in any case. (4)

Although Hoffman and Schleitheim both make reference to Matthew 5:33-36 on the oath, their positions are nevertheless independently argued and address totally different objections in respectively unique ways. In particular, where Schleitheim rejects oaths because of the human *inability* to keep such promises, Hoffman *equates* the Christian "yea" with the oath. In a civil context, however, both positions would have been equally radical, for both forbade baptized adults to swear civil oaths.

> *(4) Hoffman "For the Christian, 'yea' is his oath and he holds to it; those who do not keep their promises, will also not keep high oaths either. A Christian does no evil, oath or no oath. Therefore it is silly and dangerous to dig up oaths against God's Word." (Hoffman, 1526, e3v).*

Conclusion

Melchior Hoffman's political ethic stood closest to Hans Hut's within the Anabaptist camp. Like Hut, Hoffman interpreted baptism on confession of faith as signifying a thorough yieldedness to the Spirit of God–a dying to self and rising in Christ–and like Hut, Hoffman saw this baptism on the forehead as the sealing of the 144,000 elect of the Last Days with the sign of TAU. Hoffman emphasized the working of the Spirit of God in yielded believers and, like Hut, also expected the poor and simple to be more ready to yield than the powerful. The established clergy were particularly singled out for criticism.

> *Hoffman and Hut*

Like Hut, Hoffman expected the godless to be eradicated before Jesus' return partly by the agency of the Turks, but unlike Hut, he expected the "godly magistrates" to play a major role in the final cleansing, not necessarily the elect of their own initiative. And finally, Hoffman's approach to Scripture, like Hut's, focused on the prophetic books of the Bible and a setting of dates for the return of Christ, and so placed the spirit/letter tension in a lively eschatological context. The emphasis on the heightened activity of the Holy Spirit in the Last Days is also visible in Hoffman. After 1530, probably under the influence of Hut's followers in Strasbourg, Hoffman also accepted extra-biblical prophecy as revelatory.

*Hoffman's
Legacy*

On the question of how Anabaptism should relate to political authority, Melchior Hoffman bequeathed a volatile legacy to his followers in the north. Along with the conviction that these were the Last Days came the conviction that the secrets of Scripture and the "signs of the times" were being laid bare for anointed apostles and prophets. Added to the mix was Hoffman's own conviction that there would be a purging of the godless before Christ's return, and a fatal ambiguity about who exactly would be responsible for the purging, and when the purging was to begin. All of these elements, taken together and heated to a fever pitch in the Netherlands, led to the establishment of the Anabaptist kingdom of Münster, an event which, sadly, belongs firmly within the history of Anabaptism as such and which ultimately owed its existence to the teachings of Melchior Hoffman.

Rothmann and Menno on the Sword

The question of what God was revealing concerning the saints and government was nowhere more pressing than in Westphalia and the Netherlands during and after the establishment of the kingdom of Münster. Faced with Münsterite literalism on the one hand, and with David Joris's spiritualism on the other, Menno Simons attempted to keep to the middle ground between either side, although in the face of Joris's direct and continuing challenge, Menno undoubtedly came down more on the literal side of the question.

Bernhard Rothmann

Standing behind Rothmann's justification for the taking of the sword in Münster was a figurative system of reading and interpreting Scripture borrowed from Melchior Hoffman. Also central to Rothmann's system was the principle of the "cloven hoof," which held that scriptural contradictions (the two points of the hoof) were simply apparent contradictions, and capable of being resolved into one biblical truth by inspired interpreters.

Rothmann's most crucial "cloven hoof" resolution was that Scripture pointed to different "times" in salvation history. Scripture and its figures could not be interpreted properly until one knew to which "time" (we might say, "dispensation") in history a particular passage referred. Rothmann believed that there were three primary times in salvation history:

Three Ages of History

—from creation to the flood

—from the flood to Münster

—from Münster to the end of time. This third age Rothmann called the "time of Restitution."

Rothmann was convinced that since the final age of salvation history had arrived, the letter of Scripture needed to be read according to different, though very specific rules. In the time of Restitution, God would restore Israel. (5) The most relevant biblical canon for the time of Restitution, then, was not the New Testament, but rather the first five books of the Old Testament and the Old Testament Prophets.

> **(5) Rothmann** *"See! The Throne of David must be reestablished, the Kingdom prepared and armed, and all the enemies of Christ humbled by David. Then the peaceful Solomon, the eternal king and anointed God, Christ, will enter and possess the throne of his father, David, and his Kingdom shall have no end..." (Cited in Stayer, 1976, 250).*

This had direct implications for understanding the Jesus' "hard sayings" about violence. Rothmann held that in the third and final age, Old Testament injuctions concerning God's vengeance on the ungodly at the end of time were supposed to be applied once again, in a literal way. By contrast, the New Testament injunctions of Jesus (e.g. in Matthew 5) needed to be understood in a non-literal mode. The time of suffering and "turning the other cheek" belonged to the *second* age, which had now passed. In the time of Restitution, Rothmann taught, God's Kingdom would be established not by the spiritual sword alone, but by the exercise of the physical sword, in preparation for Christ's return.

Portrait of John van Leiden,
the "promised David," dressed in his royal robes,
holding the symbols of his office.

Bernhard Rothmann writes
about Jan van Leiden and the
Restitution:
"Now, dear brothers, the time
of vengeance is here. God has
raised the promised David and
armed him for vengeance and
punishment over Babylon and
its people. Therefore, dear
brothers, arm for battle, not
only with the Apostles' humble
weapon of suffering, but also
with vengeance, the magnificent
armor of David, to stamp out
the entire Babylonian power
and the entire godless establish-
ment with the power and the
help of God. Think that you can
do to them everything that they
have done to you; indeed, they
shall receive in the same
measure with which they have
measured out..." (Cited in
Stayer, 1976, 251-52).

Thus it was that in answer to the question of why Münsterite Christians seized the sword, when according to the New Testament, Christians were called upon to suffer, Rothmann replied that one must understand that it was now the time of Restitution, when the true Kingdom was being erected, and the ungodly were supposed to be brought to an end by the true Israelites of the Last Days. (6)

*(6) **Rothmann** "The Lord wishes ... that we and all true Christians in this time not only be allowed to turn away the power of the ungodly with the sword, but even more, that the sword be put into the hands of his people to avenge all that is unjust and evil in the whole world... The time is at hand." (Stupperich, 1970, 282).*

One further step was necessary for Rothmann's explicit justification for the events unfolding in Münster, and this was the argument that faithful Christians *themselves* were to take up the sword in preparation for Christ's arrival, rather than waiting for God to initiate the final "cleansing"–perhaps through "godly rulers," as Hoffman had said.

Although he initially appealed to visions and signs that had appeared to the faithful in Münster, Rothmann's more fundamental argument was scriptural and was based on his interpretation of the figure of the "throne of David." Here Rothmann used Melchior Hoffman's figurative exegesis, and turned it to his own purposes.

Throne of David

Rothmann argued that the David of the Old Testament was not a "figure" for Christ (a common interpretation), but rather, it was King Solomon who must be understood as the Old Testament figure for Christ. With this step, Rothmann felt free to apply all the Old Testament prophecies concerning the raising up of the fallen throne of David–the Restitution of Israel. Those prophecies applied, he argued, to the kingdom of Münster and to King Jan van Leiden–the second David.

Once Rothmann had established (to his satisfaction) that he was living in the time of Restitution, that the time of the Gospel had passed, and that the throne of David was being reestablished in Münster under the second David (Jan van Leiden), Rothmann could apply, in a literal way, the Old Testament prophecies concerning the judgement that would befall the "godless." Rothmann was convinced that all the divine signs pointed to the fact that God was calling his elect to take up the sword. Although they had been ready to suffer death for the sake of the Kingdom, said Rothmann, God had other plans for His saints in these Last Days.

God had made it clear that the "time of restitution" was at hand, the time of grace and mercy was over, and the time of divine vengeance had begun. (7)

---

(7) Rothmann *"God will make for his people bronze claws and iron horns. They will make plough-shares and hoes into swords and spears. They shall choose a captain, fly the flag, and blow the trumpet. They will incite an obstinate and merciless people against Babylon. In everything they will repay Babylon with her own coin, yes, in double measure." (Klaassen, 1982, 335).*

The still-smoking remains of this Old Testament-based "glorious aggression" confronted Menno Simons when he began working to reorganize the Melchiorite movement in the north, following the collapse of the Münsterite kingdom.

Menno Simons and the Sword

Menno Simons worked continuously to overcome the negative image that Münster had created. Nevertheless, Menno belonged solidly in the Melchiorite tradition, and spoke Melchiorite theological language, even while he attempted to combat what he called the errors of the Münsterites.

Menno, unlike Rothmann, did not rest his interpretation of Scripture on a three-fold periodization of history. Menno's main point was to emphasize the centrality of Christ in matters of teaching and practice. His biblical principle was summed up in the one verse Menno inscribed on the title pages of all of his writings:

Christ at the Centre

For no other foundation can be laid, than that which is laid, which is Jesus Christ (1 Corinthians 3:11).

The most crucial distinction for Menno was that the Bible as a whole needed to be read from the Cristocentric perspective, that all prophecy had to be tested by Christ and, further, that the time of the Gospel would last until Christ himself came again in glory. For Menno the Old Testament was authoritative only in a provisional and exhortative sense, by supplying examples of true faith, for example. But Christ's words, commands, and example provided infallible guidelines for doctrine and action.

Menno's rejection of a literal reading of the Old Testament had its roots in an earlier disagreement among the Melchiorites concerning the proper use of the "cloven hoof." In the Fall of 1535, at the height of the Münsterite kingdom, a debate took place in Amsterdam between Jacob van Campen and Obbe Philips on this very question. Jacob van Campen defended the use of the "cloven hoof" as it was being interpreted in Münster, and insisted that "the Old Testament 'types' must have both a literal and a spiritual fulfillment in the Christian era."

Cloven Hoof

Obbe argued, to the contrary, that Old Testament figures were to be applied only in a spiritual, figurative sense. Echoes of Obbe's spiritualized, figurative approach, which rejected the literal application of Old Testament practices to Münster, are found in Menno's writings, but they were expressed most fully in the later writings of Obbe's brother, Dirk Philips.

The first writing we have from Menno's hand, "The Blasphemy of John of Leiden" was written around April, 1535 as a direct refutation of the Münster events. From the beginning his argument placed Christ at the centre. Menno repeatedly attacked Rothmann's claim that Jan van Leiden was the "second David" preparing the way for "Solomon" (Jesus). (8)

> *(8) Menno* "*Greater antichrist there cannot arise than he who poses as the David of promise. This David is Christ as the Scriptures testify abundantly.*" CWMS, 37.

In his earliest writing, Menno read the Old Testament as providing figures which pointed to Christ. The similarity to the figurative exegesis of Hoffman and Rothmann is striking. But Menno was using what he considered to be the *proper* figurative interpretation. Menno read the Old Testament figures Christologically (or "spiritually," as he said), and argued against their literal meaning or application, as had Obbe against van Campen. (9)

MENNO   SIMONS, WT FRIESLANT.

Menno Simons, pictured with his crutch (he had trouble walking in his later years) holding a Bible open to 1 Corinthians 3:11: "For no other foundation can anyone lay than that which is laid, which is Jesus Christ."

(9) Menno *"One should not imagine that the figure of the Old Testament is so applied to the truth of the New Testament that flesh is understood as referring to flesh; for the figure must reflect the reality; the image, the being, and the letter, the Spirit." (CWMS, 42).*

With Christ placed back at the centre of Scripture, Menno insisted that one must look to what Christ had taught about warfare, violence and vengeance. Christ left us an example, that we should follow, said Menno; He was minded to suffer, and so must all Christians be minded, overcoming their foes with the spiritual sword of the Word of God. The literal words and the concrete example of Jesus' life became the central ethical measures for Menno, as they had become also for the Swiss and the Hutterites. (10)

(10) Menno *"If Christ fights His enemies with the sword of His mouth, if He smites the earth with the rod of His mouth, and slays the wicked with the breath of His lips; and if we are to be conformed to His image, how can we, then, oppose our enemies with any other sword?" (CWMS, 44).*

"They who are baptized inwardly with Spirit and fire, and externally with water, according to the Word of the Lord, have no weapons except patience, hope, silence, and God's Word. . . . Iron and metal spears and swords we leave to those who, alas, regard human blood and swine's blood about alike." (CWMS, 198).

There remained the matter of the End Times calendar, which had played such a central role for the political ethics of Hut, Hoffman and Rothmann. Against the Münsterite argument that God wished to punish Babylon by means of His Servants (the "true Christians," meaning the Anabaptists), Menno said that the "times and the seasons" were known to God alone. Babylon would indeed be punished, justly and soon, for its iniquities against the saints, but God would do the punishing, not Christians.

Prophetic Calendar

Menno did spend some time assuring the Melchiorites that the enemies of Christ would receive their just reward (punishment), but first Christ had to return in glory.

On the question of prophetic authority–a pressing matter in Melchiorite Anabaptism–Menno again set forward a Christological measure. (11) The foundation which is Christ cannot be moved, and is the measure by which all Scripture and all prophecy is to be measured. Furthermore, that foundation remains "until the end of the world"; there is no dispensation remaining between the time of Jesus' birth and His second coming.

> *(11) Menno* "*Even though Elijah himself were to come, he would not have anything to teach contrary to the foundation and doctrine of Christ and the apostles. But he must teach and preach in harmony with them if he would execute the office of the true preacher, for by the Spirit, Word, actions, and example of Christ, all must be judged until the last judgement. Otherwise the whole Scriptures are false.*" *(CWMS, 220).*

The sharp distinction that Menno drew between the spiritual and the earthly kingdoms puts one in mind of Michael Sattler, and the strict polarity seen at Schleitheim, which consigned all use of the sword (and hence all ruling and judging functions of the magistrates) to a realm "outside the perfection of Christ." But Menno's position on the magistracy was more Melchiorite than Swiss. It grew out of Hoffman's own view, and did not echo Schleitheim. Menno repeatedly admonished princes and rulers to repentance, but he did not consider them non-Christian (outside the perfection of Christ) simply by virtue of their office. Nor did Menno assume that if rulers became Christian they would have to abandon their ruling offices, in imitation of Christ (such as Schleitheim and Riedemann both argued).

Throughout his writings Menno assumed the possiblility that rulers could repent and become true Christian *rulers*. In his early writings especially, Menno went beyond an ambiguous granting that God had ordained the sword of government, and called on rulers to use their power for good, even in matters relating to the church.

Although Menno soon moved away from counselling rulers to legislate and enforce true religion, nevertheless he maintained to the end the possibility of the existence of pious Christian rulers. Menno hoped that princes and rulers would repent, and then *rule in a Christian manner*. (12) This understanding marked Menno as a Melchiorite. It put him at a good distance from Schleitheim, much closer to Denck and Marpeck in his conclusions. In spite of similarities in approach to Scripture between Menno and the Swiss (the priority of the New Testament; Christocentrism in personal and corporate ethics) Menno Simons stood in the Melchiorite, not the Swiss, tradition in his understanding of the sword of government (his political ethics).

---

(12) Menno writes to rulers.

"Yes, dear sirs, if you could thus convert yourselves with all your heart; if you could change yourselves and humble yourselves before God, could deny yourselves and seek and follow Christ and His righteousness; if you could renounce the world and flesh and its lusts, as you have heard, then you would be kings and priests not only in natural things, but also in spiritual. You would possess your souls in peace, rule your land in Christian wisdom, in the pure fear of God; then you would be victorious against all harmful enemies of our souls, live in grace, die in grace, and deserve to be called in truth, without hypocrisy, Christian kings and believing princes." (CWMS, 363).

Menno and the Oath

Whether to swear oaths or not to swear oaths does not seem to have been an issue in Münster. In spite of Melchior Hoffman's rejection of oath taking, as outlined above, Bernhard Rothmann did not address the issue at all. This would stand to reason, given Rothmann's explanation that

Jesus' commands in the New Testament had been superseded in the "time of restitution."

Menno Simons apparently did not consider the oath to be as urgent a matter as the sword, or perhaps he became convinced only gradually that oath taking should be forbidden. In any case, he took up the issue of the oath only late in his reforming career and writings. The earliest extended discussion dates from 1552–sixteen years after Menno became an Anabaptist!

Addressing himself to those who continued to persecute Anabaptists, Menno argued in 1552 that the oaths required by the magistracy are forbidden to Christians. Menno's argument was Christocentric, emphasizing obedience to Christ's commands. Menno also traces the development of oath taking in the Bible, arguing for a progressive revelation perfectly revealed by Jesus. The treatment of oaths in the Old Testament was superseded by Jesus' words on the matter. (13)

> *(13) Menno* "To swear truly was allowed to the Jews under the Law; but the Gospel forbids this to Christians." *(CWMS, 519).*

For Menno, disobedience to the literal words of Christ was cause for damnation; therefore the oath became a life and death issue. Menno pleaded with those in power, that they accept "yea and nay" as being as binding as oaths, as a kind of surrogate oath, in which lying could be treated the same way as perjury. Unlike Schleitheim's argument, which held that no human being has the power to "promise" into the future, Menno's argument was that "affirming" was simply swearing in another fashion, and should be treated as such by the authorities. The primary reason for affirmation rather than oath taking is simply "obedience to the commands of Christ" as expressed in Scripture.

David Joris and Menno

David Joris

Faced with Münster's collapse and the need to reunite dispirited Melchiorites, David Joris explained the failure in terms reminiscent of Hans Hut after the failed Peasants' War. The Münsterites, said Joris, had tried to establish a physical restitution when they had not yet managed to attain a full spiritual restitution. What was needed was a postponement, while the spiritual "third restitution" was taking place within true believers.

Joris' position on the sword and vengeance contained some ambiguities. Immediately following the slaughter in Münster, Joris (as had Hut after the Peasants' War) dwelt upon the joys of the eventual vengeance of the Lord on the impious. (14) But who would do the bloody task of wreaking vengeance on the ungodly? Joris usually maintained that it was "God and His angels" who would do the punishing, not the "saints," but occasionally he implied that believers (once perfectly yielded spiritually) also would be able to enjoy vengeance in their own person. (15) Immediately following the fall of Münster Joris spoke often and extravagantly about the "sword of the Spirit" in ways that could easily have been misunderstood and misinterpreted.

> **(14) Joris, writing against persecutors in 1535.**
> *"Oh Behold, God's scythe will strike all of you*
> *And it shall violently cut you down to the earth,*
> *so that neither branch nor root will remain...*
> *His burnished sword will cut, yes indeed,*
> *it is grasped to hew, to strike all who are drunk,*
> *and who are unconcerned and glad."*
> *(In Waite, 1990, 101-102).*

> **(15) Joris** *"When you are advanced enough and know that your flesh is dead so that it seeks nothing for itself... then [you may] burn with wrath as Moses, Phyneas, Ehud, Jahel, David, Christ etc., [burned] against the evil ones..." (In Waite, 1990, 102).*

If there was some ambiguity in Joris' earlier teaching concerning the sword, with some hints that he might be expecting followers to take up a physical sword in due course, his increasing move towards spiritualism

from 1539 onward settled the question. Increasingly Joris became convinced of his own prophetic and spiritual authority as the "third David."
And he insisted more and more that all events of true significance would
happen spiritually and internally, in the souls of believers. The restitution
would take place there, as would the return of Christ. External actions, so
long as they did not harm the inward, spiritual person, were of little consequence. Joris wrote concerning "judges and commanders" that insofar
as they "do all things correctly in the faith and do not hinder Christians
nor the gospel," then "it is free to them." (Waite, 1994, 154).

Spiritualism

In 1544 Joris put his Nicodemite theory into practice. He moved to
Basel under a pseudonym, publicly conforming to all required practices
while secretly continuing to write treatises and letters of counsel for the
spiritual edification of his followers. For Joris there were, emphatically,
two kingdoms, but the visible and physical kingdom of darkness was so
unimportant that actions performed in that kingdom were of very little
consequence.

Menno Simons

Menno Simons had not been present at the Bocholt conference of 1536,
when David Joris had had some success in mediating between competing
Melchiorite factions, but it became increasingly clear that he and Joris
were fellow Melchiorite Anabaptists working at cross purposes. Already
in the first edition of his most important writing, the *Fundamentboeck*
(1539/40), Menno argued that the Melchiorite prophets (and this included
David Joris, of course) had gone beyond the testimony of Scripture, sub-
stituting their own authority for that of Christ. Menno emphasized repeatedly that true holiness would be in conformity to the Gospel of Christ
as revealed in the Word of God. True holiness is obedient to that Word.
The righteous live by faith, and that faith "must be conformed to the
gospel of Christ."

*Prophets and
Scripture*

In replying to this challenge, David Joris wrote that Menno was acting like the Pharisee in judging the publican to be a sinner, which was a sign of the lack of Christ's Spirit. Menno, said Joris, was judging only on the basis of appearances, which was exactly how the world judged, namely according to the flesh and not the spirit. Joris judged Menno to have grasped only the letter of Scripture.

Teaching
Authority

From this opening exchange we see clearly the difficulties that confronted post-Münster Melchiorites on the matter of teaching authority. Menno and Joris, both baptized by Obbe Philips, not surprisingly were agreed on certain Anabaptist essentials. But Menno wished to set limits on the working of the Spirit by appealing to the life and teachings of Christ, thereby denying the possibility of scriptural interpretations that went beyond Christ, and denying the possiblity of contemporary prophetic revelations.

On the substantive issue of spirit and letter Joris did add some further argumentation in reply to Menno's letter. Menno had written that obedience to Christ was central. Joris agreed, but added an important qualification. The fiery flame of the Spirit, said Joris, must come with power into one's mind and spirit, from which would come righteousness and truth with power. It is obedience to this inner, spiritual Christ and eternal truth that is true obedience. The fleshly, outer person reading the letter cannot attain to this truth. In fact, said Joris, he himself had received the spiritual power to know the truth. The same Lord who had authored the Scriptures had given him a learned tongue, had made his mouth into a razor in the spirit, and had given him knowledge of the right time to speak. The Lord had opened Joris' ears like a master does for a disciple.

Prophets

How did Menno reply to Joris' claim to spiritual and prophetic legitimacy? In a revealing passage found in a writing dating from around 1542– and most probably with Joris' criticisms in mind–Menno made no claims to prophetic authority, and denied that Joris was a prophet. (16)

> *(16) Menno* *"Brethren, I tell you the truth and lie not. I am no Enoch, I am no Elias, I am not one who sees visions, I am no prophet who can teach and prophesy otherwise than what is written in the Word of God and understood in the Spirit."*
>
> *"The Word of Christ is sufficient for me. If I do not follow His testimony, then verily all that I do is useless, ... even if I had such visions and inspirations..." (CWMS, 310).*

Likewise, said Menno, he was not a "third David as some have boasted and do even now boast." There are only two Davids in Scripture, namely the son of Jesse, and Christ, the spiritual David. "Whosoever poses as a third is a falsifier and blasphemer against Christ." With this Menno declared against both Jan van Leiden (the "second David" of Münster) and David Joris, who was considered by his followers to be the "third David."

On what basis did Menno claim his own authority to teach? Menno acknowledged that in his natural person he was "nothing but unclean slime and dust of the earth," until, he said, "the clear light of grace and knowledge appeared unto me from high heaven. This has given me such a heart, will, and desire that I willingly seek after that which is good and strive with the holy Paul to follow..." (CWMS, 310).

There was a difference between the true grace and knowledge which came to him from "high heaven," and the false visions and illuminations of the contemporary prophets, Menno insisted. The false prophets were set on "their own honor, fame, and gain," while Menno's own writing and preaching "is nothing else than Jesus Christ." Nevertheless, in the final analysis Menno too had to rest his particular (Christocentric) reading and interpretation of Scripture on a "spiritual understanding" that had come to him through "the light of grace and knowledge from high heaven."

Conclusion

The fact that Bernhard Rothmann, David Joris, and Menno Simons all stood in the tradition of Melchior Hoffman testifies both to the power exercised by Hoffman's ideas in the Netherlands, and to the pliable nature of his teaching. Crucial to the further development of a Melchiorite political ethic were Hoffman's appeals to the working of the Spirit in contemporary prophets, the exegetical freedom provided by his figurative approach to Scripture, and his conviction that Jesus Christ would return in the space of a couple of years. This truly was a volatile mix of ideas.

If Hoffman, Rothmann, and the Melchiorite prophets had been right (that is, if Christ had returned in 1535 and accepted the Münsterite "Bride"), politics as such would have come to an end. In fact, such an apocalyptic ending was *absolutely necessary* in order for Hoffman's political ethic to function. For both Melchior Hoffman and for the Münsterites, "politics" was a short-term, interim situation that soon would be rendered obsolete by the return of the "King of kings." When Christ did not return, and the prophetic edifice had been laid waste by fire and sword, adjustments needed to be made.

Apart from the desperate attempts by the Batenburgers to keep the spirit of Münster alive, adjustments to the Melchiorite political ethic were made in two primary contrasting directions, by David Joris and Menno Simons, who were competing for support among the same disillusioned Melchiorites. Given their ideological differences each man was, in effect, challenging the leadership authority of the other. In many ways, David Joris was in a better position to provide that initial leadership than was Menno Simons.

Against the background of Melchior Hoffman's teaching, which both Menno and Joris shared, Menno was more of an innovator than was Joris, for Joris was claiming little more than had Hoffman or Matthijs. Joris' claim to charismatic, prophetic authority placed him in continuity with the mainstream of the Melchiorite tradition, and placed Menno is the awkward position of appearing to be one of those "learned preachers" who appealed not to the Spirit, but to their own wisdom and knowledge in the interpretation of the *letter* of Scripture. Certainly Menno's emphasis on the letter, and the outer signs of inner regeneration, led him to work for the establishment of *visible* outposts of the Kingdom of God on earth (again closer to the Münsterite ideal). Joris was content to gather together a largely invisible, "spiritual" church.

But in the end, Joris's political ethic, like Hoffman's and Rothmann's, also was an interim ethic. It bought a little more time for the Melchiorite apocalyptic dream, but did not solve the basic dilemma. Believers, said Joris, were to stay hidden, working on their inner, spiritual lives, after which Christ and the angels would return. In this way Joris provided a logical continuation of Hoffman's ideas that exerted a certain attraction in the early going, after Münster. But the fact that Christ did not return proved the undoing of Joris's political ethic, as it had for Hoffman and Rothmann before him. Accepting the political status quo, attempting to keep a "spiritual fellowship" alive in secret, and looking more and more to a mortal prophet as its guide to blessedness (after 1544, disguised as businessman in Basel), the Davidjorists had few resources for long-term survival.

*Failed
Apocalypticism*

Menno also had to deal with the failure of Melchiorite prophecies concerning the Last Days. The apocalyptically expectant tone of Menno's earlier writings does fade over time, as one might predict. But more importantly, Menno's political ethic, while looking forward to Christ's second coming, was not simply a short-term, interim ethic depending entirely upon Christ's return. Since Menno maintained that the era of Christ (and his commandments) would remain in force until His second coming (of which no one knew the times or the seasons), Menno's ethics in general, and his political ethic in particular, were independent of the apocalyptic event. Menno Simons also stood solidly in the Melchiorite tradition, but he redefined crucial Melchiorite teachings, and developed different Melchiorite ideas than did Joris.

The most fundamental realignment was Menno's denial of the prophetic authority of Melchiorite contemporaries and his insistence that the Bible had to be read with Christ at the centre. Gone were dreams and

*Prophecy
denied*

visions, and gone too were appeals to a relativizing "age of restitution" that took away the ethical force of Jesus's commands. If this was a "literalism" that put one in mind of the Münsterites, nevertheless it was a Christocentric, New Testament reading of Scripture that made limited use of Old Testament "figures" and allegories. Menno's insistence on Jesus's command not to wield the sword (personal pacifism) and not to swear oaths brings the Swiss Brethren and the Hutterites to mind, even though important Melchiorite traces remain in Menno's political ethic.

Conclusion: Sword, Oath, and Separatism

How should the true church relate to the world of government and politics? The lack of consensus among early Anabaptists on how Scripture was to be interpreted was visibly demonstrated in the various positions early Anabaptists assumed concerning the sword of government and the oath, in all the Anabaptist streams.

Diversity

The diversity of Anabaptist views concerning government during its developmental period, first brought to our attention by James Stayer's seminal *Anabaptists and the Sword* (1976), is beyond dispute. The diversity of views among the early Anabaptists should put an end to casual appeals to the so-called "normative" position of "Anabaptist nonresistance" as given expression in Schleitheim's article 6. Schleitheim was not normative for the Anabaptist movement at the time of its composition. Schleitheim expressed one view among many, based on one way among many of interpreting and reading Scripture in search of guidelines for the reform of the church.

Consensus

However, when we look to the ongoing traditions of the Swiss Brethren, the Hutterites, and the Mennonites, we do find that a pacifist and separatist consensus did emerge concerning the world, government, the sword, and the oath. All three surviving Anabaptist traditions eventually came to appeal to a literal Christocentric hermeneutics, focused on the words and the life of Jesus. All three traditions read this Scripture as providing a rule of life to be followed obediently by disciples. And in all three cases, the sword of government and civic oaths would be forbidden to Christians, on virtually identical biblical grounds.

Agreement had crystallized by the end of the sixteenth century in the Anabaptist traditions that survived, but it was a consensus about biblical and ethical norms that emerged only at the end of a sometimes bloody and often chaotic period of history. In point of fact, consensus on the sword and the oath was achieved only after apocalyptic prophecy had spectacularly failed, and spiritualist Anabaptists had departed or been banned.

The general development in the Anabaptist interpretation of Scripture that is visible in the foregoing chapters also will be seen in the chapters to follow. The steady emergence and dominance of Christocentric, literal readings of Scripture, with the New Testament at the centre, would provide biblical answers to many of the questions under dispute in the Anabaptist movement.

2.
Anabaptism
and
Socio-Economic Reality

Chapter 15

Mutual Aid, Equality, and Marriage

Adelheit Schwarz of Watt

In the spring of 1529, Bartli Hug of the Swiss village of Dällikon, near Zurich, reported to the authorities that several women from the neighbouring village of Watt had come to Dällikon, gone into Elsa Spilmann's house, and held a suspicious meeting. The women involved included Jakob Fry's wife and Konrad Fry's wife. Furthermore, the Anabaptist leader Wilhelm Reublin had read and preached at the inn in Weiningen. Included in the audience were Hans Grossman, Elsa Spilmann, her daughter Barbara, *Adelheit Spilmann, Baltiß Spilmann's wife*, and Felix Fry's wife from Watt. Bartli Hug said that he had tried to do his duty as a citizen, and stop the proceedings. "For this they locked me out, and told me I would not be saved," he reported.

Adelheit Spilmann, Balthasar Spilmann's wife, was also known by her maiden name of Schwarz. She was from the village of Watt, although she lived with her husband and their family in the village of Dällikon. She was attracted to Anabaptism and usually was in the company of like-minded women. As a group, these women were not afraid to speak their minds or to act boldly on their convictions.

By April 1529, Elsa Spilmann and Adelheit Spilmann had both been in prison already once on account of the "Anabaptist business." Another witness testified that Elsa and Adelheit weren't attending the official state church (which they were obliged to do by law), and that he had never seen them at the celebration of the Lord's Supper in the local church. Adelheit was changing religious allegiances.

In December 1529, the Zurich authorities made a concerted effort to suppress Anabaptist activity in the region of Bülach, just north of Zurich. They arrested at least twenty-eight people from the area, of whom six or seven proved not to have accepted rebaptism. Almost half of those arrested–twelve, in fact–were women, and we find Adelheit Schwarz among them, arrested now for the second time.

The prison testimony of these women reveals their disruptive strategy of "passive resistance." Adelheit's questioning comes first in the document, and the scribe notes that she refused to give a straight answer to the questions. She insisted only that "she holds that baptism to be correct which God has commanded," but she refused to say which baptism that was. Appollonia Schnider gave the same answer. Margaret Wiener of Bülach admitted that she had been baptized about one year previous, but she refused to say who had baptized her, nor would she say anything about their practice, no matter how long she was questioned. Her mother, Annli Wiener of Bülach, was so uncommunicative that the scribe simply wrote that "one can get less out of her than out of a stone." In similar fashion Annli Sidler confessed that she held to the baptism that God commanded, namely that those who believe and are baptized are saved.

It is obvious that these women had planned their joint strategy with some care, and although they were powerless in the conventional sense, they had devised a clever way of throwing sand into the gears of official machinery. But then frustrated officials responded with the weapon of physical torture.

When Regula Kernn said little that was useful to her questioners, she was beaten with rods, but the scribe reports that they got absolutely nothing further from her. Annli Sidler simply refused to say who had baptized her, since she would not inflict more suffering on him. Appollonia Schnider, obviously responding to torture with thumbscrews, said that her jailers could "press her finger as long and as hard as they wished, but she would not say who had baptized her; for she would not be guilty of his blood."

These three women endured at least ten months more of prison before they recanted and were released. When they did recant, they also named the man who had baptized them: Conrad Winckler of Wasserberg, who had been arrested with them and then executed by drowning by the Zurich authorities. In spite of jail and torture, their testimony had formed no part of the judgement against Winckler.

Adelheit also was questioned in this second round, and admitted that she had not yet been rebaptized. Nevertheless, concerning the "main article" on baptism she answered as she had before, that she wished to hold to the baptism which God had commanded. But in her conscience, she said, she did not know which baptism was correct.

It is a remarkable fact that Adelheit chose to remain in prison with her Anabaptist friends. Since she was not rebaptized, she could have left prison at any time with few concessions on her part. But she could not, she said, burden her conscience in this way. Although in the end she consented to an official recantation concerning baptism, she soon changed her mind about that.

On March 13, 1531, Balthasar Spilmann of Dällikon appeared in "marriage court" in Zurich and asked for a divorce from Adelheit Schwarz of Watt. She was, he said, an Anabaptist who had twice been arrested. She had borne him seven children. But one night she had packed some things and left, and he did not know where she was. He wished to divorce her, he said, because he had to care for his thirteen children, and he needed a wife for that purpose! The court told him to find Adelheit so that the court could hear both sides in the case.

On April 27, Balthasar Spilmann was back before the court. He had located Adelheit, and had sent a daughter to fetch her. Adelheit had come back with the girl, and stayed overnight, but left again immediately. When Balthasar showed her the letter from the court, she had said "insulting things" and insisted that "she wished to be obedient to God, and not to the earthly authorities." Two days later the court granted Balthasar a divorce from Adelheit. The problem, noted the court, was a growing one. There were several more cases like it. As a corrective measure the court recommended "strong punishment for such unfaithful, deserting persons."

Did Adelheit simply abandon her family? Was she escaping from a life of drudgery and servitude? Had she come to a consciousness of personal worth? Was she simply more devoted to God than to husband and family? The documents do not say which of these interpretations is closest to the truth. But a comment by a later Anabaptist prisoner tells us a little more about Adelheit and the depth of her religious convictions.

In the year 1548, seventeen years after the events recounted above, a man named Hans Fisher was arrested for Anabaptism by the Zurich authorities. He finally gave a full recantation. He had been baptized nine years before, in a forest near Kaiserstuhl by the Rhine. He confessed that the Anabaptists had held their meetings in forests and woods in the Swiss district of Baden, and in the woods near Bülach. Among the people he named explicitly as fellow worshippers were "Adelheit Spilmann and her mother," as well as Adelheit Spilmann from Dällikon.

"Adelheit Spilmann from Dällikon" is Adelheit Schwarz of Watt, for Spilmann was her married name, and she had once lived in Dällikon. It is altogether possible, if not likely, that the younger Adelheit Spilmann and her mother, mentioned in 1548, were Adelheit Schwarz's granddaughter and daughter. But in any case, it is clear that Adelheit Schwarz of Watt persevered in the Anabaptist faith.

(For more, see Arnold Snyder and Linda Huebert Hecht, eds., *Profiles of Anabaptist Women: Sixteenth Century Reforming Pioneers* [Waterloo: WLU Press, 1996]).

Anabaptism and Socio-Economic Structures

The story of Adelheit Schwarz of Watt illustrates the socially subversive nature of early Anabaptism. Swiss authorities knew that "being more obedient to God than to man" was more than just a Bible verse. It was an approach to life that posed a direct challenge to the political, social, and economic status quo.

Sixteenth century society was built upon hierarchies of all kinds which were assumed to be God given, in the nature of divine order and creation. But it was a time of uncertainty and redrawing of boundaries. Some important assumptions of dominant, cultural Christianity already had come under attack by the evangelical reformers, particularly the privileged social position of the clergy. It was only natural that social and economic relationships of all kinds would be re-evaluated and tested by the authority of the Spirit and the Word of God in Scripture.

One of the unintended effects of Martin Luther's reformation efforts was that when common people turned to the Bible, they found democratic social and economic principles there. Many were convinced that Scripture called for a larger measure of equality in Christian society. Likewise the priesthood of all believers was a radical democratic principle, as was the notion that God had created the earth for all people, not for the exclusive enjoyment of the nobility. (1) Reinforcing the democratic

> *(1) Jakob Stapfer describes Hans Kruesi's teaching, July, 1525.*
> "[He] taught the ignorant common people that no one owed any more obedience to the authorities, and especially that all people are equal, and that what one person had should be divided up with the others." *(QGTS, I, #353, 259-61).*

social and economic impulses that Anabaptism inherited from the early Reformation of the common people were the core principles that were common to all branches of the Anabaptist movement.

Primary among these theological principles was the work of the Holy *Spirit* Spirit, so much in evidence in early Anabaptism. The Spirit seemed to be blind to conventional social hierarchies. It did not choose to speak primarily to the educated, to aristocrats, or only to men, but rather spoke to *all* those who humbled themselves in obedience to God, who yielded themselves to that Spirit. (2)

---

(2) Melchior Hoffman, Preface to Commentary on Revelation, 1530.
"Concerning these high gifts of the Holy Spirit or of his Mind, God pays no regard to a person's [social] station, but rather through Christ He calls, names, draws, and chooses his elect from all tribes and tongues, heathens, peoples, and groups, but especially from the poor, those who are stricken and humbled in mind, spirit and heart." (Fast, 1962, 310-311).

This understanding stood behind Anabaptist challenges to the social and economic structures of sixteenth century society. The Anabaptists believed that the inner change wrought by the Spirit in every person had to be manifested not only in "pious" acts, but in practical life decisions that were in conformity with the social and economic ordering of Scripture.

Economic Questions

In economic matters, the Anabaptists looked back to medieval social and ascetic economic ideals, rather than anticipating the coming capitalist revolution.

---

(3) Hans Denck

"It is hard for the rich man (that is, all persons who are full of the creaturely, each one according to his measure) to enter into the Kingdom of Heaven; but not impossible (Matt. 19:23). . . . Yea, it is impossible to retain the creaturely, as the false Christians do, and at the same time to receive salvation."

(Furcha, 1975, 97).

Anabaptists emphatically did not agree with the Protestant reformers that the economic life of Christians was neutral in matters of salvation. (3) The living of a life of discipleship was paramount for them, just as it had been in the monastic traditions. This meant that the economic activity of the regenerated believers needed to be carried out according to the norms of the Kingdom of Heaven. Kingdom norms were economic sufficiency (not surplus) and the sharing of any surplus with those in need. Anabaptists were convinced, as had been the ascetic tradition before them, that ample justification for this view could be found in the Bible.

Many of the same religious, social and economic impulses that fueled the so-called Peasants' War were considered legitimate issues within the Anabaptist movement, in particular the election and support of pastors by local communities (as against the compulsory church tithe) and the disciplining of those pastors by those communities. The South German and Melchiorite Anabaptists believed that the events of the Last Days would finally reform society. But in the end, of course, the Peasants' Revolt failed, and Christ did not return. Democratic reform principles were not abandoned, but were directed inward, to the church, and society was left to its own devices.

Peasants

With two important exceptions–Balthasar Hubmaier in Nicholsburg (4) and the Münsterite experience–the bulk of Anabaptist writing concerning economic matters was composed within this later, separated framework, written for the church of the faithful, not for society at large. The most fundamental points of discussion reflected in Anabaptist writing on economic matters thus have to do with the question of how the true church ought to incarnate biblical economics.

> **(4) Balthasar Hubmaier**
> *"I have ever and always spoken thus of the community of goods: that one person should always look out for the other, so that the hungry are fed, the thirsty given drink, the naked clothed." (Pipkin and Yoder, 1989, 183).*

The broad shape of Anabaptist thinking on economic matters is generally recognized and has been noted above as one of the core Anabaptist beliefs. (5) All Anabaptists agreed that the reborn, baptized and regenerated believers made up a sharing community by virtue of their re-birth, baptism, participation in the Supper, and manner of life obedient to Christ's com-

> **(5) Ambrosius Spittelmaier, "Reply to Questioning," 1527, Nuremberg.**
> *"No one can accept [the kingdom of God] except those who are poor in Christ here, for a Christian has nothing of his own... He should have nothing of his own in such a manner that he would [not] wish to say 'the house is mine, the land is mine, the coin is mine,' but rather 'it is all ours.' This is why we say 'Our Father.' In sum, a Christian ... looks more to his neighbour than to himself (I Cor. 13)..." (Schornbaum, 1934, 49).*

mands. It was inconceivable to the Anabaptists that there could be reborn and regenerated Christians, baptized into the one Body of Christ, who would cling to surplus goods or wealth when they saw a fellow member of the Body in need. Such an understanding was universally Anabaptist, present in the Swiss, South German, and North German/Dutch manifestations. The most consistent Anabaptist pattern, seen among all Anabaptist groups, was an attempt to put into practice the apostolic pattern of sharing described in Acts 2, 4 and 5.

---

(6) Menno Simons

"[Those who are truly reborn of the Holy Spirit] show mercy and love, as much as they can. No one among them is allowed to beg. They take to heart the need of the saints. They entertain those in distress. They take the stranger into their houses. They comfort the afflicted; assist the needy; clothe the naked; feed the hungry; do not turn their face from the poor; do not despise their own flesh. Isa. 59:7,8. Behold, such a community we teach." (CWMS, 558).

The principle of sufficiency for all (particularly within the community of saints, the one Body of Christ) was accepted virtually across the board in the Anabaptist movement. (6)

Three Criticisms The Anabaptist critique of contemporary economic practices was not simply directed within, to other church members, but also was directed outside, implicitly and explicitly, against all those who wished to call themselves Christians. Three points stand out.

–The Anabaptists were critical of the poverty they saw around them, particularly since the poor were supposedly also members of Christ's Church, whether Protestant or Catholic.

–All Anabaptists were extremely suspicious of trade and commerce as means of earning one's livelihood. Christians, they said, should be engaged in "honest hand labour." (7)

–The Anabaptists uniformly rejected the charging of interest on money at loan. Such interest, according to the understanding of the time, was most often simply described as "usury" or even "theft."

In contrast to Christian groups outside the Anabaptist movement, the fundamental uniformity of Anabaptist teaching on economic matters is striking, from the common ascetic, spiritual underpinnings, to the concrete manifestations of economic community that were expected to emerge as a result of rebirth and baptism. The understanding also was common that the celebration of the Lord's Supper was a recommitment to the community in all things, including economic necessity.

> **(7) Peter Riedemann**
> *"[Christians] should labour, working with their hands what is honest, that they may have to give to him that needeth." (Riedemann, 1950, 126-27).*

In spite of this strong point of agreement, economics became a point of contention within the movement (leading eventually to schism) because Scripture provided no exact guidelines for concrete implementation. Disagreements emerged over patterns of production and ownership, not over the principle of distribution.

The crucial issue became whether the sharing of possessions was to be a *voluntary* expression of one's inner regeneration, or whether yielding possession of economic goods needed to be *legislated* by the true church, the Body of Christ. This question was argued most vigorously in Moravia.

Voluntary or Legislated?

Early communitarian Anabaptism in Moravia saw the emergence of three main groups: the proto-Hutterites in Auspitz (who emigrated from Nicholsburg), the followers of Gabriel Ascherham (the Gabrielites), who originated in Silesia, and the followers of Philip Plenner (the Philipites), who had migrated from Swabia. By 1530 the latter two of these groups numbered several thousand in their membership. They recognized Gabriel Ascherham as their lead bishop, and practiced a voluntary form of community of goods.

Gabriel Ascherham

All of this came to head in 1533 when Jakob Hutter brought a stricter vision of "true community" to the Auspitz group. Community of goods was to be legislated, not voluntary, Hutter maintained. The end result, besides mutual recrimination, excommunication and schism, was the es-

Jakob Hutter

tablishment of a strict and legislated community of goods in the Auspitz community under Hutter's leadership. In this move to outward legislation (*Ordnungen*) concerning behaviour in the community, the previous emphasis on *Gelassenheit* was retained, but now linked indissolubly to an outward condition of total yieldedness in economic matters. This linkage is common in subsequent Hutterite writings. (8)

> **(8) Hutterite bishop, Peter Walpot, makes the case for linking inner and outer.**
> *"It should be realized that where there is genuine spiritual communion, there is also external community of goods; the one cannot exist without the other and it does not endure without the other. Otherwise it would also follow that the interior baptism of the Spirit were sufficient and the external confirmation of water baptism unnecessary, although here, too, the one cannot exist without the other." (In Stayer, 1991, 157).*

The question of voluntary versus legislated community of goods remained a permanent point of contention between the Hutterites and all other Anabaptists. The Hutterites argued that Acts 2, 4 and 5 outlined the proper biblical economic order for a Christian community. The typical non-Hutterite response to this argument was to say that even in the Jerusalem church there had been no coercion, and furthermore, the practice was not extended to all the early churches.

In spite of significant commonalities, in the end the practical specifics governing the economic life of the reborn came to divide the Anabaptist fellowship, driving a permanent wedge between the Hutterites and other Anabaptists. The issue was central to Anabaptist theology. If the "outer" and the "inner" lives of believers are indissolubly linked and determine salvation, as the Anabaptists maintained, must not a spiritual union of believers also result necessarily in a life of radical economic sharing?

> **Anabaptist women testify before the Bernese court, May 1529.**
> Barbli with the wooden leg. *"Whoever has a true faith will share with a needy member and not keep anything as personal property... but indeed, no one should take anyone else's possessions forcefully."* Margaret von Sigrißwil. (Heinrich Seiler's wife). *"She does not accept infant baptism, and she is speaking for herself alone. She has not been baptized again, but she wishes with all her heart to be, because with the [infant] baptism she received, she was muddied with papal laws like the Mass, praying to the saints, and other things." (QGTS, III, Aarau, Bern Solothurn, #306).*

Depiction of a Hutterite family in Moravia,
standing in front of their communal dwelling (Haushaben).
This woodcut was the cover illustration for a Jesuit polemic written against the Hutterites:
Christof Andreas Fischer, Der Hutterischen Widertauffer Taubenkobel (1607).

The Equality of Men and Women Before God

Many Anabaptists cited the text "God is no respecter of persons" (Acts 10:34-35) in their court testimonies and other places. A Swiss Brethren biblical concordance dating from around 1550 devotes twelve pages to this theme, collating and citing a variety of Scriptures to make the point. What the Anabaptists meant by citing this passage in Acts is plain. In matters of faith and salvation, the way in which the world views "the person" is immaterial. Every person, woman or man, stands equally accountable before God.

Individual
Responsibility

The three-fold understanding of baptism in the Anabaptist movement gave visible expression and form to the idea of personal equality and accountability before God. Both the inner baptism of the Spirit and the outer baptism in water were radically individual events. No priest, wife, husband, parent, or godparent could take these steps for anyone else. Salvation was not granted by a powerful church with its clergy, but rather was a matter between the believer and God.

The Anabaptists believed that all individuals were required to pass through the same process of yielding personally to the Spirit of God, and of exercising their free will either to accept God's grace and its consequences—above all, obedience (water baptism, community discipline, economic sharing)—or to reject grace and its visible, communal consequences. And, of course, the acceptance of water baptism signified not only an inner yielding to God and a visible commitment to a radical new community of brothers and sisters in the Lord. It also signified a willingness to bear the cross of persecution and possible martyrdom—the baptism of blood.

All of these steps—from an openness to the Spirit, to the acceptance of water baptism, to the steadfastness unto death called for by state persecution—were steps that could be taken only by individuals who had freely chosen (and who continued to choose) the "narrow way" by means of God's grace.

Communal
Accountability

Nevertheless there was a tension in Anabaptism between individual choice and communal commitment. In the Anabaptist understanding, individual choice (that is, openness to the Holy Spirit) led to the Body of Christ on earth, which required accountability, obedience and conformity. This two-fold movement, from radical individual choice to the limitation of choice by the community of believers, framed the question of equality in the Anabaptist community of saints.

Swiss Anabaptism

Early Swiss Anabaptism emerged as a movement because it emphasized the work of the Holy Spirit in individual believers, both women and men. Consequently, spiritualistic manifestations among early Swiss Anabaptist women and men were not uncommon.

Arrest of Catherine Muller in Zurich, 1637

Agnes Linck of Biel testified in Solothurn in 1528 that she had been baptized in the Spirit. She denied having been instructed by any Anabaptist, but rather said that she had been instructed "by Christ her Lord." She was literate and confessed to having instructed two younger people.

Margret Hottinger of Zollikon was noted for her piety and her prophetic gifts. The chronicler Johannes Kessler of St. Gall complained that "she undertook to speak of things that nobody could understand, as if she were so deeply raised up in God that nobody could comprehend her speech." (Harder, 1985, 548). The circle around Margret included Magdalena Müller, Barbara Mürglen, and Frena Buman of St. Gall who, under the "inspiration of the Spirit" carried out some bizarre prophetic actions, much to Kessler's outrage.

Margret Hottinger

As we have seen above, the Schleitheim Articles, with their critique of those who "practice and observe the freedom of the Spirit and of Christ," restricted individual and prophetic manifestations of the Spirit in Swiss Anabaptism. This limitation did protect Swiss Anabaptism from some of the excesses that appeared in the rest of the movement, but it also limited leadership possibilities for women.

South German Anabaptism and the Hutterite Communities

The appeal to a direct and spiritual call from God as the basis for preaching, teaching and action was even stronger in Hans Hut's circle than among the Swiss. Linda Huebert Hecht's study of court records for the Tirol revealed a high percentage of female participation in the early Anabaptist movement there, from 1527 to 1529.

Ursula Binder

Ursula Binder and her husband were baptized by Hans Hut, who then sent them to missionize in Salzburg. The court record suggests that she was as active in this mission work as was her husband, but gives no further relevant details. One would like to know more about the woman who, it was reported, said that she had "made six new Christians in a short time," but again no further information is available.

Helena von Freyberg

More is known about Helene von Freyberg. She was a member of the lower nobility who used her castle at Münichau to give refuge to Anabaptist preachers, and also gathered and led an Anabaptist conventicle there. She later instructed converts in the Anabaptist faith.

While there is good evidence for the proselytizing activity of Anabaptist women in the Tirol in this earliest period, there is little evidence shedding light on the spiritual calling of these women. This undoubtedly is due to the nature of the surviving evidence, rather than to fundamental differences in Anabaptist regional movements.

Moravia

As persecution increased in the Tirol, more and more Anabaptists fled to Moravia, where many joined the communal groups that had emerged there in 1528. The Tirolean refugees encountered a very different social ethos when they entered the Moravian communities, especially the Hutterite ones after 1533. The strong emphasis on a biblical rule of life necessary to sustain a communal endeavour soon restricted the scope of activity for women.

In 1545, in his influential *Rechenshafft (Account)*, the Hutterite leader Peter Riedeman outlined what he understood to be the proper divine order governing the relationship between men and women, especially within

marriage. Riedeman empha-
sized the traditional hierarchical order of creation, rather
than spiritual equality. (9)

In this way did "spiritual
equality before God" become
a practical inequality within the
Hutterite communities. Men,
as those "in whom something
of God's glory is seen" were
to have compassion on the
"weaker vessels" even as men
"went before" and exercised

(9) "Since woman was taken from man, and not man from woman, man hath lordship but woman weakness, humility and submission, therefore she should be under the yoke of man and obedient to him, even as the woman was commanded by God when he said to her, 'The man shall be thy lord.'" (Riedemann, 1950, 98-99).

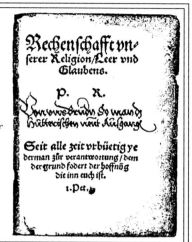

spiritual and physical leadership and authority. Women, for their part, were
to be humble, submissive, and obedient. Leadership within the Hutterite
church and community was in exclusively male hands; individual choice
for women remained in the initial commitment to baptism and the community, in the freedom to leave "unbelieving" spouses, and in the ultimate testimony of martyrdom. This pattern was not peculiar to the
Hutterites, but became the accepted structure in the surviving Anabaptist
communities.

Melchiorite Anabaptism

Nowhere in the Anabaptist movement did women achieve and maintain as
lofty a pastoral and leadership role as in the Strasbourg Melchiorite community. For this reason the contrast between the early and late Melchiorite
movements is quite dramatic.

Of the 18 active prophets in Hoffman's community, 8 were women.
The theological justification for the involvement of women in these positions was provided by Joel 2:28-29 and Acts 2:17-18: "In the last days ... I
will pour out my Spirit upon all flesh, and your sons and your daughters

Prophets

shall prophesy..." Given Hoffman's conviction that he was living in the Last Days such scriptural justification undoubtedly was considered self-evident and not requiring further proof.

Two of the most prominent of Strasbourg prophets were Ursula Jost, whose visions have been described above, and Barbara Rebstock. Ursula is perhaps the best known because of the publication of her visions in 1530, but Barbara Rebstock seems to have been considered by contemporaries the more important of the two prophetesses. She was widely renowned for her prophetic powers of discernment.

Barbara
Rebstock

In a testimony dating from April 1534, Franz from Hazebrouck in Flanders testified that he had been baptized in Münster by Bernhard Rothmann. He had heard about Barbara in the Netherlands and come to Strasbourg specifically to see her, where he had been arrested. Barbara also led regular gatherings in her place of residence in the Kalbgasse. She exercised direct leadership in the Strasbourg Melchiorite congregation, not only through visions and prophecies, but also as an inspired counsellor, teacher, and long-term elder in the congregation.

The cases of Ursula Jost and Barbara Rebstock demonstrate how, under certain conditions, sixteenth century gender barriers were overcome in the Anabaptist movement by demonstrations of spiritual inspiration. What was remarkable about Barbara Rebstock in particular was the long-term leadership and counsel she continued to provide to the Strasbourg Melchiorite community.

(10) Bernhard Rothmann
"God has placed the woman below the man, that she be submissively obedient to her husband and honour him, and follow and hear him only."
(Stupperich, 1970, 262).

Melchior Hoffman's openness to prophetic leadership by women was not transferred wholesale to the Netherlands, although there were also some notable prophetesses in the north in the early going. The prevailing theology and mood in the "New Jerusalem" of Münster was patriarchal and restrictive. (10) It was an attitude that culminated in a male-dominated polygamy, justified in Old Testament biblical terms.

This patriarchal attitude was carried forth by David Joris after the fall of Münster, although he numbered many women in his following. Joris wanted men to assert leadership and women to take a subservient place in the community of saints. Joris liked to advise men to "let your beards grow." (Waite, 1994, 117). How would such teaching concerning men and women be heard in the original Melchiorite setting (Strasbourg), and by Barbara Rebstock, whose husband clearly occupied a spiritual role second to hers in the congregation? The question came to a head in 1538, when David Joris came to Strasbourg in an effort to convince the Melchiorite elders of his prophetic and leadership authority. One of those elders was Barbara Rebstock.

David Joris

Barbara Rebstock

In Strasbourg Joris insisted on his spiritual authority over the Strasbourg brethren. At some point in the discussion, Barbara "spoke out of turn" (according to Joris' account) and suggested that Joris was going too far, and trying to "pluck the fruits of our tree before they are ripe." She counselled silence, and the other Strasbourg elders heeded her counsel. Joris was furious: "I warn you that you not let yourselves be misled. Men, regard yourselves above the women, then you will not be deceived." (Waite, 1994, chapter 7).

Barbara Rebstock's place of leadership in the Strasbourg congregation was secured by Melchior Hoffman's institutionalization of the prophetic office, which was open to men and women alike, and depended only on the prophetic gifts of the individual in question.

While the Strasbourg Melchiorites and David Joris disagreed about the gender limits of the prophetic office, Menno Simons simply denied Melchior Hoffman's prophetic office to men and women alike. Menno turned resolutely to Christ and the letter of Scripture, to be interpreted by duly called male preachers and teachers.

Menno Simons

The movement away from a prophetic office to a more literal biblicism had the effect of restricting pastoral and leadership possibilities for women in the north. Nevertheless women did continue to exercise informal leadership in the Mennonite setting, as they did also in the rest of the later

Anabaptist movement. The case of Elisabeth Dirks, who appears to have functioned as such a leader, is well-known to readers of the Martyrs Mirror. (*Martyrs Mirror*, 481-83). In some cases women were better-educated than their husbands and were able to give them help in reading Scripture. Women in the north also became notable hymn writers. Soetjen Gerrits of Rotterdam, who was blind, composed an entire book of hymns that was published in Haarlem in 1592; the hymns of Vrou Gerrets of Medemblick also were published in 1607.

Conclusion

A fundamental tension is visible within Anabaptism because of the central role played by the Holy Spirit in calling men and women alike to lives of costly discipleship. The necessary call of the Spirit was never considered to be gender-specific. Furthermore, the Spirit was to accompany believers throughout their walk on the narrow way in this world, right up to the moment of death.

How then did it come to be decided that it was beyond the power of the Spirit to call women to preach, teach, or baptize? Societal norms undoubtedly played important roles here, but part of the answer also was the steady movement away from spiritual beginnings to increasing reliance on literal Scripture as providing the rule of life and conduct for the Body of Christ on earth. The stress shifted from an individual spiritual call, to one validated by male leaders of communities.

Nevertheless, care should be taken not to claim too much here. Even in the earlier, more pneumatic phases of Anabaptism there were clear restrictions on the activity of women. It would be a mistake to characterize early Anabaptism as a "golden age" of pure spiritual equality that opened up the same leadership possibilities for men and women alike. Such was not the case.

At the same time it is evident that the early spiritual phase of Anabaptist development opened up many *more* possibilities of direct participation and leadership for women than was the social norm in the sixteenth century, or than would become the norm in later Anabaptism.

As individuals called to faith and discipleship, women needed to respond personally to that call. No husband or guardian could take that step. If their faith commitment were threatened by an "unbelieving" spouse, women were free to leave that relationship. Women exercised remarkable informal leadership in proselytization, Bible reading (in some cases), in teaching and hymn-writing, and (especially in the early movement) in prophetic utterance and spiritual guidance. And finally, women chose of their own volition to suffer imprisonment, torture, and death for their faith. From available figures, a third or more of all Anabaptist martyrs were women. In all of these ways Anabaptist women were empowered to choose for themselves, contravening common societal restrictions on their gender.

Anabaptist Marriage

From the very beginning of the Anabaptist movement fundamental questions were raised concerning the marriage relationship. On the one hand stood the medieval ascetic legacy which valued celibacy as a more worthy state than marriage. An ascetic renunciation of the flesh played a salvific function in the medieval church.

For Martin Luther, on the other hand, rejection of "the flesh" could not contribute to salvation, since human beings are saved by grace through faith. For Luther and the mainline Reformers, marriage was not relevant to salvation, except only insofar as it demonstrated the uselessness of celibate renunciation.

> **(11) Thomas Müntzer** *"Do not these passionate desires impede your sanctification? How can the spirit be poured out over your flesh and how can you have living colloquy with God when you deny such things?"* (Matheson, 1988, 44.)

Thomas Müntzer had critiqued Luther and Melanchthon at precisely this point already in 1522. (11). Müntzer's central point was that marriage had to be considered part of the sanctification process. The Anabaptists agreed with him.

As in so many other matters, the Anabaptist position on marriage was worked out in the theological middle ground between late medieval Christianity and mainline Protestantism. Following the Protestant and early Radical Reformers, the Anabaptists rejected vows of celibacy. Anabaptists also were unsparingly critical of the immorality of the clergy. Anabaptists were in agreement with the Protestants in seeing marriage as an honourable, God-given estate. But, in keeping with their more ascetic understanding of spiritual regeneration and the life of discipleship that was to follow, the Anabaptists insisted that marriage had spiritual consequences.

The highest state of marriage for the Anabaptists was the spiritual marriage to Christ and the Body of Christ. "Natural" marriage (that is, the simple physical union of men and women) was of secondary importance. The language of "spiritual marriage" was used in the Swiss, South German, and Melchiorite traditions alike, although it received its loftiest emphasis in the Melchiorite stream. The need to be spiritually united to Christ applied to men and women alike. (12)

> **(12) Hutterite bishop Peter Walpot.**
> *"The husband cannot give account for his wife, nor the wife for her husband, but rather each must render account personally on that day, and bear their own burden."* (Müller, 1938, 256).

The Anabaptist baptismal vow paralleled in uncanny ways the vow of monastic profession, which also was seen as a "marriage to Christ," and commonly was called a "second baptism" in the monastic tradition. But the Anabaptist rejection of celibacy meant that marriage itself would have to be redefined, and not simply eliminated.

What was to be done when a person who was already married "in the world," was then "reborn of the Spirit" and joined the community of saints by water baptism? Was a former marriage still valid if the spouse of an Anabaptist remained an "unbeliever?" If it was granted that the unbelief of one marriage partner constituted adequate grounds for separation, was unbelief also grounds for divorce? Might one remarry after having separated from an unbeliever? How was marriage between two Anabaptist believers to be understood and carried out?

These questions and many others would be resolved in a variety of ways in the Anabaptist movement, generally depending upon where particular Anabaptist groups stood on the spirit/letter and inner/outer questions, and depending also on where in the developmental process a particular community found itself.

Separation, Divorce, and Remarriage

Mixed marriages posed a particular problem, especially if the faith and practice of an Anabaptist believer was threatened or prevented by a spouse. All Anabaptists allowed a believer to leave an unbelieving spouse, if faith was threatened, because believers had made their highest commitment to Christ and the Church. This ranked "natural" marriage as a secondary consideration, but how far was this to extend? The practical working out of this common principle was anything but uniform, especially in the early years of the movement.

Among the Swiss, who very early circulated a tract on divorce, a *Swiss Brethren* distinction was made between separation for reasons of faith, which was defended for women and men alike, and divorce, which was rejected except in cases of adultery. This was the ideal. But the court records in the first half of the sixteenth century give ample evidence that not all Swiss Brethren lived up to the ideal. To cite only one example, in October 1543,

Margaret von Ringgenberg (near Interlaken in Bernese territory) told the court that she had married Ulli Bucher eight years before. He had become an Anabaptist, had left her after two years of marriage (ca. 1537), and had taken another wife, as he himself had told her four years earlier (ca. 1549). Further details are not known, but on the face of it, Ulli Bucher's behaviour toward his wife did not fit the ideal prescribed for Swiss Anabaptist behaviour concerning separation, divorce, and remarriage. Many similar cases could be cited, particularly from the early sixteenth century.

By the mid to late sixteenth century, the Swiss had become far less prone to separate from unbelieving spouses, more willing to tolerate ambiguity in the relationship between church and world, and more ready to give weight to the natural marriages of believers with unbelievers. As one example among many, Andreas Gut was a prominent Anabaptist leader near Zurich who edited an impressive Confession in 1588. He was married to an "unbeliever." Gut not only remained married to his wife, but together they became parents of nine children, all nine of whom were duly baptized into the state church against their father's protests, as the parish records note. This too was a development beyond what the early tract on divorce had visualized, but it was a development back in the Lutheran direction of holding natural marriage in high esteem, rather than a movement in a more radically ascetic direction.

Hutterites   Community boundaries among the Hutterites were more strictly drawn than among the Swiss. Communal living conditions meant that mixed marriages posed a logistical problem as well as a theological problem. Although bishop Peter Walpot claimed that provisions were made for such "mixed" couples, the Hutterites were more ready to separate spouses and families if the unbeliever became obstructive, especially in the matter of the education of the children. Opponents claimed that Hutterites allowed remarriages after such separations.

There probably were such cases, even though Hutterite teaching, strictly speaking, only allowed for remarriage in cases of adultery.

Contrasting the development of separation and divorce practices between the Swiss and Hutterite communities of the later sixteenth century suggests that where community boundaries were not stringently maintained against "the world," as they came not to be among some of the Swiss, natural marriages were given a higher status, and more ambiguity was tolerated in marriage relationships. Within the Hutterite communities, natural marriage fell firmly into second place, with pride of place given to the believer's pledge to Christ and, increasingly, to the Body of Christ on earth, the community.

Melchior Hoffman introduced some complicating elements into the mix. Hoffman's understanding of spiritual rebirth was heightened by his spiritualist Christology. Just as Christ the Redeemer did not take on human flesh, and so was able to overcome the sin of Adam and Eve for all of humanity, so likewise believers could overcome sin by uniting spiritually with Christ. They had come to partake of the "heavenly flesh" of Christ when they united with Him in spiritual marriage.

Melchior Hoffman

Hoffman's strange Christology pushed his expectations to a qualitative level not often seen among the Swiss. Perhaps the closest comparable examples among the Swiss Anabaptists occurred among the Anabaptists of St Gall in 1526. On Hoffman's principles, possession of the Spirit of Christ by believers meant that the "law of the Spirit" now dwelt within them and that they thenceforth were bound to no external law. The drastic possibilities offered by Hoffman's position are plain enough. They quickly were put to the test.

Claus Frey and Elßbeth Pferdsfelder were arrested in May, 1533 by the Strasbourg authorities on charges of bigamy. After his baptism, Claus Frey had been forced to leave his home territory. He did this with his wife's consent, leaving both her and their eight children behind. But when she later refused to follow him into exile, he separated from her,

Claus and Elßbeth

and divided his goods with her. He emerged as an Anabaptist teacher in Franconia. While living in the home of the Anabaptist Georg Groß, called Pfersfelder, he came to know Georg's sister, the widowed Elßbeth Pfersfelder. After some visionary experiences, they established a "spiritual marriage" that included the physical aspects of marriage as well. At his first hearing in Strasbourg in May 1533, Claus maintained that Elßbeth was his spiritually wedded sister, even though he had a wife and children at Windsheim.

It is to the credit of Melchior Hoffman and his Strasbourg group that the "revelations" of this couple were tested and found wanting. Not only did Hoffman and the prophet Valentin Dufft urge Claus Frey to leave his "spiritual wife" Elßbeth and return to his family, so too did Barbara Rebstock.

In the end Claus Frey and Elßbeth Pfersfelder found themselves excluded by all the Anabaptist groups in Strasbourg. Hoffman himself denounced Frey as a thief of God's glory and a satanic whoremaster. Nevertheless, within Melchiorite teaching itself, the elements were freely available for recurrences of the Claus Frey kind. With Hoffman's arrest in Strasbourg in May 1533 (shortly following Frey's arrest and his denunciation of Hoffman), the Melchiorite movement in the north was set in a new direction thanks largely to the "revelations" of Jan Matthijs, who in significant ways fit the Claus Frey profile. (13)

---

(13) Obbe Philips
"There arose a baker of Haarlem named John Matthijs, who had an elderly wife whom he deserted, and he took with him a brewer's daughter who was a very pretty young slip of a girl and had great knowledge of the gospel. [Divara, later wife of Jan van Leiden, and Queen of Münster]. He enticed her away from her parents with sacred and beautiful words and told how God had shown great things to him, and she would be his wife." (SAW, 213-14).

Less than a year after Hoffman had denounced Claus Frey as a satanic whoremaster for abandoning his wife and taking another in "spiritual marriage," his follower and disciple Jan Matthijs did exactly the same thing. While Melchior Hoffman himself continued to demand that natural marriages be honoured, his followers in the north chose to emphasize spiritual marriage to the detriment of natural marriage. Jan Matthijs's practice of putting away his natural wife and taking a spiritual wife received theological legitimation at the hands of Bernhard Rothmann.

In an early writing (1534), Rothmann cited the usual Anabaptist text concerning divorce: What God has joined let no man put asunder. But he reversed the usual understanding of the text by concluding that marriage outside the faith is simply "whoredom in God's eyes." (14) Building on this logic Rothmann concluded that since God had not joined "heathens" together, they were therefore not truly married. Even further, in the case of a mixed marriage between a believer and an unbeliever, Rothmann said, a believer was not bound to the marriage. Natural marriage had to give way before spiritual marriage.

> **(14) Bernhard Rothmann**
> *"[Marriage between unbelievers] is sin and is unclean, and is no marriage before God... For what does not come from faith is sin..." (Stupperich, 1970, 204).*

Polygamy

It was a short step from here to polygamy among the "saints," which Rothmann explained and defended in his *Restitution*. Rothmann now said that those who had accepted baptism had been washed of all sin. Therefore they were to renew their marriage vows in order to proceed henceforth in all purity. Polygamy was defended as a pure and spiritual marriage, with the end being the procreation of sanctified children.

For all its lascivious undertones, Münsterite polygamy was hardly a celebration of human sexuality or an invitation to a love-fest. James Stayer has aptly noted the "innerworldly ascetic" character of Münsterite polygamy. No "fleshly lust" was to play a role in these spiritual marriages. Sexual relations were for the purpose of procreation only. Furthermore, these polygamous relationships were strongly patriarchal.

Joris

David Joris continued the logic and argumentation that had been used earlier by Claus Frey, Jan Matthijs and Bernhard Rothmann: What God has joined together cannot be separated, but what God has *not* joined

"The New Man." Engraving after David Joris' illustration in the Wonder Book

together may in fact be separated. Since marriages between believers and unbelievers are not true marriages in God's eyes, said Joris, believers may leave unbelievers freely. The only true marriage, argued Joris, is a spiritual marriage between regenerated believers.

Like Rothmann, Joris argued for a patriarchal view of marriage and, like Rothmann, he also argued that the only "pure" union of a man and a woman is one in which lust or sexual desire plays no part. The only aim of a truly spiritual marriage, said Joris, could be the production of regenerate children.

Joris was convinced that those who had truly been regenerated spiritually would be able to overcome the "lusts of the flesh" completely. (15) In fact, Joris thought that the true test of a man's regeneration was the ability to lay naked with a woman and to feel no lust. At this point we certainly have reached the outer limits of optimism regarding inner regeneration and its influence upon outer behaviour, where the number of those "called" might well be numerous, but the number of "elect" few indeed.

Menno Simons was forced to define his own position over against the Münsterites and the Davidjorists, criticizing Münsterite polygamy, on the one hand, and Davidjorist teachings and practices on the other. Nevertheless Menno's Melchiorite doctrine of regeneration (which he not uncommonly described as a marriage between believers and Christ) opened the door to further questions concerning separation and divorce.

Suffice it to say here that the Melchiorite concern for the purity of individual believers (which was threatened, thought Menno, by mixed marriages), coupled with a growing concern for the purity of the Body of Christ (the church), combined to lead Menno to recommend the "shunning" of banned spouses, as we will see in more detail in the chapter to follow.

"The Image of the Bride of Christ"
Engraving after an illustration by David
Joris, from the Wonder Book

Conclusion

Obviously, it is difficult to generalize about the Anabaptist practice of marriage, but close attention to stages of development within the general movement is helpful. In the earlier, formative years of the movement there were many questionable cases of abandonment, bigamy, and polygamy. Nevertheless, as Anabaptist groups began to establish community boundaries, they also began to establish norms of conduct governing marriage. This historical progression towards settled communities was paralleled by a collective movement away from spiritualism towards Christocentric, New Testament biblicism. As Anabaptist communities established firmer boundaries (and as dissenters were separated from those communities), the standard biblical texts enjoining monogamy were cited and applied.

Communal Norms

Marriage practices in the settled Anabaptist communities after 1550 were surprisingly uniform. The establishment of separated communities of believers among the Swiss Brethren, Hutterites, and Mennonites dictated marriage within those groups alone, and placed the control of marriage under the authority of the congregations and, especially, the elders and leaders of those congregations. An increasing concern to maintain the purity of the separated church is evident in the later communities, as is also the concern to raise children "in the faith." If a man and a woman "married in the Lord," there would be no call for separations such as had occurred in the earlier mixed marriages. What came to the fore under the later, more settled conditions, were separations either because of the banning of a marriage partner (a contentious issue, as will be seen below), or separations that occurred because of persecution.

Diversity and Unity

The question of Anabaptist marriage highlights both the unity and the diversity of Anabaptist thought and practice. On the one hand, there was undeniable early diversity in early Anabaptist practice. This is particularly true when one surveys Anabaptist thought and practice from 1525, including the events in Münster, until around 1550. Nevertheless, there was a surprising uniformity in the ascetic and biblical argumentation used to support these various Anabaptist marriage practices.

The primacy of the inner, spiritual commitment to Christ meant that Anabaptist men and women alike were freed from earthly attachments that stood in the way of their relationship to Christ. Just how free such previously married believers were to enter into new relationships was, as we have seen, a contested issue until community boundaries and guidelines were established by the surviving Anabaptist groups at differing points during the sixteenth century. But the issue was the *extent* of freedom such believers were to have. The principle itself never was disputed among the Anabaptists: God always was to be obeyed above men.

What did become a disputed issue among them was the extent of regeneration implied by one's "marriage to Christ," and what this might mean for natural marriages "in the world." Although the inner/outer tension was taken in the most radically spiritualist direction in the Melchiorite tradition, the differences between the radical Melchiorites and the rest of the Anabaptists in marital teaching and practice were in fact differences of degree resting upon shared, fundamental assumptions.

Were the Anabaptists radical in their understanding of relationships between men and women? One's answer will depend in large part upon the historical sources one chooses to read. An historian studying the earlier, more spiritualist phases of the movement may be excused for concluding that the Anabaptists granted radical freedom to men and women alike. An historian reading the later community writings pertaining to marriage (written exclusively by men) may be excused for concluding that the Anabaptists simply mirrored the patriarchal patterns of sixteenth century society.

Both conclusions, taken together and read in a developmental manner, provide a reliable picture of the theological and practical tension underlying Anabaptist marriage relationships and how that tension was resolved. This tension emerged because of the ascetic requirements demanded by the ultimate commitment to Christ, and the simultaneous attempt to retain and define marriage as both a natural and a divine ordinance.

3.
Anabaptism
and
Religious Reform

Chapter 16

Anabaptism and Religious Reform:
The Inner and the Outer

Balthasar Hubmaier (1527)

"So all of those who cry: 'Well, what about water baptism? Why all the fuss about the Lord's Supper? They are after all just outward signs! They're nothing but water, bread, and wine! Why fight about that?' They have not in their whole life learned enough to know why the signs were instituted by Christ, what they seek to achieve or toward what they should finally be directed, namely to gather a church, to commit oneself publicly to live according to the Word of Christ in faith and brotherly love, and because of sin to subject oneself to fraternal admonition and the Christian ban, and to do all of this with a sacramental oath before the Christian church and all her members..." (Pipkin and Yoder, 1989, 384).

Pilgram Marpeck (1544)

"I also admit that the inner and the outer have to be kept distinct, but to divide the one from the other, to use one and not the other, cannot be substantiated by any Scripture." (Klassen and Klaassen, 1978, 389).

Menno Simons against followers of David Joris (1539)

"This kingdom (of Christ) is not a kingdom in which they parade in gold, silver, pearls, silk, velvet, and costly finery, as is done by the haughty, proud world; matters which your leaders defend and allow with this meaningless provision; just so you do not desire these things and live for them in your heart." (CWMS, 217).

In this section of our study we return to the question of church reform, looking especially at the fundamental inner/outer tensions that already are visible in the core Anabaptist principles. In this chapter we will outline some further developments within those core principles.

The Spiritualist Challenge

Most recent descriptions of Anabaptism have concentrated on the outer marks of the movement, and not without reason. Anabaptists insisted that salvation by faith entailed a life of discipleship. But somewhat obscured in all of this has been the inner, spiritual dimension without which Anabaptism would never have come to exist at all. It was the renovating power of the living God, the power of the Holy Spirit, that provided the fundamental groundwork for subsequent Anabaptist spirituality and discipleship, which created a church reform movement, and which eventually came to define the Believers' Church ecclesiological tradition.

Holy Spirit

The "inner" emphasis noted in early Anabaptism was not typically Protestant, but rather had roots in several related strands of late medieval piety. But the Anabaptists faced a very significant question as a result of their evangelical critique of the medieval church. What role, if any, were the external ceremonies to play in *making possible* the life of the spirit? The inherent connection in late medieval Catholicism between the reception of the sacraments and growth in holiness was severed by the Anabaptists, following as they did the initial Protestant (and more specifically, Zwinglian) lead in these questions.

Sacraments

The more spiritualist Anabaptists naturally played down the importance of the outer marks of the church, especially the ceremonies of baptism and the Supper. They found such ceremonies divisive and, given their secondary nature, saw no problem in dropping them altogether under certain circumstances. The more literalist Anabaptists naturally emphasized obedience to the words and commands of Christ–and there are clear

Ceremonies

injunctions in the New Testament to baptize, discipline, be nonresistant, not swear oaths, celebrate the Lord's Supper, and share with those in need.

There was, however, a third option represented in the developmental Anabaptist period. Pilgram Marpeck argued for a middle way between the spiritualist rejection of the outer ceremonies and the literalist insistence on obedience to the letter. Although Marpeck's continuing influence is seen primarily among the later Swiss Brethren, and no "Pilgramite" Anabaptist branch managed to survive to the present, Marpeck's insightful perspective provides a useful Believers' Church commentary still today.

Spiritualism Defined: Hans Denck and the Ceremonies

Hans Denck took a contemplative and mystical approach to the Christian life. The same inner emphasis in Denck that we have noted above, concerning the priority of the living, inner Word over that of the outer, written word of Scripture, is visible also in Denck's understanding of the value of external ceremonies. The essential distinctions were drawn clearly in Denck's *The Law of God*, written in 1526, after he had accepted water baptism (Furcha, 1975). In that writing Denck distinguished between commandments, customs, and laws.

The highest observances ordered by God, said Denck, are the "com- *Commandments*
mandments," which cannot be overlooked. The highest command is to love God and neighbour. This is an inner, spiritual commandment, with ethical implications. It is the only truly necessary Christian observance.

"Customs," on the other hand, are "external ordinances," which re- *Customs*
mind human beings of eternal and divine things. Into this category fall all outward observances and ceremonies which might be ordered by Scripture, such as circumcision, baptism or the Supper. To the one who has the highest commandment written in the heart (the law of love), such outward

> *(1) Denck* "Whoever fulfils the law of love, truly fulfils all ceremonies also, even though he may never give them a thought." (Furcha, 1975, 52).

ceremonies are secondary and even useless. (1) Outward ceremonies have a secondary, derivative usefulness. They must promote love in others. In such cases, believers may well keep the outward ceremonies, for the sake of the highest commandment to love the neighbour.

Laws

Finally, the "laws" are civil ordinances, instituted to maintain social order. These laws, while they have been instituted as part of God's general ordering of the world, do not "point beyond themselves" to God's highest commandment, as do customs. Laws have merely practical function in human society.

It was a particular strength of Hans Denck's thought that he insisted on focusing continually on the living character of God's presence with human beings. By repeatedly pushing back to this point, that the Christian life is, most fundamentally, a life immersed in the living Christ, Hans Denck was sounding a venerable theme of Christian spirituality. Nevertheless, Denck's rejection of the medieval sacraments removed a crucial lynch pin of late medieval spirituality, which had linked together the inner and the outer worlds, and had provided outer, visible, and tangible mediators of grace.

Dual Universe

Hans Denck and the spiritualists assumed a dualistic universe in which the outer, physical world was of no essential use in the saving process. The only reality to be heeded was spiritual and in the heart. Physical reality could, at best, provide the "proving ground" for the genuineness of inner regeneration and provide reminders and pointers to that more real spiritual world.

It is important to note that the literalist Anabaptism of Grebel, Sattler, Riedeman, and Menno Simons (which called simply for obedience to Scripture) assumed the very same dualistic premises as did the spiritualists. The literalist Anabaptists agreed: the spiritual world is the more important one. Furthermore, they agreed that the physical world shares nothing essential with the spiritual world. To the obvious question of why one would continue with divisive secondary ceremonies, the literalists could only add the proviso "we do it because Jesus said so." Pilgram Marpeck recognized the dilemma, and attempted to re-establish the essential centrality of the outer ceremonies of the church as necessary for the *spiritual life* of its members.

Spiritualism Challenged: Pilgram Marpeck and Hans Bünderlin

Hans Bünderlin was an Anabaptist missionary and leader, baptized in Augsburg in 1526 and active in Austrian and Moravian territories. By 1528 he had moved to Strasbourg, but by 1530 Bünderlin had joined the spiritualist ranks. He abandoned external ceremonies and the Anabaptist congregations that continued such usages.

Bünderlin argued that "ceremonies" had been perverted by the papal church, and so needed to be abandoned altogether. Jesus, Bünderlin said, revealed the fact that ceremonies were only external signs, with no validity of themselves. True Israelites were those who had the Word in their hearts, and performed the true sacrifices "in spirit and in truth." Furthermore, said Bünderlin, Jesus' commands to baptize and celebrate the Supper was given only to the apostles themselves, and not to the church they founded. Since true Christianity is inward, Bünderlin said, the restoration of the true church must begin by abandoning the ceremonies.

Ceremonies Abandoned

In writing against Bünderlin, Pilgram Marpeck agreed that ceremonies had been misused in the church, but he maintained that the Spirit was bestowed on the elect in order to purify the ceremonies. A purely spiritual kingdom, Marpeck maintained, was not instituted with the birth of Christ, but rather would arrive only when Christ returned at the end of the age.

Ceremonies Defended

Marpeck mistrusted the radical individualization represented by Bünderlin and the spiritualists. He could not agree with "these spirits," he said, because they would not submit themselves to communal discipline.

<table>
<tr><td>

(2) Marpeck against the Spiritualists.
"I sense that [these spirits] lack the Holy Spirit dedicated to the common good (1 Corinthians 12), who uses the gifts of the Holy Spirit for the edification of others (1 Corinthians 14; Ephesians 4), and thus serves them (1 Peter 4)." (Klassen and Klaassen, 1978, 52-53).

</td></tr>
</table>

Against the radical individualism advocated by Bünderlin, Pilgram Marpeck returned to the note sounded by Hans Denck in his most Anabaptist writings: love of neighbour cannot lightly be set aside. (2)

With this note, Marpeck anticipated a second crucial point to be made in his following observations. The inward, individual spiritual life (the love of God) cannot be neatly separated from the outward, social and physical life (the love of neighbour). The two are linked together in the highest commandment of the Lord. Love demands external "preaching, teaching, or action toward others," and not simply attention to one's own internal spiritual condition. Personal spirituality cannot be nurtured at the expense of the community.

Of equal significance is Marpeck's accompanying argument, for it provided a strong rationale for a visible church. The "external order" cannot be dispensed with, Marpeck argued, for it is *through* the external that human beings are "led from the visible into the invisible." The outward ceremonies, although they can be misused, nevertheless were instituted for human benefit in the same way that Christ took on a human body in order to serve humanity. (3)

(3)Pilgram Marpeck
"What the Father does, as Spirit and God, the Son immediately does likewise, but he does it as an external man who performs outward works. The Father loves the Son, and has given all things into His hand. Those who are born anew in Christ, according to the inner working of the Holy Spirit, are those who are baptized with fire, who are aglow with love. Moreover, these children, born of the Spirit, see what the Father, working through Christ, does for the inner man; they, too, by co-witnessing in the Holy Spirit, immediately do likewise for the external man. Thus, the body of Christ is also built inwardly through the Holy Spirit, and externally through the co-witness of works. His church of communion is His bride, internally in the Spirit and truth, externally with praise to God, and to be a light before the world. But this church is separated from the world, for it is a witness over it." (Klassen and Klaassen, 1978, 423).

Marpeck's insistence on a visible "co-witness" to the invisible activity
of the Holy Spirit led him away from the dualism of radical spiritualism,
and also away from a Christology that emphasized Christ's divinity at the
expense of His humanity.

While Marpeck agreed that there was a higher spiritual realm and a
lower physical realm, nevertheless he insisted that the two were *indivisibly linked*, as the two natures of Christ had been. Marpeck refused to
deny spiritual significance to the physical realm. The outward ceremonies
instituted by Christ were tangible *means* by which believers would be "led
from the visible to the invisible." The visible church and its ceremonies,
then, were an "extension of the incarnation," and a "prolongation of the
humanity of Christ." (Rempel, 1993, 155).

Spiritualism in the North: Menno Simons and Nicolaas van Blesdijk

Apocalyptic elements were notably absent in the debate between Marpeck
and Bünderlin. In the north it would be otherwise, because the basic elements for that discussion were provided by Melchior Hoffman. The central scriptural issues in the north had to do with the role of the Spirit in the
utterance and interpretation of prophecy (both biblical and actual), while
the inner/outer debate had to deal with Hoffman's spiritualized Christology,
his optimism concerning human regeneration, and Melchiorite attempts to
establish a visible kingdom of righteousness on earth.

The situation in the north was ripe for a spiritualist challenge. The
brethren at Münster had insisted on the establishment of a highly visible
Kingdom of God on earth, and had taken the sword as a means to this end.
Was not one of the failures of Münster precisely the fact that too much had
been made of *externals*, when in fact the kingdom of God was spiritual,
not physical? Should not the essential life of the spirit be emphasized, and
outer manifestations of religious life de-emphasized?

David Joris and his followers, Like Hans Denck and Hans Bünderlin, emphasized the priority of the inner, spiritual life. But David Joris concluded further that deception was allowed in the insignificant "outward ceremonies." This position has been called "Nicodemism," after Nicodemus who came to see Jesus secretly, at night. The usefulness of being a "nicodemite" in the midst of the horrific persecution of the sixteenth century is obvious. Anabaptist followers of Joris could easily avoid detection by attending state churches and in all things appearing to conform to the required religious practices. Davidjorists did not have to bother with water baptism at all, thus avoiding an imperial crime. Nicodemism was a position that Menno Simons could not abide.

Nicodemism

Nicolaas M. van Blesdijk, David Joris's son-in-law, became the most able defender of Joris's spiritualist views in the north, after Joris withdrew to Basle to lead his own nicodemite life. In 1546 Menno Simons, Dirk Philips and others engaged in a debate with Blesdijk. In a letter to Blesdijk, Menno charged that participating in the public services of Catholics or Protestants was "idolatry." Blesdijk's opening line of defence followed, as one might expect, the logic of David Joris's emphasis on the inner spiritual life. Blesdijk agreed that idolatry was always a sin, but he insisted that true idolatry was a matter of inwardly loving created things above God, and not mere attendance at a church service.

Nicolaas van Blesdijk

Blesdijk explicitly stated the spiritualist belief when he maintained that the "evangelical, apostolic teaching" demonstrated the true way to serve God, namely by means of righteousness, purity and truth in one's heart. These virtues, Blesdijk maintained, *cannot be brought about by any ceremonies or outer things*, but rather are the fruit of faith in the heart. Such a heart is the result of the inward work of the Holy Spirit. Faith in the heart frees one "from the laws and darkness of all ceremonies."

Blesdijk appealed explicitly to the apostle Paul in defending his position. In Colossians 2, Paul had said that faith in Christ frees believers from ceremonies and the penalty of sin. Eating, drinking, and the use of any earthly thing (*elementisch dinck*) was thus made free in Christ. In fact, holding to ceremonies as though they were necessary demonstrated an unclean heart. Condemning others simply on the basis of their use of outer ceremonies was a greater abomination than any use of ceremonies could be.

A case in point for Menno was the question of baptism. Holding to the *Baptism* necessity of this external ordinance had been a central defining characteristic of the Anabaptist movement from the start–except of course that its necessity had been challenged (at least temporarily) by Melchior Hoffman himself and was now being challenged by the spiritualists. Menno argued that Christ had most clearly *commanded* the church to baptize believers on their confession of faith. (4) For Blesdijk it was all a needless argument

---

(4) Menno Simons
"If now I do not believe and do not suffer myself to be baptized in accordance with God's Word, but allow my little children without Scriptural warrant to be baptized, am I then obedient unto the voice of the Lord? Can I then inherit the promise given to the believers? The answer is no." (CWMS, 1025).

---

over a secondary and unessential question. To argue over whether to baptize a child that is two days old, or rather wait until the child is twelve years old, is an argument over nothing more important than the timing of an outer ceremony–as if salvation depended on the ceremony.

It is worth noting that Blesdijk agreed with Menno that the "proper" and biblical mode of baptism was water baptism of adults on confession of faith. On this point, said Blesdijk, "we have no disagreement." The question was, rather, whether Christians were free to use or not to use outer ceremonies such as baptism. But ceremonies, said Blesdijk, really were not of the essence, since ceremonies did not lead to a change of heart.

At this point Menno might have argued, as had Marpeck against Bünderlin, that the outer ceremonies of the church community did in fact lead to and build up the inner life of faith, and that the outer testimony of the church was essential to the church being church. But Menno did not take up this

Obedience

line of argumentation, preferring rather to reiterate the necessity of obedience to the "commands of Scripture" in the maintenance of purity.

For Blesdijk, Menno's attempt to prove that outward actions are idolatrous was an instance of literal proof-texting. "There is nothing so evil," noted Blesdijk, perhaps thinking back to the Münster experience, "but that people will find some letter of Scripture that appears to command or defend it." Menno refused to grant the point. The pure bride of Christ is espoused to one husband (2 Corinthians 11:2). It is a pure church, which separates from drunkards, the covetous, fornicators, the idolatrous, and the proud, as the apostle said: avoid them and don't eat with them (1 Corinthians 5:11). Any who preach another gospel are accursed (Galatians 1:8). In short, said Menno, "How then can some say this is a matter of liberty? Of this liberty any sensible Christian may judge." (CWMS, 1023).

Scripture Interpreted

What are the limits of Christian freedom, and what does the "obedience of faith" demand? The debate between Menno Simons and Nicolaas van Blesdijk is particularly interesting because Blesdijk took up the argument on Menno's ground, namely that of Scripture itself. Further, he acknowledged the priority of the New Testament over the Old and did not disagree with the Christocentric reading of the Bible.

But Blesdijk and Menno approached Scripture with very different attitudes and presuppositions. Blesdijk was convinced that love was the "highest summation and foundation of all the Scriptures" (*die Hooftsomma ende gront aller Schriftuyren*), by which all other scriptural statements must be measured. Menno continued to insist that Christ's "commands" must be obeyed. For Menno, what was not "implied or commanded" in the New Testament was forbidden and false. For Blesdijk, what was not forbidden in the New Testament, was allowed.

However, Blesdijk and the spiritualists wished to push the logic of Christian freedom even further. Since the inner is what really matters, the outer is practically inconsequential. Thus they came close to severing the link between the inner and outer lives of believers. Furthermore, this radical individualizing of the Christian life left little room for the community of believers. Blesdijk could grant that the proper biblical procedure was water baptism for those who have been baptized inwardly, but he would argue further that infant baptism was simply of no real consequence, and that water baptism was optional.

Menno's answer, although expressed in a more legalistic mode than that of some other Anabaptists, nevertheless reiterated a central point made in most other parts of the movement: Baptism is administered following confession of faith because that is the *biblical order*, and believers are and ought to be *obedient* to the commands of Scripture.

Menno in effect sidestepped the deeper question concerning the essential relationship of the inner lives of believers and the outward ceremonies or ordinances of the gathered community. Marpeck's point, that the outer and inner lives are indivisibly linked, was not pursued by Menno. In all likelihood, Menno was not familiar with Marpeck's writings. In any case, rather than challenging Blesdijk's argument that inner changes are radically disconnected from "any ceremonies or outer things," Menno simply insisted upon obedience to what has been commanded.

Sin, Discipleship, and Discipline

With the exception of Pilgram Marpeck, Anabaptists agreed that the visible, outer world and the inner, spiritual world belonged in separate spheres. Therefore, one could not reach the spiritual world by means of temporal things or actions. Said another way, with the exception of Marpeck, all Anabaptists rejected any hint of sacramental power or revelatory participation of the temporal in the divine. The divine needed to be reached by means of pure immaterial spirit, mediated at best by the Word of God.

As we have seen, the spiritualists argued that since this was the case, external ceremonies needed to be done away with. David Joris went further and argued that since only the spiritual mattered, what one did externally was of no consequence. Dissembling to escape persecution was prudent and theologically defensible as well.

Dualism Modified

At this point it becomes evident that the non-spiritualist Anabaptists were not prepared to accept the full consequences of the dualist position. Although the world of the spirit could not be reached by material means, those who had been reborn in the spirit needed to *incarnate* that rebirth in visible ways, in the material world. Faced with the spiritualist challenge, those who remained Anabaptists accepted only half of the dualist equation.

Insofar as Anabaptists continued to insist that the spiritual rebirth had to have specific material consequences, the manner, means, and thoroughness of regeneration became crucial questions.

–Did the Holy Spirit regenerate believers directly, through no outward means except perhaps the hearing of the Word?

–Was this regeneration thorough and complete to the point that the regenerate could expect to remain essentially free from sin?

–How far and how deep does the efficacy of grace extend?

–What sins deserve to banned, and which not?

Debates on the concrete results of regeneration took place in several Anabaptist contexts. The Swiss Brethren disagreed with both Balthasar Hubmaier and Pilgram Marpeck. Among the Dutch similar issues emerged in disagreements concerning marriage and the enforcement of the ban.

Regeneration and Ban: the Swiss Brethren and Marpeck

The Swiss Brethren position on the ban was premised on a two kingdom understanding: Christians have been called out of the world, and now have their citizenship in heaven. The church is the community of heaven, living now according to the pattern and model of Christ. Obedience to the command to "go and sin no more" is possible because regenerated believers have been granted the ability to carry out Christ's commands.

Balthasar Hubmaier, as we have seen in his disagreement concerning the sword of government, did not agree. He believed that sin was too deeply rooted in human reality for obedience to be perfectly effective in particular churches. Christians are regenerated, said Hubmaier, and they must strive to do their best by struggling against sin and the flesh, but in the final analysis, only Christ can say "My kingdom is not of this world."

Between the position of the Swiss Brethren, which was strictly separatist, and that of Hubmaier, which tended to bless Christian participation in many activites of the world according to one's office, stood that of Pilgram Marpeck. Although his argument concerning the proper exercise of the ban was directed primarily against the Swiss, and what he viewed as their excessive legalism, his outline of the proper Christian ban in effect mediated between the Swiss and the Hubmaierian positions, and opened new avenues of understanding.

Swiss Brethren and the Ban

Article 2 of Schleitheim dealt with the ban, basing itself entirely on Matthew 18:15ff. The ban applies to those who have "given themselves over to the Lord" in baptism, and who have thereby pledged obedience to Christ's commandments. If any such regenerated brothers or sisters "still somehow slip and fall into error and sin," they are to be admonished and corrected, according to the pattern outlined in Matthew 18. Michael Sattler, who was responsible for framing the Schleitheim Articles, and the Swiss Brethren who followed Schleitheim, understood the ban primarily in its excommunicatory function of maintaining purity in the Body. The reason for this was Sattler's very optimistic view of the power of regeneration by the Spirit of God.

Schleitheim

In the monastic setting from which Michael Sattler emerged, growth in the spiritual life was understood to be a long, slow process. Communal prayer, the liturgy, obedience to a superior, and communal tasks all became vehicles through which the monks were to grow in the spiritual life. Michael Sattler's Anabaptist writings, while reflecting a strong ascetic emphasis on the renunciation of the flesh in favour of the life of the spirit, contained no hint of the monastic scheme of progressive sanctification. Rather, "Sattler spoke as if his hearers had already arrived, had already received the 'spirit of Christ' in its fullness." (Snyder, 1984, 166).

Sattler believed that those chosen by God to be God's children received Christ's spirit at the time of election. For Sattler and the Swiss Brethren, believers already were the saints, although they had to be on the watch lest Satan overtake them through temptation. Seen in light of Jesus' coming, which Sattler was convinced was soon to occur, the church's central concerns were unity, prayer, and purity, in separation from all sinfulness.

We can see here a crucial distinction between Michael Sattler and Balthasar Hubmaier. For Hubmaier, sin remained rooted in the very being ("flesh") of the regenerate and perfection in this life was impossible. Nevertheless, for Hubmaier growth in the spiritual life was possible and necessary, and it was towards such growth that the church was oriented. Hubmaier remained close to the Roman Catholic conception of gradual sanctification, in that he structured the worship life of the church with a view toward spiritual growth. Sattler remained close to the Roman Catholic understanding that a measure of perfection was possible in this life—but Sattler would hold that this high degree of perfection had already arrived with the Spirit of Christ and was sealed by believers' baptism.

The Swiss Brethren after Schleitheim continued to hold Sattler's basic position concerning the ban. The teaching of Scripture was clear and unequivocal and demanded obedience. Christians were called to admonish sinners to repentance according to Matthew 18, and to separate from those who persisted in sin and so maintain the purity of the Body of Christ. Such was Christ's teaching and the practice of the apostles. Love meant separating from evil.

Pilgram Marpeck and the Ban

Marpeck's initial critique of Swiss Brethren banning practices made use of Luther's distinction between law, and gospel. The law contains the threat of punishment, instils fear of God, and functions for the bringing about of repentance. As such, law is preliminary to Gospel. But the law, be it divine (scriptural) or human (ordinances), was not meant to, nor is it able to bring about the true peace of God. The Swiss Brethren, argued Marpeck, had turned the Christian life into one of obedience to law, and even if that law were based on Scripture (or more narrowly, the New Testament), it remained external law nonetheless.

Law

By contrast, the living Gospel is a setting free from the imprisonment of the law which condemns. Echoing Hans Denck, Marpeck maintained that the law cannot rule in the kingdom of Christ, but rather freedom in Christ must rule there. When the focus falls on the spiritual regeneration that occurs in the heart of believers, then the ban takes on a different dimension. The measure of Christian obedience is not then adherence to law or the maintenance of purity according to a legal standard, but rather adherence to the mercy, patience and love of Christ, whose spirit had come to rule regenerated hearts.

Gospel

On the other side of the issue, however, Marpeck agreed that the Christian church should maintain its responsibility in administering discipline, but with the caution that no one should judge individuals "before the time of the fruit." A true understanding of Christ's life and commands would put "long-suffering, forebearance, and meekness"–in a word, love–at the centre of the Christian life, and not a quick and strict application of excommunicatory discipline.

Discipline

A second point of contention between Pilgram Marpeck and the Swiss Brethren concerned Marpeck's understanding of the "freedom of the spirit in Christ" which freedom, Marpeck noted, some had accused him of stretching too far. In defending himself against this charge, Marpeck emphasized his understanding of the rebirth and regeneration that every believer must undergo. This rebirth is the result of grace, and a manifestation of the love of God. (5) The same regeneration continues in all believers. But on the other hand, Satan retains a hold even on regenerated believers, because of the weakness of the flesh. Therefore the distinction Hubmaier made between Christ and the Christian was deemed valid by Marpeck. (6) For Marpeck the crux of the problem was not so

> *(5) Marpeck* *"All who have, in baptism, died to the law of sin (Col. 3:3) and have been buried with Christ (Rom. 6:4), do not themselves live. Rather Christ lives in them, through the law of grace and the voluntary spirit in Christ Jesus."* *(Klassen and Klaassen, 1978, 320).*

> *(6) Marpeck* *"In Christ the fullness of Godhead dwells bodily; in us, in this time, it is only in part."* *(Klassen and Klaassen, 1978, 532).*

much in external behaviour, as in internal disposition. In Christ, love was complete and had no defect; human beings, on the other hand, "are full of weakness."

Besides the human propensity to outward, sinful acts, human beings have an equally great capacity for self-deception. Marpeck counselled caution. The most fundamental root of sin is in the heart, not in external actions–even though actions eventually reveal what is in the heart–and therefore even the regenerate must realize just how difficult a battle is the struggle of the spirit against the flesh.

Pilgram Marpeck could not countenance the Swiss Brethren "rush to judgement" on the basis of some external negative evidences. (7) People in such a hurry, he said, apparently had not experienced either the stubborn depth of their own sin

> *(7) Marpeck* *"No one may judge except he who has first judged and sentenced his own life through the grace and mercy of God, whereby he has pulled the beam out of his eye. Then, very properly, in patience, humility, meekness, and love, he may with the greatest care pull the sliver out of his brother's eye without hurting or irritating the eye. That is, after all, how he has been treated by God."! (Klassen and Klaassen, 1978, 326).*

and self-deception, or the loving mercy of God which was extended to those who, with true contrition, repented of their willfulness. Love, patience, and forbearance most befit forgiven sinners who still struggle against the flesh. Those who have been broken to contrition and brought back to life by Christ the Physician will want to live out that same gentleness within the Body of Christ.

Love

The Swiss Brethren and Pilgram Marpeck agreed on many crucial issues concerning the ban, but their disagreements also were extremely important for the way in which the inner change of regeneration would express itself outwardly in the church. On the question of grace and sin Marpeck steered a middle course. He insisted that God's work of grace was not completed or brought to perfection with initial repentance and rebirth. God's grace continued to be needed throughout the Christian life, not merely for the maintenance of initial purity, but rather for growth in the Christian life. Human sin, Marpeck noted, is not easily displaced.

Grace

Sin

On the other hand, against the reformed preachers, Marpeck also insisted on obedience, growing from grace, according to the model of Jesus Christ. Love may cover a multitude of sins, but love does not cover willful disobedience. Those who wish to avoid obedience by appealing to God's all-forgiving grace are, in fact, denying and resisting the working of God's grace in their own lives. On the matter of discipleship or *Nachfolge* (following after Christ) Marpeck was insistent. The Christian is to live as Christ lived, for Jesus' life is the highest example of how his disciples are to manifest the love of God and the love of neighbor.

Menno Simons: The Church of the Regenerate

The Melchiorite legacy led to its fair share of internal tensions. In particular, the Davidjorist emphasis on inner, spiritual purity carried with it the threat of an invisible church, to the point that (as Menno described it) the Jorists believed that "to the pure, all things are pure." But by 1546 an opposite trend had become evident. The problem of legalism became a

Dirk Philips

pressing issue among Menno's followers. Without a doubt two younger and more rigorous leaders, Dirk Philips and Leenaert Bouwens, played a role in this development. It appears that Dirk, Leenaert and others appropriated themes present already in Menno's earlier writings but brought them to the fore in such a single-minded fashion that they virtually determined the course of later developments.

Historians have long observed that Menno Simons' writings reflect a shift as one moves from the concerns of the early Menno, to those of the later Menno. In his earlier writings, Menno was concerned with placing Christ at the centre of Scripture, and with individual faith, regeneration, and the new life, all of which would lead to the community of saints. One finds in the early Menno an emphasis on the mortification of the flesh, which results from and makes visible the spiritual rebirth that is witnessed to in baptism. In later years Menno became much more concerned with the pure community.

Community Purity

This shift in accent from Christ to community has often been attributed, not without reason, to the influence of Dirk Philips and Leenaert Bouwens. The issue that emerged was whether excommunicated members needed to be "shunned" as well as banned. That is, was it necessary to avoid physical contact in eating, drinking, and daily life, with members who had been expelled from the church?

Swaen Rutgers

In 1555 an open crisis erupted when Leenaert Bouwens banned the husband of Swaen Rutgers, and then demanded (although she was a pious woman and had herself done nothing worthy of discipline) that she shun all

contact with her husband, under threat of excommunication. Menno was
asked to intervene in the case and wrote a letter in 1556 to the church at
Emden, in which he took up a moderate position, apparently on the side of
Swaen Rutgers, against Bouwens.

Shunning

By 1557 the lines had hardened between the moderate and the strict
parties concerning the ban. Menno was now old and weak, nevertheless he
travelled first to Franeker and then to Harlingen in order to try to find a
solution. He managed to gain some agreement with the leaders in Franeker,
but on arriving in Harlingen he was overcome by Dirk and Leenaert. According to the report of an eyewitness, Menno was threatened with excommunication by Leenaert Bouwens if he did not support the strict view.
Faced with this opposition, Menno capitulated. The official position now
became that shunning was a necessary accompaniment to banning. The
result was schism with the "moderate" party of Waterlanders, with the
Swiss Brethren and the Brethren of the Lower Rhine. In spite of the warm
pastoral tone of Menno's early writings, the redemptive aim of the ban
faded into the background as concern to maintain church purity assumed
more and more importance.

Already in 1550 Menno and Dirk had to address a series of specific
questions concerning rules of conduct. The questions and the answers
illustrate the climate within the Dutch church.

*Rules of
Conduct*

–May church members eat common meals with someone who has
been banned? Answer: No. Banning means exclusion not only from the
Lord's Supper, but from all eating.

–May one buy and sell with a banned member? Answer: Only in exceptional cases, and not as a general rule.

–May one greet or receive a banned member? Answer: Beyond common courtesy, no.

–May one do acts of mercy for a banned member in need? Answer:
Yes, although Dirk's reply suggested that he was suspicious about the possibilities of leniency or abuse.

–Must banned family members be shunned? Answer: Yes. Menno and Dirk used virtually identical language here: "the ban is a general rule, and excepts none; neither husband nor wife, neither parent nor child." (CWMS, 478; WDP, 613).

Both the Waterlanders and the Swiss Brethren objected to the hard line assumed by Dirk and Menno. The earliest Waterlandian confession, in agreement with the Swiss Brethren objections, says that marriage is so binding "that it may not be separated or broken for any reason except adultery, according to the words of Christ, Matthew 18." (Dyck, 1962, 13).

Menno and the strict party argued, to the contrary, that the "external marriage bond" must give way to the "spiritual marriage bond made with Christ through faith." If one truly loves one's spouse, Menno added, then shunning will be observed so that the banned and shunned spouse may be shamed unto salvation. Although Menno concluded by admonishing elders and pastors to "prudence and paternal care," the thrust of his presentation was "willing obedience unto Christ." (CWMS, 970-974).

If it be said that Menno and his followers avoided the shoals of spiritualist antinomianism in overcoming the David Jorists, it appears that they did so only to run aground on the rocks of legalism. The combination of an optimistic doctrine of regeneration ("marriage to Christ"), a strong emphasis on obedience to the external Word, and an equally strong emphasis on a church maintained "without spot or wrinkle" by strict church discipline, was particularly disastrous for church life among the Dutch Anabaptists. Through all of this the inner regeneration, by God's grace, that enables discipleship faded further and further into the background, replaced by external measures of faithfulness and obedience.

Conclusion

The Anabaptist insistence on the necessary conjunction between the inner and the outer lives of believers was both its genius and its burden. A fine balance was required to keep from erring either to one side or the other.

The Moravian and Dutch schisms, and disagreements concerning the depth of sin, regeneration, obedience, the ban, and the role of the church, all point us back to spirit/letter and inner/outer tensions, visible within Anabaptism from the start. In the eventual development of these controversies we may note the steady victory of the letter of the law over the spirit of the law, of the outer over the inner.

Of course the disputants recognized the danger of the legalistic tendency too, and strove to overcome its negative consequences. But the repeated appeals to love, humility, forbearance, and patience–all desirable, if elusive, Christian virtues–inevitably gave way before the more brittle obedience to "thus saith the Word of the Lord." It was as if once the basic presuppositions of regeneration, obedience to the Word, sinless living, the pure community, and community discipline were in place, the very logic of those assumptions drove to legalistic conclusions and results. What became obscured in the process was the role of God's enabling grace and the spiritual renewal upon which true obedience must rest.

On following the course of the events in Dutch Anabaptism in particular, one is reminded of the medieval practice of classifying sins into mortal and venial categories, each having correspondingly severe penances. If there is no salvation outside the Church; if the Church holds the keys to bind and to loose the sinner; if the measure of sin is obedience to external law; then salvation becomes a matter of satisfying the eternal judge and (even more importantly) that judge's earthly representatives. Law engulfs Gospel. Regardless of how one ultimately judges the

Davidjorists and other spiritualists, Blesdijk had a relevant point to make when, in his admonition to Menno, he stressed freedom from the law in Christ.

| *Marpeck*

Pilgram Marpeck pushed inner/outer issues to profound levels, both in the matter of church ordinances and also in the question of discipleship. What makes it *possible* for followers of Christ to live as disciples? Against those who wished simply to insist upon "obedience," Marpeck observed that not even the divine law can convert the heart. Only God's grace can change one's very being. One might be able to achieve a certain measure of outward conformity without inner regeneration, but true discipleship will be the result of a fundamental change in one's being. And church ordinances perform an essential function in the conversion of the heart. They are the means of grace, enabling the fundamental changes that are needed.

In a context in which the ban was increasingly used as a "spiritual sword" against fellow believers, Pilgram Marpeck conceived of the ban according to the image of Christ the Physician. What was crucial about the ban, said Marpeck, was its medicinal function, not its separating function. If a member of one's body is "failing or weak," medicine is first lovingly applied, and then one waits, and hopes for improvement. (8) But, Marpeck

(8) Marpeck *"Certainly, the true shepherds will not drive a patient, humble, meek, and loving heart any further than the chief Shepherd, Christ has driven and bound it, but will let it go out and in, find full and sufficient pasture, and be and remain victorious over all temptation in Christ Jesus." (Klassen and Klaassen, 1978, 346).*

granted, if the medicine did not work, excommunication might have to be undertaken as a last resort.

Marpeck's observations are significant because although they too were built upon Anabaptist presuppositions, they re-visioned the Christian life as a process of spiritual growth into Christlikeness. Discipleship, Marpeck said, will not come easily, given the deep roots of self love that dwell in the human heart. (9) The Christian life for Marpeck was not the desperate defense of a perfect state, but rather a growing continually into the divine nature by means of individual and communal spiritual disciplines.

> **(9) Marpeck**
> *"Ah, my brethren, how diligently and carefully we have to take heed that we do not consider our own impulse the impulse of the Holy Spirit, our own course the course and walk of Christ." (Klassen and Klaassen, 1978, 511).*

The result was that Marpeck had a less militantly sectarian vision of the church. He conceived of the church less as a "pure body," and more as the place where those in need of the "Great Physician's medicine" come for healing and wholeness. And, as we have seen, Marpeck insisted further that the ceremonies of worship were essential *means* to spiritual healing and wholeness. And finally, Marpeck insisted that although the life of faith is rooted in the personal, interior action of the Holy Spirit, growth in the spiritual life will take place in the larger context of the community of faith. (10)

> **(10) Marpeck** *"The salvation of the soul depends upon love for the neighbor. Whoever does not love his neighbor does not love his own soul, and foolishly seeks his own profit to his highest damage." (Klassen and Klaassen, 1978, 54).*

In all these ways it appears, from the vantage point of the late twentieth century, that Pilgram Marpeck had the keenest sense of balance of all the sixteenth century Anabaptists.

HET
BLOEDIGH TOONEEL
DER
DOOPS-GESINDE,
EN
WEERELOOSE
CHRISTENEN.

Die / om het getuygenisse JESU hares Salighmaeckers/
geleden hebben / en gedoode zijn / van Christi tijde af/
tot dese onse laetste tijden toe.

Mitsgaders:

Een beschrijvinge des H. Doops, ende andere stucken van den Gods-
dienst, door alle de selve tijden geoeffent.

Begrepen in Twee BOECKEN.

Zijnde een vergrootinge van den voorgaenden MARTELAERS-SPIEGEL, uyt
vele geloofweerdige Chronijcken / Memorien / Getuygenissen/ &c.

DOOR

T. J. V. B.

Gedruckt tot DORDRECHT, by Jacob Braat,
_____
Voor Jacobus Savry, woonende in 't Kasteel van Gendt.
In 't Jaer 1660,

Title page of the first edition of the *Martyrs Mirror*
(1660),
compiled by Thieleman van Braght

Chapter 17

The Church

Ulrich Zwingli (December 1526/January 1527)
Zwingli reported to the Zurich magistrates that he had heard from "reliable witnesses" that George Blaurock was claiming miraculous occurrences, including escapes from prison in both Zurich and Chur, through locked doors. (QGTS, I, 215).

Wilhelm Reublin reports on events following Michael Sattler's martyrdom in May, 1527.
"His right hand could not be burned up, nor the heart, until the executioner had to cut it into pieces, and then the blood at first spurted high heavenward. In the night, many observed the sun and the moon standing still above the place of execution, three hours long, with golden letters written within. Such a bright light went out from them that many thought it was midday." (Yoder, 1973, 78).

Pilgram Marpeck (1531) writes against those who were claiming that "miraculous signs" ended in the apostolic age.
"Not only through external ceremonies but also through the power of Christ ... these people bear witness both in death and blood. And they do so uncoerced –freely, deliberately, and joyfully through the abundant comfort and power of the Holy Spirit of Christ in this world. Thus they seal and confirm the power of Christ. . . . One also marvels when one sees how the faithful God (who, after all, overflows with goodness) raises from the dead several such brothers and sisters of Christ after they were hanged,

drowned, or killed in other ways. Even today, they are found alive and we can hear their own testimony." (Klassen and Klaassen, 1978, 50).

Reformed Preacher at Aetingen, Switzerland. (1537)
Report of a miracle that was circulating far and wide among the people.
"When an Anabaptist had been sentenced to death [in Bern], the executioner asked him for a distinctive sign (*ain warzeichen*) so he could see that the Anabaptist had died in a just cause (*das er recht sterbe*). The Anabaptist was supposed to have answered that the hangman should go to Breitfeld at night [after the Anabaptist's death], and he would offer him his hand, and the sun and the moon would appear." These events were supposed to have taken place, as the Anabaptist predicted. Rumour also had it that the executioner was unable to continue his duties, and quit his job. (QGTS, III, #955).

God's Vengeance (1563) on a priest who betrayed several Anabaptists.
"Such putrefaction entered his flesh, that it fell off piecemeal, or was cut off from time to time, from his body, no physicians being able to cure the disease. Thus it happened on one occasion, a large piece of putrid flesh having dropped, or been cut off from his body, that the same was eaten by a dog, while he beheld it with his own eyes... And in this way he at last died most miserably..." (*Martyrs Mirror*, 665-66).

Miraculous delivery of seven Anabaptists (1565)
"In the year 1565, under the same intendant, who was a very bloodthirsty man, ...seven other persons, four brethren and three sisters, had been previously apprehended. These four brethren were also sentenced that they should be put to death, if they refused to renounce their faith. But the Lord protected them, and delivered them all out of prison unharmed in their faith, for this bloodthirsty tyrant was smitten by God with sudden death, so that the prisoners were liberated from prison..." (*Martyrs Mirror*, 687).

What did it mean in the sixteenth century, to make the claim that one belonged to the true church? Within the small Anabaptist movement it meant being where God was present and confirmed with power. (1) There had been the understanding, from the start, that the Holy Spirit was the real power behind the birth of personal faith in individuals, and behind the calling into being of the church. Being a part of the true church, then, meant occupying a zone of divine activity while still living in the world.

> **(1) Hans Hut, 1527**
> *"The Gospel [is] not a speech but a power of God, which is given by God alone and makes a man entirely new from his mouth and heart and in all behaviour and bearing."*
> *(Rupp, 1969, 391).*

With such a point of departure, differences proliferated, as could be expected. What marks would daily contact with the living power of God leave on the true church? Some early Anabaptist answers to this question met with spectacular failure. The apocalyptic, prophetic Anabaptists were convinced that the Holy Spirit would grant them privileged information about events of the End Times, for example–a conviction that proved false.

The growing distrust of individual prophets, and the corresponding growing importance of the church, the visible *Gemeinde*, the sober flock of the faithful, is evident in the Anabaptist historical records. Nevertheless, it is important not to lose sight of the deeper dimensions of "divinity" that remained in the continuing Anabaptist conception of the church.

We have already noted the importance of the image of the church as the "Bride of Christ," an image that pervades Anabaptist writings and testimonies. Two further images of the church are also helpful. Members of the Anabaptist churches were often described as the "Saints," a term that had a specific resonance when heard in a late medieval context. In the second place, the church itself was often described as the "Body of Christ," a phrase that resonated with sacramental connotations in the sixteenth century.

Saints

Body of Christ

The image of the church as the "Body of Christ" also brings us back to Christology and images of Christ, which were central to the Anabaptist understanding of the church.

The Fellowship of Saints

Dirk Philips, Enchiridion.
"*The Holy Spirit teaches and reigns over the Christian congregation which is a fellowship of the saints, that is, of the believers and newborn children of God...*" (WDP, 65-66).

It is instructive to return once again to the late medieval setting, and to place the Anabaptist image of true believers as "saints" within that context.

(2) "By belonging immediately to both worlds, the [medieval] saint was also included in two temporalities. As a man, he was a captive of the imperfect earthly world, but his saintliness was not of this world–it was a reflection of eternity–and in this sense while alive he dwelled in the Other World too. As a saint, while he was alive eternity was included in earthly time; he was its bearer among people, more perceptible and, owing to his miracles, more convincing than any other higher power." (Gurevich, 1988, 137).

In the sixteenth century, the claim to sainthood was still heard with medieval ears. The temporal world was dominated by a cosmic struggle between good and evil forces, in which one hoped to ally oneself with the community of good. In the medieval period, popularly acclaimed saints (not necessarily persons canonized by Rome) were persons who possessed and demonstrated divine charisma. They demonstrated that charisma by the performance of miracles, both before and after their deaths. Saints were, in effect, human emissaries of the divine, and bearers of divine power. (2)

The Reformation introduced some important changes to the way saints had been understood. Martin Luther opposed any and all notions of sainthood. In the realm of salvation, the saints could play no role of mediation at all, said Luther. In the realm of this world, any appearance of sanctity was no demonstration of the fact. Human beings were, Luther insisted, fatally flawed and could be saved by faith in Christ alone. Someone who appeared "saintly" was more than likely a hypocrite, a person relying on his or her own merits rather than having faith in Christ. The Anabaptists accepted only the first part of Luther's critique.

Critique of Medieval Saints

The medieval church had a judicial understanding of salvation, in which only those purged of sins would be accepted into the presence of God. Penances were performed in order to atone for specific sins committed. Most people, not being full time monks or nuns, sinned more than they could cover by acts of penance. Because of this, it was believed that after death, most people went to reside in purgatory (the place of cleansing, or purgation).

Purgatory

The exceptions to the general rule were the saints and the reprobates. The latter went directly to hell; the former directly to heaven. The saints could not only provide help through miracles while they lived in this world, they also could provide aid and mediation from their location in heaven for friends and devotees on earth and in purgatory.

The Anabaptists followed the Protestant lead in reconceiving the process of salvation. It was the mediation of Christ alone that atoned for human sin, said the Anabaptists. The saints (as understood in medieval Christianity) could play no role at all in the saving process. (3) Likewise, purgatory was written off as a human invention. The few references to purgatory in Anabaptist testimonies radically reconceived it as a process of cleansing that must happen in the here and now, by means of repentance and commitment. (4)

> *(3) Hubmaier, "Catechism"*
> "If you want to obey and honor Mary, do not call upon her or the other saints, but alone upon her Son, Christ Jesus…"
> *(Pipkin and Yoder, 1989, 357).*

> *(4) A. Spittelmaier, "Reply to Questioning," 1527.*
> *"I know of no other purgatory than when a Christian gives himself here under the cross of Christ and allows himself to be cleansed by God and Christ, inwardly and outwardly, in soul and body, with spirit, water, and blood." (Schornbaum, 1934, 55).*

Continuation of Medieval Piety

While the Anabaptists agreed with the Protestant critique of the cult of saints, they did not agree that therefore there were no more saintly people on earth. They made the amazing claim that God had chosen them to be the living saints, and had called them to gather together in a fellowship of

---

(5) Hubmaier, "Twelve Articles"
"I believe and trust that the Holy Spirit has come into me, and that the power of the most high God has overshadowed my soul like that of Mary, so that I might be conceived a new man and be born again in thy living, indestructible Word, and in the Spirit..." (Pipkin and Yoder, 199, 236).

---

saints. They insisted that a spiritual power had been granted to true believers, just as it had been granted to the Blessed Virgin and the saints. (5) This did not mean (in answer to Luther's reproach) that great claims were being made for human abilities or for human righteousness. It meant, rather, that great claims were being made for the power of God to produce new human beings and to continue working miracles in the world through the reborn. (6)

(6) Hubmaier, "Catechism"
"Leonhart: Do you believe that the saints can perform wondrous signs and miracles?
Hans: No. God alone performs miracles through them." (Pipkin and Yoder, 1989, 358).

The Anabaptist understanding of salvation was not a repudiation of the presence or activity of saints in the world, even though it was a denial of the medieval tendency to venerate saints for their supposed personal power and ability to provide miraculous help. The

Become Saints

Anabaptist message was: Don't count on the saints for help. Pray to God for help so that through the power of the Holy Spirit, you can *become one of the saints*. The latter was not what Luther had in mind.

When we read Anabaptist descriptions of the process of rebirth, regeneration, and new life, we have returned to a world of piety that would have been thoroughly familiar to medieval Christians. At the conclusion of chapter 1, we listed some ideals of medieval piety that remained important to the Anabaptists. We can now provide more specific content.

–An ascetic understanding of salvation and the Christian life.

Asceticism is the belief that spiritual growth occurs in tandem with a process of self denial. This belief was central to Anabaptist spirituality, as it was also in medieval Christian thought.

Gelassenheit

There was, first of all, the yielding (*Gelassenheit*) that must take place inwardly. Human beings needed to get out of the way so that the Holy

Spirit could accomplish God's will. Medieval mystics provided the basic vocabulary and grammar for this inward process, which Anabaptists continued to use.

The process of yielding inwardly to God's will was assumed to be a painful one. From the start, suffering was expected to be a part of the process of inward rebirth. (7) But from an early understanding of inner suffering and purgation, Anabaptists soon elaborated a theology of external suffering. The experiences of fierce persecution and martyrdom cemented a theology of suffering that insisted that the true church would *necessarily* suffer in the flesh, as Christ had suffered on the cross.

> *(7) Hans Hut*
>
> "No man can come to salvation, save through suffering and tribulation which God works in him, as also the whole Scripture and all the creatures show nothing else but the suffering Christ in all his members." *(Rupp, 1969, 386).*

Numerous martyr hymns and martyr accounts reinforced the necessity of suffering for reborn Christians, as did Anabaptist Scripture collections, prison testimonies, and writings for edification. (8) Notable in some of this testimony is the related theme of purification from sin by means of physical suffering. In other words, the cleansing function of

> *(8) Ausbund Hymn 35, by Georg Steinmetzer, martyred in 1530.*
> Stanza 2: *"It cannot be any other way on all this earth:*
> *Sin cannot be undone, except through suffering and pain."*
> Stanza 3: *"If we wish to be saved, be we great or small,*
> *We must be purified through much sorrow on earth...*
> *Whoever follows Christ the Lord is walking on the right path."*

purgatory was transferred by some Anabaptists to life in this world. The links to medieval piety here are clear, particularly the continuation of the notion of a necessary penitential cleansing and the pain associated with that purification.

Also in tune with the medieval ascetic stream, Anabaptists invariably emphasized the ascetic ideals of humility, patience, resignation, and renunciation of personal gain. The ascetic ideals held up for the Anabaptist "saints" looked thoroughly familiar in the medieval context. (9)

> *(9) Pilgram Marpeck (1547)* "All the saints of God must learn the depths of Christ, these same depths of humility and damnation, into which the leaven of our sin brought Christ. . . . Whoever does not grasp that he must be condemned with and in Christ in the depths can never understand nor achieve the height of Christ." *(Klassen and Klaassen, 1978, 434).*

–A linking of spiritual charisma to moral purity

Saintliness in the medieval period was linked to exemplary and holy living. Medieval heretical groups made many converts by insisting on that fact, and pointing to the moral deficiencies of the church clergy. Many of the same anticlerical themes run through Anabaptist testimonies. (10) Some

> **(10) Martin Weninger's Vindication, 1535**
> *"It is evident that the priests have neither the doctrine nor the manner of life of apostles; yet they say they are apostles and that the Lord is among them. . . . Christ teaches that we should guard ourselves from those of this world who lead astray..." (Wenger, 1948, 185).*

modern historians have complained about a "puritanical" tendency among the Anabaptists, and have suggested that things were not so bad in the state churches. There is good evidence to the contrary in parish visitation records. An overwhelming majority of the Reformed clergy in the canton of Zurich, for example, were the same priests as before, and many of the same problems persisted. In parishes with clerical problems, Anabaptism did very well as an alternative church movement. (11)

> **(11) Testimony, Grüningen Anabaptists, 1528**
> Rudolf Michel: *"The preacher does not rightly proclaim God's Word."*
> Heini Reiman: *"When his priest stops telling lies, and rightly proclaims God's Word and lives in love, then he will listen to him."*
> Jacob Karpfis: *"He does not want to attend the preaching because God said: 'Guard yourself from false prophets.'"*
> Hans Füsi: *"He does not wish to go to church to hear the preaching because his preacher does not live or teach according to the word of Christ." (QGTS, II, 286-87).*

> **(12)** *"[The common people in the Middle Ages] were troubled by observing bishops priding themselves on intimacy with saints and yet absorbed in earthly affairs such as taking part in wars and obtaining earthly riches." (Gurevich, 1988, 64).*

Anabaptists expected a "saintly life" from all their members, but especially from their leaders and "shepherds." Like religious dissidents in the middle ages, folk wisdom led to the conclusion that clergy who lacked a saintly life were not saints, their "holy orders" notwithstanding. (12)

Martyrdom and Miracles

The ultimate test of one's renunciation and "contempt for the world" was the willingness to accept death rather than renounce one's faith and so dishonour one's Lord. The "baptism of blood" was a daily mortification of the flesh, in preparation for the ultimate sacrifice, if such was needed. (13)

> *(13) Balthasar Hubmaier*
> *"For whoever wants to cry with Christ to God: 'Abba, pater, dear Father,' must do so in faith, and must also be cobaptized in water with Christ and suffer jointly with him in blood. Then he will be a son and heir of God, fellow heir with Christ..." (Pipkin and Yoder, 1989, 301).*

All too often, the ultimate sacrifice was called for. A recurring theme in the Anabaptist martyr accounts is the assertion that God gives the saints the miraculous strength needed to endure suffering. Part and parcel of most Anabaptist martyr accounts are details concerning the "steadfastness" of the martyrs in the excruciatingly painful moments leading up their deaths. These details of death agonies, which seem grisly to us, were of great interest to sixteenth century people. They were demonstrations that in spite of horrible suffering, God had not forsaken the martyrs in their need, and indeed had confirmed the justice of their cause by granting them supernatural strength. (14)

> *(14) Ausbund Hymn 17, Martyrdom of Ursula and Mary van Beckom.*
> *Stanza 43: "Therefore let us praise God,*
> *who gives humankind such grace and power from on high,*
> *who wants to make us worthy of victory, along with all the saints,*
> *so that we win the crown when we are put to the test,*
> *as we have witnessed that they (Ursula and Mary) have done."*

The medieval stories and legends of the saints appealed to the steadfast martyrdom of the saints as proof of their sanctity. Anabaptist martyr accounts, of course, did the same.

Although Anabaptist martyrs outnumbered those of other traditions in the sixteenth century, all Christian groups had their martyrs in that bloody century. In the face of competing claims to truth, miraculous confirmations carried with them the argument that the death of the martyrs of one's own tradition had been "true" deaths, blessed by God. The church of such divinely confirmed saints and martyrs surely was the true church.

The Body of Christ

Ambrosius Spittelmaier, 1527.
"[The body of Christ concerns] all those who belong to Christ through his godly Word, who are his members, that is hands, feet or eyes. Such members must be joined to Christ spiritually and not physically. Christ, the true man in the flesh, is the head of such members through which the members are ruled. With such a head and members it becomes like a visible body, for just as in one body there are many members doing different (unequal) things, nevertheless they serve one another, for what one member has the other member has as well. The members are also humble with each other, and obedient to each other (Luke 22; I Cor. 12; Rom. 14)." (Schornbaum, 1934, 49-50).

An even more important Anbaptist image of the church was provided by the description of the church as the Body of Christ. This language, like the language of believers as "saints," was taken directly from biblical usages. But in the sixteenth century, "body of Christ" language, like "saint" language, carried literal medieval resonances and answered medieval questions in a particular way.

Sacrament of the Altar

In what way is God present here and now to humanity, in Christ? The medieval church had a very specific answer to this question: The Body of Christ is located in the consecrated elements of bread and wine. When medieval people celebrated the Mass they were given the host with the words "The Body of Christ." Veneration of the body of Christ as contained in the consecrated host was a common devotional practice.

All Anabaptists–excepting perhaps Pilgram Marpeck–were in essential agreement with Ulrich Zwingli in their radical rejection of the sacramental mediation of grace. Again and again we read that "the water is just water"; "the bread is just bread"; "the wine is just wine." There is no divine power in the priestly blessing of these physical elements that can render them

Christ in Heaven

sacraments. In other words, the Anabaptists denied that the "body of Christ" was contained in the physical elements of bread and wine. They argued that Christ had "ascended into heaven and sitteth at the right hand of God the Father."

We have noted that one possible outcome of the radical anti-sacramental view is to deny any value to the outer elements altogether, a point pressed by the spiritualists. One further step was then possible, namely denying that the presence of Christ's Spirit would necessarily result in any particular external characteristics of the church. If the church of Christ is a purely spiritual church, there will be no physical "body of Christ" on earth, but only an invisible spiritual membership.

The Anabaptists who continued to insist upon and practise the visible, external church ordinances were not willing to press their anti-sacramentalism to the point of invisibility. They were not as throroughly anti-sacramental as we might be led to think. The sacramental substratum underlying Anabaptist view of the church became visible in the debates with the spiritualists.

Visible Church

Even though the Anabaptists denied that the Body of Christ was made physically present to humankind in the elements of the Mass by the action of priests, they nevertheless insisted against the spiritualists that the true church itself was a physical presence of Christ on earth, present in Christ's members. Christ the Head was in heaven, at God's right hand, but the Body of Christ was incarnated in this world, in the members.

Members of Christ

In our century, we tend to read Anabaptist statements describing the church as the Body of Christ, and individual believers as members or limbs of that Body, as an extended metaphor, not a literal description. There is much evidence to suggest that for the Anabaptists it was intended as a literal description, and not a metaphor at all. As the church assumed more importance, so too did an incarnational conception of the church.

When we encounter the claim that the Anabaptist church is a bodily presence of Christ, incarnated in the world in the saints (baptized human members), we must hear this claim with medieval ears. For increasing numbers of Anabaptists, the gathering of the regenerate saints fulfilled one of the functions of the medieval sacrament. Christ was incarnated, made really and bodily present, in the members of the church. It was the church that was the visible sign of invisible grace. *Ausbund* Hymn 55, for example, makes the explicit connection between the true celebration of the Lord's Supper and the Body of Christ, the church. (15)

---

(15) Ausbund Hymn 55
Stanza 7: *"All members of His Body strive to do His works all the time, following His will unto death. They are one loaf with Christ..."*
Stanza 8: *"Christ is the bread of life, His flesh and blood were given for us, His Spirit teaches us how to partake worthily. He measures us for new clothing when we come to know Him. His love burns within us so that we show forth His work in this flesh."*
Stanza 18: *"You must truly eat the little Lamb here in all its forms..."*
Stanza 19: *"You must become a stranger along with Him, with no citizenship on this earth, and live in love, with patience even if you are hated for no fault of your own. You must love enemies, deceive no one, turn your flesh into the dust of the earth."*
Stanza 20: *"You must also go with Him into the garden, and await the chalice according to the Father's will..."*
Stanza 22: *"For with the bread He means to show that whoever has His Spirit is His own. Such a one is a member of His body and community, of His flesh and limbs..."*

Once we hear Anabaptist claims for the church as the Body of Christ against the medieval sacramental background we can begin to appreciate more fully the concrete parallels the Anabaptists drew between their own experiences and those of Christ.

Individuals are bodily members of Christ Himself because of their heavenly rebirth, regeneration, and baptismal incorporation into the Body of Christ on earth. (16) Therefore they must manifest a Christ-like life in all things, according to the model of Christ and His concrete commands in Scripture. (17) Likewise, just as Christ suffered, so must the physical

---

(16) Pilgram Marpeck (1544)
"All who are thus kissed by the mouth of God, and who have conceived a divine nature by the seed of the Word, are brought to this bride and mother, the church, by the Holy Spirit. In her, as the mother, spouse, consort, and church of Christ, are they born. Conceived by the action of the Holy Spirit, she bears the children of the Word in her body. ...that body is the body of Christ for while Christ is the husband and Head, the two are one flesh." (Klassen and Klaassen, 1978, 393).

members of His Body suffer sacrificially. Just as Christ was persecuted, so must His Body on earth also be persecuted. Just as Christ forgave, rendered unto Caesar, refused to judge or take the sword, so His Body will also do. The Body of Christ on earth, the true church, will incarnate in a visible way, the mind and the spirit of Christ, by lives that conform to His life.

> *(17) Menno Simons (1545)*
> *"...if you would be a member of the holy body of Christ, you must follow the Head and obey Him. John 3:36; II Thes. 1:8."* *(CWMS, 1024).*

Against this background, it is not difficult to see why an ethics of purity was so emphasized in Anabaptist churches. When the "Body of Christ" was understood to be contained in the sacramental host it was at the same time understood to be divine, pure, undefiled by earthly stain. *Purity* Some of this thinking also is present in the Anabaptist conception of the church as the Body of Christ. Members of the Body of Christ will also manifest the same purity as the Head. This purity was maintained by the exercise of the ban.

Conclusion

The Anabaptist images of the church as the fellowship of saints and as the Body of Christ gave concrete shape and substance to the Anabaptist church. When seen against the late medieval background, it is evident that the Anabaptist conception of the church developed medieval themes in original ways that did not fit with either the Catholic or the Protestant traditions. Furthermore, responding to internal debates, the Anabaptist conception of the church assumed more precise shape as the sixteenth century wore on. We may summarize these developments as follows.

–The baptizing spiritualists were optimistic about regeneration, but they safeguarded the individual and subjective nature of the Christian life. The spiritualists resisted a communal, legislative restriction of the Spirit. Their insistence upon freedom from all law, except the law of love as manifested in Christ, meant that the boundaries of their communities were amorphous, and over time tended to become virtually invisible.

–The Anabaptists who insisted upon linking regeneration with obedience to a literal New Testament law were, by that step, elevating community guidelines above the individual reception of the Holy Spirit. The baptism of the Spirit would entail, they said, very specific visible evidences of regeneration, as defined by the true church's reading of Scripture. The Spirit was present in tightly governed communities, it appeared, and nowhere else. These Anabaptists believed that water baptism and a visible commitment to the Body of Christ on earth would naturally follow faith; outside of this progression there would be no salvation.

–Hubmaier and Marpeck were among the few Anabaptists who took up positions between the spiritualists and the literalists on questions of regeneration. Their questioning of the actual thoroughness of regeneration was a significant theological and practical objection. If human beings remain in need of significant further regeneration after repentance and coming to faith, then the church will be structured not so much to preserve purity among the regenerate saints, but rather to encourage growth for the "weak and imperfect," which would include all members.

The tradition passed on by the surviving Anabaptist groups was a very optimistic one indeed. The concrete and visible church was where the physical presence of Christ (in His members) would be incarnated in the world. This understanding suggested the Christological question: Given that believers were to represent Christ on earth, how had Christ been incarnated? What exactly were believers supposed to mirror in their own lives? Christological debates pointed to a further philosophical question that, although rarely acknowledged, underlay many of these discussions: Is the nature of reality essentially dualistic, with an impregnable division between the worlds of spirit and matter? If so, what will "incarnation" mean in such a world? How these questions were answered had significant implications for the eventual shape of the Anabaptist church.

Chapter 18

Christology

Agreement made by the brethren and elders at Strasbourg, assembled because of the question of the origin of the flesh of Christ.

"Since we brothers and elders many times are forced and often and in many ways and forms are driven, time and again, to speak concerning the incarnation [birth] of Christ ... we servants and elders were invited again by the brothers that are called Hofmanites, and by the brothers in the Netherlands, and have gathered together in Strasbourg from many places. And when we earnestly considered this article, we discovered by God's grace, that through a misunderstanding on both sides, the birth of Christ was pushed too high, or too low. Because of this, peace and fraternal unity disappeared. Therefore we justly measured our ignorance, and called to the Lord; and so we have seen our lack, guided above all by the Scriptures in the fear of God, which we rightly should believe above all, and which we should in no way change, overturn and falsify.

For it is true that the Scripture in many places seems to indicate that Christ brought his flesh from heaven, John 1, 3, 6, 7, 8, 14, 16, 17; I Cor. 15; Heb. 1, 7, 13; Revel. 1. But likewise the Scripture also seems to indicate that Christ took flesh and received it from Mary, Gen. 3, 22; Deut. 18; II Samuel 7; Isa. 11; Psalm 131; Acts 2; Rom. 1; Phil. 2; Heb. 2; Rev. 5. . .

Therefore it happened for us just as for those who wished to build the useless tower [of Babel]: in the same way the Lord confused our speech, so that no one could understand the other. Perhaps this occurred because we tried to know more than one ought to know, Rom. 12, and because we did not pay enough attention to the Scripture which says: Don't inquire after things that are too difficult for you, and don't attempt to investigate what is too great for you. But strive for what lies before you here, for you cannot grasp hidden things, Eccl. 3.

Therefore we confess that from now on we should and will, by God's grace, keep his commandments, John 13, 14, and ordinances, Matt. 18, so as to keep ourselves in a given-over [lit.: dead] life, with pure and yielded hearts, in order to walk in true righteousness, for therein is found salvation, and in the knowledge of God and Jesus Christ, John 17. Therefore it is written, to know you is the perfection of righteousness, Wisd. 15. And, 'In this way we confess that we have known him, if we keep his commandments. Whoever says "I know him" and does not keep his commandments, such a one is a liar, and there is no truth in such a one. But whoever obeys his Word, in such a one truly is the Love of God perfected,' I John 2.

In this we must give him honour, that we believe his Word above all, and confess it to be true: [that we] confess and declare in our inmost persons that Christ is truly God, Eph. 2. ... And in our simplicity we wish to remain with the Scripture, which declares and confesses: 'The word became Flesh, and dwelt among us,' John 1.

Now since it is not only dangerous but also condemnable, not to fulfill the Word, Deut. 4; Prov. 30; Rev. 22, therefore we wish to make our consciences captive under the obedience of Christ, and confess him in all places, according to the Scripture. A godless life and evil appearance should be opposed more by a Christian and Godly walk, than with the mouth. And from now on we will not speak, outside of the clear Scripture, how far or near, high or low, Christ became man, and we will give a faithful warning to any that we hear speaking concerning this, outside of what Scripture says." (Cramer and Pijper, 1910, 226-28)

> **John Rempel**
> *"In Christian theology, belief about the incarnation logically determines belief about sacraments: the manner in which God took on flesh becomes the archetype for the relationship between spirit and matter." (Rempel, 1993, 169).*

The most widespread doctrinal unorthodoxy to be found in the Anabaptist movement was a peculiar Christology found among virtually all of the followers of Melchior Hoffman.

From the start the Anabaptist movement had been Christocentric, continuing a medieval stream of piety that emphasized following after Christ in life, according to the witness of His life and His words as recorded in the New Testament. This stream of piety was not given to speculation, but was given rather to simple, pious obedience or "imitation." When Melchior Hoffman became an Anabaptist, he went beyond "simple obedience" and taught an accompanying spiritualized Christology that scandalized sixteenth century mainstream theologians and drove a doctrinal wedge between the Melchiorites and other Anabaptists.

Christology outside the Melchiorite Tradition

The Anabaptists who gathered in Strasbourg in 1555 attempted to heal the Christological breach, with only partial success. The solution was more "Swiss" than "Dutch," in that it emphasized a pious life over speculation about "things that are too high for us." There is good evidence that the Strasbourg solution did not meet with widespread success in the north, even though it pointed the way to an eventual solution.

The Swiss Anabaptists and the Hutterites were not given to Christological speculation, and were content to repeat orthodox formulations about the nature of Christ. Jesus Christ, said the Hutterite elder Peter Riedemann, is the Eternal Word and Truth, the Saviour and Christ, fully human and fully divine, the only begotten Son of God. The versification of the Apostles' Creed in the Swiss Brethren hymnal, the *Ausbund*, stuck even closer to orthodox language: Jesus Christ is the true Son of God, the only begotten Saviour, present with the Father before the world began, begotten not created, of the same substance (*Wesen*) as the Father through whom all things were made. Conceived by the Holy Spirit of the Virgin Mary, he was born "a human being like any other common person." (*Ausbund*, hymn 2). There is no hint among the Swiss Brethren or the Hutterites of speculative unorthodoxy in Christology.

> **(1) Peter Riedemann**
>
> *"[Only Christ has the power to] quicken whom he will and to give his fullness to whomsoever and in what abundance he will. And those who take from and receive of him become through him likewise 'God's anointed' or Christians–failing this, they have the name in vain."* (Klaassen, 1982, 29).

Nevertheless, Riedemann's exposition of the Creed points to the particular Anabaptist interpretation (or Christocentric extension) of orthodox Christology. After confessing that only Christ can overcome death, Riedemann adds the point that all Anabaptists felt constrained to add, namely that "confessing Christ" verbally in this way means nothing, unless the Christ that is confessed is followed in life and deed. (1)

For the Anabaptists, the point of Christological formulations was not simply to affirm who Jesus Christ was and is, in a philosophically and linguistically correct manner, but to insist further that "confessing Christ as Lord" can only be done by one who, in Riedemann's words, "experience(s) such a victory in himself, namely that Christ has overcome the devil in him also, and rent and removed his snare, that is sin." To confess Christ as the Son of God meant, for Riedemann, that this "brightness of the glory of the Father ... has now taken us captive into his obedience and leads us in his way, teaches us his character, ways, and goodness..." (Klaassen, 1982, 30-31).

In typically Anabaptist fashion, for Riedemann affirmations about the nature of Christ became quite naturally affirmations about the necessity of regeneration, obedience, and discipleship in Christ's human members.

Swiss Brethren and Hutterite Christological statements, affirming as they do the joint divinity and humanity of Christ, can quite naturally go on to affirm both the "divine birth" of the Spirit of Christ in believers, and the concrete life of discipleship that must issue from rebirth and regeneration. It was the life of Jesus that provided the model for discipleship. Just as Jesus in His humanity had lived, so should true disciples live.

The Dutch Anabaptists, however, had to deal with a slightly different set of problems, for they were heirs to Melchior Hoffman's very spiritualized Christology and heightened expectation for regeneration. In what follows we will outline Hoffman's view, inherited and modified from Caspar Schwenckfeld, consider Pilgram Marpeck's response to Schwenckfeld's Christology (which served as an indirect response to Hoffman's view), and conclude by looking at Menno Simons' appropriation of Melchiorite Christology.

Caspar Schwenckfeld and Melchior Hoffman

Melchior Hoffman's concern with the question of how Jesus Christ assumed human form was based on his concern about the atonement for sin. Hoffman came to believe that Satan's hold on human beings could only be loosed by a perfect sacrifice. (2) If Jesus Christ had "taken flesh" from

> *(2) Melchior Hoffman, 1530*
> *"He did not take flesh upon himself but became himself flesh and corporal, in order that he might himself give salvation and pay for the sin of the whole world by means of his guiltless suffering, dying, and the pouring out of his blood." (SAW, 198).*

Mary, his death could not have atoned for sin because it would have been just another human death. The devil would have been paid back "in his own coin."

Hoffman's concern about the atonement and salvation, and his rejection of the orthodox understanding of the two natures of Christ was related to his understanding of the Lord's Supper. Hoffman believed that the orthodox two-natures Christology had led to a false teaching concerning the real presence in the Eucharist.

Word became Flesh

The key biblical text relating to all of this was John 1:14: "The word became flesh and dwelt among us." The key word in the phrase was *became* flesh which, Hoffman emphasized, was used by the evangelist rather than "the word *took on* human flesh." By means of this distinction, namely that Christ brought a pure flesh from heaven and then *became* human, Hoffman believed that Christ's essentially pure and spiritual nature could be maintained, both in the matter of the atonement and in the understanding of the Supper.

Melchior Hoffman and Caspar Schwenckfeld had come to know each other in Strasbourg beginning in 1529. They shared some important commonalities, both having begun reforming careers in the Lutheran camp, both having rejected key elements of Luther's theology, and both holding to a similar spiritualized understanding of the Lord's Supper.

From these similarities grew their similar Christological concerns. Hoffman's solution paralleled Schwenckfeld's very closely. Klaus Deppermann concluded that Schwenckfeld was the source of Hoffman's teaching, but that Hoffman was less careful than was Schwenckfeld about

Docetism

the danger of docetism–the view that Jesus was essentially divine, and merely took on a human *appearance*. Hoffman, like Schwenckfeld, held that God alone must be considered the progenitor of Jesus, but unlike Schwenckfeld, he did not agree that the Virgin Mary played any essential role in providing Jesus with human flesh–even of a unique and distinctive kind of human flesh. Hoffman said, rather inelegantly, that Jesus had "passed through Mary like water through a pipe."

Mariology

The differences in Christology between Schwenckfeld and Hoffman come to rest in their respective Mariologies. Schwenckfeld held, against Hoffman, that Mary herself had been immaculately conceived, and so could pass on "uncorrupted" flesh to Christ. Hoffman denied the immaculate conception of Mary. For Hoffman, to the contrary, any essential motherhood attributed to Mary would taint Jesus with "creatureliness."

In spite of the close similarities in their Christologies, then, Schwenckfeld resolutely combatted Hoffman's view, and considered it a gross mistake. He said later that Hoffman had "sucked [his] error out of our truth, as the spider sucks poison out of a precious flower."

Hoffman's rejection of the sacraments—in both its Roman Catholic and Lutheran forms—was complete and in accord with the Anabaptist view. It was strengthened by his Christology. Salvation could not be mediated by a real, physical presence of Christ in physical elements, but would be mediated by a spiritual process leading to repentance, regeneration, and baptism. Hoffman described this process as a "spiritual marriage to Christ."

Hoffman also rejected the Reformers' view of justification, joining other Anabaptists in emphasizing rebirth in the Spirit, regeneration, and a life of actual righteousness. "The elect" were those who had yielded to the living Spirit of their own free will. True believers were those in whom the Spirit of Christ had come to dwell, and they would live visibly new lives according to the Spirit, not the flesh.

Justification

As a consequence of his spiritualistic Christology, Hoffman's view of human regeneration was extremely optimistic. Just as Christ had conquered the flesh perfectly by means of an immaculate, spiritual conception and pure birth, so those who had been regenerated by Christ's Spirit were "wedded" to Christ and joined by Christ to His spiritual Body, the church. The regenerate had, through Christ, conquered the flesh by the Spirit.

Regeneration

Hoffman's marked optimism concerning regeneration, based on his spiritualized Christology, made even more explicit the inner/outer tension already present in the movement. Hoffman's stronger emphasis on the Spirit is evident in his acceptance of contemporary prophecy, in his willingness to allow water baptism to lapse when persecution intensified, and in his spiritualized understanding of discipleship.

 Hoffman also taught that believers were to "follow after Christ," but his teaching differed from that of the Swiss Brethren and the Hutterites primarily because he understood following after Christ in more figurative than literal terms. For Hoffman, the life of Jesus Christ was the "figurative model" believers were to follow, particularly his example of yieldedness to the Father's will, which led to the establishment of a new covenant sealed in baptism, and a time of testing in the wilderness.

In the second place, Hoffman (like Hut) understood discipleship, or following after Christ, within a calendar of End Times events, in which the actions of believers–especially those of the "pious rulers"–would be carried out in accordance with the demands of God's final justice. The yieldedness of believers, and their willingness to suffer as Jesus had suffered, was thus tempered in Hoffman by the expectation that God's justice would avenge that suffering before Christ's return, and that this vengeance would be carried out very soon.

Caspar Schwenckfeld and Pilgram Marpeck

Pilgram Marpeck did not enter into a written debate with Melchior Hoffman, but he did engage Caspar Schwenckfeld's Christology at some length. As a result of this debate, Marpeck was forced to clarify his own Christology and understanding of the Lord's Supper, from an Anabaptist perspective. Marpeck's views, although unique to Anabaptism and not destined to survive in an ongoing tradition, nevertheless remain valuable theological perspectives as such, given his Anabaptist presuppositions. Furthermore, because of the close similarity between Schwenckfeld's and Hoffman's Christologies, Marpeck's objections to Schwenckfeld's Christology applied equally well to Hoffman, and to the Dutch Anabaptists, like Menno and Dirk, who accepted Hoffman's basic view.

Already in 1531 Marpeck had made the connection between the two natures of Christ and his view that the physical and the spiritual formed one essential reality. The debates with Schwenckfeld in 1538 and 1539 forced him to clarify and refine his views. Marpeck was thoroughly opposed to any Christology which seemed to deny the full humanity of Christ. (3) But by 1538 Schwenckfeld had come to the conviction that even Christ's human nature was "uncreated," and so came to oppose Marpeck's further elaboration of the meaning of the two natures of Christ.

> **(3) Pilgram Marpeck**
> *"He [Jesus Christ] was a true natural human being ... the true seed of Abraham ... fruit of the body of Mary, therefore he can truly be called our brother... with all our weaknesses except sin..." (In Boyd, 1992, 117).*

In 1542 Marpeck argued not only that Christ's nature was an essential union in one person of the human and divine natures, but also that this union continued after Christ's death, resurrection, and ascension. The "physical" part of the union was carried on, through Christ's spirit, by the church: the baptism, the Supper, and the acts of mercy of the gathered community are "prolongations of the incarnation."

Schwenckfeld, in reply, accused Marpeck of mixing the spiritual and the bodily, to which Marpeck answered in 1543. Marpeck argued further that Christ has two bodies, "the transfigured body of Christ at the right hand of the Father and the untransfigured body of Christ (composed of earthly members gathered by his Spirit)." Marpeck argued that Christ's Spirit "secures" the human spirit, which then carries out physical acts and deeds in conformity with Christ's Spirit.

This much Marpeck held in common with other Anabaptists. But because of his emphasis on the incarnational doctrine of "two natures, one body," he drew a non-dualist conclusion: regenerated human beings are integrated spiritual and physical beings, empowered to act by Christ's Spirit. (4) Likewise, the community of believers "is constituted by the Spirit through the concrete acts of believers."

> **(4)** *"The new human being is one integrated entity which enjoys participation in ... the divine Spirit." (Boyd, 1992, 124).*

Marpeck thus maintained not only the full divinity and humanity of Christ, but also the essential unity of the spiritual and the human in individual believers and in the Body of Christ, the church. Because of this essential unity, which included the physical and the human as essential parts of the reborn Christian, the perfectionist strain was softened by

Marpeck. Believers are being regenerated, but they have not yet sloughed off their humanity nor been perfectly wedded to Christ.

Furthermore, because of this unity, the ceremonies and acts of love in which that community participates reveal the divine in an essential way, rather than being simply physical signs pointing to another reality. Because of their essential link with the divine reality, the ceremonies cannot be done away with, for they are of the essence of God's revelatory order as prolongations of the incarnation. In fact, Marpeck would argue against the spiritualists that "a person can neither know nor be saved by the transfigured Christ apart from the concrete life of [the] community." (In Boyd, 1992, 125).

Menno Simons, Melchiorite Christology, and the Church

Menno Simons inherited Melchior Hoffman's spiritualized Christology, and consistently defended it. One must agree with Cornelius Krahn's observation that Menno's defence of the Melchiorite position on the incarnation was no mere "bagatelle," but rather was tightly integrated with his own understanding of salvation and the nature of the church.

Two writings in particular outline Menno's Christology: the "Brief Confession on the Incarnation" (1544) (CWMS, 422-454), and "The Incarnation of Our Lord" (1554) (CWMS, 785-834). In these writings Menno reiterated and defended the essence of Hoffman's spiritualized Christology as being in accordance with the letter of Scripture.

Against the orthodox position that holds two undivided natures in one person, Menno wrote: "The Lord Jesus Christ is not an impure and divided Christ of two persons or sons, but an undivided and pure Christ, a single person, God's own first-born Son and only begotten Son." (CWMS, 793). Granting that Menno misrepresented the orthodox position here (which does not hold that Christ was "two persons"), the key words are "impure" and "divided," as against "undivided" and "pure."

Menno appealed to the words of John, and repeated Hoffman's key verse, adopted also by the Münsterites. John, Menno insisted, says, "The Word became flesh. He does not say, The Word assumed a man of our or of Mary's flesh and dwelt in this, as our opponents say" (CWMS, 795). (5)

---

(5) Menno Simons

"Recall that Christ calls Himself the Son of man, and says that this Son of man descended from heaven. But the son of Mary, whose flesh is of Mary did not descend from heaven, did He, but must have sprung from Adam's flesh, if the position of the learned ones is correct." (CWMS, 797).

And so Menno concludes, in good Melchiorite fashion: "It follows irresistibly that the entire Christ Jesus, both God and man, man and God, has His origin in heaven and not on earth. . . . Fast and immovable is the testimony, The Word became flesh." (CWMS, 797-98).

In his earlier writing on the incarnation, Menno made it clear that he drew the same regenerationist conclusion from this Christology as had Hoffman. (6) Believers are those who have been born again, of Christ's

---

(6) Menno Simons

"[The true brethren and sisters of Jesus Christ are] the well-disposed children of God, who with Christ Jesus are born of God the Father and the powerful seed of the divine Word in Christ Jesus, who are regenerated by Christ, partake of His Spirit and nature, who have been made like unto Him, are Christian and heavenly minded..." (CWMS, 423).

Spirit. When these believers gather together into the "rightly believing, Christian church" they can be described only in superlative terms, as follows:

> They are the body and bride of Christ, the ark, the mount and garden of the Lord, the house, people, city, temple of God, the spiritual Eve, flesh of Christ's flesh and bone of His bone, children of God, the chosen generation, the spiritual seed of Abraham, children of the promise,

branches and trees of righteousness, sheep of the heavenly pasture, kings and priests, a holy people which is God's own. (CWMS, 448).

Menno held with Hoffman that the Body of Christ, made up of those who had been regenerated and "married" to Christ spiritually, would partake of the essential divinity of Christ in its sojourn on this earth.

As we have seen, however, Menno was not willing to draw all the same spiritualist conclusions from this Christology as had Hoffman and other Melchiorites. Whereas Hoffman had been willing to suspend outer ceremonies, Menno linked the performance of those ceremonies with obe-

Obedience

dience to Scripture. Where Hoffman had spoken of following after Christ in an essentially figurative way, Menno insisted upon a literal discipleship, based on the testimony of the New Testament. Whereas Joris and Blesdijk continued further down the spiritualist path outlined by Hoffman and his Christology, Menno attempted to hold on to Hoffman's spiritualist Christology *while at the same time* applying literal measures of spiritual regeneration.

Purity of the Body

The result for Menno was a heightened emphasis on the visible purity of the Body of Christ, for the Body of Christ would of necessity need to manifest in word and deed, in the world, the spiritual perfection of having been united to the essentially divine Christ. It is in this way that the controversy concerning the ban in Dutch Anabaptism, which was a controversy about the limits and possibility of purity, had significant roots in Melchiorite Christology.

Conclusion

The debates between Marpeck and the spiritualists, and Menno and the Davidjorists provide two contrasting Anabaptist responses to the challenge of spiritualism. It is important to note that the primary role of the Spirit of God was not at issue in either debate. Marpeck and Menno, no less than Denck, Bünderlin, Schwenckfeld and Blesdijk, maintained that a personal experience of the renewing Spirit of God was necessary in order for one to become a Christian believer. Furthermore, both Marpeck and Menno maintained resolutely that the true church must be a visible church, in which the ceremonies and ordinances were practised and which showed forth, in an unmistakable and visible way, the inner regeneration which both they and the spiritualists held to be primary. Nevertheless, the contrasting responses of Marpeck and Menno to the challenge of spiritualism are instructive.

Marpeck and Menno

Marpeck worked consciously to avoid a legalistic and literalistic response to the spiritualist challenge, while yet not losing touch with the demand for a renewed life of discipleship and following Jesus. Marpeck's insistence on the integrity of the spiritual and the physical dimensions of creation was grounded in an appreciation for the deeper meaning of the incarnation. Not only did a good God bring a good creation into being, the centrality of the physical side of creation in the saving process was revealed, confirmed, and cemented by the incarnation of Jesus Christ. The only way to salvation, Marpeck would affirm in many of his writings, is through the humanity of Christ. Consequently, the human dimensions of the Body of Christ also form a crucial and continuing part of Jesus' mission to the world.

Incarnation

Pilgram Marpeck insisted further against the spiritualists that the practice and expression of divine love must take place within the community of love, and cannot exist in splendid spiritual isolation. The ceremonies which define the community, and which are practised within the community of love are, said Marpeck, remembrances, pledges and memorials of Christ's historic love for humanity. Nevertheless, the ceremonies are much more than mere memorials, performed out of a blind obedience to the law. They are also, said Marpeck, integral means of growth into divine love and the mature spiritual life. With this insistence, Pilgram Marpeck moved the Anabaptist discussion back again towards

Community

the Catholic sacramental insight: the physical ordinances and ceremonies commanded by Christ and celebrated by Christians in communal worship are necessary means of grace, physical windows and doors that participate in and open the way to the divine, and without which the way to the divine will not be known.

Marpeck challenged the dualist presupposition of the spiritualists. Menno, the Swiss, and the Hutterites did not. But Menno had the added handicap of an inherited Melchiorite Christology which was built upon the stark division, and even enmity, between the spiritual and the physical dimensions of reality. Christ could only atone for human sin by not being tainted with creatureliness; believers could only be saved by overcoming creatureliness by a divine birth and life.

Having acccepted this spiritualist Christology, Menno still faced the need to move beyond the prophetic apocalypticism and spiritualism that had accompanied it in Melchiorite Anabaptism. He did this, as we have seen, by appealing to the words and the example of Christ as witnessed to in Scripture, but he built this New Testament biblicism on the Christology

he had inherited from Hoffman. That is, Melchiorite Christology simply heightened Menno's optimism concerning the ethical possibilities of the spiritual rebirth of believers, and thus heightened his expectations for the obedience of the pure Bride of Christ, the church.

The community of believers played several crucial roles in Marpeck's understanding of the process of redemption and salvation that are missing in Menno, the Swiss and the Hutterites. For Marpeck the church as the Body of Christ was a sacramental offer of God's grace, mercy, and salvation to all. As in the incarnation, God's grace continues to be offered through the physical Body of Christ to individuals and to the wider world by means of external and visible testimonies, ceremonies, and acts of love.

But Marpeck took the incarnational point further: The Body of Christ is also the place where believers are expected to grow in Christian love by means of the practice of the disciplines of worship, love and service. This step moved Marpeck's ecclesiology away from the temptation of isolated separatism. For Marpeck, a central reason for the church's being was proclamation of the good news and a showing forth to the world of the way to God. Christian worship was crucial for evangelization, and also for the spiritual development of believers, for it was through the church that believers were to be challenged and helped in the process of growing into the nature of Christ.

Proclamation

Such pastoral concerns were not lacking in Menno, the Swiss, or the Hutterites, of course. But for them, the church was to be, above all, "without spot or wrinkle," as Christ also was. Apart from Marpeck, it was the divine Christ, not the incarnate Christ, that inspired the Anabaptist understanding of the church as the "Body of Christ." Consequently, it was above all divine purity, not human growth, that was expected to be "incarnated" by believers. It was separation and purity, not evangelism, that defined the true church.

Here Marpeck's Christological emphasis on the humanity of Christ, along with a more tempered optimism concerning regeneration, toned down the perfectionist, sectarian tendency that had been part of Anabaptism from the start and that asserted itself increasingly in the ongoing Anabaptist church traditions.

There was an uncanny parallel between Marpeck's critique of Swiss Brethren legalism and Blesdijk's critique of Menno's reading of Scripture. Menno's strongest argument against Blesdijk for the continuation of a visible church was to insist that Christ's commands must be obeyed. Blesdijk's objection was based on his Pauline appeal to Christian freedom, and his conviction that love was the "highest summation and foundation of all the Scriptures" by which all other scriptural statements must be measured.

One suspects, from other statements he made, that Marpeck would have agreed with Blesdijk, against Menno. While Marpeck would have disagreed with Blesdijk's conclusions regarding the visible marks of the church, he shared an appreciation with Blesdijk for the spiritual freedom of a Christian that Menno, the Swiss Brethren, and the Hutterites did not.

Historically speaking, it was the conception of the church without spot or wrinkle that became the consensus view in the surviving Anabaptist groups, and that was passed on to succeeding generations. Marpeck's answer to the spiritualist challenge, in spite of its rich possibilites, was not passed on to succeeding groups.

Among the followers of Menno, the Melchiorite Christology that had provided the theological support for the emphasis on the pure Body of Christ on earth faded during the seventeenth century, although among the more conservative descendants of Menno, defences of Melchiorite Christology were still being reprinted as late as 1825. The majority of Dutch Mennonites no longer held to Menno's Christology by 1800, but the emphasis on the church without spot or wrinkle survived and flourished nevertheless.

The Swiss Brethren and the Hutterites, while they elaborated more sophisticated scriptural defences of their understandings of the church as the sixteenth century proceeded, maintained their views of the church as the fellowship of Saints, the pure Body of Christ, untroubled by Christological speculation. Marpeck's view disappeared, to be recovered only as a result of modern historical investigations.

D.
The Surviving Anabaptist Traditions: 1560 to the Present

Swiss Brethren in Alsace, from a later century

Chapter 19

The Continuing Anabaptist Tradition

Thieleman J. van Braght, Author's Preface to the *Martyrs Mirror*

"This book, the humble work of our hands, but which is nevertheless a precious jewel, in view of the persons and matters contained therein, we have dedicated to you [most beloved brethren and sisters]. Receive it, then, with the same love with which it has been dedicated to you. Read it again and again, and with the same attention and emotion with which we have written and re-written it. We are fully confident that, if you do this, it will not be unfruitful to you. But, before all things, fix your eyes upon the martyrs themselves, note the steadfastness of their faith, and follow their example. . . . With inseparable love ought we, most beloved in the Lord, to be joined to our blessed fellow brethren who have been slain for the testimony of the Lord, that we might follow their footsteps unto the end; for surely, the God whom they confessed and served, is also our God; the Saviour on whom they placed their hope is our Saviour; the faith which they all confessed is our faith (we speak of Anabaptists in general); the law and commandments of God which they received as their rule of life are also our laws and commandments; they bowed their knees before God; they obligated themselves by the words of their lips to render obedience to God, and thereupon received holy baptism; we have done the same; they promised to continue steadfastly all the days of their life in the faith and due obedience, without departing therefrom, yea, if necessary, to suffer death for it; we have promised the same. What difference, then, is there between us and them? Certainly only this: that they all persevered unto the end nay, unto a cruel death, without departing to the right or to the left; which we have not yet done. They have therefore entered into rest, yea, have come to the Lord; while we are yet in unrest, proceeding in our pilgrimage in the absence of the Lord.

Therefore, my most beloved friends in Christ Jesus, let us also in this last respect seek to be conformed to our beloved slain fellow brethren, that we may continue steadfastly unto the end in the most holy faith which we have confessed with them. Oh! be careful in this matter; watch over your dear-bought souls; for it is highly necessary, yea, more necessary than at any former time." Dort, July 25th, 1659.

(Martyrs Mirror, 1972, 8).

The words of Thieleman van Braght, compiler of the huge *Martyrs Mirror*, locate us at some historical distance from the events and debates we have described in the foregoing pages. By the middle of the seventeenth century, when van Braght completed his enormous task, many of the issues faced in the first decades of the Anabaptist movement had been settled and a recognizably Anabaptist theological tradition had taken shape. But at the same time, new lines of internal division had emerged that divided Anabaptist groups from one another. In remembering and appealing to the common Anabaptist experience of persecution and martyrdom, van Braght was hoping to provide a unifying centre for a people who, in his view, shared "the most holy faith."

The preceding section of this study has looked in detail at internal Anabaptist debates and developments, as a variety of theological and practical options were tested and tried. But these developments did not take place in a vacuum. Standing behind internal debates were the historical realities that provided the real context for the debates.

The first significant external factor shaping the development of the later Anabaptist tradition was political persecution. The second significant external factor was that Jesus did not return, as expected and predicted.

Political persecution meant an underground existence for virtually all Anabaptists, and a severe testing of their convictions concerning biblical church reform. The spiritualist option, which provided attractive alternatives to visibility and martyrdom, provoked one of the central theolgical debates to take place in the mature movement. It was driven by political persecution, and the need to find ways of continuing to live "in the world," even if not "of the world."

Persecution

The victory of the "anti-Nicodemite" Anabaptists meant the survival of a visible church, but at the cost of thousands of martyrs. The common Anabaptist tradition to which van Braght was appealing came into being in the crucible of prison, torture, and the gallows. Sometimes brethren of different persuasions found themselves together in these prisons, tarred with the same Anabaptist brush in spite of differences they considered important. In part, an Anabaptist theological tradition took shape because, to the world outside, an Anabaptist by any other name was still a heretic.

Anti Nicodemite

But it is important also not to lose sight of the phenomenally important strength of apocalyptic expectation in shaping the early movement. It does not seem an exaggeration to say that in the absence of the expectation that Jesus was on the verge of returning to earth to rule in glory, there would have been no Anabaptist movement. The early missionizing efforts were driven by apocalyptic excitement and hope, as was the openness to the Spirit, to prophecy, and to the emergence of a new world.

Apocalyptic

The later Anabaptist traditions took shape in the shadow of failed apocalyptic expectations, in the realization that the triumph of Christ and His saints would be delayed for a long time yet. The early Anabaptist saints, who had looked forward to participating in the thousand-year reign with Christ, came to see only the cross of suffering on this earth.

The later Anabaptist tradition was thus shaped by unremitting external political pressure, the failure of apocalyptic hopes, and the internal victory of anti-Nicodemite Anabaptists.

In this chapter we will return briefly to the external historical forces that helped to shape the theological tradition that came to survive in the Swiss Brethren, Hutterite, and Dutch Anabaptist groups. We will conclude by summarizing the revised, shared core of teachings and practices that had solidified by the end of the century.

External Forces that Shaped the Anabaptist Tradition

Standing just behind the debates concerning the proper Christian stance towards government were relationships with actual governing authorities. Although the prevailing context for Anabaptists was one of political persecution, nevertheless realities varied widely for Anabaptist communities towards the end of the sixteenth century, depending upon geographical location. Dutch Anabaptists living in Amsterdam in the 1590s, under an official policy of toleration, would take a different view of government and "the world" than would Swiss Brethren in Bern or Zurich, where Anabaptists were still being sought out, arrested, and martyred. In what follows we will try to give an impression of the various realities in which the later Anabaptist tradition took shape.

Moravia

Hapsburg

Moravia was the land of religious freedom, but only to the extent that local lords could continue to exert their independence from the house of Hapsburg. Ferdinand, Archduke of Austria and later Holy Roman Emperor, was ruler of Austrian territories. Besides being militantly Catholic, he was determined to establish firm political control over the territories of Moravia and Silesia, which had fallen into Austrian hands in 1526. Local lords, who offered religious toleration to communal and non-communal Anabaptists, resisted Ferdinand in what became, ultimately, a losing battle. Many of these lords had sympathies with the fifteenth century Hussite movement of reform, and no great love of either the Hapsburgs or their attempts to impose Catholicism. Furthermore, the Anabaptist refugees were good for local economies. They brought an infusion of new people, skills, and energy in farming and the crafts.

Because of a lack of records, we do not know how many Anabaptist refugees fled to Moravia in the 1520s and 1530s, but the number was in the thousands. Leonard Gross estimates that by 1529 more than 12,000 Anabaptist refugees had come to Nicholsburg and the neighbouring area.

The three communal Anabaptist groups, the Gabrielites, the Philipites, and the Auspitz brethren numbered several thousand members. They experienced a bitter schism in 1533. Jakob Hutter led the Auspitz group and enforced a rigorous, legislated community of goods. There were, in addition, Swiss Anabaptists living in many communities in Moravia in these decades, as well as small numbers of Pilgramites (followers of Pilgram Marpeck).

All of this came to a sudden end as a result of the disaster of Münster. *Persecution* The scandal of crusading and polygamous Anabaptism meant that Anabaptists everywhere were identified as Münsterites, whether they were or not. Ferdinand managed to unleash a vicious persecution in 1535-1536, and again in 1547-1551 in his Moravian territories.

The 1535-36 persecution was especially disastrous for the communal Anabaptists, who were driven out of their communities and forced into exile and hiding. Ferdinand came in person to Moravia to see to the expulsion of the "heretics" from the territory.

The Philipites, who had numbered a few thousand members, never recovered from the 1535 disbanding of their communities. A large number of Philipites who were attempting to flee were arrested and imprisoned in the castle at Passau. While in prison they composed over fifty hymns. Many of these Philipites later joined the Swiss Brethren, and their prison hymns formed the core of the *Ausbund* hymnal. The Gabrielites likewise never recovered from the 1536 persecution. Some fled back to Silesia; some eventually joined the Hutterites, as did some of the Philipite remnant.

Little is known about the Swiss Brethren and Pilgramites during these years. Presumably they also were scattered hither and yon.

The first wave of persecution was intense but short lived. By 1537 the Hutterites were setting up new Bruderhofs (communal farms) again. It is assumed, because of later evidence, that the Swiss Brethren and Pilgramite refugees returned once again.

The second wave of persecution, from 1547-1551, was more serious. The Austrian authorities now had some freedom to do as they wished. The Turks had been driven back, and in the rest of Europe, Protestant states were in retreat. This breathing space allowed the Hapsburgs to renew their efforts in Moravia. At this point the Hutterites began settlements further to the East, in Slovakia, but conditions there soon became difficult as well. During these years the Hutterites were literally without homes. They dug elaborate caves and tunnels in remote parts of the country, and somehow subsisted there.

A renewed threat from the Turks and Protestants around 1551 meant trouble for the Hapsburgs, but renewed space and toleration for the Anabaptist refugees. In 1564 the dreaded Ferdinand of Austria died. Under his successor, Maximillian II (1564-1576) religious refugees were allowed to live in peace in Moravia. The Hutterites remember the period from 1565 to 1578 as their "golden age." We know that Swiss Brethren also enjoyed prosperity and freedom in Moravia during this period, because of some of the correspondence that has survived. Leonard Gross estimates that in the 1570s there were probably around twenty Swiss Brethren congregations in Moravia, with an unknown number of members. This compares to more than seventy Hutterite communities with an estimated membership of around 20,000. Followers of Pilgram Marpeck, never numerous, faded away as the sixteenth century progressed. The last document pointing to a Pilgramite presence in Moravia dates from 1571.

In 1620 the Moravian territories fell decisively under Hapsburg control. By 1622 it was impossible for Hutterites or other Anabaptists to

Golden Age

continue in Moravia. All Hapsburg territories were aggressively re-Catholicized. Hutterites continued a precarious existence by migrating progressively further East, into Slovakia and beyond. All trace of Swiss Brethren and Pilgramites is lost in seventeenth century Moravia.

Switzerland

Swiss Anabaptists fled in great numbers to Moravia throughout the sixteenth century, but the small numbers who remained in Switzerland showed amazing determination in the face of implacable hostility by the Swiss authorities. There were Anabaptist communities living underground in the cantons of Zurich, Appenzell, Bern, and Basel. They managed to survive to the present only in isolated regions in the canton of Bern.

The Swiss authorities utilized every sort of pressure imaginable to produce religious conformity. Property confiscations were common, as was the expedient of declaring the children of Anabaptists illegitimate and therefore not eligible to inherit property. Parish records, begun in 1525, provided legal documentation of marriages and baptisms in the state church. Swiss Anabaptists, of course, were not included in these records.

The last Anabaptist to be executed in Bern was Hans Haslibacher in 1571; the last to be executed in Zurich was Hans Landis in 1614. But fines, lengthy imprisonment, banishment, and other forms of legal harassment continued. As late as 1657 there were a reported 170 Swiss Anabaptists in prison in Zurich, living on a meagre diet. As the Moravian refuge closed down, Swiss Anabaptists migrated to Alsace and the Palatinate. By 1700, their numbers in Switzerland were few indeed.

Martyrs

The Netherlands

The political situation in the Netherlands was dominated by a growing resistance to Hapsburg rule. In the sixteenth century the Netherlands was ruled by Charles V, and then by his son Phillip II, king of Spain. Charles and Phillip were equally intent on stamping out heresy in their territories, and to the extent that they could, they applied the methods of inquisition in the Netherlands as had also been the case in the Austrian territories controlled by Charles' brother Ferdinand.

Anabaptist martyrs were most numerous in the Netherlands, where perhaps as many of 1500 Anabaptists lost their lives in the most horrifying ways imaginable. Persecution was lightest in Friesland and other northern provinces; it became most intense in the southern province of Flanders (present day Belgium). The last Anabaptist martyr in the north was put to death at Leeuwarden in 1574; in the south Anna Uttenhove was the last Anabaptist martyr, buried alive near Brussels in 1597.

William of Orange

Successive military victories by William of Orange wrested the northern provinces of the Netherlands from Hapsburg control. William granted religious toleration (with some limitations) in 1578. The southern provinces (now Belgium) were won decisively by the Hapsburgs in 1585, leading to the virtual extinction of Anabaptism (and Protestantism) in Flanders. Flemish Anabaptists fled north, and subsequently many Mennonites migrated east along the Baltic coast, settling as far east as the city of Danzig and the Vistula delta in the later sixteenth century.

Conclusion

Political realities shaped Anabaptist communities in different ways. In the rare situations of toleration, closely-knit communities, with strongly enforced boundaries, seemed to flourish. Certainly the Hutterites did in the last half of the sixteenth century in Moravia. In situations of intense persecution, the more brittle communities were less able to survive. In these situations, some accomodations were called for. The Swiss Brethren in Switzerland survived by accepting degrees of dissimulation and conformity, such as allowing their children to be baptized in the state church, often by an intermediary. But perhaps the most serious external threat was encountered by the Dutch Mennonites, namely the threat extended by assimilation and acceptance into society at large, thanks to religious toleration. It was the threat posed by acceptance that so concerned Thieleman van Braght.

The Anabaptist Tradition of Doctrine and Practice

The previous major section of our study traced the process of internal development of the Anabaptist groups, up to ca. 1560. At the most general level, we see the resolution of two major issues that had been contested early, namely apocalyptic expectation, and spiritualism. Furthermore, a series of practical, ethical matters had also been resolved, most notably the questions of the sword and the oath.

By the last quarter of the sixteenth century, all surviving Anabaptist *Apocalypticism* groups had abandoned the expectation that the return of Christ could be predicted with accuracy by combining contemporary prophecies with an an inspired interpretation of prophetic Scripture. Apocalyptic expectation did not disappear altogether. We still read about "these dangerous Last Days" in Anabaptist testimonies, but the apocalypticism of the later Anabaptists was a chastened one, still carrying the scars of Münster. Münster closed the door on apocalyptic Anabaptism.

Likewise, the spiritualist substratum that had undergirded Anabaptist *Spiritualism* doctrine and practice from the start, came to be muted and subdued in the subsequent decades. As we have seen above, an appeal to the direct activity of the Holy Spirit was essential to the emergence of Anabaptism. Under the pressure of persecution, a spiritualist interpretation of Anabaptism offered the attractive option of invisibility. True religious practice could be considered something essentially spiritual, of the heart, and not something visibly illegal.

The anti-Nicodemite reaction of the surviving Anabaptist groups meant *Anti Nicodemite* that the visible practices of water baptism and a Lord's Supper were retained as necessary to salvation. It also meant that these practices were deemed important enough to die for. In contrast to those who were prepared to dissimulate, the surviving Anabaptist groups developed a growing martyr tradition that was remembered in songs, writings, and printed works. It was to this tradition that van Braght appealed.

Later Anabaptist Doctrinal Emphases

The Work of the Holy Spirit.

Early Anabaptism was, as we have seen, a very charismatic movement, with some parts of the movement (especially South German Anabaptism) outlining in detail the process of individual yielding to the Spirit. Other parts of the movement expected the Spirit to reveal God's will in the form of prophetic dreams and visions.

The later Anabaptist traditions continued to insist upon the inner work of the Spirit which produces faith, but in contrast to the early movement, the emphasis fell more on the ethical and communal results of the Spirit's work. Scriptural measures tested the genuineness of the inner work of the Spirit. Those Scriptural measures were defined by elders within communities, and enforced by the ban. In short, we may say that in the Swiss Brethren, Hutterite, and Mennonite traditions, the church came to define and set the limits of the Spirit's work.

Spirit and Letter

The Anabaptist understanding of how God's will is revealed to humanity also underwent significant changes. Of the three interpretive tendencies outlined earlier, only one survived in the ongoing tradition, namely the emphasis on the letter of Scripture, read Christocentrically, with an emphasis on New Testament.

The spiritualist reading of Scripture continued to pose challenges to the Anabaptist movement long after the prophetic/apocalyptic tendency had been discredited, but in the end both of those tendencies were excluded from the Swiss, Hutterite, and Mennonite traditions of biblical interpretation. From the point of view of scriptural interpretation, the later Anabaptist traditions reached a consensus that had been lacking in the origins.

Doctrine of Salvation (Soteriology)

The characteristic Anabaptist insistence that salvation is granted to those whose inner change (faith, regeneration) is manifest in outward behaviour (a new life of discipleship) remained unchanged throughout the sixteenth century. But, as has been sufficiently noted in the preceding chapters, as time went on the emphasis came to fall increasingly on the outward signs of regeneration (and legislation concerning outward behaviour), rather than the process of regeneration as such.

The historical record suggests that the most significant change in the Anabaptist understanding of salvation was not in the *principle* of an inner/outer correspondence (which remained constant), but rather in the various outward signs that the different groups came to hold as *necessary* evidences of inward regeneration, and upon which salvation rested.

The Human Person (Anthropology)

The later Anabaptists continued to defend a doctrine of free will: once they had been empowered by the Holy Spirit, human beings could choose to accept or reject God's regenerating grace. In their understanding of salvation the later Anabaptists continued to agree with the early Anabaptists, and to disagree with the Protestant emphasis on predestination and forensic justification by faith alone. To be saved meant that one had done one's small human part, and had persevered to the end.

Gelassenheit

The call for *Gelassenheit* did not disappear in the later Anabaptist traditions, but the understanding of *Gelassenheit* did change. The understanding of "yielding to God's will" in the early movement was directed primarily within, to the inner struggle of faith that human beings undergo when faced by the call to die to self and rise in Christ. This emphasis on inner, spiritual struggle took on increasingly public and visible dimensions, thanks to widespread persecution.

For the later Anabaptists, *Gelassenheit* meant accepting what God had decreed should happen in the world. Rather than continuing to mean simply struggling with private and personal faith issues, *Gelassenheit* came to mean something akin to what we might call "accepting Providence." Many later testimonies of the martyrs speak about yielding to God's will in accepting the world's persecution.

Eschatology

By the end of the sixteenth century the enthusiastic apocalypticism of the early Anabaptists had been muted. The later Anabaptist literature looks forward not so much to the End Times as it does to the resurrection. Walter Klaassen has noted that in the End Times excitement of the early sixteenth century, rigorous Anabaptist discipline is best understood as a "short-range holding action." The emphasis fell on purity in view of the imminent return of the Head. "That would mean," he concludes, "that the concentration on the forms of congregational life and holiness never did, in their minds, constitute an alternative ecclesiology for the future, but that it became such when the apocalyptic expectations were not fulfilled." (Klaassen, 1992, 117-18). This observation is important given the increasing importance of the "pure church" in defining the later traditions.

The Later Anabaptist Doctrine of the Church (Ecclesiology)

The later Anabaptist doctrine of the church, when contrasted with that of the early core, is notable primarily for the increasingly specific answers that were given to the question "What are the marks of the true church?" Thus the proper manner of interpreting Scripture, the proper stance regarding the sword and the oath, the proper role of women in the community, the proper form of marriage, correct economic relationships, and the biblical form of binding and loosing all came to be rigorously defined in the later Anabaptist communities. As we have seen in sufficient detail in the foregoing chapters, on some of these issues a consensus was reached. On other issues, differences among the various Anabaptists resulted in permanent schism.

Baptism

Two factors may be noted concerning baptism in the later Anabaptist groups. First, the apocalyptic tone given to baptism by Hans Hut, and later by Melchior Hoffman and Bernhard Rothmann, faded in importance as the expectation for the imminent arrival of the End Times also faded. Although the peculiar form of baptism on the forehead seems to have persisted among some of the Dutch Anabaptists (Dirk Philips appears to have baptized in this way), the enthusiastic expectation had faded that the 144,000 elect, so marked, would very soon reign with Christ. In the second place, baptism was the rite in which the later Anabaptists continued to recognize the interior work of the Holy Spirit. There is little apparent movement from early Anabaptism to the later traditions in the matter of baptism, except for the fading of the strong apocalyptic overtones seen in certain parts of the early Anabaptist movement.

The Ban

The emphasis on community discipline also continued throughout the period of Anabaptist development. Changes concerning the ban had to do primarily with the increasing willingness to utilize excommunication in order to keep the communities pure. As more specific external measures of faithfulness were adopted by Anabaptist groups, by so much more was the ban used. The milder possibilities suggested by Hans Denck, Pilgram Marpeck, and the spiritualist Anabaptists were not heeded in the later movement, and faded from view.

The Supper

As John Rempel has demonstrated, some interesting alternative theologies of the Supper were proposed in the developmental period of Anabaptism. The understanding of the Lord's Supper in the Swiss, Hutterite, and Mennonite traditions, however, continued to reflect the broad, anti-sacramental view visible in the early movement. The Supper continued to be seen as a memorial celebration of Christ's sacrifice, to be celebrated only by baptized members in good standing.

Mutual Aid

The early Anabaptist insistence on mutual aid in the Body of Christ remained visible as a general principle in the later traditions. The one noteworthy development concerning mutual aid was the divisiveness caused by the question of whether a full and legislated community of goods was necessary, or not. This matter, more than any other, came to divide the Hutterites from the Swiss Brethren and the Mennonites. Nevertheless, the tradition of economic sharing continued to be strongly held, even when other aspects of the Anabaptist heritage had dropped away.

Sword and Oath

Although there had been no consensus on matters of the sword and the oath among the early Anabaptists, consensus on these issues did emerge over time among the surviving Anabaptist groups.

As we have noted above, the option of a state-Anabaptism, as put forward by Balthasar Hubmaier, did not outlive the 1520s. After the von Liechtensteins, there were no rulers anywhere in Europe who were willing to consider Anabaptism as the religion of their state. Hubmaier's argument that it is legitimate for Anabaptist citizens to take the sword when ordered to do so by rulers, disappeared with Hubmaier and the collapse of Nicholsburg as an Anabaptist state.

With the collapse of Münster came also the collapse of the argument that the saints of the last days were to take the sword in a crusade against the impious. With Obbe, Joris, and Menno leading the way, a consensus emerged in the North that regenerated Christians would follow after Christ into suffering. The apocalyptic Christ of vengeance faded from view, replaced by Jesus, the man of sorrows, who marked out the way of the cross for the elect.

When this shift was completed in the North, the Melchiorites joined the Swiss Brethren and Hutterites in espousing a doctrine of "living without weapons" (*Wehrlosigkeit*). Likewise, the Mennonites came to agree that Christ had commanded that oaths not be sworn, following Christ's command in Matthew 5. Anabaptist confessions of faith from the last quarter of the sixteenth century, from all regions, always include refusal to take the sword, and refusal to swear oaths, as necessary marks of regenerated Christians.

Foot Washing

The later Dutch Mennonite tradition incorporated the ordinance of foot washing in addition to baptism and the Lord's Supper. Foot washing, according to the Dordrecht Confession of 1632, was instituted because of Jesus' example; it was to be performed "as a sign of true humiliation; but yet more particularly as a sign to remind us of the true washing–the washing and purification of the soul in the blood of Christ." (Loewen, 1985, 67). With the later influence of the Dutch confessions on the Swiss, foot washing entered that tradition as well. Foot washing is still celebrated among the more conservative groups descended in the Swiss Brethren line.

Marriage and the Role of Women

While early Anabaptist practice concerning separation and marriage was a bit chaotic, the later Anabaptist groups reached a consensus that true believers would marry only within their Anabaptist groups. Marriage was one more case where outer behaviour needed to reflect inner regeneration. In the early days of the movement, "mixed" marriages led to crises of conscience and separations. The later Anabaptists sought to avoid the problem by avoiding mixed marriages. The church community and its elders functioned as the custodians of proper marriage for the later Anabaptists. The marriage issues that emerged later had to do with whether banned marriage partners needed to be shunned as well.

As spiritualism faded, charismatic and prophetic openings for Anabaptist women narrowed and virtually disappeared. Corresponding developments in the larger movement, which shifted from spirit to letter, and from individual to community, likewise tended to narrow the options for Anabaptist women. Still, the martyrdom of hundreds of Anabaptist women from the later period testify to the continued strength of their faith commitment and choice as individuals.

Conclusion

Revisiting the core Anabaptist teachings in the last quarter of the sixteenth century clarifies elements of continuity as well as elements of change in the Anabaptist story. The core doctrines and practices, present from the beginning, continued to define the movement throughout. All the same, the Anabaptism of the 1520s could have developed in a number of different ways. It was not a foregone conclusion that the Anabaptism of the 1580s would look the way it did.

One way of thinking about the internal development of Anabaptism over the course of 75 years is to think in terms of a series of fundamental internal polarities and tensions, present from the beginnings:

–Inner and Outer

–Spirit and Letter

–Individual and Community

–Church and World

–Gospel and Law

As these polarities worked themselves out in the historical movement, Anabaptism asumed clearer definition and firmer boundaries.

In short, the separatist and more tightly structured communities of Anabaptists found at the end of the sixteenth century came into existence as the result of an historical process that interpreted the foundational polarities and resolved theological tensions in particular ways. External political pressures played their part in drawing forth non-charismatic, literal, separatist conclusions. At the end of the day, these interpretations of the Anabaptist core came to define the tradition that would live on. But there was no historical *inevitability* to the end result. The Anabaptist story includes the disappointed, the disillusioned, and the unsuccessful, as well as those who succeeded in defining the on-going tradition.

The changes and developments noted above gave a strongly separatist shape to the surviving Anabaptist traditions, resulting in disciplined and regulated bodies of believers. The internal strength of these tightly structured communities was demonstrated throughout the sixteenth century and beyond, as they endured exile, persecution, and martyrdom. There is no better source than the *Martyrs Mirror* to shed light on this aspect of the surviving tradition.

The later Anabaptist groups were supported by their separatist ecclesiology, living as they were in conditions of exile in a world almost inevitably hostile to them, although in varying degrees. The evangelizing fervour of early Anabaptism did not survive under these later conditions. The price to be paid for survival in a hostile world was that Anabaptists needed to agree to be "the quiet in the land." With that proviso, they managed to find political authorities here and there who would tolerate their presence and exploit their labour.

The notable exception to this rule occurred among the Dutch Mennonites who remained in the Netherlands. Dutch Anabaptism had always been strongly urban, although represented in the countryside too. It remained in touch with the economic currents of the day. By the mid-seventeenth century, Dutch Mennonites were experiencing social and political acceptance. They came to enjoy a golden age of prosperity that mirrored the emergence of the Dutch as a world economic power. With increased wealth, however, came also a growing tradition of generosity. Dutch Mennonite aid was extended liberally not only to needy Mennonites, Swiss Brethren, Amish, and Hutterites, but also to the needy at large.

The printing of the *Martyrs Mirror* embodied some of the contradictions of inheriting a tradition for which suffering had become a central virtue. The *Martyrs Mirror*, with all good intentions, exhorted Dutch Mennonites to emulate the martyrs of old. But it was, in fact, a huge and costly book, expensively bound and, by its second edition, illustrated by the sophisticated engravings of the well-known artist Jan Luiken. As Brad Gregory has noted, it was a book that could have been conceived, produced, and bought only by a people who were no longer being persecuted and martyred. (Gregory, 1996).

The story of the development of the Dutch tradition in a more spiritualist, pietist, and eventually liberal direction cannot be told here. Suffice it to say that after acrimonious church splits and eventual reconciliation (in 1811), the Mennonites who remained in the Netherlands adopted not the name of the rigorous disciplinarian, Menno Simons, but the name of the more liberal Waterlanders: the "baptism minded" (*Doopsgezinden*).

In a pattern that would repeat itself among Swiss and Mennonites elsewhere, at different times and places, toleration and prosperity in the Netherlands wore down the walls of separation that divided Anabaptists and their descendants from the rest of "unredeemed humanity." The surviving Hutterite communities and the Old Order Amish and Mennonites, on the other hand, have continued to this day attempting to live in communal islands of faith, in the world, but not of it.

Chapter 20

Epilogue

The Continuing Conversation

What kind of a movement was Anabaptism? Was it a supremely Bad Thing, which thankfully was supressed by political authorities in the sixteenth century? Was it a surpassingly Good Thing, the fount of true Christian discipleship, the proper and courageous Reformation, and fore-runner of democratic freedoms?

Readers know by now that in this author's understanding of the story, Anabaptism cannot rightly be described as either one or the other. Anabaptism was a sixteenth century church reform movement that gave voice primarily to the piety and reforming aspirations of common people. It reflected all of the chaotic genius of popular movements, with its generous mix of visionaries, seekers, saints, sinners, and the deluded.

Anabaptist testimonies and writings often spoke about the need to endure the "refiner's fire." They were describing their own historical experience. As the Anabaptist movement progressed, the tragi-comic elements (such as an Anabaptist "king of the universe") faded away. The story becomes one of heart-wrenching hope in the midst of a profound and almost universal cruelty. There really was a "world" out there, over against the church. And this "world" seemed intent upon physically obliterating the Anabaptists from the face of the earth. The recovery of Anabaptist court testimonies has allowed us to reclaim the stories of the everyday women and men whose conviction and persistence passed on an Anabaptist church tradition to this present century.

Refining Fire

Is there anything to be learned from an historical tale such as this one? Although it is not currently in fashion to say so, this author believes that there is. Granting the potential dangers of addressing contemporary issues "historically," still it is important for the faith children of the Anabaptists to reflect on how current issues in the Believers' Churches have been shaped by the inherited theological tradition. With such an examination comes the possibility of a conscious acceptance of the presuppositions of the inherited tradition, or of re-evaluation and conscious change.

The intent of this chapter is to encourage reflection and conversation. It does not pretend to draw normative conclusions about the proper content of an Anabaptist/Believers' Church theology and ecclesiology. Rather, it seems a fair question to ask what might have been lost as well as gained in the sixteenth century process of defining the borders of the Believers' Church tradition.

The Holy Spirit

It is not an overstatement to say that Anabaptism came into existence because of fundamental spiritualist premises. The emergence of Anabaptism as a church renewal movement would not have taken place apart from the spiritual rationale and impulse that underlay its more visible features.

But it is no mystery why the spiritualist side of Anabaptism fell out of favour. The spectacular failures of specific prophecies and apocalyptic projects certainly led to sober second thoughts. And, the more individualistic and spiritualistically oriented Anabaptists lost the battle to convince others to make their Anabaptism a predominantly interior one, and withdrew (or were expelled) from the movement.

As the sixteenth century progressed, letter took priority over spirit; conformity to outer ecclesial rules of behaviour took priority over experiences of inner regeneration; visible lines of demarcation separating church from world were defined with increasing precision.

A serious question confronting Believers' Churches today would seem to be: Can there be a genuine "Believers' Church" in the absence of a strong and vital appeal to the activity of the Holy Spirit?

Scripture: Spirit and Letter

There are some obvious negative lessons to be learned from the Anabaptist experience, as has been amply pointed out by church historians since the sixteenth century. One need only recall some of the concrete historical results of prophetic Anabaptism to see how an expectation of immediate visions, dreams, and revelations can lead to self deception and disaster. There is a "spiritual" manner of reading and interpreting the "hidden secrets of Scripture" that remains a live temptation in every age, in spite of the fact that the misbegotten fruits of such interpretations litter every generation of our church's history.

The corrective that was passed on in the Anabaptist tradition was to emphasize the letter of Scripture, read with Christ at the centre, as we see in the writings of the Swiss, the Hutterites, and Menno Simons. In the context of the events that had overtaken the Low Countries, Menno's response may seem self evident. Certainly to those who carry the name Mennonite, Menno's appeal to a New Testament biblicism does seem self evidently correct.

Menno's insistence that Christ must be placed at the centre of Scripture and the Christian life remains a valid and helpful heuristic principle, and even more so when contrasted to the revelatory claims of his prophetic contemporaries. Menno had a point: the witness of canonical Scripture, read with the life and words of the incarnate Christ at the centre, is the bedrock of divine revelation for Christians. David Joris' visions and "revelations" did, in an important sense, usurp the place of Scripture; and in the end, Joris turned out not to be the "third David" after all.

Even if we agree that Scripture with Christ at the centre must be the revelatory measure for Christians, important questions remain: How is the

Interpretation

New Testament witness to Christ to be interpreted? In what way does the New Testament witness to Christ provide a rule of life for believers? What might the freedom of the Gospel signify? What specific Christology underlies the appeal to Christ?

These questions take on more urgency if we can agree that not all that was planted along Menno's path can be said to have borne good fruit. Legalism sometimes became the response to the danger of antinomianism; obsessive purity the answer to the danger of libertinism. The pendulum swung to the opposite side of its arc, and brought with it not only solutions, but also a fresh set of problems. The Swiss, the Hutterites, and Menno tended to make a new law of the Gospel, making of Christ a new law giver, and making of the church (more specifically, the church elders) the enforcers of the divine law. This legalistic, Christocentric reading of Scripture and definition of community boundaries became the norm for all surviving Anabaptist groups, whose descendants (not coincidentally) have had a long history of schism and division.

There were other approaches to the spirit/letter issue in the sixteenth century that we would do well to recall. Hans Denck's attempts to hold together spirit and letter provided an alternative Anabaptist Christocentric example, as did Pilgram Marpeck's efforts. In both of their cases, it was the love of Christ in the hearts of believers (always measured against the scriptural witness to Christ) that provided the crucial measure for the Chris-

Love of Christ

tian. A Christocentric reading of Scripture for Denck and Marpeck meant that the law of love must take precedence over the legalistic application of less universal commands—even those of the New Testament. We may think here too of Marpeck's Christological formulations, forged in the midst of his debates with the spiritualists.

Looked at historically, the appeal to the highest commandment of love, in dialogue with the witness of Scripture, appears to be the more profound answer. Arguing, as did Menno, the Swiss, and the Hutterites, that the spirit will *necessarily* be linked to particular understandings of literal scriptural commands, has more than once proved to be misguided. We may think of shunning as one such example, or the North American Mennonite issue of a particular head covering for women as another. From our vantage point at the end of the twentieth century, it appears that the love of Christ as revealed in His words and His life provides a heuristic principle that survives the interpretive predilections of any age–although the principle of itself does not prescribe behaviour in the appealing, normative fashion that humanity on the whole seems to desire.

The problem with an appeal to the love of Christ as an heuristic principle would seem to be primarily sociological: it weakens visible, enforceable community boundaries. The strong assertion of biblical laws of conduct, to the contrary, makes clear who is in and who is out. Perhaps for this reason neither Denck nor Marpeck founded groups that survived. Nevertheless, historical survival is a dubious measure of truth. Believers' Churches today must face the sixteenth century reformational question: To what extent must traditions be confronted anew by the Spirit and the Word?

Communal Boundaries

Regarding the question of the spirit and the letter, it must be said that in the historical experiences of the Anabaptist movement, positions at either end of the continuum revealed their limitations and dangers. In view of this, the obvious answer is to suggest a healthy *via media*–but this would be to give far too glib a reply to what is in fact a very difficult question.

Still, one lesson of history is hard to miss in all of this: Christians need to exercise a profound dose of humility concerning what they claim to know, biblically and spiritually. This humility needs to be exercised especially in our relations with those who disagree with us. Sixteenth century Christians were inclined to measure Christian truth by the intensity of assurance it could generate. In retrospect, we may say that Christian truth is proven rather by the intensity of love that it generates. In this sense Hans Denck ultimately may have more to teach us than does Michael Sattler.

A particular *tradition* of biblical interpretation has been part of the Believers' Church inheritance. To be part of the Believers' Church tradition has meant to have received a well established "canon within the canon" that already provides the answers to what a "pure and simple" reading of Scripture should conclude. These interpretations have been passed on as traditional (self-evidently true) teachings.

Part of the conscious reappropriation of the Believers' Church tradition must include a fresh reading of Scripture that is prepared to test the received tradition not only against Scripture, but also against other theological traditions. It will no longer do to operate under the fiction that the Believers' Church tradition is "purely biblical" whereas other readings of Scripture are tainted with "human tradition." The Believers' Church reading of Scripture is also a human tradition. Those who doubt that this is so are invited to consult the emerging volumes of the "Believers' Church Bible Commentary" series (Herald Press).

The question may well be: How far are Believers' Churches today willing to trust the Spirit of God in the interpretation of Scripture? The tendency to formalism and legalism, and the largely unexamined acceptance of a received tradition of biblical interpretation, all beg for a breath of the Spirit. It may well be that the broadest Anabaptist scriptural principle, namely that spirit and letter must be held together in order to be revelatory, could prove helpful in our own time. The further recognition that all readings of Scripture are shaped by our humanity should open the doors even further to ecumenical dialogue with other Christian traditions.

Priesthood of all Believers

The question of interpretive authority was a critical one in the Anabaptist movement, as we have seen. It was made all the more critical because the

Protestant Reformation had removed the doctrine of interpretive authority through apostolic succession (from Christ through Peter to the Bishops of Rome). In its place, the Reformers had placed Scripture–but who was then vested with the authority to *interpret* Scripture?

One answer of the mainline Reformers–that this authority rested only with those who had been called and then sent to preach by a legitimate political authority–was rejected by the Anabaptists, and continues to be rejected by Believers' Churches today. Historical events since the sixteenth century, particularly the genocidal insanities sponsored by "legitimate political authorities" in the twentieth century, have demonstrated the worth of the Anabaptist insight: the Gospel cannot be handed over to the "world" to use as it pleases. But who, then, will decide when an interpreter of Scripture is genuine?

When pressed, the early Anabaptists said that they had been called by *God* to preach the Gospel. It is no surprise, then, that in all varieties of early Anabaptism, we return in the end to the working of the Spirit of God as the fundamental basis for teaching and interpretive authority. As William Keeney has noted, this was the unrecognized "subjective factor" that caused so many problems for sixteenth century biblicists. (1)

It was the "convincing power of the Holy Spirit in the heart of the believer" that led to something approximating the priesthood of all believers in early Anabaptism, but this "spiritual democracy" was not destined to last. With the growing emergence of a tradition of textual interpretation came also a different kind of leadership. Congregations began to look to bishops and elders–a movement in Anabaptism that parallels almost exactly developments in the first century of Christianity.

> *(1) "... [since] ultimately the appeal could not be to the letter alone but to the convincing power of the Holy Spirit in the heart of the believer, no objective test could finally resolve the differences. Each also had an unswerving belief that the correct understanding had been granted by the Holy Spirit." (Keeney, 1968, 42-43).*

Although anticlericalism was crucial in Anabaptist origins, by the end of the sixteenth century the settled Anabaptist groups had drawn clear

Clergy

lines of distinction between their own clergy and laity. Bishops or elders were those empowered to baptize, to preside over the Lord's Supper, to perform marriages, to make definitive interpretations of Scripture and, in more than one instance, bishops and ministers decided disciplinary matters and saw to the ordination of other pastors and elders.

The qualifiers entered first at Schleitheim, then by the Hutterites, and finally by Menno Simons were decisive: the only true pastors would be those who were commissioned or chosen by the elders and/or the congregation. This insistence in fact rendered the priesthood of all believers functionally obsolete, even if in comparison to mainline Protestant churches, the surviving Anabaptist groups allowed for a much higher participation of the laity in church life.

Leadership

Believers' Churches today routinely train professional pastors (clergy, in other words) in seminaries, recognizing that theological and pastoral education is helpful in the task of pastoral ministry. At the same time, at a rhetorical level at least, many Believers' Churches extol the virtues of an idealized Anabaptist priesthood of all believers–all members are pastors, it is said, and minister in a variety of ways.

But in practice, most Believers' Church members today do not function as "priests" who interpret Scripture within the congregation or who carry out other traditionally pastoral tasks. In most cases, Believers' Church congregations become the employer of a professional Believers' Church minister.

The sixteenth century situation suggests that pastoral questions are settled in tandem with the settling of broader ecclesiological questions. If the church is understood as the faithful remnant expecting Jesus' return momentarily, the emergency election of leaders may well suffice (Schleitheim). If the church is understood to be a longsuffering minority in a persecuting world, pastors are needed who will instruct, strengthen and maintain community boundaries, and nurture succeeding generations (Menno). What is the pattern of leadership needed when a Believers' Church is accepted as part of the social/cultural landscape in a pluralistic, secular, and democratic society? Or conversely, what does the current pattern of pastoral leadership say about the state of Believers' Church ecclesiology?

Understanding of Salvation (Soteriology)

A sure way of inviting open dispute is to attempt to identify what "lay at the heart" of Anabaptism: Was it discipleship, a doctrine of the church, existential theology? I will grant, even before I am challenged, that my own reading is partial, and may well be wrong, but in my view the heart and soul of the Anabaptist movement is found in its understanding of salvation, its *soteriology*. Central to that soteriology was the integral linking of the inner and outer lives of believers which the Anabaptists were sure was true to the witness of Scripture. Salvation, said the Anabaptists, is by grace through faith; but saving faith must be expressed in works of love, or it is no faith at all. Human beings must yield to the inner working of the living Spirit of God (*Gelassenheit*), they must assent to this grace (exercise human free will) and, thanks to the regeneration by the Holy Spirit, they will live lives of visible obedience and discipleship. The church is thus the Body of Christ, visibly composed of these saints of the Lord.

Regeneration

Beginning at the personal level of individual regeneration, we may ask whether Anabaptist optimism in this regard was in fact justified. Historically considered, the answer seems to be "no," in spite of some astounding examples to the contrary. On the whole, Anabaptist optimism concerning the extent and throroughness of regeneration was not borne out in church practice over the long run.

This is not to say that there were not faithful disciples in the tradition, or that the ideals of regeneration and discipleship should be abandoned, but only to say that human sin was not as *easily* overcome as most Anabaptists had anticipated. A negative way of saying this would be: the Anabaptist "regenerationist" tradition did not take sin seriously enough. Optimism concerning regeneration became part of the received tradition. The Melchiorite stream, resting as it did on a docetic Christology, went even further along this road than did the Swiss and Hutterite traditions, but they did not lag far behind.

Ban

Some modern appropriations of the "Anabaptist Vision" have argued that the Anabaptists were not "perfectionists," for if they had been, they would not have instituted the ban and used it. This caveat misses an important point. The Anabaptist practice of the ban, far from negating a perfectionist attitude towards sin and the law, is the primary example of that attitude, and the instrument used to maintain a theoretical ideal of sinless perfection in the Body of Christ. This perfectionism was not incidental to the received tradition, but rather was central to it. The personal and ecclesiological implications for Believers' Churches have been profound.

One of the drawbacks of the perfectionist tendency has been the lack of an adequate means for dealing with personal failure and sin in Believers' Churches. As long as a perfectionist regenerational principle was accepted as the sum and substance of the Christian life, one had either visibly failed at discipleship or was visibly (or at least adequately) succeeding. The grey areas in between–where, quite frankly, the majority of Christians reside–were theologically and pastorally inaccessible. Yet it is precisely in the grey areas of life that Christians need mentoring, admonition, and help in order to grow and progress in the spiritual life. The "successful" disciple does not need the help; the disciple who has failed does not get attention until it is obviously too late.

The ban in the later Anabaptist tradition was an ecclesiological instrument attuned to spiritual failure, not spiritual growth. In such a setting the danger of hypocrisy–long a reproach on the side of mainline Protestants–

could not be avoided completely, especially in close knit communities, where appearances could be as important as realities.

Part of the continuing theological conversation for Believers' Churches is to return again to the question of sin, regeneration, discipleship, admonition, forgiveness, and growth. The pastoral issues related to sin, regeneration, and admonition need to be thought through with some care, particularly in light of the importance of discipleship in the tradition.

It was Pilgram Marpeck who insisted on the importance of the distinction between law and Gospel as one that provided a crucial counter balance for those who tended to emphasize literal obedience to the commands of Scripture. The Gospel of Jesus Christ, Marpeck maintained, is a setting free from the law, which we were not able to keep perfectly in any case. Marpeck emphasized, from a thoroughly Anabaptist perspective, human dependence on God's love and grace; recognition of our dependence on grace, he maintained, acts as a hedge against human presumption.

Law and Gospel

A further related point made by Marpeck is well worth repeating: the law is not now, nor has it ever been, *capable* of changing the heart. Only God and God's gracious Spirit can do that. Discipleship, then, is not fundamentally an issue of obedience to the law, but rather it depends upon God's grace and regeneration. True discipleship grows from the heart, and not as a result of an external legal code or the threat of punishment.

If regeneration is not perfectly accomplished in this life (as Hubmaier and Marpeck argued), and if the church is not the spotless Body of Christ on earth (as historical evidence suggests), what then becomes of the ban? Either the ban must be abandoned altogether as a misguided attempt at maintaining legalistic perfection, or radically reconceived as an instrument of admonition, growth, and spiritual medicine.

It is this author's conviction that the integration of the inner and outer lives of believers was a spiritual insight of great worth that lay at the heart of the Anabaptist theological tradition. But the external, ethical, and legalistic dimensions of discipleship that came to be stressed in the tradition, coupled with a very optimistic regenerationist conviction, have not worn well.

A possible avenue to explore further in the present day may well be the path indicated by the more mystical and spiritualist Anabaptists, who explored in some depth the process of *Gelassenheit* and growth in the interior, spiritual life. Early Anabaptism suggests that there are inner dimensions of regeneration that must precede and accompany any genuine outward walk of discipleship. These dimensions can and should be cultivated by means of the spiritual disciplines–of which obedience is one.

Perhaps focusing again on the spiritual life as a walk, a progression, a practice in obedience, a pilgrimage of growth–rather than focusing on the perfect obedience to be expected from the baptized–will allow Believers' Churches to develop a more humane and realistic pastoral understanding of the admonition and discipline that can offer positive aid to disciples on their pilgrimage.

The Nature of the Church (Ecclesiology): Sect or Church?

We can see in Michael Sattler and Balthasar Hubmaier two very different Anabaptist visions of how the church is to be structured: either in a separated, sectarian fashion, or along mainstream, church lines.

Sect: God has responded to human sin in such a way that the world is allowed to proceed under the dominion of Satan for the time being, with governments necessarily ruling according to violence and coercion as befits the kingdom of darkness. True believers have nothing to do with the kingdom of darkness.

Church: God has ordered the world in the best way possible, ordaining governments as benevolent servants, the best means available for restraining sin. Christians therefore participate in God's ordering of the world.

The New Testament provides crucial texts in both cases, but it was the sectarian, two kingdoms interpretation that prevailed as the Anabaptist tradition.

Many present-day Believers' Church members in North America seem to have concluded that the Anabaptist understanding of the two kingdoms no longer serves as an adequate framework for church life. Today the Believers' Churches, including the Mennonite denomination, are moving rapidly away from the counter-culturalism of "sects" and much closer to the culture-embracing position of "churches." What this means is that Believers' Churches generally no longer call their members out of "the world" to an exclusive citizenship in Christ's Body, which takes precedence over all else, to the point of death if necessary.

It is my impression that in the Believers' Churches of our day, the line separating the two kingdoms is becoming increasingly invisible and subjective–a dualism experienced privately and personally, rather than a visible, external church/world dualism.

–Salvation is now often described as justification by means of Christ's vicarious atonement, and not necessarily related to a life of discipleship.

–Fraternal admonition is no longer practised, adding to the invisibility of the saving process.

–Economic activities are seen as essentially personal and neutral, not matters which the church at large need consider (except perhaps in extraordinarily embarassing cases, which never seem to include cases of excessive wealth).

–More and more ethical questions are relegated to the personal sphere, such as questions concerning marriage and sexuality.

As the visible division between the two kingdoms is erased it may appear that the very nature of the Believers' Church also is erased. But there are options outside the stark extremes of Hubmaier's culture affirming church and Michael Sattler's sectarianism.

Hans Denck (in his early writings) and Pilgram Marpeck both maintained that the line between the two kingdoms, while real, was not to be marked by law, but rather by Gospel. They insisted that there would be a visible distinction between the two kingdoms of church and world. But at the same time, they insisted that it was Christ's love and mercy that rendered the Kingdom of Christ visible on earth. There is, then, at least this third Anabaptist response to a two kingdoms view, standing between the better-known extremes of church and sect. Can there be a Believers' Church marked by love rather than law? Or is such an appeal simply the "slippery slope" leading to the practical extinction of Believers' Church boundaries?

Love marks the line

The Sword

The Mennonite church of today is known as one of the historic "peace churches" because of a principled refusal to participate in warfare. Early in this century, some Mennonite historians described the historic "Anabaptist/ Mennonite" position as one of "nonresistance." The term drew upon the non-retaliatory command of Matthew 5:39 and a host of sixteenth century Anabaptist examples.

Although reasons can be given for continued usage of the term, it is my view that the term nonresistance is of limited historical and descriptive usefulness, for several reasons.

"Nonresistance" is, first of all, an inaccurate historical description of the full scope of Anabaptist reality in the sixteenth century. It is not true that this was the "Anabaptist" position on the sword. The early Anabaptists were not united in promoting nonresistance.

In the second place, even when we turn to the post-Schleitheim Swiss Brethren and exclude all other Anabaptists, nonresistance still is inadequate to describe their position as a whole. Matthew 5:39 certainly was applied by the Swiss to the "evil" of government and the sword of government. The sense was that governments were to be obeyed, not resisted, insofar as they did not command something contrary to God's Word. Likewise, armed resistance was excluded in all cases–*Wehrlosigkeit* (being weaponless) was the term often used. Nevertheless, this "nonresistance" had very definite limits for the Swiss, precisely when governments (as they consistently did) commanded "evil" things. When governments ordered the Anabaptists to attend state churches, participate in the Lord's Supper in those churches, swear oaths of loyalty, bear the sword in defence of territories, or abjure their belief in believers' baptism, the Anabaptists *resisted*, though not with the sword. Contrary to its passive connotations, nonresistance had definite limits for the Anabaptists.

Weaponless Resistance

Anabaptists refused to participate in a violent reformation of society, which was seen as bound and delivered to Satan. They refused to participate in any governing function. Nevertheless, when the integrity of the Anabaptists' own witness was jeapordized by what they saw as evil, resist they did.

In short, a re-appropriation of the Anabaptist pacifist position which portrays it as an apolitical passivity simply does not fit the historical facts. There is an important sense in which "weaponless resistance" is a descriptive term that fits even the Swiss Brethren and Mennonite reaction to governments much more accurately than does the term "nonresistance." The Anabaptists of the first few generations were anything but passive or free from resistance.

There is a further sense in which the word nonresistance is inadequate to capture the full Anabaptist position. All Anabaptists emphatically did "resist evil" in their own midst, by means of the ban. Nonresistance did not apply when evil needed to be opposed by the "sword of the spirit." The danger represented by the ban, the spiritual sword, was that it could quickly become legalistic and coercive, as un-Christian as physical violence itself.

Pilgram Marpeck's comments concerning the ban provide us with helpful guidance here. As we have seen, he insisted that the crucial principle was loving patience, and it applied equally inside and outside the church. It was not a question of *whether* to resist or not. There simply *is* evil which must be resisted. But it was rather the *manner* in which evil was resisted that made one's faithfulness Christian, or un-Christian.

Pilgram Marpeck's observations extend the question of the sword and the two kingdoms in helpful ways. Marpeck insisted:

–Not the automatic, culture-blessing acceptance of government calls to warfare

–Not the non-engaged passivity implied by "nonresistance"

–Not the focused political action often implied in our day by "nonviolent resistance" (all too often without deep spiritual roots)

–But rather, Christ's patient, loving resistance which recognizes and names evil and attempts to overcome it with good, ever depending on God's grace for the final victory.

This loving resistance, furthermore, focuses not simply or exclusively on the violence and coercion that takes place *outside* the church, but looks with equal urgency to the manner in which all human relationships are carried out, most particularly *within* the church, where the flame of love should burn the brightest. The misuse of power to violate and coerce others is not exclusive to "the world." Violence occurs also in the church. This painful reality reveals (it should come as no surprise) hearts in need of the redeeming and empowering love of God.

Economics

A further dimension that arises from the inner/outer linkage has to do with the economic activity of Christians. We know that we live in a different century when we realize that all the Anabaptists agreed that economic questions were, in the end, spiritual questions.

This observation has a pressing contemporary relevance, need it be said, in a social context where the relationship between one's Christianity and one's level of economic prosperity is increasingly being severed–that is, in a culture that tempts Christians continually to separate the inner life of faith from the outer life of discipleship.

There are no easy answers. Spirituality and economics are bound up in the larger cultural webs in which we all live. The question may be how to maintain the essential Anabaptist insight (rather than their practice). That is, a "life of the spirit" and a life of discipleship in this world can never be separated.

The early Anabaptists (and the mainstream Christian spiritual tradition that preceded them) had it right: The Christian life in this world grows out of, and is an integral expression of, the new life in Christ. Where there is true love of God, there must needs be a radical love of neighbour. What kind of "discipleship" is left when the economic dimensions of the love of neighbour are passed over in polite silence?

Equality

On the topic of equality much can be said that is painful to hear. One way of continuing the conversation begun in the sixteenth century would be to ask again whether we believe that the Holy Spirit calls all of humanity to salvation, and that the response of faith will entail a pilgrimage of discipleship.

If the Holy Spirit does call men and women alike to faith and to lives of costly discipleship, what will be the outer manifestations of this call? At what point in the Christian walk may we suppose that the Holy Spirit begins to recognize gender, begins to restrict the activities of women in the church, and proceeds to grant more and more ecclesial power to men alone? How are we to discern when we have arrived at such a delimiting case? Do males have some special "spiritual" receptivity that makes them uniquely suited to interpreting the purposes of God? If a woman were to think that the Holy Spirit had called her to ministry, is it true that her "call" cannot be considered legitimate until male elders have bestowed their confirmation on the Spirit of God?

Here we have, without a doubt, returned again to questions of the Spirit's role in the interpretation of the letter of Scripture. The role played in Believers' Churches by the literal reading of selected Pauline verses needs no elaboration. Those few words about "women remaining silent" are as threadbare from overuse and misuse as are Paul's words in Romans 13, concerning governments and obedience. Is this what the Holy Spirit had in mind? Is this the Gospel?

As in all cases involving power and the imbalance of power, there is good reason for Believers' Churches to apply the "hermenutics of suspicion" not only to the appropriation of the Gospel by governments, but also to the appropriation of the church by men. All human beings stand equally before God. So said the early Anabaptists, and they were right. As in the political question, so also in the matter of women and men in the church: We would do well to focus on how the Holy Spirit actually calls human beings and works in human history, rather than rehearsing endlessly the few lines of Pauline advice that have so dominated our conversation on these issues. The words "God is no respecter of persons" provide more profound guidance.

Church Ordinances

Sixteenth century developments that led to the establishment of an Anabaptist tradition had implications for the most visible church ordinances, namely baptism, the ban, and the Supper. The progressive weakening of Anabaptist spiritualism in the sixteenth century had implications for the way in which these ordinances functioned and were conceptualized.

Baptism
The solidly biblical rationale for adult baptism was one of the most visible parts of the theological/biblical tradition that was passed on in Believers'

Churches. Biblical references buttressing the practice of believers' baptism were among the first that new converts learned. The standard verses are repeated interminably (to our ears) in thousands of court records. At one level this inherited literalist biblical rationale worked well: there is a biblical order that states, first teach, then baptize. On strictly biblical grounds the Anabaptists had a very strong case indeed for the baptism of adults following confession of faith. But when pressed beyond some literal limits, the rationale begins to weaken.

Would we agree with the later Anabaptist tradition that *salvation* depends upon obedience to the particular, literal "biblical order" concerning baptism? Should we be willing to excommunicate from our churches those who question the *salvific* necessity of following the "proper order"? Should we be willing to suffer martyrdom for the sake of this particular order of "first teach, then baptize"? Do we believe that infants who are baptized with water, but who are then confirmed in their faith as adults (in "mainline" churches) nevertheless are damned because they did not undergo the step of consciously chosen *water* baptism as adults? How far are we willing to push our inherited traditional literal reading of Scripture? Probably not nearly so far as were the later Anabaptists.

We may be able to learn something from Pilgram Marpeck, or even Nicolaas van Blesdijk. They argued that the central point of water baptism following confession of faith was not "obedience to the biblical law" but rather an outward pledge to a community of an inner conversion by the Spirit of God. Without the inner change, the outer was to no avail, be its observance biblical or not, because the water is just water and has no power. When the focus mistakenly falls on the outer obedience to the rite of water baptism, does this not give undeserved salvific power to the water and the rite? Did not the original Anabaptist critique of the Roman Catholic sacrament oppose precisely this point?

Part of the difficulty here was the fact that first generation Anabaptists actively converted from one faith to another. Freely chosen adult baptism sealed that inner conversion. But what would be the pattern in the second generation of Anabaptist believers and beyond? From what, and to what, would the children of Anabaptist parents convert? Although Ulrich Zwingli's argument attempting to link infant baptism to Old Testament circumcision was not convincing biblical exegesis, his point that the children of believers ought to be recognized as a part of the people of God was an argument that proved to have some historical force. With the coming of adult confirmation to mainline churches, the practical distinction between those traditions and the Believers' Church tradition was drastically reduced.

Being of the second generation Anabaptist leadership, and also because he had the freedom to think and write over a longer period of time, Pilgram Marpeck was able to conceive of the church not only in its apocalyptic role as the "pure Bride" awaiting the Groom's coming, but also as a place of growth, where children of Anabaptist parents could be nurtured in the faith, and the weak (that is, *all* believers) could be strengthened.

Already in 1532, Marpeck described a ceremony of infant dedication in which the congregation gives thanks for its children, prays for them, and admonishes the parents "to do whatever is needed to raise the child up to the praise and glory of God, and to commit the child to God until it is clearly seen that God is working in him for faith or unfaith." (Klassen and Klaassen, 1978, 147). The current practice of infant dedication in Believers' Churches has an Anabaptist referent; more importantly, the practice of infant dedication recognizes the different initiatory needs of children who are born and raised in the community of faith.

The other part of the problem of second generation children has been more difficult to address, namely "What will 'conversion' mean to children who have been raised in the faith?" The danger, especially when the outward rite is stressed as a point of salvific obedience, is that the water is received even though a spiritual transformation or inner commitment has not really taken place–again, the very critique the early Anabaptists made of infant baptism. The fundamental rationale underlying believers' baptism certainly is not being addressed when entire Sunday school classes dutifully receive the waters of baptism simultaneously, at an "appropriate" age.

For a time, in the North American Mennonite experience, revival meetings provided a context for public repentance, conversion, and commitment, which could then be followed by baptism into the church. This approach worked for some, but not all. It was an method that claimed its share of psychological victims. How may the practice of baptism on confession of faith be rejuvenated in the Believers' Churches? How might the inner dimensions related to this powerful symbol of dying and rising in Christ be recaptured in churches long accustomed to fairly "automatic" performances of the outward rite?

The Ban

Sufficient attention already has been given to a critique of the kind of "discipline" exercised in the later Anabaptist tradition. Here we wish to make only one point: while the conception and practice of the ban was, on the whole, literalistic and legalistic in the sixteenth century, there are dimensions of the ban that call for thoughtful reconsideration.

The linking of the ban to believers' baptism cemented an important factor of accountability between church members that emphasized the communal nature of the fellowship. The inner spiritual change led not only to individual water baptism, but led necessarily to the community and to a mutual accountability within that community. Can there be "Believers' Churches" in the absence of such accountability? How might this dimension be recovered in a secular and individualistic age such as our own?

There also were confessional, penitential, and absolutionist (forgiveness) dimensions in the early Anabaptist practice of the ban that need to be considered in our own time. There must be positive and helpful ways of confessing human sin and failure, and ways of being forgiven and of accepting forgiveness, within Believers' Churches.

The Supper

In this concluding discussion we have made much of the inner side of the Anabaptist conversations as possible correctives to the strong traditional emphasis on the outer dimensions of the Christian life. Our point has not been to urge a spiritualist or subjective reading of Anabaptism to the detriment of the outer expressions of inner renewal. Our point has been, rather, to suggest that there is wisdom in maintaining a balanced inner/outer integration. Nowhere is that balance, or lack of balance, more evident than in sacramental teaching, especially as it relates to the Lord's Supper.

In the ancient Christian tradition, the Eucharist was a thanksgiving and celebration of the mystery of God's incarnation and redemption in Christ. What was defined precisely as transubstantiation in the late medieval period was earlier simply regarded as a mystery. In an inexplicable way, God became present to humanity again in the celebration of the Supper. In the celebration of the "sacrament of the altar" there was a "communication" between God and humanity in which God's grace was again offered to the communicant.

This is not the place to elaborate necessary historical and theological details. Interested readers are encouraged to consult John D. Rempel's excellent study. Suffice it to say here that Anabaptist sacramental theology was based on a common philosophical critique of the day which denied the possibility that material things could mediate the divine. But the Anabaptists did not completely sever the divine/human link. It was precisely concerning the "Body of Christ" that Anabaptists made the bold claim that the Body of Christ is the visible congregation of saints. As John Rempel notes, the Anabaptists "portrayed Christ as present in the church in his humanity." (Rempel, 1993, 35). This was a radical sacramental and christological claim in a sixteenth century context–and remains so in the twentieth! Underlying the necessity for visible purity in the Body of Christ was a late medieval understanding of what the Body of Christ is: a pure and holy sacrament.

We have suggested above that this expectation for sacramental purity made excessive demands on church members. In the context of the Lord's Supper there is here a serious reversal of traditional eucharistic theology. Rather than sinful humanity coming to the table to *receive* grace and forgiveness, in the Anabaptist tradition believers were to *bring* pure and regenerated selves to the table as an offering. The Supper thus became a celebration of grace already given and accepted, a remembrance of Christ's sacrifice which had offered forgiveness once and for all, a Supper of solidarity between "pure members" of the Body of Christ on earth.

Pilgram Marpeck did not agree with the image of perfectly regenerated believers bringing that perfection together to constitute a pure church. The image he used more frequently was that of the church as a place where the broken could be healed. "We do not ... do wrong," said Marpeck, "if we, who are weak and ill, employ the Great Physician's medicine, and if we extend it to one another, to those who are hungry ..." (Klassen and Klaassen, 1978, 87).

The "Great Physician's medicine" comes to us, said Marpeck, in the forms of outward worship, in ceremonies and ordinances. They were meant to lead us to a deeper and more profound understanding of the love of God and neighbour. They can and ought to be sacraments for us, that is, "visible signs of invisible grace," or physical ways in which we may receive grace. Marpeck appreciated the spiritual power of communal symbols and ceremonies, which he saw as physical means of growth into love and the mature spiritual life.

Marpeck's observations may well be helpful for Believers' Churches today, as they work their way back from radically "non symbolic" forms of worship to ones that are beginning to recognize again the spiritual power of visible ceremonies, symbols and rituals. Marpeck's vision of the church as the place where the Great Physician's medicine is lovingly (and visibly) dispensed still speaks powerfully in our century. His alternative Anabaptist conception of the Christian life as one of growth "through instruction and knowledge of Christ's mind," and of the church as the place where the healing of Christ the Physician is made manifest, is an Anabaptist vision for believers who fall short of perfection, and yet believe that Christ's call to discipleship was meant to be followed.

Conclusion

The concluding comments made above undoubtedly have concentrated too much on a critique of the received Anabaptist theological tradition, particularly focusing on the external aspects of that tradition. Our intent was not to suggest that there was little of worth passed on by that tradition–far from it! It is because they stand on the solid foundation of what was passed on that the Believers' Churches have the luxury of being able to look back over a theological and ecclesial tradition that now spans almost half a millenium, and to reflect upon it.

In reflecting upon the historical development of Anabaptism, one central point spoke repeatedly to this observer: the vitality of early Anabaptism and of the received tradition rested upon an encounter with the living Christ. It was the grafting of lifeless twigs onto the living vine that, in the final analysis, brought into being a "church of believers."

Believers' Churches are now venerable old plants, with deep and strong roots. May the caretakers and labourers in this corner of God's garden have the courage and wisdom to prune with care and patience, all that may hinder a life rooted in the living God; and may they have the foresight and wisdom to cultivate lovingly all that encourages that same life-giving rootedness.

Appendix

Anabaptist Historiography: An Overview

Origin and lineage have always been important in Christian history. Historical descriptions of Anabaptism–and there have been many–have returned again and again to the question of origins. Who started this movement? By answering this question it has been thought that one has described the essential character of the movement. There was no lack of opinion on these matters already in the sixteenth century.

Anabaptism defined in the sixteenth century: Origins and Character

Heinrich Bullinger

Without a doubt the most influential contemporary description of Anabaptism was published in 1561 by Heinrich Bullinger, who was Ulrich Zwingli's successor in Zurich. He said that Anabaptism began in Saxony,

---

(1) Heinrich Bullinger describes Anabaptist beginnings, 1561.

"Around the year of our Lord 1521 and 1522 there emerged some restless spirits in the land just below the Saar river in Saxony (among whom Nicholas Storch was a leader). They had some dreams, and ... God spoke to them from heaven (as they would have it) through visions and revelations, and they took this to be true... From this same school and mob emerged Thomas Müntzer... [who] boasted that God spoke with him... He also had a very low opinion of water baptism: in fact he maintained that infant baptism was not of God, therefore one must baptize with a more correct spiritual baptism.

[Müntzer's influence at Mühlhausen is described, along with his involvement in the Peasants' War, his capture, recantation, and execution in 1525]. Note well, you pious believers: here is the true parentage and the first beginning point of the Rebaptizing sect. And Müntzer, the rebel, is its patriarch or the first of its authors who indeed, before his end, confessed his error and misdeeds. Nevertheless his followers and disciples, the Anabaptists, continued to persist in them."

Heinrich Bullinger, Der Widertöufferen Ursprung... *(Zurich: Froschauer, 1561; photoreprint, Leipzig, 1975), pp. 1-3, passim. Translation by Arnold Snyder.*

---

in Lutheran territory, with the spiritualist and visionary Zwickau Prophets. What they began was continued by Thomas Müntzer, the "devil from Alstedt," who was involved in the Peasants' War of 1525. (1) Bullinger described the Zurich baptizers as former followers of Luther and Zwingli, who became followers of Müntzer, considering him to be a true prophet.

Bullinger's description of Anabaptism provided an origin far away from Zurich, and pointed emphatically to Luther's own backyard. The original Anabaptists, said Bullinger, were Lutherans gone bad. But Bullinger also painted Anabaptism as an essentially heretical, spiritualist, and insurrectionary movement. It was this description of the origin and character of Anabaptism that continued to exert a long influence on historical descriptions, for later historians simply continued to rely on Bullinger's description, century after century. (2)

> *(2) Twentieth century description of Anabaptism, showing signs of Bullinger's influence.*
>
> *"[The Anabaptists] proposed to reach a state of perfection worthy of the early church; the members communicated to each other their visions and prophecies. The spiritual temperature gradually rose, recalling that of certain contemporary sects such as the pentecostists... Here a popular, fervently mystical and anti-social religion was being opposed to that of the reformers. . . . Opposition to the baptism of infants entered rather late into their programme and then doubtless under the influence of Thomas Müntzer."*
>
> *J. Rilliet,* Zwingli, Third Man of the Reformation *(London: Lutterworth Press, 1964), 140.*

Sebastian Franck

Most sixteenth century writers were as hostile to the Anabaptists as was Bullinger. Sebastian Franck was one of the exceptions. As a religious dissenter and a spiritualist, Franck felt a kinship for the marginalized and persecuted Anabaptists. According to his description, the baptizing movement began only in 1526, *after* the end of the Peasants' War. The "origins" of Anabaptism were biblical and in no way insurrectionary. Franck's description was so positive that it was still cited as contemporary evidence in the twentieth century by Mennonite scholars. (3)

(3) Sebastian Franck's description from the Chronica (1531).
"In the year 1526, ...following the Peasants' War, a new sect and special church began based on the letter of Scripture, which some called Re-baptizers and others Baptists. . . . ...they taught nothing but love, faith, and the need of bearing the cross. They showed themselves humble, patient under much suffering... They helped each other faithfully with aid and loans, taught that all things were to be held in common, and called each other brothers. ...the world feared they were plotting rebellion (of which, as I hear, they were in all cases innocent)."
In John Horsch, Mennonites in Europe *(Scottdale, Pa.: Mennonite Publishing House, 1942), 293.*

The "baptizers" describe their own origins and nature

The basic story as told by the sixteenth century baptizers themselves began by describing a fallen, apostate papal church. The marks of this fallen church included the "worship of images," an idolatrous "presence of Christ" in the bread and wine of the Lord's Supper, and of course, the "unbiblical practice" of infant baptism.

(4) From the Martyrs' Mirror (1660)
"The church of God on earth ... though never perishing entirely, does not always show herself in her full form, yea, at times she seems to have vanished altogether...
It is expressly stated that the Waldenses, from ancient times were designated by the papists by the name of Anabaptists; doubtless, because they baptized those who had been baptized in their infancy again, or, at least, aright, afterwards, when they had attained to the faith. . . . It is certainly clearly and plainly said, that the Waldenses were anabaptists, as the ungodly now call the Christian baptists..."
T. J. van Braght, The Bloody Theater or Martyrs' Mirror, *trans. by Joseph F. Sohm (Scottdale, Pa.: Herald Press, 1972), 25; 279.*

In spite of the "fallenness" of the papal church, the story continued, there had been faithful and devout Christians in every age. These "true Christians" had protested the abuses. These true believers always were labelled "heretics" by the apostate majority, and were inevitably perse-

(5) *From the Ausbund, the Swiss Brethren hymnal.*

Hymn 31: Wir Bitten dich, ewiger Gott, by Leonhard Schiemer (d. 1527).

Thine holy place they have destroyed,
Thine altar overthrown,
And reaching forth their bloody hands,
Have foully slain Thine own.
And we alone, a little flock,
The few who still remain,
Are exiles wandering through the land
In sorrow and in pain.

We are, alas, like scattered sheep,
The shepherd not in sight,
Each far away from home and hearth,
And, like the birds of night
That hide away in rocky clefts,
We have our rocky hold,
Yet near at hand, as for the birds,
There waits the hunter bold.

We wander in the forests dark,
With dogs upon our track;
And like the captive, silent lamb
Men bring us, prisoners, back.
They point to us, amid the throng,
And with their taunts offend,
And long to let the sharpened ax
On heretics descend.

Translated by Burrage, in Paul M. Yoder, et al., Four Hundred Years with the Ausbund *(Scottdale, Pa.: Herald Press, 1964), 41.*

(6) *From the Ausbund*
Hymn 18: Anna Jansz of Rotterdam (d. 1539).

2. Annelein received permission
To see her son in Rotterdam,
As her death drew near.
Isaiah hear my testament,
My last will before my death
Now comes from my mouth.

3. I am going on the path of the prophets,
The martyrs' and apostles' way;
There is none better.
They all have drunk from the cup,
Even as did Christ Himself,
As I have heard it read.

13. They are despised and rejected
By this wretched world.
They must carry Christ's cross,
And have no secure place
Because they keep God's word.
They often are hunted down.

14. God lives with such people,
Who are mocked by the world.
Keep company with them.
They will show you the true way,
Lead you away from the path of evil,
Guide you away from hell.

Translated by Pamela Klassen, in C. Arnold Snyder and Linda H. Hecht, eds., Profiles of Anabaptist Women *(Waterloo: WLU Press, 1996), 345-56.*

cuted by the fallen church–just as Jesus had been persecuted and crucified. The Waldensians were often cited as a prime example of such faithful, persecuted Christians of a previous age. (4)

The persecuted and hunted Anabaptists were often depicted as walking the path trodden by Christ, the Apostles, and the faithful martyrs of all
ages who had followed after Christ. They stood in the line of the "true
church," which in their understanding had always been labelled an "heretical" church by the apostate church of the majority.

In the literature of the Anabaptists, the origins of the baptizing movement were biblical and Apostolic. The true church was characterized by
faithfulness and hope in the face of persecution by "the world." (5)(6)

"Anabaptism" in modern scholarship

For several centuries, descriptions of Anabaptism ran along one or the
other of two well-worn tracks. The vast majority of church historians,
Protestant and Catholic, continued to describe Anabaptism in the negative
terms first set out by Heinrich Bullinger. On the other hand, descendants
of the Anabaptists, always in the minority, continued to remember their
parents in the faith as the "faithful few" in a fallen world. Books like the
Martyrs Mirror (1660), which were continuously reprinted and translated
by the Mennonites, contributed to keeping the minority view alive among
Anabaptist descendants.

A new chapter opened around 1850. The emergence of modern historical studies, with a corresponding emphasis on the critical use of primary sources, led to the compilation and publication of archival sources.
Among these sources were volumes of collected "Anabaptist legal documents" (*Täuferakten*) organized regionally. Scholars interested in telling
the Anabaptist story now could make reference to primary documents
originally preserved as legal evidence in the sixteenth century.

The Anabaptist story is still being reshaped by the interpretation of
primary documents, as more are discovered in European archives and

more are published. While interpretive differences have countinued to flourish in the nineteenth and twentieth centuries, as will be seen below, the appeal to the sources has introduced an important, objective corrective to the process of historical description.

Friedrich Engels: The Marxist Reversal

In 1850 Friedrich Engels, Karl Marx's friend and co-worker, published a work called "The Peasant War in Germany" in which Reformation events were interpreted in light of a materialist, revolutionary understanding of history. For Engels, the heroes of the story were the oppressed peasants, led by Thomas Müntzer; the villains were the propertied classes, led by Martin Luther. Engels accepted the majority view that had Anabaptism originating with Thomas Müntzer. But rather than concluding that this was a bad thing, he concluded that the progressive forces of history were on the side of Müntzer and the Anabaptists, who were people ahead of their time.

---

(7) Friedrich Engels: Anabaptism as proto-Communist.

"Only in the teachings of Müntzer did ... communist notions find expression as the desires of a vital section of society. . . . The rising agitation among the peasants and the plebeians had enormously lightened Müntzer's task of propaganda. In the person of the Anabaptists he found invaluable agents. This sect, having no definite dogmas, held together by common opposition against all ruling classes and by the common symbol of second baptism, ascetic in their mode of living, untiring, fanatic and intrepid in propaganda, had grouped itself more closely around Müntzer. Made homeless by constant persecutions, its members wandered over the length and breadth of Germany, announcing everywhere the new gospel wherein Münzer had made clear to them their own demands and wishes."

    Friedrich Engels, The German Revolutions *(Chicago: University of Chicago Press, 1967; original edition, 1850), 38; 39; 50-51.*

Engels argued that since the peasants lacked an appropriate secular language, they were forced to utilize religious language to express their socially revolutionary ideas. In effect, Engels believed that the religious language used by the peasants in the sixteenth century had to be read as a kind of "code" for revolutionary ideas. And, Engels argued, the revolutionary mastermind was none other than Thomas Müntzer, aided by his "secret shock troops," the Anabaptists. (7)

Engels' work set the direction for official Marxist scholarship, which with the collapse of the iron curtain has now effectively come to an end. But for many decades Marxist scholars furthered the Marxist view. They alerted church historians to the importance of social and economic realities that had often gone unnoticed in more traditional church histories.

Anabaptism a continuation of Medieval Heresy (A Good Thing)

The opinion that Anabaptism was connected to medieval heretical movements, such as the Waldensians, and that this connection was a positive thing, was taken up by some church historians in the nineteenth century, and continued to find defenders in the twentieth.

---

(8) Delbert Gratz: Bernese Anabaptism is Medieval Heresy Reborn (a good thing)
"The idea of Waldensian descent has been handed down by word of mouth as well as in writing through the Anabaptists themselves. The modern Mennonites in Canton Bern hold to this theory although they have had little contact with literature that would have taught them this. It is the story of their origin that has been told by parents to their children for generations... It may well be concluded that there are two strains of Anabaptism in existence during the Reformation period in Bernese territory, the one located in the cities of Bern, Biel, and Aarau and being nourished (and perhaps founded) by Anabaptists from other Swiss cities as Basel and Zurich, and the other movement of a much older origin in the more secluded rural areas in the state of Bern. It was the latter strain that survived two centuries of persecution and has lived on to the present day."
Delbert Gratz, Bernese Anabaptists *(Goshen, Ind.: Mennonite Historical Society, 1953), 3-7 passim.*

In 1885, Ludwig Keller argued that Anabaptism was a "renewal" of the medieval "evangelical brotherhoods." The thesis was furthered ten years later by Ernst Müller, who maintained that at least one strain of Bernese Anabaptism grew directly out of Waldensian roots, rather than being an import from Zurich or elsewhere. The North American historian, Delbert Gratz, continued to argue this thesis in his monograph on Bernese Anabaptism published in 1953. (8)

Anabaptism a continuation of Medieval Heresy (A Bad Thing)

Whereas being part of the "heretical" tradition could seem to be a good thing to Mennonites, to some Pietist historians, and perhaps to others on the margins, to historians located within majoritarian churches all heresy was detestable. To connect Anabaptism to medieval heresy, then, was to condemn it.

To the English historian Ronald Knox, the similarities between Anabaptism and medieval heresy were undeniable. What characterized them both was an identical spirit of "enthusiasm" which had threatened to destroy the church in every age. It was the emergence of this unbridled enthusiasm that brought the Protestants to their senses, and put an end to the dangerous notion of a "priesthood of all believers" in the Reformation. (9)

---

(9) Ronald Knox: Anabaptism is Medieval Heresy Reborn (a bad thing).

"[The ambition of the Waldenses] was to live the Sermon on the mount; they would have no treasure on earth, they contested the right of the secular power to inflict capital punishment, they would take no oaths. . . . It is difficult not to see, in this Waldensian, then Beghard, then Lollard mentality, the culture from which, at the Reformation, the Anabaptists sprang. . . .

[Anabaptism's] chief historical importance surely lies ... in the recoil of official Protestantism from the very notion or mention of enthusiasm. The idea of a prophetic ministry, native to the Protestant genius, disappears everywhere, and ordained ministers spring up to replace it, no less institutional in character than is the Catholic priesthood."

Ronald Knox, Enthusiasm *(Oxford: Clarendon, 1950), 105; 137-38.*

Ernst Troeltsch: Sociological Typology

One of the most influential models for North American scholars was provided by Ernst Troeltsch. In his classic work, *The Social Teaching of the Christian Churches*, Troeltsch explained the development of Christianity in the West according to development of three sociological "types": the church, sect, and mystical types.

For Troeltsch, Anabaptism was the quintessential "Protestant sect type": Anabaptists "separated from the world," claiming religious and civil freedom, forming communities of the "truly converted" and rejecting the majoritarian "churches" of their day.

When Troeltsch read Reformation history through his sociological prism, it appeared to him that Anabaptism had nothing essential to do with spiritualists, mystics, or revolutionaries. Anabaptism began in Zurich, he said, and was a purely religious, peaceful movement. From Zurich the movement spread outwards. There were excesses later, due to the pressure of persecution, but they had nothing essential to do with the original nature of the movement. (10)

(10) Ernst Troeltsch: Anabaptism as a Protestant Sect Type.

"The Anabaptist movement broke out in 1525, in Zurich, in radical Reform circles, to whom Zwingli's application of the principles of Scripture seemed inadequate. The following were its main characteristics: emphasis on Believers' Baptism, a voluntary church, the precepts of the Sermon on the Mount, the rejection of the oath, of war, law, and authority, and, finally, the most far-reaching mutual material help, and the equality of all Church members, the election of elders and preachers by the local congregations, and, to a large extent, the unpaid character of the pastoral office; these principles were in close agreement with the democratic tendencies of the masses. ...

From Zurich the movement spread with great swiftness and intensity... The whole of Central Europe was soon covered with a network of Anabaptist communities, loosely connected with each other, who all practised a strictly Scriptural form of worship. ...

(The) terrible pressure of persecution ... drove the Baptist communities into an excited Revivalism and Chiliasm, and thus some fanatics in the Netherlands ... came to the conclusion that the Last Days were at hand... This led to the horrors of Münster, which was a disaster for the whole movement, and only made their persecutors feel still more sure that their oppressive attitude was justifiable and right."

Ernst Troeltsch, *The Social Teaching of the Christian Churches, 2 vols., trans. by Olive Wyon (Chicago: University of Chicago Press, 1981; reprint of the 1931 edition, Allen and Unwin), II, 694; 703-5, passim.*

Karl Holl: Troeltsch Challenged

The older, mainstream interpretation of Anabaptism begun by Bullinger did not take kindly to Troeltsch's revisionism. The Lutheran historian Karl Holl contested Troeltsch's methodology as well as his conclusions.

Holl argued that at the heart of the "enthusiasm" that Luther had opposed was a spiritualistic mysticism, and that by creating a separate "sect type" and placing Anabaptism within it, Troeltsch's "types" obscured the historical connection that existed between mysticism and Anabaptism.

---

(11) Karl Holl opposes Troeltsch's conclusions.

"What Troeltsch added of his own, ...namely a sharp distinction between Anabaptism and mysticism (or spiritualism), I am not able to consider an advance. With such a distinction, first of all, all historical connections are torn up: Zurich Anabaptism is pushed to the summit, as if it had emerged purely out of itself, Müntzer appears subsequently among the "Mystics and Spiritualists," Denck came before, following which there is a lengthy conversation concerning [Sebastian] Franck, and Melchior Hoffman is not mentioned at all.

But even insofar as the sketch is intended only as a working out of the "Types," I cannot agree with it. What Troeltsch explains precisely ... is indeed abstractly clearly thought, but it corresponds not at all to reality. There is no Anabaptism which did not support mysticism however simply."

Karl Holl, "Luther und die Schwärmer" (1922), in Gesammelte Aufsätze zur Kirchengeschichte, *I, (Tübingen: Mohr, 1948), 424, n. 1; 434-35, passim. Trans. by Arnold Snyder.*

The Anabaptist movement, Holl insisted, emphasized the Spirit and originated with Thomas Müntzer, as Bullinger had said. The sociological "types," while they formed neat abstract intellectual categories, didn't relate to historical reality. (11)

Harold S. Bender: the Mennonite rediscovery of Anabaptism

Troeltsch's approach, combined with the reinterpretation of published court records, led to a vigorous historical rehabilitation of Anabaptism by North American Mennonite scholars. Bullinger's description of Anabaptist origins and character–and the majoritarian historical accounts derived from it–came in for special criticism as an instance of special pleading that obscured the true nature of the Anabaptist movement.

No one did more than Harold S. Bender (1897-1962) to place a rehabilitated Anabaptism at the center of church historical circles, and at the heart of North American Mennonite consciousness. In Bender's reading of Anabaptist origins and character, the movement originated with Zwingli in Zurich. It departed from the larger reform only because Zwingli (and Luther as well) compromised their original biblical principles. "Anabaptism proper," according to Bender, had everything to do with

Zwingli, Zurich, a rediscovery of the Bible, and a serious following after Jesus; it had nothing to do with Thomas Müntzer or rebellion. True Anabaptism was an undefiled Protestantism.

---

(12) Harold S. Bender, "The Anabaptist Vision."

"...we know enough today to draw a clear line of demarcation between original evangelical and constructive Anabaptism on the one hand, which was born in the bosom of Zwinglianism in Zürich, Switzerland, in 1525, and established in the Low Countries in 1533, and the various mystical, spiritualistic, revolutionary, or even antinomian related and unrealted groups on the other hand, which came and went like the flowers of the field in those days of the great renovation. The former, Anabaptism proper, maintained an unbroken course in Swintzerland, South Germany, Austria, and Holland throughout the sixteenth century, and has continued until the present day in the Mennonite movememt...

Anabaptism is the culmination of the Reformation, the fulfillment of the original vision of Luther and Zwingli, and thus ... a consistent evangelical Protestantism seeking to recreate without compromise the original New Testament church, the vision of Christ and the Apostles."

Harold S. Bender, "The Anabaptist Vision," in Guy F. Hershberger, ed., The Recovery of the Anabaptist Vision *(Scottdale, Pa.: Herald Press, 1957), 35; 37.*

In Bender's account, Anabaptism of the pure and "proper" kind proceeded to spread from Zurich across Europe. It was characterized by three points of emphasis: discipleship, the church as a brotherhood, and an ethic of love and nonresistance. (12)

Harold Bender's emphasis on the Swiss Anabaptists was a natural outgrowth of his doctoral research into the life of Conrad Grebel.

---

(13) Harold S. Bender, Anabaptist Nature and Origins.

"That Grebel and his Swiss Brethren derived their faith solely and directly from the New Testament without any apparent literary or personal antecedents is one of the most striking things about the new movement. Every attempt to trace connections to earlier sources has failed, whether to the Waldensians or the Hussites as Ludwig Keller believed, or to the Franciscan Tertiaries as Albrecht Ritschl suggested. The Anabaptists were biblicists and it was from the biblical fountains alone that they drank. Having taken altogether seriously the sola scriptura of the Reformation, they were able to break more completely with the ecclesiastical and sociological forms of the Middle Ages and thus to return to the original ideas of the New Testament."

Harold S. Bender, Conrad Grebel *(Scottdale, Pa.: Herald Press, 1950), 214.*

Grebel was one of the originators of the Anabaptist movement in Zurich. In pursuing his research on Conrad Grebel, Bender utilized the full range of archival resources to good advantage. (13)

Bender's biographical work on Grebel has stood the test of time. Less successful has been his extrapolation from Swiss beginnings to a "proper Anabaptism" running in an identifiably clear stream throughout all the varieties of "baptizing" expression throughout Europe. If Bullinger's Anabaptists looked suspiciously like Lutherans gone bad, Bender's Anabaptists looked a bit too much like ideal twentieth century Indiana Mennonites: committed to the Bible (but not fundamentalist), apolitical (but responsible citizens), pacifist (but loyal), and dedicated to following after Jesus within a close church community.

George H. Williams: Anabaptism and Radical Reformation

North American church historians outside Mennonite circles also discovered the broad stream of Reformation dissent in the twentieth century. Roland Bainton coined the phrase "the Left Wing of the Reformation" to describe this branch of the Reformation. George H. Williams preferred the term "Radical Reformation."

---

(14) George H. Williams: Anabaptism and Radical Reform.

"From all sides we are coming to recognize in the Radical Reformation a major expression of the religious movement of the sixteenth century. . . . Among the dissidents in the Radical Reformation there are three main groupings: the Anabaptists proper, the Spiritualists, and the Evangelical Rationalists. . . . Though Anabaptists, Spiritualists, and Evangelical Rationalists differed among themselves as to what constituted the root of faith and order and the ultimate source of divine authority among them (the New Testament, the Spirit, reason), all three groupings within the Radical Reformation agreed in cutting back to that root and in freeing church and creed of what they regarded as the suffocating growth of ecclesiastical tradition and magisterial prerogative. Precisely this makes theirs a "Radical Reformation."

(I) have found it useful to distinguish within Anabaptism itself three main subdivisions... Besides the evangelical Anabaptists, who of late have received the most attention especially from Mennonite scholars, there are the revolutionary and the contemplative Anabaptists. . . . Within Anabaptism itself the three foregoing groupings have much in common but they also display several major differences."

George H. Williams, "Introduction," Spiritual and Anabaptist Writers, *ed. by G. H. Williams and A. Mergal, (Philadelphia: Westminster Press, 1957), 19-22; 28-29, passim.*

Although Williams was not a sociologist, he utilized a system of classification reminiscent of Troeltsch's "types." Over against the culture-affirming "magisterial reformation" (which Troeltsch would have called a "church type") Williams counterposed a "radical reformation." Within this larger stream of dissent from the mainstream, Williams located three main groupings: the Anabaptists, the Spiritualists, and the Evangelical Rationalists. These groupings were further subdivided into three subsections each. Williams subdivided the Anabaptists further into Evangelical, Contemplative, and Revolutionary Anabaptists. (14)

Without getting into the contentious denominational issue of which of these three were the "true" or "genuine" Anabaptists, Williams' categories made a natural place for Harold Bender's pacifist and separatist "Evangelical Anabaptists," stemming from Zurich.

By the 1960s it appeared that Anabaptism, after centuries of automatic defamation by association, had achieved an aura of respectable evangelical radicality. Anabaptism was now one branch of a larger sixteenth century reforming movement.

The Consensus Challenged

The emerging consensus did not lack for critics, even before it had emerged as a consensus in North America. Dutch Anabaptist historians had never been convinced of the "Swiss origin and character" argument which was deduced from Troeltsch's typology, primarily because there were some clear differences and no visible historical links between the northern Anabaptist movement (Obbe and Dirk Philips and Menno Simons) and the Swiss Brethren. Marxist historians likewise were not convinced.

In North America, Robert Friedmann, Hans Hillerbrand, John Oyer, and Walter Klaassen all questioned the supposed purely "Protestant" character of Anabaptism, as well as the supposed absence of "spiritualism" and "revolution" among the "true" Anabaptists.

Claus Peter Clasen's monumental social-historical study concluded with the unflattering suggestion that far from being "ahead of their time," the Anabaptists were positively dangerous to social order and Western civilization.

Stayer, Packull, and Deppermann: Polygenesis

The thesis of the multiple origins of the Anabaptist movement (or the "polygenesis" view) was put forward as an explicit alternative to Bender's thesis that Anabaptism had had one point of origin, in Zurich, and had spread out from there. Bender's view was described as the "monogenesis" position, or the thesis of a single point of birth. (15)

---

(15) Stayer, Packull, and Deppermann: Polygenesis.

"Certainly the first adult baptisms occurred in Zurich, and equally certainly Hut and Denck in Augsburg or Hoffman in Strassburg were not ignorant of the existence of the Swiss Brethren. . . . But a number of Anabaptist movements arose that were independent of the Swiss Brethren... They had basically different memberships and theologies. The history of Anabaptist origins can no longer be preoccupied with the essentially sterile question of where Anabaptism began, but must devote itself to studying the plural origins of Anabaptism and their significance for the plural character of the movement."

"...we see that the three more or less independent points of departure for Anabaptist history were South German Anabaptism, the Swiss Brethren and the Melchiorites. The Zurich baptisms of 1525 have priority in point of time, but the South German Anabaptism which began in Augsburg in 1526 and the Low German-Dutch Anabaptism which Melchior Hoffman began in Emden in 1530 cannot be regarded as 'derived' from the Swiss Brethren."

J. Stayer, W. Packull and K. Deppermann, "From Monogenesis to Polygenesis: The Historical Discussion of Anabaptist Origins," MQR 49 (April, 1975), 83-86, passim.

The polygenesis approach to Anabaptist history brought new order and some historical sobriety to the field. It moved away, first of all, from an attempt to describe a supposedly homogeneous "Anabaptism." Instead there was an emphasis on the intensive study of regional movements and the historical connections to be discovered among persons in those regions. By bracketing the question of whether it made sense to speak of "Anabaptism," and focusing instead on specific persons and regions, significant historical discoveries were made.

It was in this way, for example, that the long-debated matter of Thomas Müntzer's role in the Anabaptist movement was finally clarified. Detailed historical studies showed that while Müntzer had exerted little direct influence on the Swiss Anabaptists (confirming Bender's contention), he nevertheless had been a central formative influence on the South German Anabaptist movement. Hans Hut had been a follower of Müntzer before accepting baptism from Denck, as had Melchior Rinck.

Was Müntzer the "father of Anabaptism?" The question was falsely put. It took too seriously the metaphor that Anabaptism was like a "child," and so must have had only one "father." Müntzer clearly was influential for some South German Anabaptists, even if not for all Anabaptists everywhere.

The polygenesis approach, by stepping away from the thesis of a supposed "common point of origin," was able to shed considerable light on the complex of multiple social, political, and intellectual influences that shaped the beginnings of different regional baptizing movements. No longer could historians simply speak of "Anabaptism," as if a monolithic movement had existed. Careful distinctions had to be made first about the regional variant of Anabaptism that was being considered.

Beyond Polygenesis

The "polygenesis" revision, while it provided a fruitful stimulus to historical research, continued to focus on the question of origins. After two decades of intensive work it has become clear that the focusing exclusively on "polygenesis" imposes some real limitations on the telling of the larger Anabaptist story.

First of all, identification of diverse historical origins does not of itself provide adequate explanation for change and development within the baptizing movement as a whole. To continue the birthing metaphor that "polygenesis" also assumed, one may ask: We now know who the various parents were, but what happened to the children as they grew up?

Focusing historical research on origins was not designed to answer developmental questions.

In the second place, the localized, regional approach to the study of Anabaptism proceeded by highlighting historical and ideological differences. As an historical approach, it opposed the previous trend of a sometimes uncritical homogenization. What polygenesis gained in local accuracy, however, was lost in broader perspective. As particular "Anabaptisms" came into clearer focus, "Anabaptism" tended to fade from view.

Was there an "Anabaptist movement" at all? Were there any commonalities at all between the sixteenth century baptizers?

This present book answers "yes" to both of these questions. In spite of the fact of multiple origins and a variety of ideological influences, there was nevertheless a coherent "core" of belief and practice that was common to all sixteenth century baptizers. In asserting this thesis, we are going beyond "polygenesis," not in the sense of abandoning it, but rather in the sense of building upon it. And in fact, the next steps beyond the polygenesis thesis have been clearly marked out by other scholars, including two of the originators of the polygenesis revision.

In concluding this brief historiographical overview, we can commend the following monographs as important works in their own right, that at the same time point the way to more "developmental" descriptions of the Anabaptist movement of the sixteenth century.

Walter Klaassen's recent study of apocalyptic expectation in the Radical Reformation reveals broad and fundamental commonalities. *Living at the End of the Ages* (Lanham, Md.: University Press of America, 1992), while illuminating differences in individual emphasis and detail, nevertheless also illustrates how common End Times themes were appropriated and used.

James Stayer's monograph on the development of Anabaptist community of goods (*The German Peasants' War and Anabaptist Community of Goods* [Montreal and Kingston: McGill-Queens University Press, 1991]) comes to the conclusion that from the start there was broad Anabaptist agreement on economic principles, based on a similar reading of Acts 2 and 4. This broad but fundamental agreement cut across the regional "faultlines" indicated by the polygenesis paradigm, and defined an early "pan-Anabaptist" position on these questions.

Likewise, Werner Packull's detailed study of the origin and development of communitarian Anabaptism in Moravia points out surprisingly permeable boundaries between communities of very different historical origin. Packull's book, *Hutterite Beginnings. Communitarian Experiments during the Reformation* (Baltimore and London: Johns Hopkins University Press, 1995) details in a masterful way the extent to which dialogue, interaction, and mutual influence were operative in early communitarian Anabaptism. In particular, Packull's work documents the extensive influence of Swiss Anabaptism in the development of South German Anabaptism, providing a partial corrective to the polygenesis corrective of Bender's view.

And so the historical work goes on.

Bibliography

(Books cited in the text)

Ausbund
Ausbund, das ist Etliche schöne Christliche Lieder... First edition, 1564; second expanded edition, 1583. Subsequent editions to the present reproduce the 1583 edition, with minor additions.

Baumer, 1970
Franklin Le Van Baumer, *Main Currents of Western Thought*, 3rd ed. (New York: Knopf, 1970).

Bente, 1921
F. Bente, ed., *Concordia Triglotta* (St. Louis: Concordia Publishing House, 1921).

Bettenson, 1975
H. Bettenson, *Documents of the Christian Church*, 2nd ed. (London: Oxford, 1975).

Bergsten, 1978
Torsten Bergsten, *Balthasar Hubmaier. Anabaptist Theologian and Martyr,* trans. by W.R. Estep, Jr. (Valley Forge: Judson Press, 1978).

Boyd, 1992
Stephen Boyd, *Pilgram Marpeck. His Life and Social Teaching* (Durham: Duke Univ. Press, 1992)

Cramer and Pijper
S Cramer and F. Pijper, eds., *Bibliotheca Reformatoria Neerlandica* ('s-Gravenhage: Martinus Nijhoff, 1910).

Chronicle
The Chronicle of the Hutterian Brethren, Vol. I. (Rifton, N.Y.: Plough Publishing House, 1987).

CWMS
The Complete Writings of Menno Simons, trans. Leonard Verduin (Scottdale, Pa.: Herald Press, 1956).

Dillenberger, 1961
J. Dillenberger, *Martin Luther* (Garden City, N.Y.: Doubleday, 1961).

Deppermann, 1982
K. Deppermann, "Melchior Hoffman," in H-G Goertz, ed., *Profiles of Radical Reformers* (Scottdale: Herald Press, 1982).

Dyck, 1962
Cornelius J. Dyck, "The First Waterlandian Confession of Faith," MQR 36 (Jan., 1962), 5-13.

Erkanntnuß, ca. 1570
Ein kurtze einfaltige erkanntnuß uff die dryzehen artickell so verlouffens 1572 (sic) Jars zu Franckenthal in der Pfaltz disputiert worden... (Manuscript in the Berner Bürgerbibliothek; microfilm copy in the Mennonite Historical Library, #203).

Fast, 1962
Heinold Fast, *Der linke Flügel der Reformation* (Bremen: Carl Schünemann Verlag, 1962).

Franck, 1536
Sebastian Franck, *Chronica, Zeitbuch unnd Geschichtbibel* (Ulm, 1536; reprint, Darmstadt, 1969).

Furcha, 1975
Edward J. Furcha, ed. and trans., *Selected Writings of Hans Denck* (Pittsburgh: Pickwick Press, 1975).

Furcha, 1995
The Essential Carlstadt, trans. E.J. Furcha (Scottdale: Herald Press, 1995).

Gregory, 1996
Brad Gregory, "The Anathema of Compromise. Christian Martyrdom in Early Modern Europe." PhD dissertation, Princeton University, 1996.

Gross, 1980
Leonard Gross, *The Golden Years of the Hutterites* (Scottdale, Pa.: Herald Press, 1980).

Gurevich, 1988
Aron Gurevich, *Medieval Popular Culture: Problems of Belief and Perception* (Cambridge: Cambridge University Press, 1988).

Harder, 1985
Leland Harder, *The Sources of Swiss Anabaptism* (Scottdale, Pa.: Herald Press, 1985).

Keeney, 1968
William Keeney, *The Development of Dutch Anabaptist Thought and Practice from 1539-1564* (Nieuwkoop: de Graaf, 1968).

Kirchhoff, 1970
Karl-Heinz Kirchhoff, "Was There a Peaceful Congregation in Münster in 1534?," MQR 44 (Oct., 1970), 357-370.

Klaassen, 1973
Walter Klaassen, *Anabaptism: Neither Catholic nor Protestant* (Waterloo: Conrad Press, 1973).

Klaassen, 1982
Walter Klaassen, *Anabaptism in Outline* (Scottdale, Pa.: Herald Press, 1982).

Klaassen, 1992
Walter Klaassen, *Living at the End of the Ages* (Lanham, Md.: University Press of America, 1992).

Klassen and Klaassen, 1978
William Klassen and Walter Klaassen, *The Writings of Pilgram Marpeck* (Scottdale, Pa.: Herald Press, 1978).

Ladurie, 1979
Emmanuel Le Roy Ladurie, *Montaillou. The Promised Land of Error*, trans. by Barbara Bray (New York: Vintage, 1979).

Lasswell, 1948
Harold Dwight Lasswell, "The Structure and Function of Communication in Society," in Lyman Bryson, ed., *The Communication of Ideas* (New York, 1948).

Laube, 1988
Adolf Laube, "Radicalism as a Research Problem in the History of Early Reformation," in Hans Hillerbrand, ed., *Radical Tendencies in the Reformation: Divergent Perspectives* (Kirksville, Missouri: Sixteenth Century Journal, 1988).

LeGoff, 1988
Jacques Le Goff, *Medieval Civilization, 400-1500* (Oxford: Blackwell, 1988).

Loewen, 1985
Howard John Loewen, *One Lord, One Church, One Hope, and One God: Mennonite Confessions of Faith*, (Elkhart, IN: Institute of Mennonite Studies, 1985).

Maier, 1959
Paul Maier, *Caspar Schwenckfeld on the Person and Work of Christ* (Assen: VanGorcum, 1959).

Martyrs Mirror
Thieleman J. van Braght, *The Bloody Theater or Martyrs Mirror*, trans. by Joseph F. Sohm (Scottdale, Pa.: Herald Press, 1972).

Matheson, 1988
Peter Matheson, *The Collected Works of Thomas Müntzer* (Edinburgh: T&T Clark, 1988).

Müller, 1938
Lydia Müller, ed., *Glaubenszeugnisse oberdeutscher Taufgesinnter* (Leipzig: Nachfolger, 1938; New York: Johnson Reprint, 1971).

Oyer, 1964
John S. Oyer, *Lutheran Reformers Against Anabaptists* (The Hague: Nijhoff, 1964)

Packull, 1982
Werner Packull, "Hans Denck: Fugitive from Dogmatism," in Hans-Jürgen Goertz, ed., *Profiles of Radical Reformers*, (Scottdale, Pa.: Herald Press, 1982), pp. 62-71.

Petry, 1962
Ray C. Petry, ed., *A History of Christianity,* vol. 1 (Englewood Cliffs, N.J.: Prentice-Hall, 1962).

Petry, 1987
Ray C. Petry, ed., *A History of Christianity*, vol. 1, (Grand Rapids: Baker, 1987).

Pipkin and Yoder, 1989
H. Wayne Pipkin and John H. Yoder, trans. and eds., *Balthasar Hubmaier: Theologian of Anabaptism* (Scottdale, Pa.: Herald Press, 1989).

Pries, 1992
Edmund Pries, "Oath Refusal in Zurich from 1525 to 1527: The Erratic Emergence of Anabaptist Practice," in W. Klaassen, ed., *Anabaptism Revisited* (Scottdale: Herald Press, 1992), 65-84.

QGTS, I
L. von Muralt and W. Schmid, eds., *Quellen zur Geschichte der Täufer in der Schweiz*, I. Band, Zürich (Zürich: Theologischer Verlag, 1952).

QGTS, II
Heinold Fast, ed., *Quellen zur Geschichte der Täufer in der Schweiz*, II. Band, Ostschweiz (Zürich: Theologischer Verlag, 1973).

QGTS, III
Unpublished, typescript copy of projected QGTS, volume III (Aarau, Bern, Solothurn), ed. by Dr. Martin Haas. Typescript in Stadtbibliothek, Winterthur.

Rempel, 1993
John Rempel, *The Lord's Supper in Anabaptism* (Scottdale, Pa.: Herald Press, 1993).

Riedemann, 1950
Peter Riedemann, *Account of Our Religion, Doctrine and Faith* (London: Hodder and Stoughton, 1950). (Originally written in 1542).

Rupp, 1969
Gordon Rupp, *Patterns of Reformation* (London: Epworth Press, 1969).

SAW
George H. Williams and Angel M. Mergal, eds., *Spiritual and Anabaptist Writers* (Philadelphia: Westminster Press, 1957).

Schornbaum, 1934
Karl Schornbaum, *Quellen zur Geschichte der Wiedertäufer, II. Band, Markgraftum Brandenburg* (Bayern I. Abteilung) (Leipzig: Heinsius Nachfolger, 1934).

Scott and Scribner, 1991
Tom Scott and Bob Scribner, *The German Peasants' War: A History in Documents* (New Jersey: Humanities Press, 1991).

Scribner, 1987
Robert W. Scribner, "Oral Culture and the Diffusion of Reformation Ideas," in Robert W. Scribner, *Popular Culture and Popular Movements in Reformation Germany* (London: Hambledon Press, 1987).

Seebass, 1982
Gottfried Seebass, "Hans Hut: The Suffering Avenger," in Hans-Jürgen Goertz, ed., *Profiles of Radical Reformers* (Scottdale, Pa.: Herald Press, 1982), 54-61.

Seebass, 1986
Gottfried Seebass, in Peter Erb, ed., *Schwenckfeld and Early Schwenckfeldianism* (Pennsburg, Pa.: Schwenckfelder Library, 1986).

Sessions, 1968
Kyle C. Sessions, *Reformation and Authority* (Lexington, Mass.: Heath, 1968).

Sider, 1974
Ronald J. Sider, *Andreas Bodenstein von Karlstadt* (Leiden: Brill, 1974).

Snyder, 1984
Arnold Snyder, *The Life and Thought of Michael Sattler* (Scottdale, Pa.: Herald Press, 1984).

Snyder and Hecht, 1996
Arnold Snyder and Linda Huebert Hecht, eds., *Profiles of Anabaptist Women: Sixteenth Century Reforming Pioneers* (Waterloo, ON: WLU Press, 1996).

Snyder-Penner, 1991
Russel Snyder-Penner, "Hans Nadler's Oral Exposition of the Lord's Prayer," MQR (Oct., 1991), pp. 393-406.

Stayer, 1976
James Stayer, *Anabaptists and the Sword* (Lawrence,Kan.: Coronado Press, 1976).

Stayer, 1991
James Stayer, *The German Peasants' War and Anabaptist Community of Goods* (Montreal and Kingston: McGill-Queens University Press, 1991).

STAZ
Staatsarchiv, Zurich.

Stupperich, 1970
R. Stupperich, ed., *Die Schriften Bernhard Rothmanns*, I. Band (Münster: Aschendorff, 1970).

Tappert, 1967
T.G. Tappert, ed., *Selected Writings of Martin Luther 1517-1520* (Philadelphia: Fortress, 1967).

TA, *Hesse*
G. Franz, ed., *Urkundliche Quellen zur hessischen Reformationsgeschichte* (Marburg: Elwert'sche Verlagsbuchhandlung, 1951).

Waite, 1990

Gary K. Waite, *David Joris and Dutch Anabaptism, 1524-1543* (Waterloo, ON: Wilfrid Laurier University Press, 1990).

Waite, 1994

Gary K. Waite, *The Anabaptist Writings of David Joris, 1535-1543* (Scottdale, Pa.: Herald Press, 1994).

Wenger, 1948

John C. Wenger, *"Martin Weninger's Vindication of Anabaptism, 1535,"* MQR 22 (Jan., 1948), *180-87.*

Wapler, 1913

Paul Wappler, *Die Täuferbewegung in Thüringen von 1526-1584* (Jena: Fischer, 1913).

Williams, 1992

George H. Williams, *The Radical Reformation* (Kirksville, Mo.: Sixteenth Century Journal Publishers, 1992).

WDP

Cornelius Dyck; William Keeney; and Alvin Beachy , eds. and trans., *The Writings of Dirk Philips* (Scottdale, Pa.: Herald Press, 1992).

Yoder, 1973

John H. Yoder, *The Legacy of Michael Sattler* (Scottdale, Pa.: Herald Press, 1973).

Index of Selected Names and Topics

About Pandora Press

Pandora Press is a small, independently owned press dedicated to making available modestly priced books that deal with Anabaptist, Mennonite, and Believers Church topics, both historical and theological. We welcome comments from our readers.

Later Writings by Pilgram Marpeck and his Circle. Volume 1: The Exposé, A Dialogue and Marpeck's Response to Caspar Schwenckfeld
>   Translated by Walter Klaassen, Werner Packull, and John Rempel
>   (Kitchener: Pandora Press, 1999; co-published with Herald Press)
>   Softcover, 157pp. ISBN 0-9683462-6-X
> $20.00 U.S./$23.00 Canadian. Postage: $4.00 U.S./$5.00 Can.

[*Previously untranslated writings by Marpeck and his Circle*]

John Driver, *Radical Faith. An Alternative History*
>   *of the Christian Church*, edited by Carrie Snyder.
>   (Kitchener: Pandora Press, 1999; co-published with Herald Press)
>   Softcover, 334pp. ISBN 0-9683462-8-6
> $32.00 U.S./$35.00 Canadian. Postage: $5.00 U.S./$6.00 Can.

[*A history of the church as it is seldom told – from the margins*]

C. Arnold Snyder, *From Anabaptist Seed.*
>   (Kitchener: Pandora Press, 1999; co-published with Herald Press)
>   Softcover, 53pp.; discussion questions. ISBN 0-9685543-0-X
> $5.00 U.S./$6.25 Canadian. Postage: $2.00 U.S./$2.50 Can.

[*Ideal for group study, commissioned by Mennonite World Conference*]

John D. Thiesen, *Mennonite and Nazi? Attitudes Among Mennonite Colonists in Latin America, 1933-1945.*
>   (Kitchener: Pandora Press, 1999; co-published with Herald Press)
>   Softcover, 330pp., 2 maps, 24 b/w illustrations, bibliography, index
>   ISBN 0-9683462-5-1
> $25.00 U.S./$28.00 Canadian. Postage: $4.00 U.S./$5.00 Can.

[*Careful and objective study of an explosive topic*]

Lifting the Veil. Mennonite Life in Russia before the Revolution,
    ed. by Leonard Friesen, trans. by Walter Klaassen
    (Kitchener: Pandora Press, 1998; co-published with Herald Press).
    Softcover, 128pp., 4pp illustrations ISBN 0-9683462-1-9
    $12.50 U.S./$14.00 Canadian. Postage: $4.00 U.S./$4.00 Can.
[Insightful memoirs of a leading Mennonite pastor and author]

Leonard Gross, *The Golden Years of the Hutterites, revised edition*
    (Kitchener: Pandora Press, 1998; co-published with Herald Press).
    Softcover, 280pp., index, one map. ISBN 0-9683462-3-5
    $22.00 U.S./$25.00 Canadian. Postage: $4.00 U.S./$5.00 Can.
[A classic study of the second-generation Hutterites, available again]

The Believers Church: A Voluntary Church, ed. by William H. Brackney
    (Kitchener: Pandora Press, 1998; co-published with Herald Press).
    Softcover, viii, 237pp., index. ISBN 0-9683462-0-0
    $25.00 U.S./$27.50 Canadian. Postage: $4.00 U.S./$5.00 Can.
[Papers read at the 12ᵗʰ Believers Church Conference, Hamilton, Ont.]

Jacobus ten Doornkaat Koolman, *Dirk Philips. Friend and Colleague of
    Menno Simons*, trans. W. E. Keeney, ed. C. A. Snyder
    (Kitchener: Pandora Press, 1998; co-pub. with Herald Press).
    Softcover, xviii, 236pp., index. ISBN: 0-9698762-3-8
    $23.50 U.S./$28.50 Canadian. Postage: $4.00 U.S./$5.00 Can.
[The definitive biography of Dirk Philips, now available in English]

Sarah Dyck, ed./tr., *The Silence Echoes: Memoirs of Trauma & Tears*
    (Kitchener: Pandora Press, 1997; co-published with Herald Press).
    Softcover, xii, 236pp., 2 maps. ISBN: 0-9698762-7-0
    $17.50 U.S./$19.50 Canadian. Postage: $4.00 U.S./$5.00 Can.
[First person accounts of life in the Soviet Union, trans. from German]

Wes Harrison, *Andreas Ehrenpreis and Hutterite Faith and Practice* (Kitchener: Pandora Press, 1997; co-published with Herald Press). Softcover, xxiv, 274pp., 2 maps, index. ISBN 0-9698762-6-2 $26.50 U.S./$32.00 Canadian. Postage: $4.00 U.S./$5.00 Can.
[*First biography of this important seventeenth century Hutterite leader*]

C. Arnold Snyder, *Anabaptist History and Theology: Revised Student Edition* (Kitchener: Pandora Press, 1997; co-pub. Herald Press). Softcover, xiv, 466pp., 7 maps, 28 illustrations, index, bibliography. ISBN 0-9698762-5-4 $35.00 U.S./$38.00 Canadian. Postage: $5.00 U.S./$6.00 Can.
[*Abridged, rewritten edition for undergraduates and the non-specialist*]

Nancey Murphy, *Reconciling Theology and Science: A Radical Reformation Perspective* (Kitchener, Ont.: Pandora Press, 1997). x, 103pp., index. Softcover. ISBN 0-9698762-4-6 $14.50 U.S./$17.50 Canadian. Postage: $3.50 U.S./$4.00 Can.
[*Exploration of the supposed conflict between Christianity and Science*]

C. Arnold Snyder and Linda A. Huebert Hecht, eds, *Profiles of Anabaptist Women*: *Sixteenth Century Reforming Pioneers* (Waterloo, Ont.: Wilfrid Laurier University Press, 1996). Softcover, xxii, 442pp. ISBN: 0-88920-277-X $28.95 U.S. or Canadian. Postage: $5.00 U.S./$6.00 Can.
[*Biographical sketches of more than 50 Anabaptist women; a first*]

The Limits of Perfection: A Conversation with J. Lawrence Burkholder 2nd ed., with a new epilogue by J. Lawrence Burkholder, Rodney Sawatsky and Scott Holland, eds. (Kitchener: Pandora Press, 1996). Softcover, x, 154pp. ISBN 0-9698762-2-X $10.00 U.S./$13.00 Canadian. Postage: $2.00 U.S./$3.00 Can.
[*J.L. Burkholder on his life experiences; eight Mennonites respond*]

C. Arnold Snyder, *Anabaptist History and Theology: An Introduction*
(Kitchener: Pandora Press, 1995).
Softcover, x, 434pp., 6 maps, 29 illustrations, index, bibliography.
ISBN 0-9698762-0-3
$35.00 U.S./$38.00 Canadian. Postage: $5.00 U.S./$6.00 Can.
[*Comprehensive survey; unabridged version, fully documented*]

C. Arnold Snyder, *The Life and Thought of Michael Sattler* (Scottdale:
Herald Press, 1984). Hardcover, viii, 260pp. ISBN 0-8361-1264-4
$10.00 U.S./$12.00 Canadian. Postage: $4.00 U.S./$5.00 Can.
[*First full-length biography of this Anabaptist leader and martyr*]

Pandora Press
51 Pandora Avenue N.
Kitchener, Ontario
Canada N2H 3C1
Tel./Fax: (519) 578-2381
E-mail: panpress@golden.net
Web site: www.pandorapress.com

Herald Press
616 Walnut Avenue
Scottdale, PA
U.S.A. 15683
Orders: (800) 245-7894
E-mail: hp%mph@mcimail.com
Web site: www.mph.lm.com